KU-465-710

Crash

Crash

Ten Easy Ways to avoid a Computer Disaster

Tony Collins

With
David Bicknell

SIMON & SCHUSTER

A VIACOM COMPANY

First published in Great Britain by Simon & Schuster Ltd, 1997
A Viacom company

Copyright © Tony Collins, 1997

This book is copyright under the Berne Convention.
No reproduction without permission.
All rights reserved.

The right of Tony Collins to be identified as author
of this work has been asserted by him in accordance with sections 77 and 78
of the Copyright, Designs and Patent Act, 1988.

Simon & Schuster Ltd
West Garden Place
Kendal Street
London W2 2AQ

Simon & Schuster Australia
Sydney

A CIP catalogue record for this book is available from the British Library

ISBN 0-684-81688-1

Printed and bound in Great Britain by
Butler & Tanner Ltd, Frome and London

To Caroline, Hannah and Benjie for the time I didn't
give them while working on *Crash*.

Acknowledgements

This book is written as if it expressed the view of a single person. This is a sham. The book forms a poultice of experiences, suggestions and opinions derived from many people, each one of whom knows a great deal more than David or I about the causes of computer disasters. Therefore, sincere thanks to the following . . .

Steve Larner, an 'expert witness' who is asked by companies and suppliers to investigate the causes of computer disasters to help resolve legal actions. He was once described by a judge as the most credible of all expert witnesses in a civil action over a computer project failure. His help on the common events leading to disasters and his knowledge of the legal processes has been invaluable.

The clear-thinking John Rathbone, who became head of IT at the Performing Right Society after its computer disaster, and who has steered the organisation into safe waters. I am particularly grateful for his patience under the duress of my countless telephone calls to discuss ideas on the possible common causes of project failures.

Catherine Griffiths (IC-Parc) and Leslie Wilcocks (Templeton College, Oxford) for their excellent paper 'Are Major IT Projects worth the risk?'

Mike Allen, a senior civil servant who has successfully managed several major projects. Nobody knows more about managing suppliers. Also to Peter Roney, Chief Executive of the Save and Prosper financial services group who confirmed the wisdom of delivering big IT projects in small manageable chunks over short periods; to Roger Toms, former head of IT at Surrey

County Council; Matt Devereux, IT Director at Southern Electric; Phil Reed, Head of Global Technology Services of Standard Chartered Bank; Geoff Doubleday, Managing Director, Nomura Research Institute; Mike Ribbins, Business Systems Director of Thames Water; and Andy Mealing of American Express, for their thoughts on what makes an IT project successful.

Anthony McConnell, Director of Tiptree Book Services, who patiently explained the lessons learnt from his company's project. Jason Cowley of the *Bookseller* business title, who provided further invaluable help on the impact of Tiptree's problems in the book trade. Thanks also to District Auditor Richard da Costa for his clearly written and incisive reports on the Wessex Regional Information Systems Plan; Tim Kelsey, now a *Sunday Times* journalist, who helped to investigate the Wessex affair; and to certain people who used to work at Wessex and whose keen sense of public duty helped to expose what went on there. They cannot be named but know who they are. I am also grateful to the MP John Denham, whose revelatory and bold speech in the House of Commons and tenacious questioning of ministers kept the Wessex affair in the public eye and led to the longest-ever hearing of the House of Commons Public Accounts Committee.

Senior executives in some supplier organisations whose advice on project or contract management leaves little or nothing to be desired: Charles Cox of Cap Gemini Sogeti; Frank Jones of the Sema Group; Rod Watts of ITnet; Vince Padi of CFM; David Thorpe, European head of Electronic Data Systems (EDS); Phil Sissons, Director of Shared Medical Services; and various partners at Andersen Consulting, including the former UK managing partner, Keith Burgess, his successor James Hall, and other partners, who include Hugh Morris and David Andrews. Also thanks to the executives at Andersen and at Barclays Bank for their help on the Barclays chapter.

Laurence Holt, Chief Executive Officer of the consultancy Quidnunc; consultants at the government's computer advisory bureau, the CCTA, who include its former Director Alan Healey; Robert Burford of Data Logic; and MPs, who include Sir Robert Sheldon, Stephen Byers, Alan Milburn, Alan Williams, Richard Page and Michael Stern.

Lawyers John Yates, Robert McCallough and Stephen York

Mark Macgillivray, H&M Consulting, Sunnyvale, California; Jim Ross, Florida Attorney General's Office; Nancy Simmons, US General Accounting Office; Siovonne Smith, Bill Seebeck, Seebeck International, Wilton, Connecticut; Marshall Toplansky, Core Strategies, Northbrook, Illinois, USA; Jim Johnson, The Standish Group, Dennis, Massachusetts, USA; Christine Mambourg, The Open Group, Brussels, Belgium; Howard Grant, Image and Integration, Ottawa, Canada; Randy Dove, EDS USA; John Watson, Coopers & Lybrand UK; Tom Temin and Vanessa Jo Grimm, Government Computer News, Silver Springs, Maryland, USA; Robbin Young, Windows Watcher Newsletter, Redmond, Washington, USA; Bruce Nelson, Auspex Systems, Santa Clara, California, USA; Bill Jacobs, UK; and Stephen Luxford of the UK's National Audit Office.

Parliamentary copyright material from 'Committee of Public Accounts - Wessex Regional Health Authority: Management of the Regional Information Systems Plan Minutes of Evidence' is reproduced with the permission of the Controller of Her Majesty's Stationery Office on behalf of Parliament

Contents

Preface

Ten Ways to Avoid a
Computer Disaster

Success breeds success, as the cliché goes. By the same logic does disaster breed disaster? If so, this might explain why computer failures are so common. Any regular readers of the computing trade press and increasingly the front pages of the national newspapers, could be forgiven for believing that computer managers are either genetically disposed to failure, or that common sense flies out of the window as soon as big money is allocated to a major information technology project.

This may give an overly harsh impression. Not all computing projects fail – only most of them. Now and again serendipity sees a company or government department buying and implementing a system that does as much as half of what was originally intended.

But these moderately successful aberrations are rare and tend to be on a small scale, barely noticeable among the debris of the crashes.

So this book studies the good and bad to compile a pragmatist's guide to avoiding computer catastrophes.

There are many management books on how to avoid computer disasters, many of them written by consultants or representatives of supplier organisations. These books give sound, carefully worded advice but most of the project managers in the disaster case studies in *this* book were aware of the general rules of project management.

It is easy to forget or put general rules to one side when you come to implement a new system, because your project appears, to you, to be unique.

More memorable, however, are the mistakes made by others. This is the reason that *Crash*, seeks to show how and why the calamities occurred.

Therefore *Crash* does not give a summary of the events leading up to a project collapse. It tries to plot every major event, every major decision, every circumstance that influenced the outcome.

When you can see clearly how others in front of you have become ensnared in project traps, it is easier to take a different path and avoid the same pitfalls; or you may decide that it would be safer turning back. And this is one of the clear messages of this book: that *not* embarking on full-scale computerisation projects can be much better for your organisation's long-term health than going into them without laying excessive stress on seemingly trifling matters. Often it is the accumulation of little problems that causes a project to fail, rather than a single disastrous event.

This book is necessary – and it is to be expected that there will be many more of its kind in the decades to come – because the computer industry is new, at least compared with, say, bridge building.

When a bridge collapses it is not something that can be covered up, particularly if it is carrying people. Therefore the lessons from bridge failures are learned as a result of a public or engineering industry inquiry. Yet bridges have collapsed frequently for centuries.

As recently as the 1940s the collapse of the first suspension bridge across the Narrows of Puget Sound, connecting the Olympic peninsula with the mainland of Washington, was regarded as a landmark failure in engineering history. The bridge was found to be highly vulnerable to aerodynamic forces which were insufficiently understood at the time. The failure spurred aerodynamic research and led to important advances. So lessons about bridge disasters are still being learned – 2,000 years after the Romans thought that they had invented the archetypal arched bridge.

In contrast the computer industry has had only a few decades to learn from its mistakes. And it seems to learn little or nothing because silence usually follows a computer disaster. Nobody knows how many computer failures have extinguished an entire company, though computer problems are often cited by administrators and liquidators as a contributory factor. Alternatively, companies can sometimes afford to absorb the costs of the collapse without telling shareholders, although the perpetrators will usually take early retirement or will be 'let go'.

However in some instances it has been possible to ascertain all the relevant facts; and these are the case studies in this book. Those disasters where it has been possible to obtain only superficial accounts of a project crash have not been included because the simple fact that they have occurred tells us nothing. What is interesting is how and why.

Yes, the book contains a small number of maxims, some of them blunt and obvious – yet they were not perceived as obvious at the time of the disaster. They are picked out in bold type for quick reference at a later date.

In virtually all the disasters, the same ten themes occur:

1. A tendency to be overambitious;

2. A feeling among computer managers that they should know it all, and cannot admit when they don't;

3. A belief among the entire project team that computerisation must be a good thing, and to suspect otherwise is an Orwellian thought-crime;

4. A chief executive who is in the best position to judge a computer project because he knows nothing about computers but fails to intervene – because he knows nothing about computers;

5. A readiness to accept it'll-be-all-right-on-the-night assurances from suppliers – assurances that suppliers studiously avoid writing down;

6. An over-reliance on consultants who, like some vets, may have a financial interest in prolonging ills;

7. An avoidance of cheap, proven, off-the-shelf packages in favour of costly, unproven, custom-built software; or, worse, the tailoring of a standard proven package;

8. An unwillingness by middle and senior management to impart bad news to the board – mainly because the board will make known its resentment of anyone who tries;

9. The buck stops nowhere;

10. A mistaken belief that the contract makes it easy to sue the supplier if all goes wrong.

In short there is an exaggerated view of what computerisation can achieve, an illusion that flourishes because of the popular belief that computers are synonymous with efficiency.

Occasionally this is true. Banks, for example, use computers in the job they do best: as a sophisticated form of calculator. But it has cost banks hundreds of millions of pounds to master the art of computerising without *losing* hundreds of millions of pounds. The rest of us don't have quite as much to spare.

Above all, the banks learned how dangerous it is to put faith in suppliers who suggest that computers can transcend inefficiency.

Companies may find that unless their manual or semi-computerised business procedures are so sleek, well-honed and transparent to anyone from the humblest programmer to the chief executive, then full-scale computerisation may seize on every administrative weakness and gleefully magnify it a hundredfold.

Computers, then, tend to be much less flexible than the inflexible paper-based systems they replace.

They also have a habit of making your business inescapably dependent on them, and, because they work so much more quickly than the human brain and are savagely unforgiving of human error, are just the thing for turning a molehill of a problem into a mountain of corporate debt.

If this sounds like exaggeration you need only glance through the following case studies. They are the sorts of user stories that don't fill the sales team's brochures.

Naturally enough, some technologists will be scandalised by the repeated suggestions in this book that some companies may be better off without full-scale computerisation.

Yet those companies which step back from all-out computerisation, resisting the temptation to follow the herd, may live to see off competitors who have seen the advantages of technology but, to their detriment, have not fully understood the risks and disadvantages.

I am not suggesting that, merely because most projects seem to go wrong, companies shouldn't computerise. Most will already have some form of computerisation. The questions they are constantly asking are: do we need to upgrade now? Will we fall behind if we don't? Don't we need to better empower the end-user?

These are all legitimate questions, which this book may help to answer. It may also provide some comfort to those chief executives and computer managers who instinctively want to exercise caution, who would prefer to computerise bits of the organisation rather than everything at once, and who want to leave nothing to chance.

Further, it will hearten executives who have felt they are alone in having their normally good judgement impaired by seeing a wondrous demonstration of new technology by a supplier they trust.

In one case I followed the experiences of a small family

company which fell victim to such a demonstration. There were only two people doing the accounts. It wanted to install computers to reduce the administrative staff by 50 per cent – one employee – and so spent a long time choosing a system. In fact, much of the time of the managing director was spent being impressed by the suppliers' systems, and hardly any time was devoted to considering the consequences of computerisation, or of a failure.

No sooner was the new system installed than the company found that it needed one person to enter all the data onto computer, another to manage the system, and a third to make sense of the seemingly superfluous management information.

And when something went wrong, which seemed to be most of the time, nobody knew how to fix it. As a result, a great deal of time was lost ringing suppliers and ineffectually fussing around the needs of the computer system.

The misery did not stop there. The fact that the main software supplier had included many more features in its programs than the administrators had the time to understand, did not stop the managing director and his staff spending prime company time trying to learn how to use all of the features.

What little quality time was left to the administrators to update the books was spent learning things about the system they didn't need to know. Worse, they became so enthralled with what the computers could do (potentially) that they ended up programming databases instead of helping to run the business.

Since then I have seen similar things happen on a much grander scale in other companies: **people become so absorbed in the technology that they lose sight or even interest in the benefits to the business.**

Originally corporate computers were merely a business tool but machines that once took the drudgery out of corporate accounting, have now become a structural support without which the company will collapse.

With so much dependence on computers, the major suppliers have been able to defend themselves against criticism by building fortresses of credibility, which are sustained by enormous financial muscle and seemingly unimpeachable ethics.

There was once a saying: 'Nobody was ever sacked for buying IBM', which gives an indication of the strength of computer suppliers but also promulgates the illusion that they are infallible.

The truth, of course, is that computer companies are in business to sell computers, software and services as profitably as they possibly can, and this does not always accord exactly with the interests of their customers.

That is not to say suppliers verge on the unscrupulous. The companies themselves are the guardians of rectitude . . . but few of their computer sales staffs will tear up a big order to retain their halos of integrity.

I mean this in the nicest possible way. Of course there are no armies of sales staff cheating and lying their way into the hearts of big business. That would be easy to detect. They are far more dangerous because the salespeople believe genuinely in what they say even when they are wrong – yet their sincerity can take in everyone they encounter.

But deception and self-deception are not the only dangers. The computer industry is still new, and computer law is barely more mature than the legislation governing genetic experiments. The rights and wrongs are still being debated.

Thus the computer industry is to some degree a law unto itself, so customers may feel they have little choice but to place all their trust in Providence and the suppliers, preferably the former.

Yet they will usually discover that most suppliers go about their business ethically. They will bid, and offer products that they believe are good for the customer and good for the supplier.

But sometimes economics and ethics are hard things to reconcile, and in any fight it's not difficult to imagine which one loses.

So suppliers will often fatally underestimate the amount of hardware needed to win an order, and will morally justify this artifice to themselves on the basis that, if the eventual system costs three or four times the price originally budgeted, at least the customer is in the hands of the most honourable of all suppliers. Is this immoral?

Probably not. But it behoves the prudent buyer, computer manager or chief executive to remember that suppliers come to most projects knowing that the chances of failure are much higher than it would be in their financial interests to tell.

And this is the most ticklish problem of all. For the supplier who speaks its mind may be crucified for doing so. When Joan of Arc was asked at her trial by the Inquisition if she would swear on the Gospels to tell the whole truth, she replied with extraordinary maturity for a woman of about eighteen that those who tell too much truth are bound to be hanged.

Similarly, suppliers who quote a realistic price for a project are unlikely to win the order. So they may quote an uneconomically low price in the hope of recovering losses through inevitable system enhancements and unforeseen changes.

Thus, with the supplier encouraging changes, and the end-users only too willing to suggest them, projects can drag on interminably, never reaching the point of end-user acceptance.

Before long it is apparent that the project is a disaster. The software will never be acceptable to the end-users because every change has slowed down the system to the point where it's unusable.

And buying bigger hardware means such a major new investment that it is probably worth starting the project afresh, particularly as the technology has advanced by two generations since the project specifications were drawn up.

At this stage lawyers usually become involved and suppliers and customers will blame each other, even though, when disaster strikes, it is rarely the fault of one party.

One good thing about disasters, however, is that they have now become so common that a small number of suppliers, protective of their good reputations, are refusing to bid for certain contracts if they sense that the customer does not know exactly what it wants.

Some of the more scrupulous suppliers are also declining business when they feel the customer has unrealistically high expectations. But for every supplier with a conscience that disqualifies itself from the bidding for noble reasons, there are a hundred others that will gladly proffer all the bland, authoritative, anodyne assurances that the customer wants to hear. And who will win the business?

Yet when it all goes wrong, the naïve supplier is usually as aggrieved and financially damaged as the naïve customer; but, whereas the supplier can go on to recover the losses from insurance or by winning another order, the customer may never recover.

Now and again, it is the well-meaning supplier that falls prey to a Mephisthophelean customer – where, for example, the supplier has to the best of its ability delivered what was asked for but the system is a disappointment to the customer.

To recover from the embarrassment and potential losses arising from inadequately specifying the system, the customer will then sue.

While this was being written, one small, well-meaning supplier, which delivered systems costing about £70,000 to a large company, was being sued for millions of pounds because the customer's computer department was hoping to transfer the blame for its mistakes onto the supplier and so deflect the wrath of its chief executive.

The computer department had hired a shrewd lawyer who claimed that systems problems depressed his client's turnover by more than £1 million – a claim that the supplier could not afford the time and money to defend. It will have to settle at a considerable loss whereas in this case both supplier and customer seem to have been equally culpable.

But cases like this are fairly rare. More common and memorable are the disasters that have occurred when suppliers who are only too aware of the risks of failure, have marketed their products too aggressively to customers who have little understanding of computerisation.

The lesson here, perhaps, is that if you know little or nothing about computers and everything about the running of your business you know 90 per cent of what it is necessary to know about computerisation. You can pick up the other 10 per cent by reading this book, by visiting other businesses that have been through difficult computerisations (there's no such thing as a major implementation during which nothing went seriously wrong), or by asking suppliers and their customers the most naïve questions you can think of asking.

Indeed anything is preferable to slipping into the perilous position of allowing yourself to be overawed by salespeople who seem to know so much more than you. This is the first step towards disaster. The French playwright Molière didn't know much about multimedia PCs, VRAM and 64-bit architectures, but he had an insight into the psyche of salespeople when he remarked that a learned fool is more dangerously foolish than an ignorant fool.

Yet the credibility of major computer companies and their sales staff continues to grow despite evidence of increasing corporate misery due to computerisation.

And the once-derided 'tekkies' are now among the world's most powerful engines of industrial production.

With revenues of £300 billion[*] ($480 billion) a year, the computer – or as it is often described, the 'information technology' industry – has become the world's most dynamic sector, outstripping the car and aerospace industries in revenues.

Only the oil business currently generates more money. Garish car advertisements may still catch the eye, but the worldwide lust is for

---

* Throughout *Crash*, the word 'billion' is taken to mean a thousand million.

processing power rather than horsepower. Street credibility will soon be measured not on whether you have a Porsche, but a triple 300-Mhz P6 chip-powered PC with 254M bytes of RAM and 24-speed CD-ROM.

But this wholesale addiction to technology, to symmetric and massively parallel computing, to client server systems, to issues about the death of the PC and to the downloading of corporate software from the Internet to the servers that feed dumb terminals, are the fashionable topics that hide the industry's darker corners.

The number and scale of the problems involved in installing computer systems have become so serious that Sir Robert Sheldon, chairman of the House of Commons Public Accounts Committee, which monitors public spending, has issued a health warning to organisations on the dangers of computerisation.

In fact there is a scarcely an industrialised country that has not seen its businesses seriously damaged by computer disasters. Yet these major incidents are not always so dangerous for the suppliers.

If the surveys are correct, and more than 60 per cent of new computer projects fail, does it follow that the computer supply industry has been built on the proceeds of corporate blunders?

So, if it is accepted that disasters are increasing, both in number and scale, then an incorrigibly sceptical view of computerisation is called for.

But being a heretic is not an easy reputation to sustain. Anyone who suggests that the reliable old computers were better than the petulant new 'intelligent' system will be ostracised as a reactionary, a Luddite who simply does not understand technology; will be told that once you have learned to use the new system properly and understood its complexities, you will see that it is the only way forward for the company.

One member of the computer industry's professional trade association, the British Computer Society, who dared to question the rush towards all-embracing computerisation, had to contend with his peers refusing to sit next to him at a formal function.

There again, progress depends not on the reasonable but unreasonable person, as Bernard Shaw observed.

In the 1950s the reasonable people were the proponents of nuclear power who said in effect: here is an unlimited source of energy created from merely splitting an atomic nucleus into smaller nuclei. The cost is so small that everyone will be able to have free electricity. What's more there's no soot to damage the lungs of the workers, no slag heaps to ruin the environment and, unlike coal, nuclear fuel will last indefinitely.

The argument was seductive, so much so that it became a heresy to oppose nuclear power, and few residents objected strongly to reactors being built in their neighbourhoods.

Now we know that the costs of generating electricity, whether using nuclear fuel or coal, are comparable – except that *not* running a nuclear power station costs a great deal more. You cannot dismantle it and build a block of flats on it when it has completed its useful service. You may have to encase its core in concrete and wait a while (about 10,000 years) until the fissile material is no longer radioactive.

It has taken forty years to understand that, although nuclear power has many advantages, it also has a few drawbacks. And at the moment the information technology industry is in the 'free electricity' phase, with suppliers attributing an almost talismanic quality to the computer.

But is it a cure-all? Customers know it isn't, so suppliers have stopped selling it as a panacea, but are touting the fear factor.

The UK managing partner of a major international computer consultancy told me that his new year's resolution was to help companies change to become more successful.

His view is that companies that do not master technology will find their competitors doing so at their expense.

However, there is a counter-argument: that companies should not change for the sake of change. And rather than attempting to conquer new technology some companies might be better off launching a new marketing campaign or introducing improved products onto the market.

I am not suggesting that the technology-wary know better than the technology zealots; but they deserve to be heard as well. And this book is in effect their forum.

However, there are also several examples of outstanding success stories in the following case studies, wherein the lessons from disasters have been applied.

But it must be said that more can be learned from mistakes than successes. Little is learned from the millions of planes that land safely, only from the one that crashes.

Incidentally failures due to fire, earthquakes, a broken uninterruptible power supply, logic bombs, hacking and sabotage have been excluded because they have been covered before in many excellent technical and managerial publications. This book concentrates on the systems that should never have been built in the first place.

It is directed as much at the chief executive and non-technical senior executives as at computer managers, prospective computer managers and anyone who is interested in what can go wrong with information technology.

The objective is not only to extract the lessons from disasters, but to help people to spot the early signs of them.

For this reason some of the case studies go into considerable detail because, although the mistakes are nearly always the same, they manifest themselves in many different ways. Yet the lessons that can be learned from them are often remarkably simple.

For example many of the disasters in this book would not have happened *if the costs of the new systems had been calculated meticulously and then multiplied by three.*

And here, in this one aphorism, we may have one of the secrets to designing and implementing a successful computer system.

Seasoned project managers will say this advice is nonsense – that to multiply a project's costs by three will render the system uneconomic and kill it before it is born. My response would be: 'Fine – so kill it. Isn't it better to anticipate the real costs than to learn of them only when millions has been spent?'

However I must stress that the advice given by David and me is fallible. Neither of us is an expert, unless judged by the only true definition of an expert – someone who has made more mistakes than anyone else.

CHAPTER ONE

The First Deadly Sin: Overambition

An over-ambitious computer project is an ordinary scheme rendered impracticably complex by accommodating end-users who want the new system to do everything the current one doesn't.

In short it is a good idea turned into an impossible implementation – and unnoticeably so. Computer disasters don't tend to advertise themselves: they creep up insidiously like a wound that turns gangrenous.

In fact long experience has taught the latent, skulking disaster that it can produce a much more catastrophic result if it can remain hidden until the project is all but complete.

Any connoisseur of disaster case studies should nevertheless be able to spot a technological Iago a mile off. The signs are:
• A project that was supposed to take a year goes a day late because of changes to the original specification. It's only a day. So what?
• A day turns into a week, then into three weeks; everybody agrees that the original timetable was impractical, given the necessary changes, so the deadline is pushed back six months.
• Then, as each problem solved has a knock-on effect on the performance of the system, the hardware is deemed inadequate.
• There are further complications and software changes, which are justified by the project managers as improvements or vital modifications to the specifications, and the six-month extension becomes a year.
• By this time a new technology such as client/server has leapfrogged the project, so it's necessary to look afresh at the whole approach*.

*A client/server system involves using one or a series of larger machines (the server/s)

- But, rather than throw away the old coding work, it is blended with the new, so creating the perfect conditions for a meltdown. What started as a simple project has turned into an excursion into the technological outer solar system.

Yet at the start of the project 'ambitious' is a word that shines edifyingly on all parties, basking the project team, suppliers, and subcontractors in the glow of being pioneers, innovators and technical Masters of the Universe in a world understood by few.

The word 'ambitious' also masquerades as a means of justifying, internally, the disruption that will be caused by the project, and its high cost. In reality, as our case studies show, the words 'ambition' and 'pioneering' are no friends of a computer project.

They are in fact the most common cause of failures, largely because the warning signs are not recognised early enough. But here are some of them:

- **Trying to use the latest hardware, which is unproven by time and comprehensive sales**. An insurance company Tindall Riley bought a Mapper 10 machine because it was recommended as being the best piece of equipment for its needs. But it has been alleged that, at the time, salesmen privately knew that the new hardware range was not up to the job.
- **Too tight a timetable for implementation**. Most of the case studies in the book depict projects that were given unrealistic deadlines. The London Ambulance Service, for example, insisted on allowing only a year for its massive new ambulance-dispatch system. Four years later (at the time of writing, at least), it is still waiting for its new system – having aborted two costly projects.
- **An underestimation of the costs**. When the Department of Social Security embarked on a computerisation of all its welfare offices, it told Parliament that the estimated costs of £713 million would probably come down as technology prices fell. Today the costs of the project are £2.6 billion – an increase of nearly 400 per cent. And still the promised integration of the various welfare benefit systems has yet to materialise.
- **An overestimation of the benefits to the business**. The American Department of (war) Veterans' Affairs thought that its new computer would cut the time required to process healthcare claims from four months to six weeks. Two years into the project,

to hold most of the data and/or to do the hard work of processing before passing it down the chain to a small machine such as a PC or dumb terminal (the client).)

it was taking eight months to process a claim.

• **Commissioning software that is bespoke**. Most of the disaster case studies in this book involve customised software rather than faults in an off-the-shelf package.

• **Buying an off-the-shelf package and then modifying it**. The London Stock Exchange thought it would keep its new settlement system simple by buying a US package. Three years and £70 million later, it gave up, conceding that it had been overambitious in trying to adapt a US package to the UK market. Changing an established package is like buying a two-bedroom house because you want to live simply, then extending it to accommodate the Granny's annexe, your snooker room and the children's home cinema.

The above are not extreme examples. Unfortunately, every major computer project – even simpler ones – seem to bring to the fore the worst deficiencies in human nature and weaknesses in the organisation of the company, and a realisation that the project has not been planned adequately. So making it complex and pioneering is only going to increase considerably the chances of failure.

As computerisation tears down empires, and jobs are changed, the chief executive will also come to realise that managing the computer project plays a small part in the process. Much of the real challenge is in managing managers, suppliers, consultants, third parties and end-users; but more important than anything, it is the managing of expectations, or, more precisely, the managing *down* of expectations.

This is the best antidote to complexity: **everyone needs to accept that a computer is not a cure-all, not the answer to Third World poverty and not, at the moment, a particularly effective anti-AIDS serum.**

In short, keep it simple. This is the glib phrase most often quoted by consultants who will go on to seek a commission for turning a silk thread into a labyrinth of interconnected spiders' webs.

But the phrase can mean something if it is applied not just at the beginning of a project but constantly throughout. The difficulty for the simplicity advocates will lie in defending themselves against the vitriol hurled by end-users who will mock or snub the new system because it doesn't offer any new features and may even be out-performed by its predecessor.

It will take some explaining, but technologically minded end-users will need to be told that new office systems are not like home PCs. One big difference is that home PCs tend to work. Large networked systems can be made to work well but usually only if they are kept simple; and that may mean starting small and building new features gradually. Even if the new system does not perform as well as the old – and that is usually the case at first – it should provide a foundation for improvement and expansion later.

Breaking this news to boards of directors and shareholders is not something a computer manager will relish. Even undemanding chief executives will expect computerisation to allow them to conduct board meetings in Barbados and cut administrative staff by at least 50 per cent.

Telling them that their vast investment in new computers may produce little or even no obvious benefit in the short term – and may indeed be worse than the existing system at least initially – will not have them clamouring to provide a multi-million-pound budget for the project.

But it has to be done. Otherwise don't computerise.

So what's the point in computerisation? This is indeed the most important question that needs to be asked – and usually isn't – before every major project begins.

Mostly new systems are installed because people get bored with the old ones or they feel they ought to replace ageing technology because it seems that everyone else is doing so. These are not the official reasons of course. The actual project justification runs into 150 pages, often written by a consultancy, which, couched in subtly impressive language, exposes the high costs of maintenance of the existing obsolescent systems, and warns that the status quo is the very worst of all possible worlds because it allows your competitors to overtake you.

This should not frighten you. Many major computerisations go awry, putting companies financially years behind – if not onto the books of an official receiver. So standing still in a technological sense may give you an advantage, especially as it may enable you to see from your high point all the chaos and confusion beneath, and help you to judge whether to computerise everything, parts of the organisation or merely upgrade whatever exists already.

A wise company learns from its mistakes. An even wiser one learns from other companies' mistakes.

But assuming you are reading this book because you want to computerise, rather than to find an excuse to avoid it, how should you go about it?

Not even Aristotle devised a sure-fire method of downsizing to Unix workstations from Amdahl mainframes, though he had one particularly useful piece of advice (paraphrased): Trust not the sophists who profess to teach, but those who practise . . . they would seem to do it from a sort of ability aided by experience rather than the exercise of reason.

Applied today this advice may mean that, when you're buying a new system, there is no substitute for talking to people who have done it before, rather than talking to suppliers who *say* they have done it before.

Don't talk to just one user site, which has a similar system to the one you want. Talk to several. Representatives of Abbey National (see Chapter 20) went on visits to the US to see several systems in operation, in advance of their project to launch a share registration scheme. They were not at all surprised or disappointed when they found that none of the US systems were suitable for the UK, but the visits helped to build an invaluable picture of what was, and what was not, technically and managerially feasible. As a result, Abbey's people – the prospective users of the new system *became experts*. They were able to reject or accept what they were told by suppliers based on their own experience, not that of the suppliers. In the end their knowledge kept the project uncomplicated, and, despite some problems, the systems were judged a success.

Wessex Regional Health Authority, on the other hand, went on site visits to the US, and, like Abbey, found nothing that met its needs, but used this as an excuse to build pioneering systems of unimaginable complexity. It tried to computerise hundreds of hospitals at a time when other health authorities were struggling to computerise a single outpatients department. The Wessex project was a £43 million failure.

Also, when talking to other sites, don't assume their system can be transposed into your company. No two companies are alike. Many case studies show that what works perfectly well on one site may well prove disastrous in another similar company.

It may be better to use the site visits as a knowledge-building exercise: find out not so much what went well but what problems the project team encountered and how they overcame them, and what limits they imposed on themselves. Had they done studies, for instance, to show whether, if they increased the number of end-users by 10 per cent, it would add 100 per cent to the project costs because the next hardware upgrade meant a machine from a new range?

By all means talk to the successful users, but companies debilitated by computers are much more interesting. And useful. They *know* what can and does go wrong – and, more importantly, what they didn't do but should have. They have already commissioned consultants to produce a £50,000 report on what to do next.

Site visits are not the entire answer. Other companies will not have exactly the system you want, and even if they did, their skills and understanding of computers will be different, not to say their structure, politics, approach to training and departmental empires. All these factors will have as direct a bearing on the success or otherwise of computerisation projects as the hardware and software.

And that is one of the key lessons that one can learn from other computer projects: that in a sense they are *all* pioneering. No two installations are the same. Even taking into account all the tens of millions of home computer users, very few have exactly the same configuration of hardware and software. Two PCs with exactly the same specification from the same supplier, and delivered at exactly the same time, may have key components from different manufacturers. So, if no two home computer configurations are exactly alike, imagine the dissimilarity of systems used by major corporations, given the vast diversity of networking and communications equipment, standard of maintenance, skills, hardware and software, to say nothing of the quality of configuration and implementation.

And when Aristotle denigrated reason over experience, perhaps he knew that reason and computer project management made an unhappy marriage. **Computers rely for their functioning on reason, but computer *projects* defy logic because of human caprice.**

You may think you have planned for everything but something that you thought was obvious to the suppliers and programmers was obvious to neither to them. So it was left out of the final system, and was crucial to its success. A book distributor, Tiptree, for example, thought it had thoroughly tested its new warehousing system on a small scale and even in a realistic live-running environment; yet when it came to the real thing small problems began to snowball in a way nobody had predicted.

This reinforces the point that, given the pioneering nature of all computerisations, the degree to which they *are* pioneering must be minimised.

Ideally one man or woman, preferably someone who is barely computer literate but has a profound understanding of how the business is run and particularly what its future needs are, should be the project leader. That person should have:
• the knowledge to go through the new system's specifications and sift the crucial from the necessary, and the superfluous from the desirable;
• the independence from the project team and self-confidence (and the ear of the chief executive) to reject as unnecessary modifications required by end-users who claim that every nice-to-have feature is a vital requirement;
• a true understanding of democracy, that is the ability to listen to everyone, to pass bad news up the chain of command and openly to admit mistakes.

This rare person, who may be found only in the celestial city, and only then after much sifting, should also be willing to accept the need for a simple system that is going to impress nobody at first sight but will inevitably have enough problems to show people how disastrous the project could have been had the specifications been more ambitious.

That is not to say that ambitious projects are always failures.

When Eurotunnel finished building a tunnel that linked Britain and France for the first time in 20,000 years, it was not only the most ambitious engineering project of its kind in the world – it was a success. The tunnel is open most of the time, the trains don't always break down or catch fire and the water hasn't come in.

However, it cost three times as much as expected, may take decades to break even and is now in danger of putting the main contractor, Eurotunnel, into receivership.

Highly ambitious computer projects are the same. You may recoup your investment sometime in the next century, but only if Providence is firmly on your side. Even then you will need to have planned the project in horrendous detail: for example, by allowing for the disruption in the office caused by an upgrade of hardware and software every time Microsoft's chairman Bill Gates says it is necessary. And once you have costed everything, right down to the new ergonomic chairs and larger desks to accommodate the bigger, higher-resolution monitors that are demanded by the more discerning computer users, you will need to multiply your meticulously calculated cost estimates by three. If at this stage your financial director needs to be scraped off the ceiling, you should be grateful that a serious problem has been identified now rather than later.

You may think this is an exaggeration of the problem, yet most of the case studies in this book show that ambitious projects are embarked upon with little real notion of the cost or the time it will take. The computer managers think they know. The suppliers also think they know – but confidence is the feeling you have before you fully understand the problem.

So how do you computerise in small, manageable chunks? Well, it doesn't mean splitting the project into four stages, each the size of the Eiffel Tower. It means computerising the accounts, then the stock control, and when everything is working demonstrably well, considering how the warehousing operation can be automated and whether this can be linked to the stock control, ledger and invoicing systems. This is the prosaic approach; it takes all the excitement out of installing new computers, and it will fail to turn your business overnight into the best and lowest-cost in the marketplace, but it is low-risk, and introduces the advantages of computerisation gradually, allowing the staff and the management to become accustomed to a new way of working.

It isn't cheap. Computerising bit by bit means that, two years on, you will feel it would have been cheaper to have computerised in one go; and you would have had the added benefit of a fully integrated system instead of a new range of disparate computers bought at different times that cannot be linked without major difficulties.

However, ambitious, fully integrated pioneering systems tend not to work first time, cost much more than planned, take three times as long, and may incapacitate your business if you are dependent on their successful operation.

It is clear, then, that, through better integration, an ambitious system *can* deliver a cornucopia of business benefits – doing more and costing less – than a simple one. The chances are, however, that it won't work. If you can keep it simple, you won't have to make contingency plans for a total write-off of the trebled cost estimate and a return to the old manual procedures.

But remember that you may not have the experience to recognise an overambitious project. One building construction company in the west of England, which was aware of the dangers of pioneering, stipulated in its contract with a multinational computer company that the software must not be pioneering: it must be a widely used, standardised package. But the construction company had also expected the package to do everything it wanted – which it didn't. So the users allowed the supplier to make some 'minor' software changes.

With a standard package there is no such thing as a 'minor' code change. It is like trying to add an appendage to a human being. Imperfect as we are, we are tried and tested and are unlikely to work better with two hearts, or run faster with three legs. If you want to keep the project really simple, buy a package but *don't modify it*.

Exactly what is meant by overambition and why it is important to keep it simple is shown by the Performing Right Society . . .

CASE STUDY

It is 1987, and one of Britain's oldest-established and most respectable institutions, the Performing Right Society, is shambling unknowingly towards a chasm. Few people outside the music business are aware of the society's existence. It advertises itself only discreetly, through hand-sized (PRS) stickers in the windows of shops and restaurants.

But the PRS is notorious among music composers. The manager of the pop group U2, Paul McGuinness, is not alone in believing that the society is 'superlatively inefficient'. It was founded in 1914 by music hall composers as a non-profitmaking association to collect royalties in return for granting a 'performing right' for music to be played in public.

The principle has come to be that public houses, theatres, clubs, restaurants, radio and TV stations, and cable and satellite operators pay the society a royalty for every piece of live or recorded music, but the span of organisations that are paying royalties – and who need to be chased to pay royalties – has been increasing. This is good for the music industry but imposes an increasing burden on the PRS.

Royalties must be paid for every piece of music used as background in drama series, advertisements and jingles; the signature tunes of TV and radio programmes; and the compact discs and other records played on the radio, in shopping precincts, clubs and discos.

For each performance a fee is paid to the society, which has a monopoly on the collection of royalties for musical performances in the UK.

The royalty rates vary from a few hundred pounds for a song on BBC TV's *Top of the Pops* to a few pence if a PRS inspector spots a piece of music being played in a supermarket. Keeping track of what music has been played, how much is owed, who should receive the money and what percentage, is what keeps the society in existence; but existence is hardly the right word.

Its jaws captured £178 million in 1995, which it distributed, less costs, to its 28,000 members, who are mostly composers and publishers.

The 'costs' part of the equation is conspicuously high. In 1914 it was assumed that administrative fees would be negligible. By 1994, the society swallowed one pound in administrative costs for every five pounds that it paid to its musicians and publishers.

And by 1995 when the society was facing an investigation by the Monopolies and Mergers Commission into allegations of unfair practices and administrative inefficiencies, Sir Bryan Carsberg, director of the Office of Fair Trading, said he had 'grounds for concern that the society may not be operating in a fully efficient and accountable manner'.

However, in 1987, when the plot begins, members' outbursts against the PRS's inefficiency were fairly infrequent, such that the society felt free to make whatever decisions it wanted, unimpeded by any compelling need to explain all its administrative affairs to ordinary members.

At this time, almost nobody outside the PRS knew what was going on inside, and not many inside knew either.

STAGE ONE

Within the computer department a decision is taken to upgrade the mainframe operating system from DME to VME. Although DME runs perfectly well from the organisation's point of view, it is out of date, and the number of people with an understanding of it is diminishing; so, at some point, it will need replacing. Also, working on an old operating system makes it difficult to recruit the best people and is not much fun for the existing computer staff. Their employability may slip if they don't keep up with the latest systems, so computer staff will often prefer, and indeed may pressurise, an organisation into buying the latest of everything.

But moving from one operating system to another, incompatible, one is a fairly big step, like replacing all the wiring in an old house. In determining how to go about it, the computer staff at the society discover that similar royalty-collecting organisations in other countries are technological light-years in advance of the PRS, particularly Austria. So the PRS computer managers decide not merely to catch up all the rest but leapfrog them.

The tedious DME-to-VME upgrade is put on the shelf, while investigations begin into the possibility of building an enormous new single database to rationalise all the small chunks of the computerised and semi-computerised processes within the PRS. It seems like a great idea, particularly as some of the software is nearly 25 years old and is costly to maintain. And so a major exercise begins in justifying the costs of the new project.

Such an exercise is easily performed. Superficially, you can justify the costs by estimating that the project will pay for itself within two years because of the savings; and the savings can be easily calculated by assuming that computerisation will mop up all wastage and redundant administrative tasks, leading to a vast reduction in staff numbers. To a non-technical chief executive, these efficiency savings will seem to have been calculated with mathematical precision. **Yet this, and other case studies, show that you cannot know what the savings will be until the new system has been in live use for some time.**

And though there may be tangible and intangible benefits from computerisation, don't assume that staff savings will inevitably be one of them. British Rail built new systems for privatisation, with the expectation that they would replace low-grade staff. In fact even some small offices had to hire extra people merely to maintain the new, complex systems.

In the case of the Performing Right Society, it argues that a new database will cut 135 staff, and save up to £4 million a year on the £20 million administration costs. The project is supposed to make a profit from soon after completion to happily ever after. This all makes sense to the PRS hierarchy because it is generally thought that computers replace people and make organisations efficient. A cut in staff would also offset the increases in the number of inspectors who were needed to police the growing number of organisations playing live and recorded music. And so the suppliers are called in . . .

STAGE TWO

As often happens on a major project, once the decision to start has been taken there is no provision for turning back. Everyone assumes that the new systems will be delivered.

Tacitly, reputations are staked on the project's success. Yet there should be every allowance, every contingency and every expectation of failure. However, the PRS is blighted by its unfamiliarity with failure, so it doesn't plan for one. Most noticeably, the project lacks any individual who has a notice on his desk saying 'the buck stops here'.

With any major computer project a single person is needed to take charge who has a profound grasp of the business and the technology, and who is empowered to take major decisions – otherwise group responsibility prevails.

And the thing about groups is that everyone hands over responsibility for his or her individual actions to the group, with the dangerous result that the project starts to control its own destiny. It takes on a life of its own, and everyone works for the sake of the project and not the business.

This is manifest in some of the documents that give an insight into the thinking of the PRS managers at the time. One report from a supplier uses many phrases that mean little to directors but are fashionable in the computer industry . . . 'the need to create a logical design study' and 'evaluate the appropriate architecture with which to provide a sound platform for development of future systems' and 'implement a new system known as the Performing Right On-Line Membership System (PROMS) in a fourth-generation language (4GL) accessing a Relational Database Management System both running under the Unix operating system.'

At this stage along the pitted route, the project managers do not appear to realise that the society's administrative processes are not in a fit state to be computerised. These processes are all too arcane, too complex, too little understood by even the staff, let alone outside suppliers and programmers.

Much work is needed on becoming familiar with and marshalling the information to be computerised, long before computerisation. The best maxim at this stage would have been: **simplify before computerising.**

Not realising this, the PRS becomes enveloped in choosing the technology rather than questioning whether the manually-held information is in a fit state to be computerised, and whether the PRS as an organisation has the skills and understands the implications of computerisation. Everyone seems to assume that computerisation and improvement will go hand in hand.

Worse, a 'Big Bang' tends to become the preferred plan: an all-encompassing rather than a step-by-step approach to computerisation.

For example, the PRS could have first tackled the computerisation of the intricate web of processes that are used to verify the entitlement to royalties of living people. If this was successful, then thought could have been given to the more complex task of automating the process involved in establishing the bona fides of descendants of deceased members who are also entitled to royalties. However, it tries to capture the living and the dead in one techno-swoop.

Another problem is that few PRS managers appear to check whether the paper-based musical legal agreements between, say, a musician and a publisher are in a standardised format that can be transferred onto a database.

In fact each agreement is as individual as the people named in it. Some of the agreements are short and some very long, and although it is vital for the database programmers to know how short the shortest is, and how long the longest, nobody goes through the hundreds of thousands of agreements to find out.

It is also uncertain what crucial information needs to be entered into database fields, and what secondary data can be relegated to the textual 'notes' sections of the database.

The assumption is, in looking at a few agreements, that they are typical of the rest, but they are not. One cannot imagine designing a new car from a specification that says the biggest person is 'quite tall' and smallest person 'pretty small'.

However the PRS goes ahead with building a new database without understanding the extremes in the size of its legal contracts – and without understanding the information and many inconsistencies in the documents.

If it sounds too fundamental an oversight to be true, history testifies to worse events. The Leaning Tower of Pisa leans because Italian engineers in the eleventh century put in the foundations without reaching bedrock first. In the seventeenth century the Swedes built a ship, the *Vasa*, so top heavy that soon after completion it sank in Stockholm Harbour. And in 1996 it emerged that the Western Isles Council had built a £2.2 million harbour with the entrance in the wrong place. It had positioned the entrance where prevailing south-westerly winds together with a large Atlantic swell made it impossible for boats to use the harbour other than in good weather – which is rare in the Outer Hebrides.

In the Society's case, a mastery of the business rather than technical problems prior to the computerisation could have made the difference between success and failure.

The Singaporean government made a success of a huge computer project (see Chapter 10) by radically changing and standardising its administrative procedures long before it chose the hardware and software. But for the Performing Right Society, such a radical change would have been impossible without a different attitude. The whole organisation would have had to be involved in the modernisation programme. And one person would have needed a profound overview of the business first and the technology second. As it was, the computerisation was mainly the province of a few specialists who seem to have been preoccupied with specifying the technology. Not that they were to blame. Understandably, there seems to have been no will in the organisation to spend unendurably tedious hours, weeks, months or even years simplifying and standardising the information in all the legal agreements before computerising them.

To do that would have required a data modernisation programme that could only have been undertaken by PRS legal and other experts, that is, the non-technical specialists.

And here the experiences of Buckingham Palace might have been helpful. Contrary to popular opinion the Queen, in her own house (the Royal Household), does not spend lavishly. Indeed, computer staff at the Palace complain that she displays every quality of the perfect computer project leader: she spends nothing without evaluating the risks; is unadventurous, unenterprising, unexcitable, deliberately slow-moving and, best of all, tight-fisted; every trait that was anathema to the PRS. Therefore, the Queen's main computer project has been a success. Over a period of eight years, the Queen will computerise details of more than one million art and other treasures in the Royal Collection. She spent less than £400,000 on the hardware and software because of the simplicity of the systems. Her household did not opt for a system that sought to dispense with 25 per cent of her Yeomen of the Guard, but for a straightforward database that could accept a vast quantity of information in a standardised format. The aim was to use computers to keep track of paintings, books and other possessions that might be lent to world leaders or borrowed by such illuminati as Prince Charles. The systems have helped to ensure that borrowed treasures and artefacts are eventually returned to the right place.

But what has made the system an obvious success is that the data is being entered onto it not by computer specialists, or cheap labour from a Third World country, but by the Palace's art historians: the experts. They know the value of the information currently held in manual form and what needs to be recorded on the database. For example only an expert will know when a painting has been restored satisfactorily or improperly and by whom, and whether this should be recorded on the new database. Their work in building the database is expected to take five or more years but the Royal Household will not be rushed.

In contrast the PRS managers convinced themselves there was a business imperative for the project's rapid implementation, as indeed there was, because, with all the suppliers and consultants involved, the cost was rising daily . . .

A project director for the PROMS project is chosen from a reputable consultancy company, but it is the same company that had helped with some of the earlier studies.

Nobody stops to question whether the consultancy is detached enough from the whole process to give an entirely independent view. Neither does it occur to the society that, in trying to modernise, it has set technical, rather than business, objectives.

Having taken the fateful decision to launch PROMS, the next step is to choose hardware and software suppliers. Problems emerge from the start but are not thought serious. Some of the shortlisted suppliers run performance tests to show that a simulated version of PROMS will run magnificently on their hardware.

However the tests are not of much use because the new database has yet to be adequately designed and nobody inside the PRS has much experience of a fourth-generation language or relational database management system, which adds a comic touch to the decision to opt for a fourth-generation language and relational database management system.

To complement this lack of skills, none of the suppliers know exactly what demands there will be on the system by end-users, nor how big the system will need to be: so they extrapolate their own figures from tests.

In fact what the tests show is that the project is fundamentally flawed, though this is not obvious at the time because all the immense problems that surface during the tests are deemed surmountable.

Perhaps it was thought that going back to square one would be politically unacceptable given that a team had been set up to manage and complete the project.

Managers then try to pick the hardware before they know the size of the software that will run on it.

In any case the software cannot be designed adequately because the PRS project staff do not understand all the business needs well enough. And if the staff don't understand, is there much hope for the suppliers?

What was needed at this stage was for the suppliers to drop completely any notion of computerising and spend the next few months doing nothing but talking to the hundreds of end-users about what they do and how they do it – extracting from them how they spend their day from sitting down at their desks in the morning to the time they leave in the early evening. Only then would the suppliers and project staff have sufficient understanding of the guts of the PRS's day-to-day work to understand its subtleties and nuances – for example, the shortcuts people use to work around bottlenecks in the system, or the problems they encounter when dealing with certain types of business or transactions.

Only when the technologists understand the business as well as the chief executive and end-users should the method of computerisation be considered. Computerisation is the very last stage of a computer project.

Until this point all the decision-making should be directed to answering one question: should we continue with the project?

Nine-tenths of the work on the project should be exploration, experimentation, fault-diagnosis, discussions with end-users, the anticipation of all possible problems, the simplification of processes, the understanding of the quality and flaws in existing data, the difficulties of transferring it to a new system (is it desirable to transfer existing data to the new system or would it be better to clean it up completely by entering data afresh?), and quantifying the tangible business benefits – *not* technological benefits – of computerisation. Every difficulty, every risk that is anticipated, should be examined. If anything, risks and problems should be deliberately magnified, so that nobody overestimates the likelihood of success. If, after all this, computerisation is still considered a feasible option, the chief executive should approve the project only on the basis that there will be numerous intermediate 'stop-go' decisions that determine whether the project will be abandoned or continued. **None of the project team should feel under pressure to suppress bad news to save their skins. They should always feel they can express the view to the chief executive that the project is going nowhere. In most failures, staff who knew there were major problems kept quiet to avoid jeopardising their jobs.** Management must encourage a spirit of openness – where problems are aired not suppressed.

If a project is abandoned before a further major investment decision is taken, and you are upset at the losses so far, console yourself with the knowledge that the losses, although painful now, could prove fatal for you or even your company if you continue. And if you've learned from the mistake the costs to date won't be an unmitigated loss.

It is also worth remembering that no failed projects are noticeable as such at the time. They fail one day at a time.

At this early stage everyone at the PRS seems to be bathing in their own ignorance – which is definitely a good thing if that ignorance is recognised and attempts are made to address it. However, an independent report would later observe that the PRS was not the sort of organisation that encourages self-criticism.

In any case it is difficult at this point for the computer department or suppliers to admit to any lack of understanding. They are supposed to be the experts.

But this façade of erudition makes it difficult for them to

communicate easily with non-technologists within the PRS who, now and again, ask how PROMS is going. The questioners are told that the decision to adopt the Unix open system means that the PRS is not constrained to roll out the production systems on the same platform as that on which they are developed.

Not understanding a word, the questioners dare not enquire of the project's progress again, for fear of further exposing their ignorance.

To its credit, the main consultant to the project, Learmonth Burchett Management Systems, warns the PRS that the computerisation is high risk, but it is felt the risks are acceptable. It is worth noting that in every would-be disaster that is categorised in the early stages as high risk, board approval is forthcoming because the risks are deemed acceptable, though the basis of this assessment is rarely scrutinised.

Meanwhile anyone outside the society who doubts the high-risk strategy is told that the PRS has invested considerable efforts and money in reducing and managing the risks. However, not everyone in the society realises the extent to which it is pioneering. No other organisation has such a large system running under Unix. PROMS is supposed to:
- have 300 on-line screens and 150 supporting batch or background processes;
- have an enormous go-live database of 16 Gbytes, growing by 10 per cent every year for the foreseeable future;
- handle up to 14 pairs of messages* every second – the requirement is that an end-user can ask a question of the system and get a reply within two seconds for 90 per cent of all message types even under peak loading; for 98 per cent of message types there must be a maximum response time of four seconds;
- have a database design containing 170 tables, with an average of six tables in every multi-table join with some joins across 16 tables (the maximum a relational database could handle at that time, according to an internal report).

The existing system runs on the PRS's mainframe, which was built to handle large, well-established routines. Therefore the work runs smoothly. But the PRS insists on moving to Unix, an operating system developed by universities *for* universities, which

* A message pair is a request by the end-user followed by a response from the system. This delay is known as the response time. In a good system, the response time will be measured in fractions of a second. With the PROMS system, response times could be measured in portions of hours.

has been adapted to the business world and therefore has many shortcomings. In particular, it was not originally designed to run high-volume, complex transactions – the type of transaction that the PRS plans to run on it.

However the PRS wants to move to Unix because that's the way the computer industry seems to be inexorably going. At this time, Unix seems to offer 'open systems', in other words, the ability to the run software on any Unix supplier's hardware.

This may be a mistake, however. The PRS was computerising partly because of the technology (the perceived need to move to Unix) rather than because of a clearly defined business need.

Aided by consultants, the PRS chooses six hardware suppliers who, it feels, can meet the PROMS criteria. All are invited to tender, but two decline. When the four who respond propose wildly different solutions, this should sound alarm bells at PRS headquarters.

It indicates that suppliers do not really know how to go about building PROMS and could end up learning about the risks of computerisation at the PRS's expense. But at this stage all is virtually lost. In a major project the point of no return is reached only when the project professionals, the computer department and suppliers talk unceasingly about the limitations, capabilities, and intricacies of the technology, not whether what they are doing is feasible.

In the corridors of the PRS computer department, the abstruse talk is of allowing conventional single-machine configurations where the application and database are on the same computer to share available resources, or whether symmetric multiprocessors with their own on-board memory cache but shared main memory are the best option . . . !

The PRS also wants to push back the frontiers of database science, and avoid performance problems by having the huge complex database run on a multiplicity of processors.

Yet, at this point, few if any databases were infinitely scaleable; that is, their speed could not always be improved simply by increasing the size of hardware. There comes a point when a Unix database won't run any faster even if you attach to it skyscrapers of computers. If, at this stage it is felt that the database cannot be redesigned more simply on Unix, it would have been advisable for the society to have considered reverting to the traditionalist approach: using the brute power of the mainframe. But the PRS never seems to have seriously considered this. By now everyone seems bent on the successful completion of PROMS on Unix.

The warning signs continue to be strewn densely across the PRS's path. For example suppliers estimate that the computer power needed to run PROMS will be between 57 and 120 millions of instructions per second. This is a little vague, rather like telling an architect: 'Build me a new house of between four and twelve bedrooms.'

None of these ambiguities impede the project's 'progress'. The next step is for the PRS to do what it does best: form a committee. This one is called the selection committee; it studies proposals from hardware suppliers.

The committee seems to consider every possibility except one: that computerisation won't work. It scrutinises the availability of fourth-generation languages for the proposed hardware, the cost of ownership, the processor's architecture, the expansion potential, the product's history of reliability, the engineering and technical support available from the supplier. It examines the track record and financial stability of the supplier. It also investigates the supplier's 'product-set familiarity and commitment to open systems'.

From this all-embracing review, two suppliers are chosen: Hewlett-Packard and Pyramid Technology. Onto the next step: running a test to see whether either supplier's systems can run the PROMS software.

There is one particular drawback with the tests: no PROMS software has been written yet. A subset of the software should have been written long before the type of hardware is selected. But it is felt that the project timescales are too tight to wait for PROMS to be developed. Much could be learned about project timescales from Buckingham (we-will-not-be-rushed) Palace.

This brings us to another factor common to almost all computer disasters: that systems are built to artificially tight deadlines.

Usually it is the suppliers who force impulsive decisions by promising a discount on purchases, or free support or other sales incentives if a commitment to buy software or, particularly, hardware is made before a certain date. Of course the incentive is still available after that date, but the sales technique always beguiles some user organisations.

In this case the PRS has set its own tight deadlines and, perhaps ludicrously, is having to compromise to meet them, though this provides some real excitement, a genuine purpose to the otherwise humdrum day to day work.

Nearly two-thirds of the PRS's entire computer department are diverted to working on PROMS. And there is no time to waste. The whole project acquires its own momentum, like a committee-driven runaway train.

Having chosen two hardware suppliers the PRS has no software to test so it decides to build a prototype or mini version of the software. The problem is how to design a mini database that is truly representative of a database design that has not yet been designed.

A further problem is how to simulate 100 to 200 active ad-hoc users of the new system. These can then link into the database that has not yet been designed. All these challenges seem insuperable until a bright manager at the PRS finds the solution: set up another committee. By the 8 October 1990 there is a benchmark team, which has been given a deadline of the 30 November 1990 to produce a project plan to develop and test systems that can be used to test other systems. But how?

The benchmark team consults the PROMS development team and they design a cut-down version of software that everyone thinks will be representative of PROMS. It is not felt necessary to mock up a full design of the database (so none of the real problems will emerge at this stage). Neither is it thought necessary or desirable to gather together 300 real-life end-users for the test. So how could an automated way of simulating users' needs be found?

To the rescue comes Hewlett-Packard with some of its own test software. This captures a typical electronic 'conversation' between a would-be end user of PROMS and the database itself, and then replays the keystrokes, extrapolating test results as it goes along. Unfortunately the software does not count the number of transactions. But there is no panic. The code is modified to log the entry and exit times to each program, recording at the same time the identity of the simulated end-user and his/her screen.

This time it is noted that the test software does not record end-user response times. More work and the problem is overcome. The benchmark team is delighted with the results. Its investigations have given a continuous and immediate indication of the new system's performance and allowed the team to detect anything unacceptable . . . with one proviso.

Nobody knows what will happen when 300 *real-life* human users try to log on . . . so more tests are organised with the help of the hardware supplier Pyramid, and, much to the relief of the benchmark team, it is found that the new database will cope with all 300 users logged on simultaneously – but response times at the terminals are looking pallid.

Far from coping with 14 message pairs per second, only two messages per second are handled by the Pyramid and 3.9 on the Hewlett-Packard. In short, neither manufacturer's hardware can meet the anticipated demands of PROMS. One unintentionally humorous report on this stage of the project concludes: 'Both systems can handle 300 users – but not running PROMS.'

The benchmark results are conveyed to the database and fourth-generation language product suppliers, who are disinclined to believe them. They say the problems are due to inefficient implementation of the database design. So a second benchmark test is devised. This time consultants from hardware and software suppliers are given access to PROMS design documents and application code. Still nobody seems to have seriously asked the question: 'Shouldn't we abandon the whole thing?'

The second benchmark on the Hewlett-Packard equipment produces some results that are worse than the first test. Instead of being able to cope with the anticipated 300 end-users it can manage up to 60.

The conclusion is that it won't work, but another solution is found: go back in technological time and replace the fourth generation language with a third generation one: the 'C' language. More benchmarks are arranged with software written in C. These show a dramatic improvement. The hardware can handle up to half of the required number of end-users.

The next step is to see whether the Pyramid hardware fares even better. It fares worse. Response times are an 'unacceptable' 14 seconds. The PRS's Pyramid benchmark team is about to abandon this test when a modification in the way queries are routed to the database is suggested.

This effects a dramatic improvement. But sadly there is not enough money, time or available equipment to run a third benchmark to test the latest changes on the Hewlett-Packard equipment.

So the conclusion at this stage is unsatisfactory. The tests show that the Unix hardware may or may not be sufficient: not a good basis for investing £11 million in a project.

By December 1990, only about £2 million has been spent and there is time to scrap the project without too heavy a loss. An independent review of the project will cost a further £200,000, but could prevent more money being wasted – but no such review is commissioned. Indeed progress reports were being issued at this time which showed long lists of issues to be resolved. But it was being claimed that the project was well under control.

STAGE THREE

It is the summer of 1991 and everything seems to be going according to plan, or rather nobody has reported any deviation from plan to the directors. A few weeks later a bombshell is dropped on the PRS's governing council: there is to be a ten-week delay to the timetable for PROMS.

By February 1992, six weeks before the deadline of the live operational use of PROMS, the deadlines are abandoned. This is put down to teething troubles, the sort of thing you would expect with any new system. The fact is, however, that the tests have so far been carried out on sample transactions: a largely theoretical process. When it comes to running the real system, using actual contracts between composers and publishers, it is found that these paper-based files are in a near chaotic condition, at least for the purposes of entering them on a database.

For example it is critically important that PROMS records the start date and end date of contracts for musical works. These dates dictate when the payments of royalties begin and end. It is found that some contracts do not seem to show an end date. An expert from the PRS needs to read through an agreement, which might be more than a dozen pages, to spot the end date for a single contract among a sea of legalese . . . it takes considerable time for an expert to pore over one document, yet the PRS has about 500,000 agreements: at any one time the PRS licenses over 16 million compositions.

It becomes horribly and patently clear that there is no easy automated way to convert all the paper-based agreements to a computerised format.

Not having ordered its own files into a standardised format, the society does not really know what size of database it will need or the size of computer or the amount of storage. Even by guessing the loads on the system, it is realised that no Unix hardware is going to be powerful enough to handle 300 end-users running the PRS's highly complex queries, and still give adequate response times at the terminal. According to one PRS executive at the time, tests showed that, instead of giving a split-second response, it would take up to half an hour to question and receive an answer from the system.

It is now realised that computerisation is going to take much longer and cost much more than expected.

By August 1992, outsiders begin asking questions about the project and are told there are no serious problems. Soon afterwards, however, following a trade press article about the PRS's computer problems, the society orders a technical assessment of the whole project, which reveals inadequacies in the July plan. This prompts yet another plan, which emerges in November 1992, proposing a new target date for operational use of PROMS by September 1994 – two years later than first expected – and at an additional cost of £6 million.

But by this time a new consultant working at the society, John Rathbone, has conducted his own study on PROMS and discovers major problems.

He recommends that work be suspended; and refuses to bow to pressure from insiders and some other consultants to re-interpret his findings to reflect PROMS in a more positive light. His report goes to PRS council, which takes a momentous decision . . .

STAGE FOUR

The PRS council orders a suspension of PROMS. Four days after the PRS staff are told that PROMS is being put on ice, Michael Freegard, the society's chief executive – a full-time employee for 23 years – announces his resignation. However there is no evidence that he is to blame. Indeed one wonders if he and some other executives who left after PROMS was suspended had offered themselves as scapegoats.

At the time, PRS's chairman, Wayne Bickerton, assures the music industry, through the trade press, that PROMS is 'not being scrapped'. The PRS council, meanwhile, asks the independent consultant Ewen Fletcher of Context Systems to conduct an all-embracing, penetrative post-mortem on the cause of PROMS's collapse. The subsequent report should hold absolutely nothing back, not even the names of those it felt were responsible for the failure.

Meanwhile a letter surfaces that shows that the PRS was warned as far back as 1989 that PROMS was heading for trouble. Written by Computer Corporation of American, a major US-based database company that supplies some of the main software databases for companies such as Marks and Spencer, the letter warned the PRS that it had, in its software shortlist, rejected two out of three of the database suppliers whose software was capable of running a system the size of PROMS.

It had picked one of the three – the German company Software AG – but had later rejected this as well. Almost preternaturally, the letter had said:

> The track record which exists for those three companies for systems of this scale would indicate that the PROMS system could only be run on a computer the scale of an IBM mainframe or its equivalent, and not on a smaller computer.

And this letter was sent to the PRS *three years* before PROMS failed; and one of the chief causes of failure would turn out to be that the software was too big and complex for the 'smaller' Unix computers that had been chosen to run it.

But it's March 1995, and Fletcher has completed and submitted his full report to the PRS's council, which decides not to publish it. As expected, it names those staff who, in Fletcher's opinion, are principally responsible for the failure.

But at a council meeting, one of those present asks why no directors are named in a sanitised summary of the report, which has been prepared for general publication. The reply is that the summary is 'not intended to be a whitewashing but a factual statement'. It is added that there is no mention of directors in the original Context Systems report 'in view of the fact that it had been prepared for the directors themselves'.

It is said in the Context report that senior managers who were involved with PROMS did not display an understanding of the needs of large development projects or the needs of information technology, behaved as if there were no serious problems, and should have sought advice from outside consultants or advisers who were not involved with the project team.

There had been an external consultancy working on the project but it had been closely involved since the preparatory work and its independence is questioned by Fletcher.

In fact, his report says that the project had been fundamentally flawed when the managers commended it to the council in 1990, and thereafter they presided over an expensive failure.

The accusations begin to fly.

The report concludes that a contractor which was paid to design the physical details of the database was not given sufficient information to do the job properly. As a result, assumptions were made that later proved to be incorrect, the knock-on effect being that the database was not designed efficiently. Fletcher believes that managers should have been warned of the risks of designing a database without adequate information.

Fletcher also confirms that the requirements for the new system were not in a format that could be easily comprehended and assessed by 'ordinary' people; and that the PRS council had not been kept informed of the state of the project.

The Fletcher report goes on to note that the project team has asked for £6 million and a further two years to complete the first phase of the project. Yet, at the same time, the team is uncertain about whether it can successfully complete the second phase.

In Fletcher's opinion, neither the project team nor the most senior managers at the PRS has understood the causes of the failure. He feels that a prudent project director would have suspended the project at the start of 1991 to check the causes of the problem and to ensure that the plans were sound before committing PRS to large items of project expenditure.

A review at that time would have cost less than £200,000 and would have revealed some deep-rooted flaws.

Fletcher considers that all project expenditure other than the first £3 million has been unnecessary. Particularly pertinent is his comment that, for the project to be successful, the managers and staff would need to be open about mistakes and failures, to learn from them, be willing to expose their work to review by their peers, and have the capacity to accept responsibility themselves for the work that they and their staff do.

Such an approach appears to us to be lacking within the PRS, says Fletcher.

If, as seems likely, this was also true in 1990 then the prevailing attitude would have contributed to the failure of the PROMS project, he adds.

His report recommends that the PRS considers dismissing certain managers, which is what happens.

Two middle-ranking managers are sacked, and the PRS is judged by the music industry to have acted decisively. Indeed the PRS's chairman, Wayne Bickerton, tells the music press that the senior managers singled out in the PROMS report have been disciplined or dismissed.

What the music industry doesn't know and is never told, however, is that the managers take legal action over unfair dismissal and quietly win substantial compensation. The PRS imposes a condition in the settlement that neither party should tell anybody about the settlement.

At an open meeting to discuss the PROMS disaster, Bickerton discloses the rift between the elected council directors and members, and the former executive management. He says the council was 'misled again and again' over PROMS. He concedes that most members of the council had misgivings about PROMS in 1991 but were advised that any changes to PROMS would have had a devastating effect on staff.

A highlight of the open meeting is a call for the directors to resign en masse, which the directors dutifully agree to consider. Five days later, they meet and decide that en bloc resignation would 'not be in the interests of the membership at a time when the society faces many problems requiring action by those with a detailed knowledge of the issues and personalities involved'.

In any case the PRS is able to point to the fact that a few of the directors have changed and that a new chief executive, to replace Freegard, has been appointed.

But the society's problems are not over. It finds itself in further trouble by confirming that it has dispensed with two managers over the PROMS failure, but it does not name them publicly. This leads to Robert Abrahams, a former deputy chief executive, suing the PRS for libel. He argues that ordinary people could mistakenly believe that he is one of the sacked managers.

In a settlement believed to cost the PRS more than £200,000, the society concedes that Abrahams is not named in the 'Context' report and that he bore no responsibility for the failure of

PROMS. In fact, he had sought to warn the society of the impending collapse of PROMS.

So the final cost of the PROMS fiasco is greater than that stated. Of the £11 million spent on the project, £8 million is written off. Then there are the sums paid to the managers over their unfair dismissal plus the settlement and payment of costs over the Abrahams libel action.

In an attempt to recover its costs, in late 1994, the PRS embarks on a legal action against LBMS, and says it is prepared for a 'long haul'. LBMS warns its shareholders that it has received a writ from the PRS, and sets aside £320,000 for anticipated legal costs, although its says this 'may or may not be enough'.

And so, in the closing stages of this serio-comedy, the PRS computer department goes back to the very thing that it had abandoned to work on PROMS: the relatively minor conversion of the DME operating system to VME. Not only that, it reverses the decision to move to smaller systems and invests in a more modern mainframe.

A measure of how bad things had become, and the anxiety of the computer department to be seen to be doing ordinary, everyday information technology tasks, is evident in a press release from the society announcing that it has 'successfully installed' a small-scale office automation system.

This is a little like stepping outside your house and declaring proudly to the neighbours: 'I've successfully installed my new fridge.'

And so the drama ends as it began – with the PRS in a muddle, but perhaps less so than in 1987. Now it understands its many weaknesses and has one big strength: John Rathbone, the consultant who in effect discreetly blew the whistle on PROMS. He is promoted to the new post of information systems director and lets some fresh air into the offices for the first time in years.

He has a solid business background and is therefore suspicious of technology and suppliers, and most importantly is not at all a glory-seeker. He is also highly employable because, having lived through a disaster, he is sensitised to the dangers, and can recognise the warning signs of an impending project crash.

He has now set about breaking down the internal empires that have encouraged staff to become preoccupied with their small sections of work at the PRS instead of being part of a team effort.

He is perhaps the best thing to come out of the PROMS fiasco.

In the spring of 1995, the society managed to recover £2.3 million from consultancy LBMS.

A few months later, following complaints about the PRS by its members, the government's Monopolies and Mergers Commission published the results of a long investigation into the PRS. The 362-page report found that the PRS's data had serious shortcomings: duplications between files, missing or incorrect data and inconsistencies or misplaced data. Key information was not where it was supposed to be. The Commission also concluded that the PRS 'failed to consult the membership adequately and that its policies and procedures were not sufficiently transparent'. The PRS response was defensive. It asked the commission whether a society run by and for its members could ever be considered non-accountable.

Yet, despite this and other criticisms of the PRS as an organisation, the commission found that the mainframe-based systems the society is using in the absence of PROMS are well proven, low-risk and are not unduly costly, although they are too inflexible to support any major business changes. It recommended that the PRS simplify its procedures and then computerise incrementally.

And it reasoned that PROMS failed because the project:

> Attempted to change too many things at once with new hardware, new software, new applications, new suppliers and new working practices. There proved to be too many innovations at once but at the time it probably seemed like a major step into a new world of low cost computing and efficient administration.

The PRS has unquestionably learned the lessons, at least as far as computerisation is concerned. It now has the best insurance policy against a further technology disaster: a new computer manager who understands that calamity and overambition are inseparable twins.

CHAPTER TWO

The Second Deadly Sin: Pride (I)

To call pride the Second Deadly Sin is an unfair demotion because it competes readily with overambition as the most common cause of project disasters.

In this context pride refers to a belief among some computer managers that they should know it all – and cannot easily admit when they don't.

The problem is that they have to live up to their reputations as technologically omniscient; a reputation founded on the inflated admiration that the technically inept have of the technically adept.

Yet computer managers are the first to admit privately that they are even more disadvantaged than most of us.

They know only too well how much new technology can achieve and, more importantly, how little it can achieve, but they dare not denigrate or even expose the limitations of computers in front of the board, given the size of the company's information technology budget.

Instead, the computer manager is burdened with an unchallenged reputation as a mysterious and all-knowing fixer, a technologically minded Zeus who costs a lot to feed but controls wondrous machines that can, if properly managed, slay every overt or hidden administrative defect.

The reality is that many computer managers have little or no technical background and are doing the job because of a happy, or often unhappy, accident. They fell into it because there was nobody else, or they showed an interest and aptitude in computers and were eventually asked to become the IT head.

Only they really understand their helplessness.

There are of course many varieties of computer manager but

emasculation seems to afflict two particular types:

There are those computer managers who are at the control of end-users – end-users who have large budgets and little responsibility to the business, other than to their own part of the organisation. At best these end-users view their computer manager as affectionately as they do a rusting double-decker bus. At worst they think of them as a progress-inhibiting troglodyte who sleeps with all the most expensive mainframe computer suppliers, and that is why the costs of computer services are rising every year for no additional benefit to the business. Naturally these end-users feel they know best, being at the sharp end of things, so they want their own departmental systems, servers and technical support. And before long the organisation will have 40 self-appointed computer managers in every section.

Then there are computer managers who are at the control of nobody. They know they are a law unto themselves, and also know that they have dominion over everything except the size of the computer budget. These are an equally common species. They are rendered helpless by being put into a position of unchallenged power because no other senior person in their organisation understands or wants to understand computers. But, not being despotic by nature, these managers grow into it, and begin to see technology not as a tool but as a weapon of control. And soon the technology supplants the ability of the manager to control it. At this point, the manager with a £10 million annual technology budget, who is in charge of £2 million worth of water-cooled mainframe machines, a host of diverse minicomputers, 6,000 PCs and 300 information specialists, has a career built on the strength of technology. They have a vested interest in keeping alive the myth that computers can solve any business problem, even when they know they can't.

These unfortunate managers have had to muster all their guile and ingenuity to maintain the budget. If a major new project comes along, this strengthens the computer department and gives it a higher profile in the company.

If successful, the project may even help to counter some of the criticism of the past performance of the computer department and/or its manager.

Conversely, the highly paid information-technology executive who says, 'No, sorry, we can't develop this major new project because it is neither technically nor managerially feasible' is confessing to a technological impotence that will have the board itching to contract out the computer department – and particularly that negatively-minded manager.

This may sound glib, but the last case study showed that PRS project managers did not pass bad news upwards. This was not because the knowledgeable conspired to suppress news from the unknowledgeable, but because the knowledgeable thought, genuinely, they could get the new project off the ground. However, their misplaced confidence led to the PRS's non-technical directors discovering the project's flaws too late.

The best protection against this is for chief executives to be aware, early on, of *all* the risks of computerisation. They cannot rely on anyone else. Otherwise they will discover, as soon as a project goes wrong, that: **nobody knows anything**.

Anyone investigating the cause of a disaster will find that everyone was working only on their part of the project and did not realise what the others were doing. Had they realised, they would have raised the alarm much earlier.

In short chief executives need to realise that there is no such thing as a computer expert. The only real expert is the chief executive; all the other so-called experts are those who know how to avoid the blame when anything goes wrong.

Of course there are specialists, rather than experts. The ones to be most trusted are those who admit that when complex computer systems interact with a complex business there is no expert on earth who could understand fully all the implications. Few 'experts' will make such an admission, though there is a new breed of computer manager beginning to take form. They are as rare and valuable as gold dust, and are as openly sceptical of what technology can achieve as any victim of a computer disaster.

They will have made their reputations by terrorising yet earning the respect of suppliers, by advocating an annual reduction in the costs of the existing systems, and by being averse to risks but also maintaining a good relationship with their computer departments and saving money by launching projects on a small scale only. In particular they care nothing for empires. One of this category even made himself and his management team redundant to meet the demands of the end-users for lower central IT department costs.

This is a little extreme (and the department dissolved into chaos after his departure) but it shows that not all computer managers are technocratic Napoleons.

Some are, however.

The UK insurance underwriter Hiscocks, which insures suppliers against computer disasters, has studied the subject extensively and one of its overriding conclusions is that catastrophes occur because:

- Sellers promote the idea that computerisation is simpler than it is, and
- Buyers want to believe them.

In short, hardware and software are sold as commodities when they are not.

Anyone who doubts this might do well to remember that a car crash can be caused by a single mistake, for example a burst tyre, but every disaster in this book has occurred because of the largely unpredictable coalescence of a series of mishaps.

But, while the actual events were in themselves hard to predict, the human weaknesses that lay behind them – such as pride – are much more readily identifiable.

So chief executives should beware of anyone who calls himself (or herself) an expert, and should not expect even the computer manager to be an expert.

That said, it is equally ominous if chief executives think a little too highly of their own technological expertise. The autodidactic chairman of a major user company who is a home PC enthusiast and has seen what can be achieved on an Excel spreadsheet, and therefore wants a Pentium P6-based workstation on the desk of every employee, is more dangerous than the most technology delirious computer manager: because he has the power to turn his techno-freakish visions into a catastrophic reality.

One chairman of a large UK company who formerly held a senior position at a computer supplier has sought to implement a computer strategy costing tens of millions of pounds to put a minicomputer on the desk of each of his employees.

He fell into the trap of seeing himself as a technology guru – someone who had seen all the problems before, and thought he know how to overcome them.

And being an enthusiast he always wanted the latest technology: but no project leader can achieve such an ambition in a large company, because technology moves on long before excessively complex projects are completed. However the chairman did not realise this and when he found that his envisioned technology was obsolete before the completion of the project, he aborted all the work to date and started afresh. The same thing happened again, and he has since begun a third attempt.

Apparently he blames the failures on the inadequacies of suppliers and project managers. I am sure he wouldn't accept that the project is simply too big for the latest Unix hardware that he wants to use.

Even today, four years at the time of writing after the project began, the date for project completion is some years away. It's the sort of the project that is perennially nearing completion.

Perhaps the answer, then, is for everyone, from chief executive to directors, computer manager and project leaders to be aware of each other's fallibility, and never assume they know more than you. The key is to be sufficiently detached to see the project's deficiencies, and be able to abort it if necessary, but close enough to know what is going on.

You may think this is a truism, and that I am preaching to the converted. However, the following study of Wessex Regional Health Authority underlines the dangers of everyone thinking that everyone else is an expert when nobody is.

It also strips away the surface of suppliers to show how they can behave when fighting for business.

Further, it is a good example – perhaps the best – of how the politics of the computer industry can become horribly enmeshed with systems projects to produce a disaster on a scale then unknown in the public sector.

CASE STUDY

STAGE ONE

The project began as so many major projects do: with a vision.

And, as you would expect of a vision, it is an excursion into the imagination. It particularly afflicts those who are in a state of delirium. In computer disaster terms, a vision is an essential first stage.

Yet it should be remembered that no sensible computer supplier will decry a vision because it is the most expensive form of computer project. In this case the customer is most especially right.

It was in the early 1980s that Wessex Regional Health Authority had a vision for an integrated information system covering the entire Wessex Health Authority region, incorporating nearly 300 hospitals. Wessex wanted to be different, indeed better than the other eleven regional health authorities in England and Wales.

It called in computer consultants, who seemed to share the vision, whereupon the health authority appears to have lapsed into an eight-year hallucinogenic technology euphoria.

It was a fantasy that cost taxpayers between £43 million and £63 million; and hence was the largest single computing strategy failure in the history of Britain's National Health Service.

More importantly, the case study shows what can happen when an organisation, unchecked by rigorous accountability to those who fund it – in this case the taxpayer – is allowed to spend as much money on computers as it feels is necessary, not only supported by successive chief executives but *encouraged* by them.

The problem here was that chief executives of health authorities were not really in control of their businesses; and oxymoronically had too much control.

The lack of control was because:

Funding was determined at a much higher level, by ministers, who base their decisions mainly on the previous year's budget plus an allowance for inflation.

Health authorities (mainly trusts these days) are answerable to the National Health Service, which is run by the Department of Health, which is run by ministers, who are run by their permanent secretaries. Everyone seems to oversee everyone else but nobody can be actually held responsible for *not* overseeing somebody else.

At the same time, chief executives have much control over their authorities because they are political appointees, with a ministerial mandate that cannot realistically be questioned by non-executives on the board of directors because ultimately, all appointments have to be approved by the government.

Even before considering the computer project it is worth noting in this flawed arrangement that there are parallels with private-sector companies because it often happens that those at a high level who agree to fund a major computer project then take no day-to-day interest in the project's progress or lack of it.

Everything is left to the subordinates who do not have the power, nerve or desire to raise the alarm when the project is slowly cracking around them.

Instead, it is the role of the staff to implement the new system and if they happen to encounter an insurmountable problem, they'll just have to surmount it.

In this case, the project was funded by ministers who, not being experts, left the job of supervising the systems to the Department of Health, which passed responsibility to the health authority, which delegated the job to the chairman, who in part left it to the computer managers and suppliers.

So it was left to these 'real' experts, the computer managers and suppliers, to do their duty and get the systems installed. They were the Light Brigade cavalry with orders to charge. And, as in most wars, the original mandate to fight comes from those who will never have to do the fighting.

Of course, there were Department of Health auditors who issued regular warnings about the lack of management control within the Wessex Health Authority, but these were ineffectual taps on the wrist. Nobody seems to have had the power to pull up the reins and ask, 'Should we be going on with this?'

The project was called RISP, the Regional Information Systems Plan. 'RISK' might have been more apt.

Conceived in 1982, RISP was the offspring of briefings by one of the main suppliers, IBM, whose headquarters was in Havant, not far from the main Wessex Regional Health Authority offices in Winchester. It was a project geared less specifically for patients or even doctors than for administrators.

With such influential sponsors, the project was to have seemingly unlimited funding. Money for computers was found by 'top-slicing' budgets that would otherwise have been used for less important things like hospital beds, new medical equipment and patient care.

The original justification for RISP had been a little vague. The stated aim was to 'use modern technology in order to optimise the use of information in the continuous improvement of the effectiveness and efficiency of clinical and other health services'.

It might have been better if the project was a specific technological answer to a specific business need, such as a new system enabling hospital staff in an emergency to call up the records of a casualty patient from a local GP's system.

Instead RISP seems almost to have been a technology project for technology's sake. A consultancy report that was written when the project was still at an inchoate stage said that the Wessex Health Authority should set a 'goal' for spending on computer systems of 'at least 2% of annual turnover'.

The report did not make any suggestions about what the computers should be used for.

In Wessex's case 2 per cent amounted to more than £10 million, a target it comfortably exceeded.

For the suppliers and consultancies, the spending goal must have seemed like manna from heaven: the health authority had £10 million a year to spend on computers, and it was looking for help in spending it.

Nobody questioned the technology visionaries because the uninitiated felt unqualified to challenge those who were assumed to know what they were doing.

In some areas of the public sector, where many practices and customs date back centuries, and mental languor can sometimes be a way of life, any dynamic executive who shows imagination and a willingness to be innovative and, what's more, understands computers is held in awe.

So even some government ministers have become experts. They are the latest generation of technology visionaries, purveyors of efficiency. Successive Secretaries of State for Health pushed hard for RISP's introduction; and when it would have been in the taxpayer's interests to cancel the project, they advocated its extension, which sent a clear message to the chairmen of the Wessex Regional Health Authority: if you can get RISP successfully developed, your political career is unlikely to suffer.

One of the Wessex authority's chairmen, Robin Buchanan, who pushed particularly hard for RISP's introduction, was later knighted and promoted to one of the most important jobs in the National Health Service, where he was put in charge of a budget of £4 billion.

That RISP and other related computer contracts within the health authority lost between £43 to 63 million was no taint on his character. He had not been responsible for RISP's failure, as most of the major project decisions had been taken before his arrival as chairman. However he had made judgements in relation to contracts at Wessex, which he himself felt could have been improved upon. Indeed, some of his decisions as chairman of Wessex were criticised by a district auditor and later by some MPs. But dispassionate observers were left wondering whether all this criticism enhanced the reputation of the chairman in the eyes of ministers. After all, he had, against all the odds, sought to do his political duty by promoting RISP, as ministers had required him to do. Indeed, when he subsequently left Wessex (for reasons unconnected with RISP: in fact because of promotion in the health service), he was warmly praised by the then Secretary of State for Health, Virginia Bottomley, who said of him, 'I should like to take this opportunity of wishing you continued success in your national role as chairman of the NHS Supplies Authority.'

The only people with no direct financial or careerist equity in the whole RISP affair were the patients and end-users. Eventually it was their interests that were subverted.

In the hundreds of internal Wessex health documents about RISP, hardly a mention is made of the end-users or the supposed beneficiaries: the patients and those whose job it is to look after them.

Almost without exception, the internal documents sought to promote the project with superficially worthy but arguably meaningless mission statements such as the need to develop management strategies that assess the 'availability of time and resources required to develop strategies for organisation and funding and at the same time to maintain implementation progress'.

This was the sort of jargon beloved of officialdom at the Department of Health, and so by the autumn of 1982 RISP was approved in concept, though it was two years before it was formally adopted as a strategy by the board of Wessex Health Authority.

The ministerial love of RISP grew from a belief that it would cut staff, improve the accuracy of information, and make it more complete and quickly available. There was also a hidden agenda. Ministers hoped that the project would provide a technological showpiece that could be flaunted to the media to prove that the political party in power was the party of the twenty-first century. In fact long before the systems were finished, ministers were staging well-publicised visits to local hospitals to see the gestative systems in development.

Little thought seems to have been given, however, to how

useful this timely, complete and accurate data would be, or how easily manually held information could be assembled and converted into computer format, or, most importantly, how local hospital managers would feel about millions being spent on computers at a time when lifesaving operations were being cancelled and wards were closing down because of lack of funds.

Local officials, however, were committed to the idea of having uniform systems around the region; so it was just a question of setting up some committees to decide how to go about it and what to buy – and the world's biggest computer company at the time, IBM, was naturally on hand to give some impartial advice.

This impartiality was conveyed to public servants in the Wessex region at a senior management course run by . . . IBM. The course showed Wessex officials how it was possible, practical and plausible to build a new-style integrated hospital information system, and convinced officials that there was a need for such a system.

The next step was for a team to examine the feasibility and costs of building an integrated system. The independence of the consultancies was again firmly established at this early stage. The authority decided to adopt a 'Business Systems Planning Methodology' – from IBM.

Five 'core' systems that would be RISP were conceived as:

accountancy
manpower
hospital
estates
community

As at the PRS, the emphasis was on 'integration' – the most dangerous word in the computing vocabulary.

All systems were to be accessible from any terminal connected to the network. So someone sitting at a computer anywhere in the region could find out anything they wanted: from when the lease on a building runs out to the quantities prescribed of a certain drug during the three months ended 31 December. A treasure chest of management information was waiting to be discovered for a price of just £26 million (at 1984–5 prices).

The problem was that Wessex was a big authority. It was a four-hour drive from one side of the region to the other. There were nearly 300 hospitals in the region and many of them were major undertakings in computerisation terms. A single large hospital was the size of a major business – yet Wessex's idea was, in effect, to computerise all or most of them as part of the RISP project.

It was a wonderful fantasy, which nobody had the audacity to expose as such. All of RISP's critics were reduced to pusillanimity by the seniority of the project's most vociferous supporters, among them the regional general manager.

Even the Department of Health and successive ministers were fully behind it. The few doctors and nurses who suspected that RISP wouldn't work could not hope to have any influence on the regional health authority, the Department of Health, and the government itself.

It was exactly the same at the PRS where nobody outside the clique of project managers dared question whether the scheme was such a good idea.

In any case it would have been professional suicide for any junior doctor to have blown the whistle on RISP. So, as the project gained momentum, the active resistance to it evaporated. Seven years later, even as RISP was gasping its final short breaths, the regional authority's management were continuing to promote the idea to hospitals and the outside world that the project was a picture of health, a technological panacea.

Yet the project began in the right way. The end-users were always consulted, though they were consulted rather than listened to. They were invited to 'participate' in the project – but the door was closed against high-level control.

Inevitably, therefore, this condescension to the end-users would backfire. In a few years the end-users who worked in the district health authorities would be given more power as part of the government's health service reforms; and in the end they would even control their own budgets – so their belief in RISP would later prove critical to the funding of the project.

This had been known at an early stage by the regional authority, which had always been anxious to avoid alienating the end-users, yet it had not wanted them to know of RISP's technical and growing financial problems either.

So the end-users were left floating in a sort of information vacuum, a bizarre transitional station between the real world and a nether region. They were given a great deal of information on the minutiae of the project, which was no information at all on its actual progress.

Another weakness in the project management was that nobody seems to have thought of simplifying before computerising. True, it is always difficult to effect even small administrative changes in a reactionary organisation, particularly one in the public sector. **It is always much easier to persuade people to accept computerisation than other more deep-rooted changes.**

Workers will always prefer to continue doing things the way they were doing them before; so their only concession to new technology will be to do what they were doing before except on a computer.

In the National Health Service, administrative change was the government's goal, but nobody else's. So computers were used to force through change. And this triggers another attempt at a maxim: **if humans cannot change their own organisations, computers won't do it for them**.

It is worth looking at this maxim a little more closely.

Computerising a business is like computerising your home finances. The new software can tell you all you need to know about how you spend your money, and even give you a bar or pie chart showing last year's babysitting costs against the projected spend next year, but only if you enter all the information the system needs to make its calculations.

This is far more time-consuming than you could imagine. You will need to keep a record of every cash-dispenser withdrawal, every supermarket credit and direct card purchase, every cash receipt for train tickets or petrol and so on.

Then data from each of these will need to be entered onto the system, together with details of every cheque written, every direct debit paid, every standing order, and every credit paid into the bank account, plus any charges, credit or debit interest. And you won't be able to do this until you have understood how the software works. One of the simplest systems on the market comes with a 400-page manual. Another major consideration is the need to back up your data – and carry on doing it every month without fail otherwise all your previous effort will be wasted. And if you make a big mistake without realising it, it will make a nonsense of the data on your overall financial position. In short, computerisation at home does not usually save any time.

It absorbs more time than you ever thought you could spare, although it could transform your home finances by making you realise how much money you spend on nothing in particular.

It is the same with a business: in general computers will make life much more complicated, and problems will take longer to resolve – if they can be resolved at all – though they will help you understand your business better and will even, *on very rare occasions*, give you a competitive edge.

In short the key to successful computerisation is giving more weight to the disadvantages than the benefits. Incidentally, computer managers, suppliers and consultants will rarely if ever talk about the disadvantages of computers.

It has taken me some time to discover that the polite synonym for 'disadvantage' is 'risk'. Suppliers will tend not to tell you that the new system will crash on average three times a day. They will say there is a 'risk' of a possible 5 per cent system unavailability.

Yet, in Wessex's case, the suppliers had been frank. They had briefed the authority on the disadvantages of computerisation. They had warned that:

- there was a considerable risk of slippage against the timetable;
- there was a danger of uncontrolled costs;
- there could be a loss of quality;
- the system might not meet the needs of end-users;
- the requirements of the system could change and the technology move on as the systems were being built.

Clearly – though it was perhaps not clear at the time – RISP was too big. It needed so much forethought that, if all the plans were as detailed as they needed to be, it would be years before the authority could go out to tender to buy the systems – by which time all the planning and the technology would be out of date.

But the warnings of the consultants were no deterrent because, once the idea of large-scale computerisation has a grip on the psyche of an entire organisation, no amount of warnings will have any effect. In fact the advice of the consultants had an effect only inasmuch as it reinforced the impression of the trustworthiness and credibility of the consultants.

As a concession to the risks, the authority compromised: it went out to tender for only three of the five main systems, though it carried on with the design work on the other two wings of the project edifice.

To complicate matters, the region had to contend with all the day-to-day planning, upgrading and operations of the existing systems – all of them proven, reliable and useful systems in their own way; so clearly they would have to be replaced.

The possibility of not going ahead with RISP and instead incrementally upgrading the existing systems, within the capabilities of the internal computer department, seems to have been too simple a solution to have been worth taking seriously.

Alternatively one or two core systems within RISP could have been implemented on their own, but it is hard to get project people motivated over small-scale systems. There's nothing better for morale than setting out to prove everyone wrong by achieving the impossible.

By the mid 1980s, Wessex officials were enthusing over the project in health trade magazines. One executive wrote: 'The benefits that can be identified for each system are far less than what we hope to achieve from a combination of them all.'

His next comment should have sounded an even louder alarm.

'As we are moving into an entirely new approach towards administrative computer systems in the NHS it is extremely difficult to identify and put a firm value upon the comprehensive management information that we hope to provide.'

If no firm value on the benefits could be identified at the beginning of the project, what hope was there at the end? If you are uncertain of why you are buying a car, should you buy one?

My comments are easy to make with hindsight. At the time, every step seemed a natural progression from the last; and indeed, in many ways, the project was quite conventional. As things got underway, consultants did what they always do at that stage: build an impressive mock-up of how the actual system will perform, but the suppliers could not be expected to understand the NHS as well as the hospital administrators. Even so, the project went ahead because the Department of Health and government auditors assumed that:

• those who were buying the systems all knew what they were doing, and

• those who were supplying the systems all knew what *they* were doing.

CHAPTER THREE

The Second Deadly Sin:
Pride (II)

Usually a simulation of a big system, on a single PC, looks so strikingly effective you want to take it home with you.

It is only when you try to switch on the same system with 300 users trying to access it simultaneously, that you realise that somebody somewhere has made a big mistake. In the PRS's case the response times to queries were up to 30 minutes when they should ideally have taken a fraction of a second.

And response times are a crucial determinant of a system's success. People will tolerate watching a soporific TV film for nearly two hours but they won't know the meaning of boredom until they have to sit uselessly in front of a computer screen for 10 seconds.

The problem for the chief executive minding a computer project is that, however thorough the tests, you won't know how bad the response times are until all the end-users are connected. The system may work perfectly well with 230, 240 or 250 users but with 260 it could be appalling. The answer is to add end-users slowly – month by month – and not all in one go, however much testing you've done.

But, to continue with the Wessex story, the regional health authority did not have the experience of other major disasters in the 1980s. So it was more than impressed by the new computerised procedural and data models, which replicated at a high level the total operation of the system. At that time big seemed beautiful. Only large-scale integration of various systems seemed to hold out the promise of a big step forward in efficiency.

STAGE TWO

So RISP began to take form, and consultants produced options for the overall RISP hardware and network architectures.

Time was short. The authority had set itself deadlines that, as it happens, could not be met without the help of more consultants.

So, as at the PRS, Wessex in effect put itself in the hands of the suppliers it had hired for guidance – and there was no going back.

In effect nobody but the chief executive had the authority to say *stop!* And the chief executive was a government appointee with a mandate to contract out more work to private companies.

An invitation to tender for three of the five 'core' parts of RISP drew 100 replies. The authority then drew up a shortlist of suppliers.

From this point on, the events seem to resemble more a television political drama than a real-life purchasing and implementation of computer systems.

Yet, after peeling back all the layers of histrionics, one can see from these events how the computer industry really works. For the Wessex project débâcle is unusual only because every twist and turn in the plot has come to our attention. Usually, when many tens of millions of pounds are lost in a computer project, only a superficial picture emerges of what went wrong.

But Wessex provides an unprecedented insight into some of the methods used by major industry suppliers to win contracts, and the conflicts that can arise among purchasers over what to buy.

To evaluate the bids for the RISP core software, the region and districts set up a joint team. Another team looked at hardware options.

Meanwhile IBM was not excluded from the bidding for the main implementation projects, although it had been involved in early discussions with the authority. The consultancy wing of accountancy firm Arthur Andersen was also allowed to bid, although it had already served as adviser on RISP in 1983 and 1984, and had later become involved in feasibility studies related to the project.

In fact IBM and Andersen teamed up to bid jointly.

That they were in a much stronger position than any other bidder or consortium seems to have mattered little. Other contenders for the huge contract were the UK computer manufacturer ICL, and the US-based suppliers McDonnell Douglas, and the Digital Equipment Company (DEC).

After the evaluation of the bids, each supplier was given a score. The theory was that the one with the highest number of points would win. The scores were:
- McDonnell Douglas 69.4
- Digital Equipment Corporation (DEC) 60.7
- ICL 53.9
- Arthur Andersen/IBM 48.2
- NCR 35.5

McDonnell Douglas was the number-one choice, but the authority was unsure whether its hardware was up to the job. So number two in the ratings, DEC, was chosen as preferred supplier and detailed negotiations began. The other bidders were not rejected out of hand but held in abeyance in case the preferred suppliers dropped out.

Then began the most intense lobbying seen on any major project in the public sector. The most active lobbyists appear to have been the consortium of IBM and Andersen, which had come fourth in the evaluation.

Usually little is ever publicised about the behind-the-scenes machinations of contract tendering and why certain suppliers are selected over others, but this time many of the facts have emerged through 'confidential' reports written by Wessex's independent district auditor.

STAGE THREE

Most of us think of lobbying as a discreet telephone call, or a dinner with the right contact, but it can be much more invasive.

In the US, suppliers bidding for government work are expected to use their influence to best effect. So in the computer industry, where many of the major suppliers are American, it is inevitable that lobbying will comprise more than a single phone call.

Yet the scale of lobbying for Wessex Regional Health Authority's RISP project surprised even the authority's independent auditor.

He would later comment on the 'aggressiveness' of the IBM and Andersen consortium.

- One of IBM's directors was on the board of health authority;
- Another of IBM's directors knew the authority's chairman;
- A lobbyist for Andersen Management Consultants also knew the chairman.

Indeed the lobbyist for Andersen was Patrick Jenkin, a former Secretary of State for Social Security, who, as a minister, had recommended the appointment of the then Wessex Health Authority chairman.

To suppose that neither IBM nor Andersen would use none of these contacts to influence the award of the contract would be naïve.

It began with Jim Foster, IBM's director of corporate relations, a main board member of the health authority. Rather than stand back from the whole affair because of a possible conflict of interest, he wrote a letter to the health authority lobbying for the RISP contract on behalf of IBM.

He later asked the authority to destroy his letter.

Dated 3 May 1986, Foster's letter to Wessex said:

> Since, so far, the appropriate IBM executive has been unable to tell you so directly, I want to do so now: we are a major resource in the Wessex area; we are competent to do what you require; above all we would be determined to make sure that it worked. With 6,000 people in Hampshire, a Scientific Centre and Laboratory within a few miles, and the headquarters plus a major plant 25 miles away, you should not doubt this resolve.

The Regional General Manager replied that he could not see IBM without seeing the other bidders and added enigmatically that the time was 'not yet ripe'.

The letter was revived many years later by the district auditor, who questioned Foster.

The reply was that Foster had wanted to remind the authority to have proper discussions with suppliers. He considered that Wessex had chosen the wrong supplier in DEC and had wanted to voice his concerns.

Foster was not the only weapon in IBM's armoury. Anthony Cleaver, another IBM director, knew the then chairman of Wessex, Professor Sir Bryan Thwaites.

A file record at Wessex shows that Cleaver asked Thwaites

what IBM had to do to remain in the running for the contract.

IBM applied further pressure. There was correspondence from the then chief executive of IBM to Wessex. When questioned about these approaches later, Cleaver said that, as IBM had not been categorically excluded from tendering, this left the door open to make further approaches. He said that information technology in the health service offered a significant market opportunity and IBM was keen to gain a foothold.

Meanwhile Arthur Andersen Management Consultants also sought to change Wessex's mind about the choice of DEC as preferred supplier. Arguably, Andersen was more influential than any of the other bidders. It had already done much of the early planning on RISP, knew the officials at the authority, and understood much of its thinking.

And Andersen's lobbyist-adviser was Jenkin, the former Secretary of State for Social Services, who had been instrumental in appointing Professor Bryan Thwaites, chairman of Wessex.

On behalf of Andersen, Jenkin made a protracted telephone call to Thwaites about the authority's choice of DEC as preferred supplier. The district auditor would later note that Jenkin appeared to have a 'greater depth of knowledge of the RISP tendering procedure than a tenderer would be expected to possess'.

Jenkin iterated Andersen's concern about the choice of DEC, arguing that Andersen had much US experience and so knew that no DEC-based systems could provide the functionality outlined in the authority's invitation to tender.

With due propriety Thwaites made a note of his conversation with Jenkin:

Patrick Jenkin, the last Secretary of State, DHSS [Department of Health and Social Security, as it was then called], rang me this morning in his role as one-day-per-month consultant to Arthur Andersen. He had been briefed in detail and it was one of those trickier conversations since he was, of course, plugging the value-for-taxpayers-money line. Also, that where Wessex leads, others will follow. Here is a brief summary of his main points . . . that no nurses had been involved in the assessment, that the DEC package is not working anywhere and so is not available for hands-on trial; that the DEC packages fail to do certain things – in particular electronic communication of certain clinical order/reports . . . that we are now in a flat spin because DEC is not coming up with enhancements that we were requiring of them.

Sadly, details of these entreaties were not considered fit for public consumption. The reports of them were kept secret until, many years later, a public-spirited civil servant saw fit to leak a copy of the 'confidential' auditor's report.

This same report also discloses in some detail what happened in the months after DEC was chosen as preferred supplier, and how the contract was finally awarded – and not to DEC.

The events are most easily explained in a chronology.

February 27 1986. Wessex chooses DEC as preferred supplier to RISP and sends rejection letters to other bidders. But the letter leaves open the possibility that the authority might change its mind if negotiations with DEC go badly.

April 30 1986. One of the losing bidders, Arthur Andersen Management Consultants, tries to dissuade Wessex from choosing the US company DEC, which had scored highly in a technical evaluation. Andersen's adviser is Patrick Jenkin, a former Conservative Cabinet Minister, who has a protracted telephone conversation with Professor Sir Bryan Thwaites, the chairman of Wessex Regional Health Authority. The two men already know each other, though there is no suggestion that this in any way affects Thwaites's judgement. Neither is there any suggestion that Jenkin did anything improper or that his judgement was affected by the fact that he had known Thwaites. Jenkin was merely acting as an influential mouthpiece for Andersen Consultants.

May 3 1986. Andersen's partner in the bid for the RISP contract is IBM, whose Jim Foster is a director of IBM and also a member of Wessex's board. Foster writes to the authority's regional general manager about the virtues of buying from IBM. The then chief executive of IBM also writes to Wessex.

May 1986. Negotiations between the authority and DEC begin.

July 1986. Wessex officials go on a fact-finding tour of the USA to see health sites where RISP-type software is in action. Controversially, Wessex officials ask Andersen to find a DEC-based solution in the US – even though Andersen is competing with DEC for the contract. Some Wessex officials, including the region's new information systems manager, express concern about the possible conflict of interests given Andersen's roles as adviser, contractor and bidder. The information systems manager writes:

> It is my view that a representative of Arthur Andersen should not accompany the evaluation team which may travel to the United States. Similarly, the 'sheep dog' assistance in the US should be curtailed beforehand. Also Arthur Andersen should not be permitted to contribute to any evaluation in the US or UK until a decision on the hospital information system [one of the five RISP core systems] part has been finalised.

But the concerns of the manager and his officials are apparently ignored by the authority.

Another consultancy company, PACTEL, which was acting as overall advisers to Wessex on RISP, also expresses concern about Andersen's involvement in the US fact-finding trip. It recommends that the tour be 'delayed, cancelled or changed in structure'.

But the US visits goes ahead as planned, with Andersen's US staff accompanying Wessex officials on each leg of the American journey. The auditor would later note that Wessex's selection team seemed unaware of Andersen's involvement in the main RISP contract, nor were they aware that the authority had awarded Andersen preliminary work on the final two of the five core RISP systems.

28 July 1986. Wessex's selection group officials return from the USA unable to identify suitable DEC-based software.

29 July 1986. The Wessex selection group attends a debriefing on its US trip. It is attended by Andersen representatives, which raises another point of concern for the district auditor, who later comments that Andersen's involvement in the debriefing would have allowed it to be 'made aware of the views of the Group and of the perceived defects of the systems offered by their competitors'. The auditor also says later that Andersen had had access to 'confidential information concerning rival bids and the evaluation process'. Andersen's knowledge also 'alerted them to defects in the software they were offering which they would have to overcome' before the retendering exercise. Andersen insists, however, it is not aware of 'ever having any sensitive information'. (See Appendices for full version of Andersen's comments in relation to its work at Wessex.)

August 1986. Wessex officials feel that negotiations with DEC are less than satisfactory. DEC on the other hand is upset that the specifications for the contract have altered since it was chosen as preferred supplier, making its bid seem less attractive. Meanwhile Wessex's information systems manager appears to be warming to the proposals put forward by IBM and Andersen. The manager writes to his superior with some positive comments about IBM and Arthur Andersen and recommends a 'revalidation' of tenders. He feels that IBM's proposal has 'not been given proper attention' and states that Arthur Andersen had declared its original implementation costings to be wrong and was in fact supplying more support than the competition. This letter seems to imply that Andersen has had access to rivals' tenders and has revised its bid accordingly, the district auditor's report would comment later. This is strongly denied by Andersen.

22 August 1986. The authority's review team rejects DEC's proposal and writes to the original suppliers asking them to reaffirm their tenders. But it says they must respond by 3 September. This gives them only ten days – including the August bank holiday period. Meanwhile, on the day that Wessex sends out this letter, it posts a draft contract for RISP to IBM – but not to other tenderers.

3 September 1986. Suppliers are asked to revalidate or reaffirm their original tenders, but at least one of them complains that ten days is not enough time. A further two days is granted. The suppliers have been told that, in resubmitting their bids, they must not alter them significantly from their original proposals. However, it appears that both Andersen and IBM do alter their original proposals by proposing solutions for perceived defects in their initial bid.

24 September 1986. Andersen and IBM give details of their implementation plan and set out the costs in a letter to Wessex. Andersen has already informed the authority that the software package it had proposed has been improved since the original bid was submitted. It is now three weeks after the final date for suppliers to submit their reaffirmed tenders. The letter proposes a start date of 1 November for the building of RISP.

26 September 1986. Wessex's selection group visits various sites in the UK where hospital computer systems are in use. The final visit is on the 26 September when the group flies to Scotland to inspect a McDonnell Douglas hospital system in operation. The group concludes that this McDonnell Douglas system is the best on offer, confirming the original decision of the selection panel, which gave McDonnell Douglas the highest score of all bidders, even above DEC. However the Wessex selection group is met at Heathrow Airport by the authority's information systems manager, who exerts considerable pressure on the group to alter its decision in favour of a joint Arthur Andersen and IBM proposal.

29 September 1986. Wessex holds a meeting attended by only two people to decide the choice of supplier for RISP. Remarkably, despite months of planning and the involvement of large numbers of public servants, the actual decision to award the RISP contract is taken by these two members only; and the Wessex Board of directors is not told of the decision until after a contract has been signed. At the meeting-of-two was a member of the information group and the chairman of the authority, Sir Bryan Thwaites. They are informed that the selection criteria have been amended to reflect more fully the views of would-be end-users, and that it is the consensus view of the evaluation group that a contract be entered into with Arthur Andersen/IBM.

The two men decide to award the contract to Andersen and IBM.

They also agree that the initial contract will be for £7 million of the total projected spending on RISP (at that stage) of £29 million. It is worth stressing that £29 million was the *official* estimated total cost of RISP. Privately, executives at Wessex calculate the costs at about £80 million but they keep quiet because they know that any revelations of the higher figure will jeopardise the future of the project.

Also, the selection criteria against which all the bidders had competed, is quietly amended in a way that happens to favour the Andersen/IBM bid. But at the meeting-of-two no mention is made of the fact that there is not a consensus in favour of Andersen/IBM on the selection panel. There is in fact considerable disagreement among the selection team.

At the end of the inquorate meeting, the details of the two members' discussions are minuted; but two sets of minutes are prepared. The first version, which is made available only to the two members of the information group who attended the meeting, records the fact that Andersen/IBM has been awarded the RISP contract.

The second set of minutes is distributed more widely throughout the authority. This does not mention who has been awarded the contract .

8 October 1986. A formal meeting of Wessex Regional Health Authority's board is held. The second set of minutes forms the basis of the agenda, so the authority is not told of the award of the contract to Andersen/IBM. Meanwhile correspondence with DEC continues as though no decision on the award of the contract had been made.

10 October 1986. Contracts between Andersen and IBM are negotiated with Wessex. These talks include Bryan Thwaites.

22 October 1986. Wessex's main adviser on RISP, the consultancy PACTEL, tries to point out, in as diplomatic a voice as it can muster, that the whole project may not be feasible.

It might just as well have told its concerns to the trees.

PACTEL warns that the specifications of RISP are 'not sufficiently detailed to provide a firm basis' for entering into a contract. It lists its other reservations:

That Wessex has to accept the assurance of Arthur Andersen that the software products are satisfactorily structured, are reliable enough and have sufficient functionality not to require source code amendment.

That the technical feasibility of integrating all the proposed software is unproven.

That there is a practical difficulty at this stage of specifying what hardware is needed to provide the right level of performance from the software.

That the price, delivery and other facets such as performance are to be tied down before entering into a contract. But ominously PACTEL adds: 'Given the timetable and other factors the Authority considers this impractical.'

11 November 1986. Andersen and IBM sign a contract for the development of RISP – the same companies that had come second to bottom in the original bid evaluation.

Also in November an internal report written by Wessex's evaluation team concedes that no system is 'wholly satisfactory and a compromise solution is inevitable . . . a lot of work will still be needed to modify and develop the software.' However RISP's unremitting and high-level political and regional support ensures that there is not even a whiff of a suggestion that the project should be cancelled.

10 December 1986. Only now, nearly a month after the contract has been signed, is the authority told of the fact that RISP has been awarded to Andersen/IBM.

Apart from anything else the signing of the contract appears to have taken place against a background of enforced haste.

Another maxim – Thou shalt not set artificially tight deadlines – springs to mind. Nearly a year had elapsed since bids were first invited, yet suddenly there was a spurious need to make a quick decision.

But this was one of a plethora of problems relating to RISP. Later on, the Wessex district auditor, in one of the most incisive auditors' reports I have ever seen, listed his reservations about the fact that the contract approved by the authority for signing was amended before it was actually signed.

The original version of the contract was commented on by the authority's legal advisers, who said that it 'affords the authority the best possible protection in any contract it may enter into with Arthur Andersen'.

At the same time, lawyers cautioned against allowing any changes to this contract that would weaken the authority's legal position. They considered that the contract should be offered to Arthur Andersen on the basis that 'we do not see it as a document for revision'.

But within days, significant changes were made to the initial contract.

The changes were listed by the auditor:

Original contract: This set out priced requirements and the time in which the supplier's work had to completed and accepted, otherwise there could be a breach of contract.

Actual contract signed: This set out only 'estimated' requirements for equipment and software.

Original contract: The original had a section that required the contractor to expedite progress at its own cost if progress on the project fell behind expected schedules.

Actual contract signed: The whole section is deleted from the signed document.

Original contract: There are clauses that give the authority the ability to terminate the contract if the system fails to function on site.

Actual contract signed: Clauses are deleted.

Original contract: This requires the systems to meet relevant construction, operating maintenance and performance criteria and standards which are set out in the authority's invitation to tender and associated user requirements of 1985.

Actual contract signed: No such commitment is given. Neither is there a commitment to the original contract's stipulation that 'equipment shall conform to contract or to best standards and practices being observed in the computer industry'.

Original contract: There is a stipulated discount on fee rates charged by consultants of 25 per cent.

Actual contract signed: Discount is 20 per cent – a difference on the original contract terms of £215, 000.

Other changes to the original and signed contracts include the removal of a section on quality provisions and another providing for a maximum price.

Of particular concern later would be the fact that Wessex was paying the consultants for 3,800 days of programming work – but the contract did not allow for the Crown to own exclusively the copyright. A clause in the original contract giving Wessex sole ownership of intellectual property rights had been changed.

The concern of the auditors did not end with contractual changes. The report of the district auditor summed up the following 'unsatisfactory aspects' of the contract award to Andersen and IBM:

• **an approach** to the regional general manager by a member of the authority on behalf of a company of which he was a director seeking to open discussions of their tender;

• **an approach** to the chairman of Wessex by a former Secretary of State on behalf of the same tendering consortium for which he was acting as consultant;

• **changes** in the criteria used to assess tenders;

• **changes** made to the invitations to tender without subsequent retendering;

• **doubts** as to the Wessex Information Group's authority to sign

contracts with IBM and Andersen;
* **information** regarding the contract was withheld from meetings of the authority;
* **a conflict** of interest in that Arthur Andersen, who eventually won the contract, had allegedly had access to confidential information regarding rival bids and the evaluation process.

Richard Da Costa, the auditor, said that his legal advice was that the decision by the Information Group on 19 September to award the contract to Andersen/IBM was flawed because it comprised only two people, including the authority's chairman.

The meeting's two attendees had no delegated authority to take the decision, and there was 'improper action on behalf of the successful contractor to influence the outcome of the tendering process, which should have resulted in that tenderer being disqualified.'

He added: 'In my view the health authority should enter into negotiations with Arthur Andersen to seek a refund of some of the moneys paid under this contract.'

After much guidance, however, the authority decided it had no legal leg to stand on. Its advice was that pursuing court action would lead to substantial legal, practical and evidential difficulties.

It would also cost so much money and take up so much management time that this would outweigh any possible benefits of winning the case. What the authority would not admit was whether its weakened contract with Andersen and IBM had jeopardised its chances of a successful outcome in any court action.

And who had authorised the changes to the contract? This was never made clear.

(Andersen and Lord Jenkin have raised concerns about district auditor's report, published in 1993, which accused Andersen/IBM of using improper influence to affect the outcome of the tendering process and of having access to 'information concerning rival bids and the evaluation process.' A full response by Andersen and Jenkin is published as an appendix.)

CHAPTER FOUR

The Second Deadly Sin: Pride III

The Wessex Story continues

All the incidents in the last chapter, worrying though they were, proved to be a highpoint of RISP. The project train was now rounding the hill and there was only one way to go.

The cost was becoming particularly noticeable; but, although estimates began to rise, the project had by now such a high profile and full political support that Wessex seems to have felt that it could justify any amount of spending so long as it came under the RISP umbrella.

When district authorities asked for more money to develop interim systems it was granted by the region on the basis that anything and everything would eventually link into RISP. That this might have struck the taxpayer as a cavalier approach to public spending appears to have worried nobody at Wessex, perhaps because they thought their spending plans would be kept secret.

In any case, the government had already issued a strong message that more money needed to be spent on computers. There was the 'goal' investment of 2 per cent of turnover. So internally officials drew up plans to spend nearly £100 million on computers over ten years.

Consultants and suppliers were employed without open competition. Invoices from suppliers went through without any detailed checking. The authority was opening the door to corruption and conflicts of interest.

In the mid 1980s the publicly quoted cost of RISP was £26 million. However an auditor writing a confidential report on RISP for the Department of Health notes: 'My concern at the escalating costs and at the difficulties the authority may experience in containing the expenditure within the £37.3m now projected is, I understand, shared at District level. My staff have examined the arrangements for financial control over this project. As a consequence, I am unable to establish the costs of the RISP development up to April 1986.'

In other words, a public authority had been spending millions of pounds in a way that auditors could not fully trace. Yet none of the auditors expressed their concern publicly.

And nobody in the authority was going to denigrate the region's pet RISP project without finding another job first.

In the finance department the post of accountant responsible for RISP was usually vacant. The lack of control seems to have encouraged financial anarchy. In a euphemistic tone of voice that almost parodies the stiff-upper-lip image of Britain's civil service, the Department of Health auditor drew attention internally to items of expenditure on RISP that 'did not seem to be appropriate' and that the Authority 'will wish' to control.

These inappropriate payments include 'two duplicate charges and payments of £16,445 and £4,502 respectively and inclusive of VAT'.

There were also 'invoices rendered by firms undertaking work on a man day basis but with no indication of the person involved'.

The auditor also referred enigmatically to the payment of removal expenses, but it is not clear whether these were for staff to move house or for suppliers to move their businesses. Other mysterious payments were for unspecified 'advertising costs'.

Meanwhile, according to other Department of Health internal audit reports in the mid 1980s, firms supplying contract staff to Wessex were charging the authority for things like legal and estate agency fees, training costs, agency fees to third parties, recruitment fees, the cost of increments and bonuses relating to the staff hired.

In addition, firms added their out-of-pocket expenses of £300 a day plus a management fee of 40 per cent on top of the total employment costs. Another supplier that was providing staff to the authority, at a rate of £300 per person per day, increased the rate to £350, apparently without any negotiations or comparisons with the charge rates of other firms.

A third supplier carrying out an investment appraisal report that was supposed to take an estimated 23 days at a cost of £300 a day charged more than double the number of days – 55 days at £300 a day.

In America the fiasco would have been stopped immediately, a congressional hearing established, and everyone suspended pending the inquiry's outcome. In the UK, the Department of Health politely requested that Wessex 'considers whether value for money is being secured'.

The problems were exacerbated by a shortage of competent staff at the authority, a lack of firm leadership and, as at the PRS, there were empires within empires that hampered communications between departments.

For example, the commercial division, which was asked to work on letting computer contracts, refused, citing a shortage of staff.

But it was known that there was mistrust between the commercial division and the computer department. The commercial division felt that the computer department had chosen to exclude it from contract negotiations.

Reservations in the district health authorities over the cost of RISP were growing but nobody in any authority voiced their concerns publicly; so development on the project continued apace – and with some very limited success.

The Royal Hampshire County Hospital at Winchester installed an impressive hospital information system based on the software proposed by Andersen and IBM. However the full cost has never been disclosed and, while it has been a workable system to show visiting dignitaries and politicians, it is not clear whether the benefits in patient care are in keeping with the cost. For some time the hospital's overall spending exceeded its budget.

The Bath district also installed part of the RISP system at its Royal United Hospital, but again the costs were deemed by some to be excessive – nearly £5 million, which is considerable for a single hospital, and the benefits were not as great as originally envisaged. These were two large hospitals in a region containing many hospitals. The original idea of linking up five core systems now seemed unthinkable, unless many more tens of millions of pounds were allocated. RISP may have been technically feasible, but not economically so. To have installed it as planned would have been like paying £100,000 for a taxi trip across London.

For the most senior Wessex officials, the dream of RISP continued to linger, and nobody could convince ministers or the authority's successive chairmen that it was only a dream.

The Conservative MP David Martin, shortly after his election in 1987 to a Wessex constituency, asked the RHA's chairman Sir Bryan Thwaites and the then regional general manager John Hoare about the 'money being ploughed into RISP with little or no accountability.' Later he again raised the issue but found that 'any criticism was taken personally and I could get nowhere'.

Martin added: 'I saw Tony Newton, the then Minister of Health. Later with the support of colleagues I did my best to see that Sir Bryan Thwaites was not reappointed as chairman. Tony Newton replaced him with Robin Buchanan. Thinking that the RISP scheme could now be considered more dispassionately I invited Robin Buchanan to lunch at the House of Commons to discuss it. To my disappointment he said that his own doubts had now been resolved and he was supporting continuance of the scheme!'

Unbeknown to Martin at that time, Buchanan had a ministerial brief to see RISP through to completion. In January 1989 the then new health minister David Mellor met Buchanan and asked him to improve financial control of RISP and complete it without delay.

In a letter to Buchanan, the health minister stated: 'We are agreed that it is important that the core systems [of RISP] . . . should be installed and operational in all districts within three years.'

However the end-users in the district authorities were by now close to open rebellion.

They saw that RISP had been rolling for five years, yet to them and everyone not connected with the project, the promised benefits seemed more unattainable than ever. Although the district end-users had always participated in RISP, they were far from committed to it. In fact, as the region began to take more money away from health care to fund RISP, the district authorities began to dissociate themselves from the whole project.

Ironically one arm of government was trying to push RISP forward while another part was promoting health service reforms that were giving the districts more autonomy over their budgets; and the districts did not want to spend their money on RISP.

The districts were nearer to the front line of day-to-day hospital work than the region. So, to them, it seemed far more sensible to spend their money directly on patient care, not on computers.

RISP's future began to look even more uncertain when computer staff within the region began to see the new systems as a threat to their jobs, particularly as the project was being run almost entirely by consultants.

Partly to counter disenchantment with RISP, Buchanan was involved in hiring two IBM project managers, at a cost of £14,000 a month, to work with the districts on managing the project. He wrote in an internal document that a major risk to the successful and timely implementation of RISP was the absence of strong project management in the participating districts. The IBM project managers, he wrote, would have the job of imparting their IBM-acquired project skills to local teams.

Buchanan was also involved in hiring an IBM executive to run the entire Wessex computer operation. Although the seconded executive was not supposed to become involved in purchasing equipment – let alone IBM equipment – the secondee is alleged by a district auditor to have offered advice in connection with the purchase of an IBM 3090 mainframe which, it transpired, was not needed. The secondee denies this. The £3.3 million machine lay unused, in its original packaging in a warehouse in Slough, for about eighteen months. When it was finally brought into service its value had dropped to about £1 million.

But the first real sign of an impending project crash came in 1989 when some of the districts decided not to continue with a personnel system called MAPS which had been developed by Andersen and was running on IBM equipment. MAPS, a component of RISP, was abandoned at a cost of £1.6 million.

The disenchantment with MAPS, and the publicity that followed its demise, confirmed in the minds of end-users that the regional management was incapable of introducing RISP within a reasonable period or at a cost that wasn't extortionate. They declared that enough was enough.

One district even commissioned an independent consultancy report on RISP, which confirmed all the end-user concerns about the project being too pioneering, too costly and too big.

STAGE FOUR

By 1990 several of the districts were steadfastly refusing to commit to RISP. One manager in the Isle of Wight said, 'We're only a tiny authority. How can we justify spending millions of pounds on RISP systems when we are desperate for more nurses and a few thousands of pounds' worth of medical equipment?'

Wessex was left with no alternative. The obstinate refusal of the districts to continue funding the project left the new regional general manager Ken Jarrold with no choice but to cancel it. In effect, the abandonment was a formality. After eight years' work and £43 million of taxpayers' money, the following progress had been made on RISP's five core systems:

Estates: no working system produced before the project was cancelled;

Hospital systems: only one of Wessex's 200–300 hospitals had implemented a hospital information system (though a hospital in Bath would later commit itself as well);

Finance: a general ledger system was provided in all districts; a purchasing system was rejected by districts following an evaluation that compared new systems with their existing ones;

Personnel: no working system implemented; subsequently a system called IPS was adopted, but, as a result of major arguments over who was to pay for its introduction, several districts declined to use it;

Community Care: a feasibility study was completed at a cost to Wessex of £188,000 and was then abandoned.

Even after cancelling RISP, with the loss of £20–£43 million – nobody knows exactly how much because proper records were not kept – the authority lost more millions of pounds on contracting out computer systems, staff and work to the private sector at rates that were considerably in excess of what it needed to pay.

Conflicts of interests became so common that they became a comfortable and integral part everyday life. For example, the authority's regional treasurer, Robin Little, left to join a private computer company, which, shortly afterwards, sold its services back to the authority. The lead consultant on the contract was Mr Little. In fact for a period of two months Little was both a director of the health authority and a director of the company that was supplying computer services to the authority.

Things began to change for the better only when the authority appointed its first information systems director Rosemary Storrs, a dynamic ex-IBM manager who, untrained in public sector thought processes, did what she thought was morally right without worrying about the internal or external political ramifications.

She accused one of the major suppliers of fraud (and issued a press release to that effect), and began taking legal advice on this and a range of other contracts.

Then she helped to negotiate the return of £10 million by one supplier and stopped Wessex sanctioning invoices until she knew exactly what they were for (she found one from a private supplier that was trying to charge the authority for a shower and towels used by its staff who jog at lunchtime).

She also handed the local police a suitcase of documents about certain matters on computer contracts unrelated to RISP. Her hard line against suppliers so impressed Wessex that it did what governmental bodies tend to do when confronted with a conscientious, publicly spirited, apolitical, dynamic troubleshooter. It made her redundant.

She was given a handsome settlement of £78,000 gross (£58,000 net) and was also promised, conditionally, an occasional consultancy contract of £400 a day, which some MPs later felt was designed to buy her silence.

The then regional general manager who had endorsed her settlement, Ken Jarrold, was later criticised by MPs who were concerned at the failure to seek Treasury approval for such a large payment.

The post-mortem reports on RISP and Wessex's other computer contracts are full of general lessons on avoiding computer disasters. Perhaps the most pertinent comment comes from Wessex itself. **It recognised that there had been 'more excitement and interest in building up new technology than in providing services for patients' and commented on the dangers of visions.**

'It is very dangerous when somebody has an idea, however visionary, and pursues that in the face of the good practical evidence that it is not working out,' said a Wessex representative.

Andersen took a slightly different view.

'Wessex represents an episode of change in the National Health Service. We regret that our initial work on preparing hospital systems has not been extended throughout the region. We believed and still believe the RISP vision was viable and the feasibility of the hospital and accounting systems have been proven by their use.'

Ken Jarrold said, 'The very substantial losses incurred by the Wessex Regional Health Authority can be attributed to the exploitation by some of the authority's staff and, it would seem, by some of those with whom they dealt.'

He also blamed the 'serious underlying weaknesses in the management structure between 1984 to 1989' – before his time. 'There can be no excuse for what certainly appears to be mishandling of public money and the resultant wastage of millions of pounds.'

The causes of the failure cited by the district health authorities include:

• The fact that systems were imposed on end-users;
• The would-be end-users were unfamiliar with information technology and had not received adequate training and naturally felt concerned and uneasy about using the new system;
• Consultation with end-users was inadequate, and when they were consulted it was not to ask their opinion but to tell them what they had to do;
• A failure to identify or produce suitable software.

The district auditor noted that the only really successful part of RISP was the introduction of the financial ledger. This was partly because Treasury end-users were already familiar with information technology and enthusiastically contributed to its successful implementation. There again, financial computer systems are a well-developed and straightforward branch of computing.

The old manual sales, purchase and nominal ledgers and other so-called day books lend themselves easily to computerisation. But many other areas of corporate life are not so well understood by computer suppliers, and there is less software that has been honed through trial and error.

Unless software has been around the industry for many years, it is likely to be undeveloped, and its implementation will therefore be risky.

The Wessex saga also showed the Department of Health's inability to prevent a disaster. It knew many of the most serious flaws in RISP and issued many warnings to Wessex, but they were always ineffectually worded using the insipid, euphemistic language of the civil service, for example: 'It would be advisable if control were to be improved in the following areas . . .'

If the department had been more assertive and said that the project should be cancelled by such and such a date if the contracted systems were not delivered by then, this would have given the authority an incentive to succeed. Conversely, the department could not have sought the cancellation of RISP because the project had ministerial support.

So the project was not cancelled long before 1990 because too much money had been spent on it, and no politician could countenance the embarrassment that abandonment would cause.

It was cancelled only when the district authorities refused to fund it.

Still, it was nearly two years before news of the project's failure leaked, and only then after press reports, whereupon MPs decide to investigate. Sir Robin Buchanan and Ken Jarrold were called to account by the House of Commons Public Accounts Committee, as was Sir Duncan Nichol, head of the National Health Service's Management Executive.

And so the Wessex affair seemed to draw to a close; but the curious may like to know what happened subsequently to some of the people and companies involved in RISP. Coincidentally, everyone who was ever directly involved with RISP seems to have enjoyed promotion or other success:

Anthony Cleaver, chairman of IBM, became Sir Anthony Cleaver.

Robin Buchanan was knighted in 1991. When he left Wessex he was promoted by the government to one of the most important jobs in the health service – running the NHS Supplies Authority, which spends £4 billion of public money a year. (His statement on Wessex-related matters is included as an appendix.)

Duncan Nichol, head of the NHS body responsible for monitoring Wessex's finances, became Sir Duncan Nichol. He left the public health service to join the private health service as head of BUPA in 1994.

Ken Jarrold, the regional general manager of Wessex who authorised the payment without treasury approval to Rosemary Storrs, information systems director at Wessex, was promoted to one of the top jobs in the health service, as director of human resources. He received a CBE in the 1997 New Year's Honours List.

John Hoare, a visionary regional general manager at Wessex, who was largely blamed by MPs for RISP's failure, left the authority with a compensatory payment of £111,940 plus a car worth £8,000.

Andersen Consulting, one of Wessex's main suppliers whose contracts with the authority were strongly criticised by the district auditor went on to become the world's most successful information technology management consultancy. It is one of the largest computer suppliers to the UK government, and its senior staff have been featured in publicity photos with Prime Minister John Major. In 1995, it won one of the government's largest computer contracts, to supply a new National Insurance system costing nearly £100 million.

CSL, a company criticised by the district auditor for giving advice to Wessex that was either 'negligent', or, at worst, 'knowingly or recklessly intended to promote its own interests and those of its subsidiary at the expense of the regional health authority and public funds', has now become one of the largest suppliers to local government. Since the Wessex affair, it has won several public contracts, each worth more than £10 million. It was acquired by the consultants Touche Ross.

AT&T Istel, having been accused by Wessex Regional Health Authority of fraud and having subsequently paid the authority £10 million in compensation, was later awarded a new multi-million-pound contract – by Wessex Regional Health Authority. AT&T felt that it had been a victim of fraud by some of its own employees. It issued writs which led to an out-of-court settlement in which the employees paid the company sizeable sums.

Postscript: The only individual at Wessex who was asked by government officials to pay back a redundancy settlement was Rosemary Storrs, the one person in authority who had sought to blow the whistle publicly on the irregularities in the Wessex health authority's contracts with outside suppliers.

CHAPTER FIVE

The Second Deadly Sin:
Pride (IV)

So what are the lessons of Wessex?

The failure of Wessex Regional Health Authority's RISP project differed from the Performing Right Society's PROMS failure in only one material respect: the losses were greater. The managers were not even certain how much had been lost because their accounting systems were so poor.

Again, this was a tale of well-intentioned but ultimately monomaniacal managers who became so enveloped in the daily technological challenges, problems and dramas that they lost sight of the bigger view: the needs of the business end-users – in this case the district health authorities running the hospitals.

They were also oblivious of the health service's customers: the hospital patients.

And, like all disaster victims, the health region became a change fetishist, blinded by irrepressible optimism, which justified wrong decisions with rhetoric and sophistry; and nobody questioned them because it was always assumed they knew what they were doing.

As at the PRS, the managers were radioing back to base that there were no serious problems as their plane was descending vertically towards the ground.

Also like the PRS, there was virtually no accountability.

All-pervasive secrecy ensured that hardly anyone outside the organisation knew what was going on and few inside knew either.

It is this strategy for concealing mistakes that seems so often to lead to disaster. Those culpable appear to rely on the fact that they are the only people who have any idea what has gone wrong;

therefore issues can be easily muddied, facts massaged, jargon used to obfuscate, reports expurgated, and if all else fails officials run into the nuclear bunker of 'commercial confidentiality'.

This secrecy is no better exploited than by suppliers. Long after the Wessex fiasco, some of the main suppliers, in their bids for other contracts, shrugged off the RISP disaster by saying that their role had been portrayed misleadingly in the press and on television. They absolved themselves of responsibility by claiming there was nothing wrong with anything delivered by the suppliers – it was all the fault of inept public-sector management.

Yet the full facts had long been known in detail by the unlikeliest of all organisations, the Prime Minister's office. This was because Downing Street became concerned about the repeated mentions in the House of Commons of the failure of RISP and had asked the Department of Health for a briefing.

Only then did the Department of Health start to ask some extraordinarily piercing questions about the nuts and bolts of the RISP and all the other contracts between Wessex Regional Health Authority and its computer suppliers. The department asked the questions of Wessex itself, and then passed the answers to Downing Street.

Only then were the full facts surrounding the disaster unearthed – not for the public's benefit, however, but so that Downing Street was in a position of knowledge to fend off pertinent questions from MPs and journalists.

Every question asked by Downing Street and every answer given by the Department of Health was kept secret. They were not even shown in confidence to MPs. Indeed, the fact that questions were asked by Downing Street about Wessex is supposed to have been a secret.

But despite all this subterfuge, a fairly comprehensive picture of what happened has emerged. But this is only after four years of investigative journalism, none of which should have been necessary if politicians had practised open government rather than merely preached it.

Has the investigative effort been worth it? The story of Wessex is not only the story of a computer disaster. It is the story of how the executive and political arms of government come together in adversity to ensure that nobody in senior positions could be held responsible for the waste of £43–£63 million of public money.

It shows how some normally principled suppliers can find it

difficult to avoid turning into artful market traders when given absolute freedom over the customer's chequebook.

It also gives an insight into how the hidden machinery of government operates on a day-to-day basis, from the most junior public servant to the Prime Minister's office.

The fall of RISP may seem merely to reflect public administration at its most inept, but the Wessex health authority was not untypical of a major public sector organisation. Its air of 'do whatever you want so long as nobody outside finds out about it' was and is not that unusual in public life.

Richard Da Costa prefaced his 1992 confidential report on the Wessex affair with the poignant remark:

'The information technology problems that have arisen in the Wessex region have been a cause for concern over the past five years. They are by no means unique to the Wessex Regional Health Authority and may well reflect a national problem.'

The reason Wessex is given so much attention in this chapter is not because it is an exceptional failure but because it is an unexceptional failure *and we know about it.*

There are many other authorities that are suspected of having lost tens of millions on computer projects but the facts have not yet emerged.

The fundamental changes needed to make public administrators more accountable to the public have yet to happen, and will probably never happen, because to make public bodies fully accountable means making central government more accountable – and that is inconceivable whatever the party in power.

All decisions about major computer purchases, in local councils, police forces, health authorities and central government departments, are made by secret coteries.

In America, details of major purchases, why they are made and even the bid prices are published to discourage corruption and because it is felt that taxpayers have a right to know how their money is spent. In Britain no such right is acknowledged. It is felt that civil servants and ministers always know best: and, if they don't, it is best that nobody knows. Between the propounded ethics of 'open' government policy and practice lies a glaring antithesis.

This provides perfect conditions for waste on a grand scale.

The total costs of failed computerisation projects in the public sector – those I know about – are nearly £5 billion, and there is no sign that things are getting better.

The House of Commons Public Accounts Committee does its best to try to keep track of the failures and admonish those responsible, but it has no powers to stop projects that are going wrong. Usually it does not get to hear about disasters until years later.

Even in the rare event that cases like Wessex come to public attention, MPs on the Public Accounts Committee are not given the full facts. In the Wessex instance, they ended up being briefed thoroughly not by public auditors but by a business journalist.

Even then the MPs were powerless to do anything other than castigate those involved and issue reams of generalised guidance about avoiding future disasters. Yet all this paternalistic advice, none of it backed up by the threat of any sanctions, hardly differs from the guidance issued by MPs in the 1970s after a series of computing failures. After Wessex the House of Lords and the House of Commons were told that it could never happen again, that all the controls were in place to prevent history repeating itself. However three years after Wessex was discussed by MPs, they were making similar criticisms again, this time over another visionary health service strategy. In this case the vision was for national hospital information support systems. Seven years into the project, £106 million had been spent and only £3.3 million of benefits had been identified. Even this £3.3 million was eliminated by the costs of administering the strategy, which amounted to nearly £4 million.

But let us not close this chapter on such a negative point – after all this is a book about disasters.

RISP was not in fact an unmitigated failure. One large hospital at Winchester, a pilot site for the main project, succeeded in going live with information systems that some staff say are quite impressive. It's not much for the £43–£63 million spent by Wessex, but it shows that, if money is no object, systems can be made to work in even the most arduous conditions.

The success at Winchester also highlights a point made in the chapter on success stories: that computerisation can work if you anticipate that it will cost far more than you originally expected, and will deliver no improvement in working practices in the short term and only a marginal improvement in the medium term. The real benefits are long-term, when the technology's limitations are so well understood that the organisation makes other efficiency changes that should ideally have been made before computerisation – and only then effects genuine administrative improvements.

But Winchester's systems were high-risk ones and cost many millions, much more than many companies could afford without being able to fall back on the public purse. And today Winchester stands virtually alone among the debris of RISP's crash, a memorial to the hundreds of hospitals that were unable to computerise, and were sapped of funds for medical services – all to feed the visions of those who even today are regarded as experts.

CHAPTER SIX

The Third Deadly Sin: Presumption

COMPUTERISATION MUST BE A GOOD THING, SURELY

The four main reasons for computerising or spending a large sum on upgrading are:
- Because everyone else is;
- Because everyone else isn't and you think you'll gain a competitive advantage;
- Because you've been sold a vision by a consultancy – usually the vision is called 'business process re-engineering';
- Because the high initial costs will be more than offset by the fact that you'll be doing things better and cheaper in the long run.

The list does not encompass every justification for a massive computer investment, just the main ones. And all four of these business cases are flawed because they are too vague.

New technology should be installed only for a specific reason, for a specific purpose, and to give a specific tangible advantage to the business.

For example, a good reason to buy a new Treasury system is if you need to trade internationally and the existing software is holding you back because it does not take account of deals which involve a multitude of currencies.

In contrast, any incorporeal justifications about improving business efficiency, or helping the business to expand into new markets, increasing technological flexibility, or becoming number one in the marketplace, should be viewed with extreme suspicion.

It is indeed surprising how many computer projects win board approval without a readily-perceived benefit. No project justifications could have been vaguer than Wessex Regional Health Authority's desire to use technology to improve efficiency and worse, to spend 2 per cent of turnover on computers.

And the Performing Right Society's technology investment was founded on its concern that it was being overtaken by newer, more impressive systems being developed by its counterparts in, for example, Austria. It also believed that the new systems would cut enough staff to reduce the PRS's administrative costs by up to 25 per cent.

Again, these anticipated benefits are too vague. They do not take account of the risks. Neither do they show how the savings will be achieved. They have credence only in as much as people tend to believe that computerisation and progress are synonymous.

Some suppliers now bid not to provide computers but a specific service. For example, they will deliver a cheque processing service, or provide an invoicing and bill collection operation, and even acquire all your staff who currently do these things.

But while this has the advantage of contracting out a problem, it does not solve it. You are putting yourself into the hands of a supplier who will most likely offer significant up-front savings (sometimes in the form of a lump sum) and low prices in the early stages of the service contract, in the hope that profits will pour in later as a result of unforeseen changes in the user company's requirements. In this case the supplier banks on the one predictable thing about computers: that there will be unpredictable changes.

Alternatively, a supplier will promise to deliver not a service but the specific benefit that you expect from a new system. For example, it will claim that its new stock control system will save £1m a year by eliminating surplus stock, so you say: 'Okay, deliver not just the system but the £1m a year savings.'

This sounds simple. In reality, when things go wrong and both sides call in their lawyers, the failure of the project will be blamed on the un-contracted-for changes imposed on the supplier by influential end-users, or on the obstreperous warehouse staff who opposed computerisation and therefore did not give the supplier access to all the information and data that was needed to make the system viable and thereby achieve the savings.

So, while suppliers will have an easy answer to every problem identified in this book, there's no avoiding the fact that every emollient they prescribe has a side-effect. In short, **responsibility for a project's success – and particularly its failure – will usually come back to the chief executive**.

Unless the chief executive sees *clearly* the distinct advantage of a new system, it is probably not worth going ahead with it. The case studies in this book, particularly the one that follows, show that computerisation is as likely to be a bad as a good thing.

In the case study in this chapter, the book distributor Tiptree, which has a turnover approaching £100 million, was the most efficient company of its kind in the industry; until it set about fully automating its warehousing operations.

CASE STUDY

The Tiptree company was justifiably proud of its reputation. In 1992, it had won the British Book Awards Distributor of the Year, the greatest achievement in its 27-year history. But getting to the top is one thing. Staying there can be harder.

So Tiptree decided to buy a £1.5 million warehousing system to handle greater volumes and speed up deliveries of books to its thousands of bookshops, library suppliers and other literary outlets.

But teething troubles with new systems set off a chain reaction of unpredictable events that led to the company losing at least one of its biggest customers and facing large claims for compensation.

Staff worked treble shifts to clear a backlog of deliveries, though the problems lasted for nearly six months.

And this was supposed to have been a state-of-the-art system.

This is a little unfair. The technology itself behaved almost impeccably – and that was the problem. It was utterly unforgiving of human fallibility. When warehouse staff entered incorrect information into the system, the computers were unable to verify its accuracy, and in effect believed everything they were told.

Not that this was a story of an unmitigated disaster. The company went through all the necessary steps of testing the systems almost to destruction.

It even tested the systems in an almost live environment – that is to say it ran a full-scale dress rehearsal, with every aspect of the hardware, software, interfaces and warehouse equipment functioning as it would when the system went live. **What Tiptree** didn't account for was that, no matter how much testing you have done and no matter how confident you are, something nobody had thought of will leap out of the dark on 'live' day and sabotage the project.

This may not sound too serious – but it is if there is no adequate contingency arrangements. There needs to be provision for a back-up, a soft landing when the undercarriage fails to come down.

In Tiptree's case it was so confident of success that the live day did not take account of any need to return quickly to the old semi-manual way of working.

Its problems also highlight the dangers of trying to computerise in one go rather than bit by bit, module by module.

I feel another maxim coming on: **advance step by step with a punctilious caution which may seem to cost more and take longer than doing it all in one go, but the cost and time disadvantages are more than offset by the benefit of reduced risk.**

Soon after the systems went live, the book trade's magazine *Bookseller* began receiving reports from Tiptree's customers of books delivered late, orders cancelled, pallets of the wrong books arriving or boxes turning up with no books inside.

'The summer is a quiet time for some booksellers but not for me. I have at least twenty thousand pounds' worth of outstanding orders from Tiptree,' said Chris Last, managing director of a library supplier, Cromwell Books. 'The situation is chaotic, absolutely diabolical. I have been unable to get hold of any big-selling Arrow titles such as *Jurassic Park* or *The Firm*.'

As a distributor, Tiptree would take into its warehouse a mass of books from a range of publishers such as Dorling Kindersley, Walker, Little Brown and Virgin, and then dispatch orders to individual bookshops around the UK.

The new system was designed to instruct warehouse staff to position pallets of books in the most efficient places, so as to make retrieval quick, simple and semi-automatic. This made sense.

With ten acres of warehousing and 25 million books, it was possible under the old manual system for warehouse staff to go to one corner of the warehouse to collect one pallet of books, then to another corner to fulfil the rest of the order – then go back to the other side of the warehouse to fulfil a second order. This was an inefficient use of warehouse staff.

With the new system, the idea was that computers would produce a stock-movement ticket. This would specify where books were to be positioned in the warehouse and would give the computer an electronic map of where everything was kept.

So, when it was programmed with orders, the system would work out the most efficient way for books to be picked off the shelves and put onto a conveyor belt. Automatically the system would also issue invoices, or advise if books were out of stock.

It worked perfectly during an experimental run. The problem was that, when it went live, the warehouse staff did not fully appreciate the need to behave as predictably as the computers. They cut corners, misunderstanding exactly how the system worked.

The system was so designed that it would give warehouse staff an exact location from which to collect the books, but, as this was sometimes awkward to reach, they would take books from a nearby pallet.

Under the previous manual process, a mistake such as this was of little consequence. At worst, it meant that one customer would receive one wrong order. With a computerised system, minor mistakes became disastrous.

Once a pallet was retrieved that was not the one picked by the computer, the system's electronic map of the location of books was wrong. The correct pallet was shown as out of stock and in need of replenishment, when it fact it was still on the shelf.

And the incorrectly dispatched pallet was shown as still being in stock when it had gone. As more of the wrong pallets were removed, the computers' electronic map became increasingly inaccurate. The problems were made worse when customers began complaining about undelivered orders, and staff circumvented the systems to take books off the warehouse racking for immediate dispatch.

The problem here was that the staff knew their customers by name and were used to giving a personalised service. But the intervention of humans into the computerised chain threw the delivery system into chaos.

After several months, the computers in effect lost track of where books were located. And there were no reliable manual stock records as a back-up.

It later transpired that, even from day one, the computerised stock records were wrong. Staff hadn't transferred stock data correctly from the old manual records to the new systems, so the computer's electronic map could not always tell warehouse staff where to find books or pallets.

With the stock records corrupted, staff were not able to find books quickly enough to put orders onto the conveyor belt within a maximum two-hour period allotted by the computer. After this time, the books were marked as out of stock and customers did not receive their orders.

Meanwhile the system was also rejecting perfectly packed orders. The reason was that the systems were designed to double check that a consignment was correct by weighing each box. But this worked only if the weight of each book had been correctly pre-programmed into the system.

They were – but the programmers had not allowed for the fact that the pages of paperback books lose some of their moisture content in the warehouse and so weighed a few grams less than the computer system was expecting.

So the system rejected consignments thinking they were underweight. This led to further orders going unfulfilled, plus the fact that the system was generating spurious error messages, which further confused warehouse staff as they tried to deal with other problems.

Only a two week complete shutdown of the entire warehousing operation would have given enough time to put the problems right. But this was impossible. The backlog of orders was growing daily and customers were losing business. They wanted orders delivered there and then.

The trusted, manually-based book picking system, which had helped to give Tiptree its pre-eminence, was not run in parallel with the new system and so there was no fallback position when disaster struck.

Booksellers questioned about Tiptree at the time had little compassion. 'The situation is a complete mess,' said Lionel Barnard, of the Mulberry Bush retailer in Brighton, Sussex. 'We have received damaged books, delivery times have been extremely extended, books have been lost; and VAT has been charged on some orders. I have lost valuable business because I have not had the books in stock.'

At the time, Kelvin Llewellyn, Tiptree's managing director said he sympathised with the booksellers.

'Our problem began in early July. When we first went live with the new automated system we had, as with any new system, a number of teething troubles. At the same time we had a tremendous increase in turnover going through Tiptree; we have just had the heaviest month in our history. Also, trying to teach the staff how to work the new system has taken up valuable time. Unfortunately this has meant that we have developed a backlog.'

He added: 'We are particularly distressed because this summer Tiptree has gone from being the best distributor in the country to probably the worst. The irony is that it takes twenty-seven years to build up your service and reputation, and seven weeks to lose it.'

One or two distributors condemned Tiptree for altering a process that may not have needed changing. Most customers, however, realised that Tiptree needed to look to the future, though they were critical of the fact that the new system seemed to have 'gone in overnight without customers being consulted'.

Tiptree refused at the time to reveal exactly what went wrong. This provided a challenge to the book trade press to investigate and report comments of customers and publishers. Some publishers commented in *Bookseller* that Tiptree's entire stock records had been corrupted; and to some extent this was true, although this was not so much a fault of the system as of the management of its introduction.

With the system unable to track where books were kept, titles were frequently shown as out of stock when they were present in the warehouse – somewhere. Some publishers ended up reprinting titles unnecessarily. Victoria Barnsley of Fourth Estate said, 'It is a disaster. The computer shows different stock levels each day. Books have simply disappeared off the face of the earth.'

With a system intolerant of human error, minor problems turned into major ones. For example, staff had to key into the system the dimensions of particular books that had been ordered, so that the computers could choose a correctly sized box, which would then be loaded with exactly the right number of books, heat-sealed and dispatched. Sometimes, however, staff mistakenly keyed in the dimensions of the box rather than the book – so the computer would think that only one book could fit into a large box.

To add to this problem, the computer would allocate a box to be filled with books it thought were in stock but which could not be found anywhere. The result was that customers received too many of the wrong books, not enough of the right ones, and sometimes a delivery of nothing but empty boxes.

One retailer received six pallets of one title, another received three beautifully packed, heat-sealed boxes, which contained no books. Waterstone's in Croydon opened a large box that should have contained many different titles to find only one book inside: *Chaos* by James Gleick.

The system also generated credit notes if it thought books were out of stock or if there was an error on the invoice. This led to further problems. One library services supplier was sent a 42-page account statement with 20 pages of credit notes.

Waterstone's received 1,400 credit notes in a single week. Some retailers had to assign staff purely to handle Tiptree consignments and invoices. 'Our purchasing controller goes into purdah for two days when the invoices come in,' said Malcolm Peters, chairman of Peters Library Services.

Eventually Tiptree issued an open letter to the book trade. The letter was signed by Gail Rebuck, chair and chief executive of Random House, the publisher which owns Tiptree.

I am writing to you about a matter of major concern to us all. Tiptree has made serious and expensive efforts to improve its service to the trade by a major investment programme in warehouse control systems and staff retraining. This investment was undertaken because despite the fact that Tiptree was voted the 1992 Distributor of the Year, the company is not complacent and has listened carefully to suggestions from all sectors of the trade about possible improvements in service. The results of this investment will be an unparalleled level of service to all customers with clear benefits to all sectors of the trade. However the implementation of the improved systems has not been as smooth as was anticipated and has caused major problems for some though not all of Tiptree's customers. These problems are short term and we recognise that they come at a crucial time for the trade. We are making every effort to shorten the period of change and ask all our friends throughout the trade for their forbearance at this time. However I do recognise that improved service for the future is of little consolation to those who are experiencing problems now.

As well as instituting a treble shift to clear the backlog, Tiptree set up a hotline, which helped a great deal. By January 1994 many of the problems had been resolved, though at what cost is not clear. Several publishers said they planned to seek compensation for lost orders and their costs. Virgin had already submitted a claim by October 1993.

Another publisher, Dorling Kindersley, spoke about claiming compensation running into millions. In the end this and other disputes were settled by negotiation. However Dorling Kindersley took its book distribution business elsewhere. And Tiptree lost its managing director and computer manager.

So what went wrong?

The biggest single problem was that staff did not fully appreciate the major changes in attitude and processes that would have to accompany the introduction of computers.

They did not fully understand how the systems worked – or rather how important the human element was in the chain. So they could not be blamed for failing to realise that keying in the wrong information could have such a devastating effect on the business.

'One small mistake caused a ripple which would have an increasingly serious effect on the whole process,' said Anthony McConnell, finance director of Tiptree's parent company Random House.

Tiptree directors also made a common mistake: they assumed that what works elsewhere will work for them. They saw a perfectly acceptable system working perfectly well at sites in the USA and France.

Every business is different, though it may not seem so at first sight. No two systems supplied to different companies at different times are identical. Two systems that may seem the same could differ in ways that may not seem obvious at first.

For instance, the hardware may have been manufactured at a different factory to different quality controls and may even be a different model altogether, which is potentially more powerful but may have incorporated design changes that make it less of a proven product. The system may run a different version of the software or operating system, or may have different memory, storage capacity, type of disks and back-up configurations. The 'standard' software may have been adapted to one company in a way that may not be obvious to the casual observer.

A supplier will often 'invest' or lose money at a particular user site in order to establish a credible reference customer who will then eulogise the supplier. But the reference site may give a sanitised and idealised view because it does not want to damage its special relationship with the supplier. That relationship may have yielded free or loaned equipment, or early versions of new software.

The best way to spot a 'massaged' reference site is to ask the supplier for a list of *all* its customers, not merely a selection. If the supplier is reluctant and quotes some nonsense about commercial confidentiality, make a judgement on whether you want to place your business with a company that, if things turn sour, will leave your name off its selected list of reference sites, quoting the need to maintain 'commercial confidentiality'. This is one of the most abused phrases in the computer industry. It is usually nothing more than a mask to hide the supplier's shortcomings.

Even if, rarely, the software and hardware are absolutely standard, the new systems will often have to interface with existing systems, which will invariably differ from site to site. These differences, however subtle, can lead to bottlenecks, or network blockages, which make response times at the terminal intolerable.

In any case, no two companies will implement projects and train staff to the same standard. Tiptree had problems finding time to train staff to use the system.

As difficulties surfaced, Tiptree tended to play them down to the point where customers became incredulous at what they were being told. For example Tiptree said at one point that all the problems would be resolved long before the Christmas rush of 1993, but by January 1994 *Bookseller* reported such issues as:

- an extension of delivery times
- duplicated orders
- loss of books
- arrival of empty boxes
- sending of inaccurate invoices

At least one retailer was sympathetic. '[Tiptree] had a very good hotline which worked well for orders we made via

TeleOrdering. They needed to redeem themselves. You don't win the award Book Distributor of the Year unless you have people who care. I don't know whether their robots got lost, dizzy or couldn't learn to drive on the left but it must have been heartbreaking to struggle with cartons emblazoned "Distributor of the Year" while everyone is screaming at you for giving a lousy service.'

By 1995, however, the system was yielding all the promised rewards. The company had used a quiet post-Christmas-and-New-Year holiday period to carry out a full stock take and ensure that the systems were programmed with the right data.

As this was being written, Marilyn Johnson, Tiptree's computer manager, said that 98 per cent of all orders are now dispatched the same day as they are received. This is 24 hours quicker than under the old manual process. The systems have also become a model for the rest of the book trade. In March 1995, the company announced that it was the first book distributor in the UK to guarantee a 24-hour, round-the-year delivery service — made possible only with the new system.

Johnson ascribed the initial failure of the system to the fact that 'people had worked in a certain way and did not appreciate the need for a major cultural change'.

Another computing executive pointed out that Tiptree, as part of a £90 million company, was big enough to withstand a heavy blow.

Other, smaller, companies might have been so debilitated by their first computerisation attempt that they would not have lived long enough to see their computer systems yield the promised benefits.

Perhaps the moral, then, is to be aware that all-in-one-go computerisation may indeed give you a competitive edge, and there's an equal chance it'll put you out of business.

CHAPTER SEVEN

The Fourth Deadly Sin: Pusillanimity

Before using such a long word I had to check what it meant. A definition in a dictionary of computer disasters might be: pusillanimity – the character of a chief executive or someone else not directly involved in a computer project who is in the best position to judge the progress or otherwise of a scheme because he/she knows nothing about computers, but who fails to intervene because he/she knows nothing about computers.

Indeed one of the strangest things about computers is the effect that they have on the most powerful people in an organisation.

Even chief executives who control their companies as if they secretly suspected Saddam Hussein of being a liberal are reduced to nodding acquiescence when listening to a Computer Expert.

All it takes is a smattering of jargon, interspersed with the names of some arcane databases, languages, hardware and networking products, tossed in a dressing of impressive-sounding executive-speak, and the chief executive is the computer expert's Most Humble Servant.

Most cleverly of all, none of the expert's bombast is in the least bit recognisable as bombast to the untrained listener because it always contains a few quickly understood phrases that allow enough comprehension to make the speaker sound credible, but not enough to expose the imposture.

You will recognise a counterfeit when you find yourself thinking you are to blame for the speaker's unintelligibility.

The real problems arise when, cowed by what they mistakenly believe is their ignorance, chief executives leave decisions that carry with them serious financial consequences to the experts. The result is that, even when intuition tells them all is not well, chief executives say nothing; until the computer department asks for a six-month extension to the deadline and a 50 per cent increase in the budget. Then it is time for independent advice.

But by this time, millions may have been spent, so it is a little late to commission a project review.

It is often the non-technical outsider, perhaps the chief executive or the newly recruited graduate in the photocopying room, who can most easily see the organisation's weaknesses, and is therefore its most objective critic.

That said, the earlier Wessex Regional Health Authority case study and others caution against the chief executive who becomes *too* closely involved in the project. Then objectivity may be lost; and worse, the chief executive can turn into a technology zealot and, as a result, become the most dangerous person in the organisation.

A power-crazed finance director might buy a larger car and acquire a bigger office and a couple of secretaries, but a Bayard of a chief executive who starts talking about needing 64 Mbytes of RAM and a RISC-based machine on every worker's desk, and a bank of parallel processor database engines in every department, has the *authority* to bankrupt the whole company.

One of the main causes of disaster in many of the case studies in this book is either the misguided enthusiasm of non-technical senior company officers for technology or their failure to intervene because of their technological timidity.

The first two case studies are typical. In the first, on the Performing Right Society, some senior non-technical officers had little direct involvement in the project, and the opposite was true at Wessex Regional Health Authority.

In the following case study the chief executive, and indeed the top-layer of civil service management, after a fixed-price contract was negotiated, seem to have distanced themselves.

Often a supplier will enjoy being left alone, but a computer project is a team effort. No supplier should be left to its own devices, even on a fixed-priced contract. Yet no supplier should allow the project to be driven entirely by end-users who have no understanding of the technology. Whatever the terms of the contract, the customer should always be in charge of the supplier, monitoring its progress, *understanding* the rate of progress, making sure that bad news is being passed on, checking that there are adequate contingency plans for a failure, and that the supplier is continuing to meet its promises. Otherwise, the chances are that, if the project is failing, you won't discover in what way until it's too late to alter course.

However, so long as there is firm leadership, and particularly rigorous control of changes, ideally exercised by the chief executive, the more people who contribute their ideas and criticisms the better. Then everyone will understand the benefits and limitations of the system before it is introduced.

In the following case, the fixed-price contract seems to have given the user organisation a false sense of security. Indeed, at the time, the Department of the Environment (Northern Ireland) had every reason to think that nothing could go wrong. If the systems did not work the supplier would not be paid. And if the cost was over the fixed price agreed, the supplier would have to pay the extra. It was as simple as that, surely . . .

CASE STUDY

This was not going to be a huge, amorphous, pioneering, uncontrollable project. There had already been too many of these in the public sector. This would be different. It would be broken into manageable chunks: into four entirely separate phases.

But rather than implement the software piece by piece, checking that each component worked well before moving onto the next, the department left the supplier to deliver most of the functions in the first phase. Instead of climbing Everest in small manageable stages, the supplier was expected to set up the first base camp at 26,000 feet.

The department preferred not to let the contract to different suppliers in separate phases, because it felt this was time-consuming and unnecessarily bureaucratic.

The end-users tended to agree, because they did not want to invest much time and effort in a system that would not be completed for years to come.

Perhaps they would have been more cautious if they had realised that the anticipated benefits of a system are as nothing compared with the costs of its failing.

This is where an informed chief executive could have intervened. His or her view might have been that no computer project is worthwhile unless it can deliver tangible

business benefits within six months or a year.

Most suppliers would say this is impossible – in which case the chief executive can instruct the computer manager to stop preliminary work on a bespoke software project and find off-the-shelf software packages. **Of course no ready-made software will fit exactly – but if the chief executive is willing to modify the company's administrative procedures to fit the package, rather than adapt the software to suit the company, the chances of a successful computerisation are greatly increased.**

The trouble with established off-the-shelf packages is that they tend to be boringly efficient – not much fun or challenge involved in their installation. But the main reason that a government department will tend to eschew packages is that they like to think themselves unique.

The idea of a whole department of state adapting procedures that have evolved over centuries to fit a mere software package is not only impractical but ignoble, like expecting a government minister to travel to work chauffeurless.

And so, for a variety of reasons, the Department of the Environment (Northern Ireland) bought a large bespoke system to control virtually everything within its remit. This included the maintenance of 15,000 miles of roads, bridges, street lighting, stores, maintenance depots, and section offices.

The system would, it was hoped, automate, among other things:
- the roads inventory;
- works planning;
- productivity and payroll;
- plant and vehicle management;
- receipts and debtors;
- purchasing;
- management accounting;
- bridge records;
- the organisation of roads maintenance.

These were only a few of the stated purposes. In fact, although the contract was not awarded until January 1988, the department had begun preliminary work on the project four years earlier. By 1986 the department had published an Operational Requirement, which set out what computerisation would achieve.

Caution dictated that all the main bidders should be given money to do a design study. This is always a good idea if it can be afforded. In this case it allowed the suppliers to interpret the operational requirement, and to judge for themselves how to overcome any technical difficulties.

By December 1987 the contract was awarded to Systems Designers, which later became part of EDS, the world's largest specialist computer services group.

The supplier had not merely given a price against the department's specifications. It had put together its own tender document and then set a price against it, which was accepted.

Under the implementation plan, the contract would start on 4 January 1988 and was due to last 169 weeks, a little over three years.

Considering this was a roads and street lighting computer system and not the Channel Tunnel, the time allowed for completion might, with hindsight, have been excessive.

By the time the project was due to be completed, hardware technology and the department's requirements would have changed almost unrecognisably. There was a danger that the system and its functions would be out of date before they went into active service. Yet nobody at the Treasury, which approved the project, seems to have given this much thought.

In fact the Treasury was habitually approving multi-million-pound computer projects on the basis of written but nevertheless largely unsubstantiated business cases which promised that the systems would save more than they cost (see appendices). I have seen business cases submitted to the Treasury which have been studded with phrases such as 'should deliver savings of . . .' or 'is expected to achieve a reduction in costs/staff of . . .' Little or no explanation is given as to how the savings or reductions in staff will be achieved in practice. At the Department of Social Security, for example, the business case for computerisation said that the systems would cut 20,000 jobs. In fact the DSS increased the number of jobs over the life of the project and beyond. Eight years after the scheme began in earnest, when everyone had forgotten the claim that the systems were supposed to cut 20,000 jobs, the DSS launched a second all-embracing computerisation project which, once more, cost hundreds of millions of pounds. Again, it was claimed by the DSS that the computerisation would help to save 20,000 jobs over the next few years.

I suspect that it is more difficult taking pocket money from a four-year-old than securing a few millions of pounds from the

Treasury for a new government computer project. It may be unkind to say so, but the only thing the Treasury seems to learn from its mistakes is that promises in relation to computer projects are made cheaply and delivered expensively, in which case approval for them should be made by as many civil servants as possible so that no blame can be attributed to any individual or any minister in the event of a disaster.

By 1991 the Department of the Environment's software should have been delivered. But by May 1990, nearly two and half years into the contract, none of the four releases had been delivered in full – and the estimated cost of finishing the contract virtually doubled the original budget.

An internal consultancy report in May 1990 stated the position succinctly.

'The potential benefit from the software and equipment that has been delivered (but not yet all accepted) to date is low in relation to the expenditure incurred under the contract. About 4% of the potential business benefits from the overall project will be available from 15% of the total software . . . for more than 50% of the contract payments.'

The department had in fact paid £5.54 million in advance of the project's completion; yet the situation was equally bleak for the supplier. It had dozens of people employed on a contract that had so far made a large loss. It believed that the department's end-users had not supplied enough information to allow Systems Designers to come up with an adequate system; a shortcoming that is acknowledged in the internal consultancy report commissioned by the department.

This was another project disaster in which neither supplier nor user was wholly to blame. But how could each party extricate itself from the perplexity of difficulties?

Even as the project was floundering, the department was continuing to pay the supplier about £40,000 to £50,000 a month; but this was insufficient to cover the supplier's costs, so in March it threatened to withdraw its project staff unless its losses were covered by the department.

A letter from a senior executive at the supplier stated that his company was 'incurring quite significant abortive costs amounting to some £150–£200,000 per month, and we are receiving revenue at an average of £40–£50,000 per month. I have stated on more than one occasion that the company cannot afford this continuous haemorrhaging of its cash which . . . will amount to £2.7 million by the 30 April 1990.'

Worse was to follow. The department had paid more than £2 million for an IBM mainframe from Systems Designers only to discover that it did not own the machine. It had signed a clause in its contract saying that, in any dispute with the supplier, it would not own any of the equipment.

So the department was left with a mainframe data centre it had paid for, and a mainframe it was not allowed to use. It was beginning to look as if the entire £5.54 million paid by the department to Systems Designers would have to be written off.

Then the supplier suggested two options:
• That all work on the project be run down, eliminating further abortive spending. However this would increase the start-up costs if work on the project were to resume. Even so, the supplier would transfer the IBM mainframe to a third party with whom the department could buy a computing service. This option would cost more money, leave the department with 4 per cent of the potential benefit from its new roads system, and there would be virtually nothing to show for the investment of £5.54 million.
• The supplier would continue work on the systems without further delay, provided that the department agree to a payment plan that covered the supplier's losses.

If it accepted this last choice, the department would have had to compensate the supplier and also bear additional unforeseen costs – perhaps another £8 million – to complete the systems.

The department did not know what to do, and so commissioned an independent consultancy report. Meanwhile the government's computer advisory agency the CCTA wrote a letter to the supplier on 24th May 1990. The author was the CCTA's director of contracts.

'I write on behalf of The Department of Environment Northern Ireland. You will be aware of your contractual obligation to complete delivery of Release 1 to the Department by week ended 2nd January 1989 . . . Enclosed is a list of the major deliverables which remain outstanding on Release 1. It is your obligation under the contract to complete terminal and hardware installation, together with implementation and setting up of the [software] application.'

The department then accused the supplier of an 'unacceptable and continuing failure to perform', adding:

'Any failure to perform in accordance with this notice by the 6 July 1990 will be a breach of condition which will entitle the Department to consider itself discharged from all further contractual obligations.'

The supplier's reply to the CCTA agency was equally forceful.

'The Agency will be aware that the Department issued no formal contract amendment(s) to reflect the agreed changes to the programme/schedule. But exchanges of correspondence, minutes of meetings and the like adequately demonstrate that the requirements of the original contract have been superseded by mutual agreement . . .

'It is the company's view that its performance of the contract . . . has been and is frustrated by the failure of the Department to a) provide data adequate to enable the company to perform the contract originally placed with the company b) to amend the contract to reflect the changes arising from (a).

'The Agency's claims of the company's unacceptable and continuing failure to perform are totally rejected.'

This was only part of the supplier's reply. The letter went on to hold the department liable for the costs of the delay.

And so, with the department feeling like a three-legged fox in the presence of salivating hounds, it then received an independent consultancy report which effectively advised that the remaining three legs were of little long-term value.

The report said that Release 1 delivered so far had 200 errors, and Releases 2, 3 and 4 would cost a further £12 million to complete. On top of the £5.54 million paid so far, that would bring the total project cost to £16 million – exactly double the original project price.

And completion would require a further 22,000 man days of further effort, to add to the six years the department had already devoted to the project.

And yet when the department had originally signed the fixed-price contract it was convinced it had negotiated a good deal.

The contract theoretically allowed it to recover from the contractor all money paid if the system was not in accordance with the contract. But the consultancy report cast doubt on whether a legal claim would succeed.

'As with most disputes there are two sides to the argument . . . it must be expected that the contractor will be able to mount a vigorous rebuttal and counter claim to the Department's charges.

'The Department appears vulnerable on the ability to express clearly its requirements on management accounting and for some time did not have an in-house capability to respond to Contractor queries. Specialist consultants were used to fill this role but there may be gaps in the defence on this and other undisclosed matters.

'The favourable points for the Department are that the Contractor had carried out a pre-contract study and so had a good knowledge of the project and of the Department.'

Most pertinent of all, the consultancy reported that:

'Some of the problems now being experienced arose from the casual and relaxed contractual dealings with the contractor. A more disciplined approach to contract administration and management should be followed within the project team.'

The warning came too late. The department refused to pay the supplier the £2.75 million it required to resume work on the project.

Work stopped completely, the project team was disbanded, the department sought further legal advice and formally terminated the contract.

By then the total cost to public funds was £6.97 million, of which £5.54 million had been paid to the supplier. The department's legal advice was that it was unlikely to succeed in any action to recover the £5.54 million. So it sought a negotiated settlement.

In August 1991 the CCTA agency reached an agreement which, from the taxpayer's point of view, was hardly attractive. The department agreed to pay the supplier a further £1.8 million . . . for a system that had delivered 4 per cent of what was originally intended.

To my knowledge this is the first time that a government department has threatened to sue its computer supplier and has settled by paying the supplier a further £1.8 million – merely for the legal right to use the hardware and software that it had previously paid for.

The only good to emerge from the debris of the project was that in 1991 the CCTA, in conjunction with the Treasury solicitor, sought to tighten up on government computing contracts ... but officials have made similar mollifying noises after each public-sector disaster since the 1960s.

Indeed, only two years after this multi-million-pound failure, the CCTA did not oppose – and was not given the power to oppose – a soon-to-be-notorious, £25 million statistics computer project that was also stillborn.

There then surfaced details of yet another government computing calamity: a £48 million system for the Department of Employment called Field, which was another high-risk, ambitious, pioneering project that most of the end-users ultimately rejected.

So where did the Department of the Environment (Northern Ireland) go wrong?

The most obvious flaw is that project executives realised too late that the project was in deep trouble. It seems that they had abdicated much of the project responsibility to the supplier, a company with which they had casual and relaxed contractual dealings.

There is also a school of thought (and I subscribe to it) that **suppliers and customers work best in a constant state of noble tension.** But this requires either that chief executives should be involved, at least to police the project, or that they should vest full director-level authority in whoever deals with the supplier on a day-to-day basis.

The Japanese have genuine and successful partnerships with their computer suppliers because the two sides are committed to each other by a code of honour that we in the West cannot fully understand. Honour means so much in Japan that nearly 2,000 Japanese pilots gave their lives to its name in World War Two kamikaze missions.

If a computer supplier in Japan dishonours itself by inflicting financial harm on its customer, it will be ostracised by the business community. In the West – and I know it is a sweeping generalisation, but one that has yet to be disproved – suppliers who carry with them a history of disasters seem to prosper more than their less notorious competitors.

What has also emerged from the Department of the Environment's failure is that this project could have been a success – but only if the costs of the new systems had been calculated meticulously and then multiplied by three.

Of course, you do not always have to multiply the cost by three. You can cut the scope of the project by two-thirds or apply a mixture of overestimated costs and underestimated benefits. Either way, this advice follows the same logic: that of introducing realism to computerisation, *of understanding the risks.*

Not that this guidance is the beginning and end of project management. A doubling or trebling of the Department of the Environment's original budget, coupled with the full cooperation of end-users, would no doubt have led to the delivery of an adequate roads and street management system for the Department of the Environment.

But would the department have *wanted* such a system? The software had been written using a highly specialised proprietary tool that generated its own unique code.

The tool was a technological chastity belt. It locked in its users for the lifetime of the software that was written using it. So the department, had it not abandoned the project, would have been committed to software that only highly paid specialists could maintain and develop.

Indeed today, the proprietary software that was used in the project is hardly in the mainstream of the computer industry. In short, highly proprietary software tools turn customers into hostages of their suppliers.

Yet, even as this chapter is being written, major organisations in the railway industry are spending millions of pounds on proprietary systems that can be maintained only by consultancies and suppliers at what can only be described as an enormous cost.

Also, the Department of the Environment (Northern Ireland) was another victim of the desire to order an innovative high-risk system. **Worse, it had made interim payments to the supplier of millions of pounds, and so was in a weak position when a dispute arose.**

Clearly its bargaining position would have been stronger if it had agreed to pay only on delivery of a system that had been proven to be satisfactory.

As it was, the department was reluctant to go to court for a number of reasons, one of which was the embarrassment of discussing what was then an unpublicised disaster in an open courtroom.

The ideal would have been for the department to have sacrificed the benefit of all-encompassing integration in favour of small systems that were each self-contained and could later have been individually bolted onto other systems. This is exactly what the department did once the main project had failed: it ordered a new system for each sub-section of the department, rather than try to computerise the whole of its operations.

The Ministry of Agriculture, Fisheries and Food (MAFF) also turned to small, unambitious systems but only after it had lost more than £1 million on a failed grandiose project.

The key to buying smaller systems is the realisation that integration is not overridingly important, but merely desirable. If the packages all work well individually and later cannot be subsumed under the whole, never mind. It is better that all the systems work individually and not in harmony with each other, than that none of the systems work individually and none of them fit together.

The building-block approach is more likely to succeed if the user organisation refuses to pay for each self-contained module until it is demonstrably successful.

It is not clear to me why all government departments seem content to pay in advance – and then to commission costly consultancy reports to advise on how to settle a dispute with an intransigent supplier.

The reason, perhaps, is that in the civil service there is no individual responsibility. Even ministers are not personally responsible for the mistakes of their departments. Instructions to ministers state in effect that they cannot be held responsible if they endorse bad decisions when not in full possession of all the facts. This has given rise to a practice – I don't know how widespread it is but I have information that it exists – whereby a minister will sometimes ask for particularly sensitive information or controversial recommendations to be given to them orally. One can only speculate that the reason for this is that, if things turn sour, ministers can argue that they were not in possession of the full facts and there is no written evidence to disprove this.

So if ministers are not accountable for their decisions, why should the heads of their departments be so? Besides, the departmental heads – the permanent secretaries – tend to move jobs as frequently as a buck climbs aboard a new doe. Even if they are in still in post when MPs come to debate a disaster, the permanent secretary will be surrounded by other civil servants who will be pre-armed with ten answers to every one question from a semi-knowledgeable MP.

Perhaps this explains why the House of Commons, whenever it debates a computer disaster, usually makes virtually the same set of reformational recommendations – and has done so since the 1970s.

CHAPTER EIGHT

The Fifth Deadly Sin: Credulity (I)

Any company that is about to spend millions of pounds on computers *wants* to have faith in the supplier's promises. And every supplier works hard to gain the faith of its customers.

Inevitably, therefore, there will be times when the credulity of the customers will become enmeshed with the excessive self-confidence of the supplier, and both parties will get the worst of both worlds.

Unfortunately the onus is on the customer to spot when this is going to happen, because sometimes not even the supplier knows when it is stretching itself too far, in terms of its promises or its prices, or both.

The problem is that suppliers cannot realistically be expected to admit their weaknesses. They must be seen always to demonstrate an unambiguous self-confidence, a belief in their products, an ability to deliver, and a specialist knowledge that is second to none; otherwise they will not win orders.

And they are always easy to believe.

Their credibility is enhanced by the trappings of their success. If you are a buyer with a large budget you may be whisked by private jet for a (strictly business) site visit in Acapulco, the South of France or the Far East. The destination is unimportant so long as the trip costs enough to leave the customer feeling unconsciously, or ideally consciously, indebted to the supplier.

I do not deny that, although I have a non-existent budget, I have fallen victim to such insufferable hospitality as chauffeur-driven trips to the opera and all-expenses-paid trips to Japan (a little work and a lot of shoeless restaurants and sightseeing before returning by executive class). My judgement has been scarred by such experiences. I have come back proselytised, believing that I must write something pleasant about the supplier; although, after a few hours in a darkened room, the feeling passes.

Many suppliers also impress their clients by occupying not mere offices, not even edifices of business respectability, but technological palaces in prime locations with over-the-top security. It is not unknown at some supplier sites for senior executives to exhibit their seniority by wearing bunches of chains around their necks, like door-to-door magnetic card salesmen. Each card allows access to a different part of the building. In one supplier's establishment the apparently solid walls of the boardroom, at the touch of a button, dissolve electronically into floor-to-ceiling windowlike liquid display panels which allow directors to see through to the company's main control room but without allowing the control room staff to see into the board room. The device exists not to allow directors to monitor staff performance covertly but rather as a technological exhibit. The company invites prospective customers to marvel, and then tells them in effect: if we can do this, think what we can do with your company's computer systems.

Then there are the verbal exhibitions. When discussing your requirements, suppliers will always have been there before.

This is not a deception, merely an exaggeration – easier to spot in, say, a car salesman than a computer sales executive.

Your assumption is that, because the supplier is so financially successful it must be right and, of course, know infinitely more than you.

With a used-car dealer you assume the opposite: that they know nothing about the car apart from things they wouldn't dream of telling you, and what they *will* tell you is obvious from just looking at it.

Computer companies are more inscrutable because they don't operate from back-street sites, and their staff don't wear cheap suits.

The burden of understanding this puts on the customer should not be underestimated because it is not a simple matter of knowing when suppliers are lying.

Few computer salespeople lie: rather they seem to convince themselves that they are telling the truth; so if they deceive you it is only because they are deceiving themselves. They believe sincerely that they can overcome all odds to deliver the systems to time and to budget.

They do not, however, always factor into the bid price all the things that can go wrong: for example the sudden departures of key people on the project, or not being able to contact people at the right managerial level in the end-user company to sanction a change of design, an additional purchase of, say, hardware or software, or the removal of a promised function because it makes the system impossibly complex.

So customers need to strip away the well-meant embellishment from a supplier's promises and apply an arch scepticism to what remains. To do this, the customer needs to know exactly what it wants from a new system. It has to be the expert.

And this ethereal state cannot be reached unless the customer does sufficient research, if necessary by looking at relevant sites abroad, so that it knows as much as prospective suppliers about what is achievable.

All this advice sounds so obvious as to be valueless, yet case studies in this book show that customers will tend to set aside their innate, ruthless scepticism almost as soon as a computer supplier's assistant executive vice-president walks through the door.

And when customers are confronted by a choice of suppliers, one promising a great deal in a short time, and another promising less in a longer time, the former will usually win the contract.

The following two case studies, which are given separate chapters, show exactly this. In both cases the customer was faced with two key choices: a short implementation and a longer one; and they went for the former.

And in each case there were prospective suppliers who withdrew from the bidding after warning that the timetable envisaged by the customer was unachievable.

CASE STUDY

The first of the studies takes a rare, microscopic look at the most sensitive period in a project's history: the last moments before disaster.

This covers the period between the pilot telling everyone aboard not to worry because a little turbulence is normal, and the search for bodies on a desolate mountainside.

The user victim in this case is the Department of Social Security, an organisation that is particularly shy of publicity.

No company likes its administrative defects discussed in public, but the department's computer division, known as the Information Technology Services Agency (ITSA), has been particularly resentful of enquiries.

In some ways its diffidence is understandable. The agency is part of the Department of Social Security, which has lost money on computerisations since the 1970s.

One of its most infamous projects in the 1970s was Camelot, the Computerisation and Mechanisation of Local Office Tasks. About £6 million was written off after the now-familiar disaster signs:
- the technicians assuring non-technicians that everything was going well when the non-technicians could see that it wasn't
- the dismissal of serious problems as teething troubles;
- a lack of project management skills;
- no individual responsible if the project failed.

Consultants who were brought in to advise on Camelot commented that earlier computerisations had failed because of a lack of end-user involvement. But Camelot suffered from the other extreme – too much user involvement. End-users made so many requests for changes that the systems tried to please everyone and soon became enmeshed in complexity.

Soon afterwards the department embarked on Camelot's replacement, called the Operational Strategy, which was trumpeted as the largest civil computerisation in Europe. (See Chapter 11, where the DSS once again comes in for scrutiny, this time under the heading of the Sixth Deadly Sin: Consultancy.)

But the department's most recent major disaster is called ASSIST.

As the department has been less than cooperative I have had to obtain information from a variety of unofficial sources and from internal memoranda. This means the account of the failure is a little dry but the documentation gives a level of detail that is otherwise hard to obtain after disaster strikes.

Most significantly of all, the department does not accept that it was in any way to blame; and the suppliers take exactly the same view. So both sides conform to the norm of a disaster case study, and it is worth remembering that norm is the right word because, in computer terms, disasters are more 'normal' than successes.

ASSIST was the sort of recondite project name that only the civil service feels comfortable with. It stood for the Analytical Services Statistical Information System, which had four purposes, the first of which was markedly unspecific.

ASSIST would, according to an internal project promotional leaflet, enable 'better quantitative evaluation of policy options and closer monitoring of their subsequent implementation'.

What this meant was that the system would provide reams of statistics on how much money was being spent on what type of welfare benefit, and the social profiles and demography of those receiving particular benefits.

It was crucial for social security ministers to have this information. Cynics, who are the bricks and mortar of realism, would say that all social security ministers like to throw a blanket of statistics on accusations by opposition MPs that government welfare policy is making the poor poorer.

With ASSIST working as intended, ministers had hoped that, at the touch of a button, they would be able to show that a particular welfare allowance had risen by at least 14.5 per cent above the real rate of inflation since the present administration had come to power.

But without such a system – and the department is without such a system – ministers have to muddle along much as before, making speeches in the House of Commons and answering MPs' questions with a plethora of statistics that may not be meaningful but are more relevant than the morsel of statistics that are available to the opposition.

A cynic would also say that the money allocated to ASSIST, £25 million, was large because this was a system not for welfare claimants but for administrators and ministers.

A fixed-price contract was awarded to a consortium of major computer suppliers, ICL and Hoskyns, in January 1993, but only after the department had closed the door on a cacophony of alarm bells sounded by another supplier, IBM.

IBM withdrew from the bidding because it did not feel it could meet the tight deadline.

This was a prime government contract at a prime site that could have provided IBM with a major reference customer, a launch pad, from which it could have won further government business in Europe.

But IBM felt it could not build, test and deliver in the time available: less than a year between signing the contract and delivery of phase one.

If IBM did not want to take the risk, did ICL and Hoskyns have good grounds for believing their chances of success were much greater?

The attitude of major suppliers who withdraw from a bid or decline to tender may seem at first to be unduly negative but their reservations should be taken at least as seriously as – perhaps more seriously than – the positive claims of their more sanguine counterparts.

Even today I still don't know why the department allowed so little time for the project's completion. Naturally, the system was needed urgently, to meet the ministerial requirement for better statistics – but was the project so *desperately* urgent?

That the department had been without such a system for years, and is even today able to carry on normally without such a system, is perhaps proof that, on reflection, the rush to implement the system may have been misjudged.

The lesson from this applies to most of the disasters in this book: **Thou shalt not set artificially tight deadlines**.

I also wonder how such a big ambitious system received Treasury approval when big ambitious systems, particularly those initiated by government, have had the survival rate of LSD gastronomes who have flown from the Empire State Building.

STAGE ONE

The first of ASSIST's project stages was particularly important because the department paid competing consortia to do a technical design study.

This is an ideal way to start because it enables suppliers to see what they are letting themselves in for. They are paid to replicate the design of the system, and often to provide a working demonstration, without any cost to themselves or any commitment to deliver a final system.

However, paid-for technical design studies by competing consortia are usually a luxury that only government departments can afford; and this case is evidence that they are no insurance policy against disaster.

The department's study contracts provided for:
- a high-level design;

- a prototype of the systems' features;
- a demonstration of proposed interfaces between the end-users and the computer programs.

So detailed was this work that it lasted three months, on site at the ASSIST team's civil service headquarters at Longbenton near Newcastle.

It was during this exercise that IBM and its consortium partner, the French-owned computer services company Sema, decided that 'they could not fully support the early phasing of the implementation timetable requested by the Department', according to an internal newsletter at the time.

The newsletter to staff also explained IBM's withdrawal: 'Recognising the importance to the Department of the timing of the phase 1 functionality, IBM and Sema withdrew their proposal.'

It is not clear whether the department officials interrogated IBM on its reasons for withdrawing so late in the bidding; but, if they did, it did not seem to make any difference to the tight timetable.

If anything, IBM's departure made the choice of final supplier easier for the department because, now, only two consortia were left in the running: one being ICL and Hoskyns, and the other was Digital Equipment and Data Sciences.

The newsletter went on to praise the department for the way it had set about choosing the right supplier.

'There then followed an intensive period of evaluation in which proposals were scrutinised for their technical feasibility and conformance with standards. As a result of this evaluation both consortia were invited to submit Best and Final Offers, which means that they submitted their lowest-price, final bid.

So pressing was the deadline that the department began to discuss a draft contract with both suppliers long before the winning bid was picked.

The eventual choice of supplier was ICL and Hoskyns, who are among the most knowledgeable suppliers to government. ICL was one of the main suppliers to the Operational Strategy; and today it remains one of the largest single recipients of government spending on computer hardware and software.

Hoskyns runs a data centre for the Ministry of Defence and has won several major privatisation contracts, including one at the Bank of England.

In its newsletter the department cited 'best value for money' over the ten-year lifetime of the contract as the reason for its choice of consortium.

The department was convinced there was minimal risk because it wrote into the contract a clause that stated in effect that in any dispute the winning consortium members would return to the department any advance instalment payments on the system.

The idea was that the two suppliers would not only supply the hardware and software but run the ASSIST service until well into the twenty-first century, and the £25 million price reflects this. A contract was finally signed on 8 January 1993, with the first phase due by 31 December of the same year.

The second phase was due by the end of September 1994, and phase three by July 1995.

With government computing projects being picked off like caged pheasants during a shoot, one might have supposed that officials would have refused to sanction payments to the contractor(s) until a system had been delivered and accepted.

In fact ICL and Hoskyns were paid more than £200,000 a month virtually from the start of the contract.

One of the ironies of the disaster is that, in the euphoria that accompanied the start of the project, ASSIST's managers were introduced by name in the internal newsletter with the proclamation that they and others had 'worked so hard to get where we are today (and can therefore take all the blame)'.

The reference to taking the blame was in parentheses lest anyone should take it seriously.

The newsletter also stated that the project was not only the responsibility of ICL and Hoskyns but sucked in a 'dedicated team' of dozens of people from the department's ITSA computer division and also an ASSIST project end-user committee.

From here until shortly before disaster struck, the suppliers and end-users would talk to each other in a euphemistic, circumlocutory, deferential language, neither side always seeming to say exactly what it felt.

The mood was one of strained optimism, whereby all problems would be described as minor, never insuperable. It was as if the project teams were too frightened to say what they really thought in case they upset their superiors.

Yet on a project of this size, plain speaking is an indispensable prerequisite – otherwise major problems will

surface only when the end-users are asked formally to accept or reject the system.

And so it was with ASSIST. There were no signs of any serious trouble until November 1993, a month before the project's first phase was due to go live.

Even then the problems were hardly described as potentially fatal. Minutes of a meeting of ICL, ITSA and the ASSIST team, not forgetting Hoskyns, state that 'whilst some intermediate dates had recently suffered minor slippage, remedial action had been taken to safeguard the final target date for completion and handover of the final elements [of phase one] by the 13 December 1993.'

The minutes continue in the euphemistic spirit of many internal government reports; in a vein similar to Neville Chamberlain's famous remark shortly before the start of World War Two: 'I believe it is peace in our time.'

The ASSIST minutes of 11 November 1993 said that, as planned, pilot testing of the software began on 1 November 1993, with the result that several PCs were 'all correctly loaded' with the 'user names, role and accept permissions.'

Sample cases were 'successfully' converted from the existing system to the new. Then came the test results: '. . . testing had encountered a slow but satisfactory start, and whilst several issues had been raised, each had been resolved or was currently being addressed.'

More ominously, the minutes record the following comment: 'None of the issues raised to date were insuperable.'

There was evidence of a large number of TIRs – test incident reports, a polite civil service term for problems. Naturally the level of TIRs was 'not uncommon' at this stage of a typical project.

Reassuringly, the minutes added that a solution to each TIR 'was being resolved as a matter of urgency', and was being 'carefully documented and controlled through the system testing process before the relevant software was authorised to be re-released into the live environment'.

The next stage of the minutes show some divergence of views between the three main groups involved. Each seemed to have a slightly different agenda.

Pragmatically, the first group, ICL and Hoskyns, wanted the work on the systems to go ahead as soon as possible with the smallest number of changes.

This was explained diplomatically by an ICL executive who said that 'whilst all efforts would be directed to providing a user-friendly service and to implementing all of the user requirements, there would need to be a trade-off between those that were essential and required immediately, and those that were simply desirable and could await later incorporation'.

The second group – ITSA directors – wanted the system in place as soon as possible and, what's more, felt it was critical to establish a time when end-users could be left to operate the system without any technical assistance. The ITSA directors felt that many of the issues were 'almost certainly of a minor nature and could therefore be readily rectified'.

The third group – the end-users – were the least confident of all. They were the ones who would be left to use the system, and it was their feeling that all the 'issues and incidents' (meaning problems) were because of three things:
• an inconsistent approach by different programmers making individual interpretations of what was required;
• environmental problems – these were not stated specifically but usually environmental problems are things like PCs being put on desks that do not have the room to take them, or noise on communication lines which disrupts or delays the transmission of data;
• user unfamiliarity with the system.

So, whereas ITSA's directors and the suppliers were talking in terms either of the timetable or of resolving minor problems, the end-users were signalling a more deep-rooted unease.

While the ASSIST end-users felt that 'many of the TIRs' would be resolved by new software releases, they indicated that there was a need to ensure the system was more user-friendly.

Then came the most serious warning yet. The end-user representative recorded in the minutes that although he had not as yet identified any TIRs of major significance 'many would need to be addressed before he could feel confident that ASSIST could be released into the wider user organisation'.

Commencement of the pilot tests, he said, would 'therefore depend upon the satisfactory clearance of these particular usability issues'.

At this stage it did not seem as if all parties were looking at each other straight in the eye. Certainly the warnings from end-users did not seem to be taken too seriously. One of the ICL executives commented that the 'overall process was going rather well'. An ITSA representative observed that the problems that had been encountered were 'not untypical' of those experienced by local office staff during the roll-out of the (aforementioned) Operational Strategy.

More reassuringly still, the minutes concluded that 'To date no major issues had been identified'.

Long before this stage was reached an independent audit of the work carried out so far would have revealed whether the problems were teething or insuperable. A relevant maxim here could well be: **Thou shalt continually seek assurances that a major project is under firm and successful control and if you believe what you are told without independent verification expect to discover a disaster only when it is self-evident.**

With the main meeting over, the need for caution-laden words evaporated. The minutes of the 'any other business' section show people starting to speak their minds, although this was perhaps a little late given the fact that it was now only a month before the 'go-live' date for the project.

The minutes of this last section also show that ICL had already missed a 'vital project milestone', which allegedly put the company in breach of its services agreement for ASSIST. The breach had led to ITSA's formally warning ICL that it would 'continue with the project for the time being'.

This short phrase had alarmed ICL's auditors, for it suggested that ITSA might cancel the project, so ICL asked whether the wording could be slightly amended. A director of ITSA gave the consummate civil service reply: 'ICL had clearly stated that they were unable to meet the contracted target date, and the Department therefore had a choice to either terminate the contract or agree to an extension to the formal acceptance procedures date. The Department had in this instance taken the latter course of action based on the knowledge that public investment had not in any way been compromised. The wording had, in effect, sought to express that reasoning.'

There was little further comfort for ICL in the comments of a senior member of the project team. He said everyone would work towards a formal acceptance of the system by 24 February 1994 and if the system should still be incomplete or unacceptable at that time the contract 'could in fact be terminated'.

By now the ICL executives appear to have been more than a little agitated. One of them stated: 'Both ICL and Hoskyns had invested quite heavily in ensuring that ASSIST was successfully completed. The investment was however regularly appraised by the Company auditors in order to justify the continued involvement.'

In the light of this, ICL asked ITSA to reword its response to the alleged breach of contract, to reflect the project team's agreement with ICL's proposals for remedying the problems.

ITSA agreed, but to little avail. Two months later, in January 1994, there were still problems. At a meeting between ICL, Hoskyns, ITSA and end-user representatives, it was stated that testing had been marred by system environment problems and delays in inputting rules for the projects under test.

'Progress had not therefore been as productive as initially anticipated.' ICL however stated that shortly before Christmas many of the test problems were solved and those that remained were 'currently being resolved'.

Matters were complicated for ICL and Hoskyns by the end-users requesting further changes to make the software more user-friendly.

Until these changes were made, it was felt by ITSA that the wider end-user community should not be 'exposed' to the initial 'frail' software release.

Reassuring as ever, an ICL executive countered by saying that 'despite the initial problems encountered by using pre-releases of some software components' he was confident that 'both the software and the associated environments would soon be stabilised'.

It was now a month after phase one was due to go live, and difficulties were beginning to knock into each other. The timetable, which was written into the contract, was beginning to become a burden.

Delays during the testing phase of one component had restricted the time available to the user and technical teams to complete other preliminary trials ready for the formal 20-day acceptance test which was due to start in about two weeks time, on 24 January.

One member of the end-user team warned against starting formal acceptance testing procedures until all the problems with the software had been corrected.

Even so, ICL was anxious to start the formal acceptance period – partly because by now its regular monthly payments from ITSA had ceased. Only when the system was shown to be satisfactory would payments resume.

An ICL executive told the January meeting that 'whilst a minimal delay to the commencement date was acceptable, he would not wish this delay to be viewed as a further formal breach of contract'.

An ITSA director replied that 'it was essential that sufficient time was allotted to the department to satisfy itself that the system was sufficiently robust to undergo a Formal Acceptance Trial'. A premature start to the formal testing could cause 'embarrassment'. She confirmed that the existing breach of contract would not be lifted until the system was formally accepted.

But ICL assured the team that although ASSIST had met some minor difficulties 'many of the issues were now resolved'.

Almost in passing, it seems, the minutes record that a key member of the civil service project team had been moved to a new position as a government statistician in Scotland.

For Hoskyns and ICL this was one of the professional hazards of winning government contracts – that the jobs of civil servants running a project development can change frequently enough to ensure instability in the project management.

But the show had to go on. Four months later all the preliminary issues had been resolved and the make-or-break Formal Acceptance Test began.

It was now a full five months after the first phase was due to be delivered and accepted.

Under the terms of the contract the Formal Acceptance Test, known by the project team as FAT, had to last 20 days during which the systems would need to be available to end-users 95 per cent of the time.

But at the end of the test nobody seemed to agree on what the word 'available' meant. To the end-users the word was obvious: there should be no faults that would result in a user being unable to perform any task, no matter how obscure.

To ICL and Hoskyns, this was too narrow an interpretation. If applied it meant that ICL and Hoskyns had failed the Formal Acceptance Test. It was the supplier's view, expressed in an internal memorandum, that 'to expect a system of the complexity of ASSIST to achieve acceptance without a single fault in a single process being identified, and resolved, is unrealistic and unnecessarily restrictive'.

The ICL and Hoskyns memo said that they had detected and resolved problems during the FAT, either by software amendments to the ASSIST code or by configuration changes to the systems or standard packages. All those changes were 'implemented speedily and there was no regression necessary'. In most cases, the problems did not render the system unusable and some user processing could have continued. If anything the faults tended to be caused by limits in the software being exceeded or users not using the system properly, according to the memo.

Despite all this, the fact remained that there had been problems during the test. On one occasion, time was lost because of a hardware fault that ICL and Hoskyns felt would have been circumvented by users during normal live operations. On a second occasion, an hour was lost because of an 'operational failure' by ICL and Hoskyns which, the suppliers said, 'should not be repeated'.

More positively, the suppliers reported that the ASSIST help desk had handled problems speedily and that performance tests had been successful. In fact parts of the test had gone better than the contract required.

However there were 76 'incident reports', many of which were due to user error or 'misunderstandings caused by unfamiliarity with the system'. Configuration or software deficiencies accounted for a quarter of all the incident reports.

The problems described as unresolved were said to be a 'relatively low proportion of the total' but were 'none the less of concern'. These could have been caused by 'network, PC or ASSIST problems'.

'In conclusion it is ICL/Hoskyns view that a large percentage of the FAT has been successful. There will understandably be residual issues which will require an extension to the testing period to allow resolution and satisfactory re-testing. The issues should be agreed and resolved speedily.'

So it was the supplier's perception that FAT was a success.

And it is worth remembering that £25 million hinged on the success of this test.

The end-users, in their report, were not as confident. Even before commenting on the FAT's results, they criticised what they saw as the limited scope of the tests, which covered only those processes 'available, developed, tested and formally released by ICL and Hoskyns'.

These features allowed for only a partial gathering of statistics on the payments of social security benefits and the profiles of welfare claimants.

End-users also felt that the software covered only those benefits that were 'straightforward' in nature and would use a minimum of system requirements. The users' conclusion was that: 'There are a considerable number of benefits which the current restrictive functionality would not be able to support.'

They had further complaints, particularly that important extra features would not be included in the software releases for some time yet.

The same end-users were also concerned about the way ICL and Hoskyns had approached the tests. They felt that the policies adopted by the suppliers seemed to ensure that 'FAT would never fail'.

One member of the ASSIST user team commented: 'My main concern was that we must be able to demonstrate to any third party that FAT consisted of a prescribed set of test scripts and that these had been completed without any significant errors occurring. I was not asking for an error-free system, but a demonstration that the system would be error free over twenty days out of the ten year contract.'

The views of the end-users and ICL and Hoskyns seemed to grow further apart. At one point, an internal report refers to the ASSIST user team and ICL/Hoskyns being at 'opposite ends of the spectrum', with the suppliers saying they could not work within the confines of producing an error-free system over a 20-day period.

No easy resolution seemed possible and both sides agreed to seek advice from their contracts departments. Guidance was also sought from the government's computer advisory agency, the CCTA.

It was the CCTA's view that FAT should be extended to 60 days, within which a 20-day availability period should be demonstrated.

'This compromise approach should be acceptable to all parties,' wrote the CCTA, which also pointed out the importance of the tests.

'Formal acceptance of the system is an acknowledgement that

the supplier has discharged its obligations.'

It was therefore essential, said the CCTA, that acceptance testing be undertaken in such a way as to enable users to accept the system without fearing that the software would prove unsuitable or unusable.

And with more than usual prescience the CCTA observed: 'With a project the size of ASSIST it is essential to get this right to prevent systems failures and potential bad publicity during live running.'

The CCTA's views at this stage, as an arbitrator, are pertinent. Its findings note the concern of an end-user representative who was 'unhappy that incidents and failures had occurred and were recorded but that full consideration was not being taken of the impact of the failures.'

More important still, the CCTA notes that the definition of what is meant by full availability is not clearly set out.

Despite the suppliers and customers having decades of computer project experience, neither had realised when drafting the contracts that there was a fundamental ambiguity in the wording of the definition of what was and was not an acceptable system.

This shared mistake was now a cause of acrimony between the two sides. Almost sadly the CCTA representative said he left the Department of Social Security premises having spent the day trying to sort out a situation that was 'not straightforward' because the criteria for the final acceptance tests had not been specified sufficiently.

'I am not suggesting that the representatives had failed to give detailed consideration to the criteria but with more careful planning and consideration of the impact of software errors or faults, and the likely time to resolve those faults, a more realistic criteria could have been developed.'

Virtually on the point of despair the CCTA representative said that he had spoken to end-users, the ASSIST business manager, ICL and Hoskyns and had tried to put forward suggestions on how to proceed with acceptance testing.

'However I have to report that it became quite apparent that there was some reluctance to give way from both the customer and supplier sides.'

But from the end-users' perspective, the system had too many faults to be considered acceptable. They also noted in their interpretation of the FAT results that they were 'a little disappointed to see that functions present within their current system were not available yet within ASSIST.'

I could not at this stage avoid feeling a little sorry for the suppliers. They had delivered a partially working system that had some errors but showed promise.

Yet end-users were in no mood for compromise. Some were even understandably disputatious. They quietly resented the heavy involvement of external suppliers in the public sector. Also, they had high expectations of a system that would cost £25 million over ten years.

Perhaps if the system had been bought on the basis that it would deliver little or nothing at the beginning, then nobody would have been disappointed. As it was, the high expectations of users and the low scope for manoeuvrability of the suppliers contributed to what would soon become a disaster.

By 19 May 1994, the Department of Social Security was expressing reservations about the speed of the system, for example the long time taken to load tables. ICL commented that the time taken was dependent on the number of columns, and that the current version of the software loaded a page at a time.

But the department wanted faster on-line access for users, and a facility to allow them to move easily down the screen through several pages.

This was yet another comment that ICL and Hoskyns had to take away with them to consider 'whether anything else can be done'.

It was also agreed that there would be another formal acceptance test after a two-week cooling-off period. This prompted another series of arguments about what constituted an acceptable system.

Despite all the above problems, the official minutes of a high-level meeting of all parties in June 1993 showed no major difficulties.

This was a meeting crowded with computer industry dignitaries. Among them was a director from ITSA, a director from Hoskyns and a senior executive in charge of the project at ICL. The minutes show that, all in all, there was nothing catastrophic to worry about. Yet this meeting was held several months after phase one had failed to go live as planned.

Almost as an afterthought the meeting decided to 'rework' the timetable because phase one of the project was now unlikely to be delivered by the time that phase two was due, and this would have a knock-on effect on phase three.

It was therefore agreed that ICL and Hoskyns would propose a new timetable taking into account the experiences of phase one.

After June, however, the project's descent gained fresh momentum. The system was already six months late and the department was holding up payments to ICL and Hoskyns.

Then the second acceptance tests again proved unacceptable to end-users. It was time to call a halt.

In October 1994 ITSA formally terminated the contract and demanded that the ICL and Hoskyns ASSIST project staff leave the department's offices forthwith. The suppliers' project teams were escorted off the site to ensure that any disaffection with the ending of the project did not lead to the current systems being sabotaged. This is standard practice in many organisations when there is a dispute between the staff and the company, or a dispute between a supplier and its client.

Even at this stage ITSA was saying publicly in effect, 'Problem? What Problem?' Its spokesman assured me that no public money would be lost because ICL and Hoskyns would 'automatically pay back the instalments plus the Department's costs'.

This seemed to me to be a little optimistic. Indeed I could not obtain confirmation from either ICL or Hoskyns that they were reaching for their chequebooks.

A long legal battle would have seemed certain – except that government departments detest press scrutiny of their affairs and so would not relish a court wrangle. An out-of-court settlement seemed likely.

So what are the lessons?

The Department of Social Security is one of the most experienced buyers of major computer systems in Europe. Long before ASSIST was even thought of, the department had commissioned the largest civil computerisation project in Europe, the so-called Operational Strategy. And before this it had, one assumes, learned a great deal from the failure of its Camelot computerisation.

Yet here it was again, expressing surprise that it had come to grief with a computer project. It is only a subjective view, but it seems that the department put too much faith in its contract, which, it thought, would allow it to recover its payments costs from the suppliers in the event of a dispute.

In fact ICL and Hoskyns, with some justification, did not want to repay the money and costs because they felt that they had delivered a reasonable system.

Contractually speaking, the department is worse off than it might have imagined at the start of the project, because there is a clause that in effect says that the ownership of the software remains with the suppliers until it is paid for in full.

So the department has paid Hoskyns and ICL about £4 million for software that it cannot use. It cannot simply resume development of the code where Hoskyns and ICL left off, but must start afresh.

Also the department is in danger of losing two years of the management time it had devoted to the project.

Yet in some ways ITSA had met the textbook criteria for buying a major new system. It had allowed the suppliers to understand the business intimately by paying them to do so in a technical design study.

Also, changes had been kept to a minimum by the rigorous control exercised by the suppliers. Neither was it a penny-pinching contract that allowed no scope for error: £25 million was a large sum even for a national statistics system.

But there were five fatal flaws, it seems to me.

1. **An artificially tight deadline** that made the customer more reliant on the supplier than was good for either party. If more time had been allowed, both sides could have sought to smooth over system flaws in a less pressurised atmosphere. However, no payments should have been made by the customer until at least the first phase of the system had been delivered and was doing what it was supposed to do.

2. **Big Bang approaches to computerisation rarely work well**. In this case the success or failure of the project hinged on the outcome of a 20-day acceptance test. It would have been better if the system had been split into small chunks, each one delivering clear benefits to the business. If one module does not work then don't start the next until it does. And if the first module proves to be fundamentally flawed, neither side has lost a vast sum of money.

3. **The system was imposed on end-users**, some of whom

questioned whether the work should have been given to external suppliers rather than carried out internally. At the time the contract was let, ITSA employed more than 4,000 computer specialists of its own. The external contract set up the perfect conditions for internal strife.

4. **An attitude of 'Problem? What Problem?'** This is an important point in computer disasters. The memos leading up to the legal problems in the ASSIST project refer repeatedly to problems as being minor and able to be overcome. **An over-estimation of the scale of problems is always safer than an under-estimation. Also, humility – an ability to admit to not knowing all the answers – is crucial to success.**

5. **Too much faith** was put by the department on its fixed-price contract. A fixed-price contract no more assures the success of a project than one in which the customer pays the supplier its costs plus an agreed profit. When things go wrong, a fixed-price contract is not going to stop the supplier blaming the customer and vice versa. In fact a fixed-price contract could be more limiting because it provides a legal and emotional straitjacket for both parties in that it cannot be unfixed without both sides suffering some embarrassment. Arguably ASSIST could have been a success had each party been more flexible, more willing to see difficulties from the other party's perspective. This is not always easy to do within a fixed-price contract . . . unless you secretly anticipate that the price will rise by 300 per cent.

CHAPTER NINE

The Fifth Deadly Sin: Credulity (II)

I experienced first-hand the problems caused by a crash of the London Ambulance Service's systems.

In 1992 I was waiting for a train at West Croydon station, fifteen miles south of the Ambulance Service's head office at Waterloo, London. It was the morning rush hour and the platform was crowded.

Towards the far end of the platform, people were forming a circle. As I joined the crowd I saw, between the stooped figures, a large bearded man lying flat, squirming and obviously in some pain, his dark blue suit variegated with fine light-coloured dust from the concrete platform.

Crouched over him was a small woman whose face was turned away. She was catching her breath, as if to stop herself crying, and was trying to say something, though I could not hear what. The man appeared to be having difficulty breathing but the passengers were doing nothing, all transfixed by their curiosity, so I ran to telephone for an ambulance.

There were no phones anywhere near the platform. I made my way to the main station concourse and dialled 999, which is supposed to be an emergency number.

'Ambulance . . . quickly, *please,*' I begged.

'I'm putting you through now. Where are you calling from?'

'West Croydon train station.'

'Please hold the line. They'll be with you right away.'

The phone rang twice, stopped and went silent; then . . .

'Your call is in a queue. Please hold the line. We will answer you as soon as possible. Please be ready to give details of your exact location.'

It was a recorded message.

The line appeared to go dead but then the recorded voice returned.

'Your call is in a queue. Please hold the line. We will answer you as soon as possible. Please be ready to give details of your exact location.'

The second message finished, and there was still no answer. I stared at the receiver wondering what to do next. No television comedy script writer would have thought of depicting Britain's capital city as responding to 999 calls by answerphone: it would not have been credible. But in a disaster reality so often mimics parody.

I left the receiver off the hook and used an adjacent phone. A minute later each of the telephone receivers was on top of its coin box, surreally repeating automated messages at each other while a man lay writhing, for all I knew moribund, in the dirt on Platform 4 at West Croydon station. What a place to die!

I tried a third telephone and still could raise no human. At such a time, a few seconds can seem an eternity . . . and I waited helplessly for more than five minutes.

Suspecting that it was already too late, I dialled the 999 operator again and railed at her like a man possessed. She said there was nothing she could do. She merely routed calls to the fire, police and ambulance services.

She advised me to hang on until I got an answer, however long that took.

Eventually I gave up and went back to platform, expecting the worst. Thank heaven that, on this occasion, there was no fatality.

The man, his suit now crushed into creases and folds, and his tie askew, was sitting on a bench, his head in the arms of the woman who had earlier been sobbing quietly nearby.

One passenger remarked that the man was apparently prone to epilepsy, an attack of which, of course, is potentially fatal.

I did not return to the telephones to replace the receivers, but later, from my office, rang the ambulance service headquarters to express my concern, and was told that the incident was an isolated occasion and that new computer systems had greatly improved the efficiency of the service. Nothing could have been further from the truth . . .

CASE STUDY

The similarities between this case study and the last one are remarkable, particularly inasmuch as they were both large pioneering projects built by optimistic external suppliers who had agreed to meet the unrealistically tight deadlines imposed by their customers. It seems that in each case the supplier and customer eliminated each other's reservations about the project and each drew strength from mutual assurances that all would work out well in the end.

Despite their similarities I think it is necessary to draw attention to both disasters if only to show the ease with which fundamental project flaws that are obvious with hindsight can be overlooked at the project's birth.

The London Ambulance Service is also a good example because it had already suffered a computer disaster and was now about to witness its second.

It is too easy to believe that the service was simply the victim of providential good humour, of the sort that lands a crossword winner a free air ticket on a plane that crashes.

More likely the service was a victim of its own credibility, a readiness to believe that complex computer projects alone can change an organisation almost overnight for the better. Computerisation *can* and often does change organisations overnight, sometimes by putting them out of business. **Successful computerisations make their presence felt only after months or even years – seldom straight away.**

It was never going to be easy computerising the largest ambulance service in the world, while at the same time profoundly changing an organisation that had existed since before World War Two.

Founded in 1930, the London Ambulance Service had previously been run by the Metropolitan Asylums Board.

Today, the service covers about 600 square miles with a resident population of 6.8 million people, and a substantially larger number of potential users in the daytime. In January 1993 it employed 2,700 people, including 200 managers and 326 paramedics.

Ironically, while the systems were in chaos, and ambulances were sometimes taking hours not minutes to reach the scene of an emergency, the ambulance's public relations experts were busy promoting the technological efficiency of the service, showing off its paramilitary capability: the helicopter rescue team and RRUs – rapid-response units.

Ideally, more attention should have been given to the response times of the ordinary 300 emergency ambulances and over 400 patient transport service vehicles, which were struggling to cope with between 1,300 and 1,600 emergency calls every day.

The ambulances also had to be prepared to respond to any large-scale incident that could affect many people, such as a terrorist attack or a major event involving the Houses of Parliament.

That the traffic in London moves more slowly than a pregnant snail does not make the life of ambulance staff any easier.

But in the 1980s and early 1990s, the speed of London's traffic was the least of the service's problems. The management's imperious attitude was resented by the staff, and management resented the staff's resistance to change. The two sides were united only by a sense of public purpose and duty.

Even this commitment was being severely tested. Long before the series of failed attempts at computerisation, morale was already sinking from low to subterranean. In the 1980s management had failed to modernise the service, there was minimal investment in staff or managerial training, and little scope for career advancement.

The conditions were ripe for insurrection, which came in 1990 with a damaging national dispute over pay. This left managers and staff more distrustful of each other than at any time in the service's history.

Worse, the dispute revitalised plans for new systems, because computerisation was seen by public service managers as a certain way to reduce dependence on recalcitrant staff.

But the London Ambulance Service perceived the need for new systems as desperate rather than desirable . . . so common sense was sacrificed on the altar of the 24-hour clock.

A sense of urgency pervaded every meeting, every decision relating to computerisation.

And, as if this wasn't a big enough impediment to successful progress, directors built a bigger barrier. One of the few certain things about major computer projects is that they will fail if they take place amid major organisational change. It is like trying to repaint the lines of a tennis court on the deck of a cruise ship during a storm. But the ambulance service tried it anyway.

Its board shed 53 senior and middle managers out of a total of 268, ostensibly to prepare the service for government health reforms, but this created instability at a time when stability was most needed.

Instead of embarking on computerisation with the service galvanised by confident dynamic managers working in a forward-looking atmosphere, the service ended up struggling to motivate managers who had never felt more oppressed by stress, anxiety and job insecurity.

Many of the highest-calibre managers left voluntarily and those who remained were often promoted or switched to positions to which they were not suited.

This had the effect of funnelling a great deal of executive power into the hands of a small number of directors whose span of responsibility was too great; they became involved in issues that should have been handled by second-line managers or local managers in consultation with the staff.

It was against this backdrop that the directors decided to introduce a 'state-of-the-art' command-and-control system to automate virtually completely the process of dispatching an ambulance to the scene of an emergency. A lesser challenge might have been to play cricket underwater.

The new systems were designed to bypass the need for what was termed 'a human allocator'.

It was claimed at the time that it would be the first system of its kind in the UK, and would involve a 'quantum leap in the use of technology'. These two phrases alone are enough to condemn any computer project to death.

The computer-aided dispatch (CAD) system would comprise several parts:

1. call-taking, accepting and verifying incident details, including location;

2. determining which ambulance to send;

3. communicating details of an incident to the chosen ambulance;

4. positioning suitably equipped and staffed vehicles in places where they were most likely to be needed, so minimising response times to calls.

All this could be achieved theoretically using:

- CAD software
- CAD hardware
- gazetteer and mapping software
- a communications interface
- a radio system linking the control centre to ambulances
- mobile data terminals in the ambulances linked to central computer systems
- an automatic vehicle location system

A first attempt at computerisation began in the early 1980s and a contract was awarded to an external supplier. The project was abandoned in 1990 because the system could not meet the performance criteria. It could not handle the demands placed on it. About £7.5 million of public money was spent before work stopped; but there was no time to grieve.

Almost immediately directors authorised work on a specification for new systems.

Under the manual process, when a 999 call was received, a control assistant wrote down the details on a preprinted form. The location of the incident was identified on a map, and the map coordinates were noted.

The form was put on a conveyor belt, which took it to a central collection point. There were 200 control assistants putting forms onto the belt. At the other end, a person decided who would deal with the forms, based on London's three main areas: North-East, North-West and South.

At this stage duplicated calls were identified. The forms would end up with a human 'resource allocator' who made several – intuitive – decisions that could not be easily computerised.

The resource allocator had to select which ambulance to dispatch to the scene, based on the location of the incident, while balancing any competing needs identified on other forms relating to the same sector, and taking into account the positions of ambulances by collating information from radio operators.

The resource allocator then recorded on the form which ambulance should be dispatched. The form was handed to a dispatcher who telephoned the relevant ambulance station or vehicle. The whole process was scheduled to take three minutes.

Clearly most aspects of the procedures cried out for automation, but how? So many parts of the process relied heavily on human judgement; and, while computers are good at a lot of things, judgement is not one of them.

There were in fact easier areas to computerise: a computer-based gazetteer could immediately locate a caller from a database of telephone box numbers; information could be passed around the control room electronically rather than on a conveyor belt; computers would be ideally suited to keeping up-to-the-second information on the whereabouts of each of 300 emergency ambulances; they could help to identify duplicate calls and, in simple cases, instruct the nearest ambulance to go to the scene by a direct link with a terminal inside the ambulances.

Each one of these computerisation tasks was a major exercise but was achievable without too great a risk of failure. But trying to integrate all the component parts – and to do it in one go – was possibly where the service went badly wrong.

Such an integrated system would clearly require perhaps years of development and testing. Or it could have bought a proven and working system from another ambulance authority and adapted itself to the package.

But the service viewed itself as unique. And it did not perceive a problem with ordering bespoke software. Also, it was not prepared to countenance the automation of only a few parts. It wanted to computerise everything, including the hardest job of all: that of the human resource allocator.

This was a mistake, not because it is impossible to computerise the job of resource allocator (in fact some ambulance services have done exactly this) but because it was too much too soon.

It was a challenging project in itself which needed careful planning, design and thorough testing in a live environment before being incorporated into a larger system.

Put in more businesslike language, of the sort used by consultants, the service was not taking full account of all the risks.

It is always better to treat computers as a potentially uncontrollable force that can, depending on the degree of responsibility and expertise exercised by the purchaser, be used for the benefit or destruction of the owner.

The idea of the service's new system would be that the first link in the command chain, the control assistant, would handle the whole process from taking the original 999 call to seeing the incident through to completion.

This would be a first. No other emergency service in the UK

had attempted to go as far. The London Ambulance Service could make a name for itself. It would be transformed from Britain's ugly duckling into a fully automated, remote-controlled swan; an electronic testimony to humanity's technological progress. What's more it would be achieved in the public sector, enabling the Department of Health and its ministers to glow in the incandescence of their own brilliance.

Years later the system's performance would indeed spread the name of the London Ambulance Service far and wide.

Yet the service had, or should have, known the risks of computerisation before it embarked on the project. There had already been a string of publicised computer disasters to learn from, all of which had happened because overly ambitious, pioneering systems were expected to do duty before being thoroughly tested. Rather than acting as a deterrent, the disasters seem to have provided a project management template for the new London Ambulance Service system.

The service decided not to prove modules of the new system one at a time before going live incrementally. It wanted to leap from a largely manual process to a wholly computerised one.

Worse, it set a deadline of a year from start to finish despite warnings from most suppliers that it couldn't be done.

Suppliers tend, by the nature of the leading-edge products and services they supply, to err on the side of optimism, so when they say that the customer is being too ambitious their words should ring true.

So why was the project given the go-ahead? There are two main reasons:

The first is that the service was fatally afflicted with 'visionitis' which proved no less speculative than Nick Leeson's attempt to show what could be achieved with £800 million of Barings Bank's capital.

A major organisation struck down with a 'vision' is seized by great excitement and the need for a rapturous frenzy of activity.

Once it takes hold, the disease is unstoppable; it brooks no protest from those who would advise that the project should be continually punctuated with stop-or-go decision points. Yet every major project needs a fallback plan for an early, unsuccessful termination. **The more you assume at the outset that the project will fail, the more likely your expectations will be defeated.**

The second reason that the project was given approval is that, like many government and public service organisations, the ambulance service suffered from a lack of accountability. This gave it a false sense of invincibility. A little humility might have made all the difference. King Canute is remembered not only for his success as a ruler but for his pragmatism and humility; hence the story about his becoming so fed up with being told by fawning courtiers that he was all-powerful that he went down to the beach to demonstrate his inability to stop the rising tide. The ambulance service, however, seemed content to let everyone believe that it was master of all that it had dominion over.

The project began in autumn 1990, when, in order to define the requirements specification – technical jargon for what the service wanted the system to do – contact was made with other ambulance services to establish whether any system currently in use could be tailored to the London Ambulance Service needs.

This was an ideal first step. However, the systems operated by ambulance services in the West Midlands, Surrey and Oxford were all rejected, either because adapting them would be too expensive, or because they were deemed incapable of further development.

None of them could live up to the London Ambulance Service's 'vision'.

So the London Ambulance Service felt it was justified in going it alone. Its executive management knew full well that it was launching a new pioneering project.

Later, in February 1991, a systems requirements specification was completed. It was highly detailed and prescriptive, containing a high degree of precision on how the system was intended to operate, but providing little opportunity for prospective suppliers to incorporate their own ideas as to how the system should work.

The Service wanted a system to comprise three distinct elements:

• computer-aided dispatch (CAD);
• computer map display;
• automatic vehicle location system.

It planned to link these three modules with existing mobile data terminals which were installed as part of the previously aborted £7.5 million system.

The specification was an ambitious document, although the previous project failure was caused partly by the supplier being unable to understand the complexity of the system specified by the service.

Yet this time, the new CAD system was to be more technically advanced.

The procurement process began with an advertisement in the *European Journal* on 7 February 1991. The main criterion on which the supplier would be chosen would be price, namely the lowest tender. There was little qualitative guidance on the choice of system.

More than thirty companies responded to the advertisement, offering to provide all or part of the system. But many of them were already uncomfortable with the proposed timetable, which demanded full implementation by a non-negotiable target date of 8 January 1992, less than a year later.

Perhaps an even more difficult objective to be met, in hindsight, was the target budget figure for the whole system of £1.5 million, which erroneously emerged from the service's discussions with the management consultancy, Andersen Consulting. In the autumn of 1990, John Wilby, the service's computing head, had asked Andersen to advise him on what action should be taken on the previous CAD system, and how the project should be taken forward.

Andersen told the ambulance service's management to abandon the project, and begin work on a new one. It recommended that if a solution could be found that used packaged software rather than purpose-written software, then a budget of £1.5 million should be provided, with a timescale of twelve months for implementation.

Significantly, Andersen warned that if an appropriate package could not be found, then its estimates should be significantly increased. Ultimately, though, the ambulance service management ignored or chose not to accept Andersen's advice. Indeed the Andersen report was not shown to the Director of Support Services, who would have responsibility for the new system.

Following discussions with suppliers, seventeen companies provided full proposals for all or part of the system, and those proposals were reviewed against a checklist of criteria, which in order of priority were:
1. ability to perform the tasks required
2. ability to handle throughput and response times

3. ease of use by staff
4. resilience
5. flexibility
6. ability to meet timetable
7. cost
8. additional features

This was supposed to be a ranking of the priorities but the ability to meet the timetable was, in effect, promoted to the top. No proposal reached the shortlist if the one-year timetable could not be met, or if the supplier was unable to meet almost the total functional requirement.

Most suppliers submitted some credible proposals while stating that the timetable could only be met with difficulty. Some suggested a phased approach that could be implemented by the deadline, but a full system would not be available until 1993.

This in fact would have been the best way to implement the system: in phases with each module able to work effectively on its own without relying on other future modules.

But it was not to be. The service wanted all the system in one go, and delivered within a year.

Of all the proposals, only a few fitted all the criteria. One of them was from a consortium of a well-known UK systems house, Apricot, a small software company, Systems Options, and a vehicle location specialist, Datatrak. An original Apricot proposal had chosen Terrafix for the Automatic Vehicle Location System – a mechanism that tells the user where an ambulance is in a given area – but this was replaced by Datatrak for both cost reasons and because Datatrak was said to have a more proven record among the emergency services.

The switch to Datatrak ultimately won the consortium the deal ahead of other consortia comprising Marconi Command and Control, Technical Software Designers, Surf Technology, and Solo Electronic Systems, working with a variety of partners.

What separated the competing consortia was price, and with the service committed to a £1.5 million target budget, the deal went to an Apricot-led team, whose bid of £937,463 was some £700,000 cheaper than the nearest competitor. Nobody seems to have asked why the Apricot bid was so much lower.

Despite the consortium's winning tender, a potentially fatal problem was already surfacing. Systems Options, better known as a reseller of Apricot computers, had originally been wary of chasing the contract. It had already bid unsuccessfully with Apricot for a more basic service at the Cambridgeshire Ambulance Service.

Yet Apricot persuaded Systems Options to propose a CAD system for the London service requirement.

Almost incredibly, the Systems Options quotation for the CAD system was only £35,000, so low that it indicated not so much a cheap bid to win the business, but an underestimation of the complexity of the requirement.

Ironically it later emerged, at a subsequent meeting between Systems Options and the London Ambulance Service, that Systems Options was told that the failure of the previous ambulance service system was largely due to the alleged inability of the supplier's software house to take on board the complexity of the system.

The project management's errors continued when a report was submitted to the ambulance service board recommending that the Systems Options bid be accepted. The report, prepared by the Director of Support Services, was confusing in that it suggested that the recommendation of Systems Options be backed by a statement that the software company had successfully developed systems for police and fire authorities, including Staffordshire Fire and Rescue Service.

Systems Options had indeed delivered systems for police and fire authorities, but only for administrative systems – which were not as complex as those to be used in the London Ambulance Service, where a failure of the systems could put human lives at risk.

Consequently, the ambulance board was given a false degree of comfort about the relevant experience of one of the main suppliers.

Considering the importance of the system, one might have thought that the choice of supplier would be made by a top information technology specialist with much experience of project management, managing suppliers and dealing with tenders.

Yet the prime responsibility for the evaluation of bids fell upon a contract analyst and the systems manager. The systems manager was no information technology specialist. He was a career ambulanceman who had taken over responsibility for ambulance service systems. It had even been made clear to him that ultimately he would be replaced by a more properly qualified systems manager.

As for the contract analyst, he had been with the ambulance service for five years, originally on secondment from the regional computer centre. His experience of the London Ambulance Service was largely as a result of his involvement in the failed original project.

Thus the purchase of this major project was put into the hands of a manager, who knew his job was going to be made redundant, and a contractor.

There then followed a debate among the consortium's partners over which one of them was to lead the project.

On sheer size of company Apricot, owned by the Japanese industrial giant Mitsubishi, would appear to have been in the best position. After all, Systems Options was only a small software house. Indeed, throughout the procurement process, on the basis of an original Apricot proposal – and until a project meeting on 21 May 1991 – both the ambulance service and Systems Options clearly believed that Apricot would be the prime contractor. This was despite Apricot's subsequent statement that it wanted to lead the contract only if it was in a position to control the project itself. Since success depended on the quality of the Systems Options software, Apricot felt it could not take on the role. So the ambulance service was left by default with Systems Options as the prime contractor – a reluctant lead contractor on a project that was underbudgeted, allowed too little time for development and testing and had failed to make any specific reference in the contract to the issue of who would be the lead company in the winning consortium.

By now the project team had put in place all the necessary building blocks for a disaster. And the development work had not started.

The ambulance service officials were also warned by their colleagues in other locations. A reference letter from the Staffordshire Fire and Rescue Service expressed concerns over the ability of Systems Options to cope with the project, pointing out that the company was already overstretched.

Indeed as Systems Options struggled to manage its own software input to the project, the management of the scheme effectively defaulted for a second time to the ambulance service through its Director of Support Services and the contract analyst.

A project methodology – a computer industry term for a plan on which completion of the project can be based – was adopted. This was called Prince, and it should have put the project on proper management guidelines, but significantly, no ambulance service staff member had any experience of applying the methodology, nor had any of the suppliers involved. A training course was provided for some members of the team, and some modules of the methodology were used, but not in a structured way. It might just as well have not been used at all.

Despite the lack of experience, there was early evidence that the project team was far from incompetent and recognised some important obstacles. A meeting of the project team held on 17 June 1991 – a month after the contract was awarded – isolated a number of issues of potential concern.

It acknowledged that the service had no full-time participants assigned to the project; there was a lack of formal clarification of how the Prince methodology was to be applied; there was a lack of a formal programme for the project group and other meetings; the timescale was 'somewhat less than the industry average for this sort of project . . . more like eighteen months'; and the draft project plan as provided by the supplier left no time for review and revision.

But, although the issues were discussed by the team, they were not followed up in detail. And before long the problems began to multiply. Suppliers could not deliver the technology on time. An inquiry team later admitted that the Director of Support Services had done the best job possible in trying to manage the project and sort out problems and disputes between suppliers, but it was not enough.

Indeed even a qualified project manager of the highest calibre might have struggled to cope with evidence, albeit circumstantial, that some ambulance crews tried to sabotage their equipment.

It might seem strange that end-users would want to disrupt the project; but not in the context of a system that had been introduced largely over their heads. One of the most important prerequisites of a successful implementation is 'buy-in' by the end-users. They need to feel that the systems are being introduced for their benefit, or at least are to their advantage. Yet the service's ambulance staff did not feel any sense of ownership of the system.

There was little consultation of employees in setting the original requirements specification or in the revised method of working. Junior and medium-grade public servants saw the system as a back-door management attempt to change long-established working practices. So they regarded it with distrust from the beginning.

Having said that, there was a positive attitude to information technology in general among staff who recognised that computerisation was essential to improve efficiency.

However, they lacked confidence in this particular system.

This distrust was, if anything, unknowingly nurtured by the project team. The various parts of the ambulance service did not fully understand the complexity of each other's jobs. This was exacerbated by those involved in different functions receiving separate training.

There would have been greater 'buy-in' if elements of the CAD training had been given to all sides, enabling them to understand that the system's successful operation could come about only if all parties worked in partnership.

A further problem was that too much of the training was completed well in advance of the originally planned implementation date, and so 'skills decay' prevented all the staff remembering how to use the system.

Meanwhile, the late deliveries of software from Systems Options were not its own fault. There were delays in the delivery of radio interface specifications and protocols, which would link into the new system. Indeed the contract for the radio interfaces was awarded some three months after the original systems design contract was given to Systems Options.

Yet up to early December 1991, it was hoped that the original deadline of 8 January 1992 for full implementation would be met. But by mid December it was clear there was not a chance.

At that point the CAD software was incomplete and largely untested, while the radio interface hardware and software were not fully delivered and tested. Other critical parts of the system were unfinished and their reporting accuracy was open to doubt. Some of the software was delivered with bugs, and there were data transmission problems.

It made matters worse when Systems Options, eager to please end-users, made extemporaneous software changes, thus circumventing the official Project Issue Report process, which strictly controlled software modifications.

This undermined the testing, as software would be amended without the knowledge of the project group. Such changes could, and did, introduce further bugs.

At this point independent and rigorous quality control could have made the difference between success and failure. But it was felt that, to keep costs down, Systems Options could be responsible for its own quality control. This robbed the project of an effective independent audit.

Irrespective of all the above problems, the deadline of 8 January was not relaxed because the service wanted to maintain pressure on suppliers.

So the tests began, but as the software was incomplete they proved inconclusive. Over the following months, various system elements were tested but not as an integrated whole.

The trials were always going to be of limited benefit. With an automated ambulance dispatch system the quality of the communications lines between the central systems and the local ambulance crews was critical.

But the myriad problems caused by communications failures cannot easily be simulated. Even in automated teller machines, or hole-in-the-wall cash dispensers, communications problems have caused the software to behave unpredictably: and that is on a relatively simple link between a fixed computer site and a fixed cash dispenser site. With the ambulance control system, the central site was fixed but the ambulances tended to move around.

Many calculations of risk can be made ratiocinatively; that is on the basis of detailed reasoning but, with complex mobile communications links, only lengthy, real-life trials can give an *indication* of some of the problems that are likely to be encountered.

As a cheaper compromise, a test script could have been designed to emulate failures and software inconsistencies but there is no evidence that one was prepared. So the impact of the system on the running of the service, and the knock-on effect of problems, was never fully appreciated or tested.

Nevertheless the service was determined to go live with something in January 1992. A decision was taken to go ahead with a partial solution. This was the service's first good idea.

The idea was that incident reports would be printed and ambulances dispatched manually. The partial computerisation was broadly successful although the screens occasionally locked up, or there was a server failure.

On one day an ambulance was not dispatched because a printer was turned off, thus losing a record of the emergency call in the printer's buffer. Many of these problems stemmed from the fact that the printers used in this way were never part of the original specification but were added by management in haste as a short-term expedient to show some positive progress at the already published implementation date.

But even this limited trial demonstrated a number of problems. These were:

• **Frequent incomplete reports by ambulance crews of where they were and what call they were handling**. Yet the systems required perfect information all of the time. The computers in effect built up an electronic map of the location of ambulances. If the system was circumvented or the location of ambulances was not correctly posted to the system, it would make an inappropriate choice of ambulance for dispatch to an emergency. The problems were compounded by inadequate training, communications failures and alleged wilful misuse.

• **Inaccurate location fixes of ambulances caused by faulty equipment, transmission blackspots or software error**. One of these involved a failure to identify every 53rd vehicle in the fleet, caused by a programming error.

• **The system's inability to cope with established working practices**. For example, the use of a vehicle different from that allocated by the system.

• **Overload of communications channels, notably at crew shift change**.

• **Problems with hardware, especially the freezing of workstations and perceived system slowness.**

None of this stopped the system being implemented across all of the London Ambulance Service operating divisions by September 1992.

Yet, even on implementation date, there were still 81 reports that had yet to be addressed. Of these 81, two were labelled category 2 – severe service degradation in which the system would not function in the operating environment unless rectified; 44 were category 3 – causing problems in an operating environment resulting in poorer quality of service to patients; and the remaining 35 were category 4 – minor problems requiring attention, but not affecting system implementation.

The two category 2 incidents related firstly to the way in which multiple-incident reports were displayed and also to the incorrect decoding of mobile data terminal status, which were potentially serious problems.

Despite this, and the London Ambulance Service's recognition of the seriousness of the faults, deployment of the system went ahead on the 26 October, with disastrous results.

On that day the system did not 'fail' in a technical sense. Response times, that is the time the system took to respond to a command, simply became unacceptable, mainly because of basic defects in the design that would masquerade as the symptoms of systems failure.

Strictly speaking, though, the system did what it was designed to do – but so slowly that it became unusable. In fact to the untrained eye the system came to a complete standstill.

The reason was that the near perfect information required by the system was not available, so the software was unable to propose the best ambulance to be allocated to an incident. As the hours went by, the system knew the correct location and status of fewer and fewer vehicles. Before long, there were duplicated and delayed allocations of ambulances to the scenes of emergencies.

Meanwhile the system generated an increasing number of exception messages and an 'awaiting attention' list. The system slowed down as it tried to cope with more exception messages and a backlog built up. This led to prolonged delays in answering emergency telephone calls.

The system had worked well when it went live at 7 a.m. Loading was light and both the staff and the system were able to cope with problems that caused the dispatch system to produce imperfect information on the fleet and its status.

But as the number of emergency calls during the day increased, the system's ignorance of the correct vehicle locations, the equipment they carried on board, and the skills of their crew, had inevitable consequences.

The system made incorrect allocations and multiple vehicles were sent to the same incident, or, conversely, the vehicle *not* nearest was sent. Eventually, the system had fewer ambulances to allocate, increasing the problems. As previously allocated incidents fed back through the system, emergency calls that had already been attended to were placed back on the 'awaiting attention' list.

Ambulance crews forgot to press, in sequence, the buttons that told the central computers of their locations, or radio blackspots meant that the system began to generate exception messages. As the number of exception messages increased, staff were unable to clear the backlog, and, as the queue grew, the system slowed. From an operator's perspective, the increasing number of 'awaiting attention' and exception messages meant it became too easy to fail to attend to messages that had scrolled off the top of the screen.

There were faults in the 'hand-shaking' routines between the mobile data terminals in the ambulances and the central dispatch systems. This led the system to think that an ambulance was engaged on an assignment when it was idle and waiting for instructions.

Some crews took a different vehicle from that which they had logged into, or crews would not respond correctly to the instructions generated by the systems.

All this led to ambulances taking an unacceptable time to reach patients.

Apart from increasing the risks to patients, the system problems also exacerbated the frustration of staff. They were under instruction to minimise voice communications between each other (thereby maximising the use of the system) but this only made it more difficult for them to restore normality.

And the staff complied with the instruction to the letter so that when an incorrect ambulance was dispatched, or several were sent to the same location, this could not be corrected because there were no voice communications.

After all, the system was supposed to be paperless and totally automated. Ironically, had the system generated paper, rather than screen-based messages, more attention would have been paid to exception reports.

After the problems of the 26th, and similar ones the following day, the Central Ambulance Control reverted to a semi-manual operation, which involved taking telephone calls on the CAD system, printing out incident details, choosing the best-placed vehicles by contact with the nearest station to the incident, and mobilising the ambulance via computer.

This worked fairly successfully until about a week later on 4 November when after 2 a.m. the system slowed dramatically and eventually locked up completely. Attempts to reboot failed, and so calls in the system could not be printed out, and mobilisations of vehicles via CAD from incident summaries could not take place.

Eventually, staff reverted to a manual, paper-based system using voice or telephone mobilisation of ambulances.

Systems Options was called in immediately to investigate the reasons for the failure – in particular why the back-up system had also not worked.

Later it was discovered that the fault lay in a minor programming error by a Systems Options programmer. A piece of program code had inadvertently been left in the system that caused a small amount of memory within the file server to be used up and not released every time a vehicle mobilisation was generated by the system.

Over a three-week period, the available memory was used up, causing the system to crash. Such an error was demonstrative of carelessness and a lack of quality assurance of program code changes.

Following the crashes of 26 and 27 October, and 4 November, the service gave up full-scale computerisation and fell back on the half-manual, half-computer system that is still in use today, with some success. A third attempt at full-scale computerisation is underway, at the time of writing.

So is this a disaster with a happy ending? In one way it is a triumph. After the ambulance service deteriorated to the point of collapse, the families of patients, the unions and MPs of all parties put pressure on the government to launch a public inquiry. The government came to a compromise. It set up an inquiry team comprising the chief executive of a new national health service trust, a senior computer audit partner at BDO Binder Hamlyn and a former chief conciliation officer of the Advisory Conciliation and Arbitration Service (ACAS).

Their 80-page report, conducted after a three-month inquiry, provides one of the most comprehensive public accounts of a major computer disaster.

The report stresses:
• a need for the system to be fully resilient and reliable, with fully tested levels of back-up;
• that the system must have total ownership by both management and staff, and staff must have confidence in its

reliability;
- that the system must be developed in a timescale and at a cost that allow for consultation, quality assurance and testing;
- the system should be introduced in a stepwise, modular approach;
- that retraining should be carried out thoroughly on the system to ensure staff are familiar with its features; the timing of the training should be met to ensure 'skills decay' does not occur; and
- that a suitably qualified and experienced project manager should be appointed to ensure the close control and coordination of all parts of the system.

The quality of training was also an issue. This was provided mainly by Systems Options or trainers at the ambulance service. One of the problems of the competence-basis training was that both trainer and individual needed to sign off to agree that the correct level of competence had been achieved. But different competence levels were needed for each job, such as call taking, and the training was not always comprehensive and consistent.

Systems Options admitted to the inquiry team that many of its programs could have benefited from tuning. Most were written in a software language called Visual Basic, a program tool better equipped for the delivery of fast systems software development rather than 'fast systems'. The inquiry team believed that, rather than use Visual Basic or the version 3.0 of the popular Windows software, the developers could have used a different language known as C++ or upgraded the operating environment to a more up-to-date version of Windows, version 3.1. Indeed at the time the Apricot/Systems Options proposal was submitted, Visual Basic was not available as a development tool – it arrived shortly afterwards. Therefore, when it came to development, Systems Options were using an unproven tool designed primarily for prototyping and non-mission-critical systems.

The inquiry said in its report that the performance of Visual Basic programs was not fast, and so filling the screen with such programs took time measured in several seconds. To overcome this, ambulance control staff preloaded all the screens likely to be needed at the start of a shift and used the Windows software to transfer around as required. But this placed demands on the electronic 'memory' available within workstations, reduced performance and led to extra 'clutter' on controllers' screens.

The inquiry concluded that the London Ambulance Service had adopted a graphical user interface that had made the system easy to use, but at the expense of system performance. A text-based front-end would have made the system harder to understand at first but might have improved its speed. The inquiry said that the trade-off of performance against ease of operator use was something that might need to be reconsidered in any future system.

The Apricot hardware was described as very powerful by the inquiry team, and generally resilient. The equipment – specifically different file servers, workstations and the network infrastructure supporting them – was able to cope with the peak loads likely to have been placed on it.

The Datatrak automatic vehicle location system was also regarded by the inquiry as reliable considering the problems of using it in an urban environment such as London. Although there were likely to be occasional problems with clean signal transmission, the difficulty facing the overall system was recognising and dealing with such rogue imperfect information.

Where the service fell down particularly badly was in the area of network management. Most network housekeeping and management was attended to by Systems Options, and on the days when the system 'failed' the software company's staff had to be called in to handle the network problems. The London Ambulance Service had not taken over this role by the time of systems implementation.

There had been an early proposal from Apricot that there should be a dedicated network supervisor with responsibility for identification and rectification of network problems, but, as the report states, the recommendation was never acted upon.

Ultimately, however, the report found that the service's technology leap was too great, and it did not really look properly first. It came close to success only when it was operating a semi-automated system.

Other British emergency services had experimented with low-level computer-based call-taking, then, after achieving some success, had begun proving and bedding down the system before adopting vehicle location mapping, and ultimately moved on to a more sophisticated scheme.

But the London Ambulance Service chose to go for broke and that is how it ended up. The whole exercise proved to be a technical, procedural, managerial and public relations disaster from which, several years after its first attempt, the service has yet to recover.

With so many lessons flooding in from the disaster, it is hard to distinguish the most important. Perhaps one of the more memorable aspects is the fact that the directors, having run aground once, and lost several millions of pounds, then set sail again like Captain Bligh, determined to make it around the Horn despite atrocious sea conditions.

And, as is tradition all in British public life, Captain Bligh was punished for his peremptoriness and cruelty on HMS *Bounty* by a promotion to Vice Admiral.

The two most senior executives of the ambulance service were, exceptionally, not so fortunate. After the problems in October and November 1992 the chief executive, whose job had been dependent on the successful implementation of the systems, tendered his resignation.

And later on, after the three-month inquiry accused the service of mismanagement, of not heeding obvious signs of problems, the chairman also resigned saying: 'We caused a considerable amount of anguish to the people of London. We failed to deliver the service we could.'

I cannot help but wonder that, if, like Bligh, the chairman and chief executives of London Ambulance Service had enjoyed high-level political support like some of those at Wessex Regional Health Authority, they might have ended up being tapped on the shoulder by the Queen rather than collecting their P45s.

More than a year after the London Ambulance Service's system collapse, the managers and staff were again criticised by MPs and ministers, this time for their excessive caution and lack of action over installing replacement systems.

The concern was prompted by the death of an eleven-year-old girl, Nasima Begum, who died after being denied an ambulance.

Nasima Begum died of renal failure after her family had telephoned four times for an ambulance and had waited for 53 minutes. She had a liver condition that needed urgent treatment. Her death had a double irony: firstly, she lived only two minutes from a hospital, where she was a regular patient, and secondly, the only available emergency vehicle was sent to a caller who turned out to have a headache.

Later, the then Health Secretary, Virginia Bottomley, issued a statement which said:

> No one can now be in any doubt about what needs to be done to improve the performance of the London Ambulance Service to the standards achieved by other ambulance services . . . the tragic death of Nasima Begum in deplorable circumstances was a graphic reminder that much more needs to be done to improve the performance of the London Ambulance Service.

The events leading up to Nasima Begum's death were investigated by a cross-party committee of MPs, which reported that 'lives may well have been lost' as a result of the failings in the London Ambulance Service. The MPs went on to accuse the regional health authority and the National Health Service executive of 'a complete failure of nerve' after the 1992 computer crash, which itself came after almost a decade of serious under-performance.

It is a notable characteristic of the disaster that, right up until the point when calamity struck in 1992, officials were assuring ministers – and ministers were passing on those assurances to MPs – that technically the new systems were satisfactory.

In other words, bad news was failing to travel up the chain of command to those who were ultimately accountable for the organisation's failings.

As at the Department of Social Security (and most government departments) accountability to the taxpayer is virtually non-existent; and this only added to the problems faced by the computer managers, because they were making decisions as if in a vacuum, not through any fault of their own but because British public affairs are always administered this way.

There are few effective checks on bad decisions because the mandarins and ministers who would be responsible for introducing outside scrutiny resist doing so because full accountability is just not the British way of doing things.

You have to trust in the competence of those who govern. The only independent scrutiny is provided by auditors, but in the overwhelming majority of cases their findings are kept secret and not always acted upon.

This emasculates the auditor as the only independent guardian of public service standards. It also explains why the ambulance service was able to move with ease from one disaster to another.

A vivid example of the lack of accountability was a ministerial letter sent to an MP at a time when difficulties with the service's second computer system were at their height. The minister wrote that the 'system itself is functioning correctly at a technical level'.

A few weeks later it was abandoned.

CHAPTER TEN

The Sixth Deadly Sin:
Consultancy (I)

An alternative computer dictionary definition of consultants might be: verbal speculators who conjecture on the guesses of their predecessors.

This is the kindest definition I could come up with. In reality many consultants tend to portray themselves as intellectual powerhouses, definers of the truth, the personification of wisdom. **Few would admit that computerisation is often a laboratory experiment, approved by the curious and the hopeful, financed by those who don't know the whole truth, and implemented by the powerless, the imaginative, the inquisitive, the hopeful, the gifted enthusiast and the inept.**

I don't want to imply that all or even most consultants are agents of ruin or woe. Some individual advisers prove to be the answer to a beleaguered customer's prayers.

At the insurance company Tindall Riley, a talented software consultant spotted what was wrong with a database that had been designed by a third party, redesigned it, and rescued his customer from a bigger disaster.

But in general the literature of computer consultancy companies should carry a health warning rather like the statutory ones given by financial advisers who must tell their clients, in writing, that the value of their investments can go down as well as up.

Computer consultants should warn their customers that the value of their new investments in computers is *more* likely to go down than up.

Some consultants already do. They go to customers armed with sincere advice about the dangers and risks of the venture they are proposing to undertake. Other consultants will also issue warnings but not with the same purity of intention. Their warnings to customers are in verbal small print which is forgotten or papered over by a florid display of salesmanship, optimism and promises of what the new system will achieve. This enthusiasm is so infectious and authoritative that it whittles away the innate caution of their clients.

In short consultants are not in themselves a danger, until they start to share the visions of their customers. And, yes, customers continue to have IT visions, even though these have contributed to some of the bigger computer industry disasters such as those at Wessex and at the PRS.

I am now looking at a recruitment advertisement in *The Times* which is seeking to attract an IT manager at a salary of more than £100,000 a year. It says, 'You must be a facilitator as well as a manager; an IT visionary.'

This trend towards the hiring of IT visionaries is especially perilous when the visionary is also a consultant. Customers will soon find themselves unwittingly conspiring with consultants to deprive each other of the realism that is a vital ingredient in any successful computer project.

Both may discover only too late that they have been trying to enact a technological fantasy.

I can already hear some consultants muttering indignantly that, in their case, this does not apply; that their secret weapon is to eliminate all risks of project failure by, for example, not accepting any money until their systems are working acceptably and are delivering the promised business benefits. This is a splendid idea in theory – and it works well in practice in some cases (see Chapter 19 on Barclays Bank) – but if the project goes wrong the customer still suffers.

Hours, months or even years of internal management time will have been wasted on the project. The anticipated benefits of the systems, such as staff and other cost savings, may not have materialised. This could throw into confusion future spending plans which may have been based on the anticipated savings. Even if the customer has not yet paid the consultancy fee for the aborted work, there may already have been major purchases related to the project, such as hardware, software, maintenance and/or services from other third parties. The cost of these could run into millions. And the project may have led to other important business projects being postponed or cancelled.

Some consultancies will even offer to work free for the first few weeks of the project, perhaps doing some rudimentary design work, but this is also dangerous. Some customers have publicly rejected offers of free consultancy because they say they do not want to feel indebted to the services supplier when it comes to awarding the main contract. This is being sensibly cautious.

The Wessex Regional Health Authority case study highlighted the conflicts of interest that can arise when advisers double up as suppliers.

One of the most wearying problems for customers, however, is spotting the good consultants from the bad because there is no such thing as a good or bad consultant. Even the best ones who have four successful projects to their name may stumble disastrously in the fifth.

This is because no computing project is wholly predictable. One maxim that holds true in any computerisation is: **no matter how well it is planned, something unexpectedly menacing will leap out of the dark on the day it goes live.**

It's not just computer projects: it happens in any undertaking that you think has been planned down to the last nut and bolt.

In 1996, for example, a security company that was supposed to keep motorway protesters off the site of a new road near Newbury, Berkshire, England, brought in large numbers of guards to occupy the proposed site from day one of the project. The whereabouts and actions of the guards on the first day were planned with military rigor. But when the time arrived, and work on the site was due to start, there were no guards.

The one thing the security firm had not considered had happened. The protesters had organised a blockade of the camp where the guards had spent the night. In the morning the guards were unable to leave the site and the start of the motorway works was delayed.

Again, and this has been mentioned in previous chapters, the customers must not leave control of their project in the hands of a third party. They must be in charge. They should have studied the marketplace, should know what they want from the consultancy, and more importantly understand the risks and dangers.

It sounds obvious that no project should be run entirely by consultants – yet this is frequently what happens.

The PRS project was run by consultants, as were some of the systems at Wessex Regional Health Authority.

In the success stories, however, customers have tended to use named individuals who come highly recommended by other user organisations. But beware of consultants bearing lists of their reference sites. This is a selective list. Ask for a list of *all* their customers, and for an unexpurgated copy of the last customer satisfaction survey.

There was a campaign in Britain's computer industry in 1995 for large consultancy companies to pass on their *full* customer list to all prospective clients, and to publish the results of their internal satisfaction surveys, but they firmly declined. Therefore distrust lists of satisfied customers – because there may be many more dissatisfied customers.

And don't just assume that a list of satisfied clients is what it seems. On several occasions, when a services company has given me a list of its satisfied customers, I have contacted a company on the list only to hear its executives vilifying the supplier.

One of the most common complaints of customers is that consultants who are hired to install a new marketing system see this as too parochial an assignment and try to oil their way into a senior, strategic post in the organisation where they can oversee all projects, not just those in the computer department. On some occasions these strategic consultants are given responsibility for hiring other consultants. This is a little like asking your garage to spend whatever is necessary servicing your car: you'll suddenly discover that the vehicle is unroadworthy without an end-to-end overhaul.

All this is because consultancies fear only one thing apart from going bust: the status quo. I have never known a consultancy that has reviewed a company's computer department and warned convincingly that making major changes could leave the customer worse off.

Here is an example of the sort of conversation a consultant will have with a chief executive after conducting a review of the company.

'The thing is, Mr Chief Executive,' says the expert, looking around the computer department dismissively, 'you have here an extremely efficient organisation, perfectly well managed, that is one of the most revered names in its sector. However, you haven't undergone any substantial technological modernisation for a number of years. And even large fish can be swallowed whole nowadays by bigger businesses that are adapting quickly to changing market circumstances. To remain beyond the jaws of the sharks, I would suggest a further, more detailed, review of your business, only one aspect of which would cover technology. This would cost very little and tell you a great deal.

'Clearly you are business-driven to an impressive extent at the moment, and that's doubtless one of the reasons for your market share, but, as you're aware, not many in your sector are still encumbered with the costs of maintaining your legacy mainframe systems, proprietary networking protocols and second-generation languages.

'Any major reputable supplier will advise you on the way forward, though naturally you might feel that we have a certain understanding, and, I would hope, a mutual respect.'

The conversation will then be sprinkled with the names of satisfied clients who have moved from strength to strength since they implemented the consultancy's recommendations.

Almost certainly the chief executive will find the consultant persuasive, not because of any persuasive arguments but because the comments bring to the surface a secret fear common to all chief executives: that they are failing to keep abreast of the times.

In the light of such a speech from a consultant, the chief executive will often gingerly and complaisantly put himself into the consultancy's hands. After all, the consultancy is already looking after some of the biggest and most successful companies in the world.

Of course, some consultants will advise against the status quo for genuinely sound reasons, but these should be specific. It is not difficult to spot the consultant whose advice comes straight off the production line. They reveal themselves as automatons if they denigrate the status quo, or dismiss it out of hand, without revealing to you in any detail the flaws in your organisation that lead to their conclusions. Glib phrases such as 'of course you wouldn't want to stand still' should be viewed as a warning sign.

It's also important to stress that the safest consultants are *named* individuals – whether they work for themselves, small, medium or large companies – who have a proven track record in your market sector and who not only come highly recommended by clients, but will give the names of those who are willing to provide the recommendations.

But you cannot rely on reputable suppliers as an indemnity against a disaster.

This is demonstrated by the following two case studies. Both concern huge projects in which consultants featured prominently.

The first example is that of an unmitigated disaster, though it is lightened by the success of a not dissimilar project on the other side of the world.

The second case study shows why Europe's largest civil computerisation project went considerably over budget and did not deliver all the anticipated benefits.

CASE STUDY: ONE

A TALE OF TWO CITIES
(or why Singapore succeeded where London failed)

The best thing about the London Stock Exchange's Taurus project disaster is that it prevents the government from claiming responsibility for *all* the biggest computing blunders.

In fact the day after the collapse of Taurus was like a Hollywood B-movie dramatisation of a computer disaster: telephone-number figures gambled and lost; burnt-out, jobless Masters of the Universe cuddling empty champagne bottles in City of London wine bars, and headlines across front pages from New York to Tokyo.

But what surprised the world's financial community should not have raised an eyebrow among computer-calamity connoisseurs. For Taurus was an everyday tale of programmers spending years trying to tighten a bolt without first securing the nut – for the design was never static.

This similitude does not do justice to the débâcle of Taurus – an acronym for the Transfer and Automated Registration of Uncertificated Stock.

It was a disaster with few redeemable qualities. Of course it is easy to see in retrospect what went wrong, but many people saw it as going wrong from the outset, and they expressed their doubts, but their reservations were thrown aside.

It is a common problem in would-be computer disasters that, once a major decision has been taken to put computers to war against bureaucracy and excess paperwork, nobody but the originator of that decision is empowered to halt the assault.

And the originator is usually the last to hear the bad news.

Formed in the eighteenth century, the London Stock Exchange is an association of dealers in stocks and shares. Seemingly founded on the principle that humility is a sin, it appeared to require as its membership card an arrogance that would admit of no human tendency to err.

This qualification has remained in force for more than a century. So when Taurus was floundering, the exchange's spokespeople ridiculed any notion that the project was or could be in trouble.

They would counter-attack by accusing Taurus's critics of being unknowledgeable. And unknowledgeable they were. So much secrecy suffocated the project that even the programming teams did not know what each other was doing.

This problem was summed up in graphic terms by a senior executive at a major computer supplier, who had hoped to provide systems linking into Taurus.

'I had good contacts with the Stock Exchange's software liaison team, and sometimes I'd know information that they didn't. We'd exchange notes, and they'd go away and come back and say "Where did you find that out from? You're not supposed to know that!"'

The first sign of the trouble came at a very early stage when, to justify the capital cost of Taurus, the Exchange produced a lop-sided cost/benefit analysis that listed a plethora of benefits and no full breakdown of the costs.

Questioned about the virtual absence of costs in its cost/benefit analysis, the Exchange's spokespeople shrugged their shoulders, and said it was too early to know exactly what the costs would be.

This was odd. If the Exchange could announce in detail what the savings and the benefits were going to be, why not the costs?

The truth was that the costs could not be fixed because the design could not be fixed. In fact nothing could be fixed, except the glossy public relations campaign to promote the idea of Taurus.

One reason for the uncertainty was the lack of a definitive template. Even by the time the project was abandoned, fundamental aspects of the design had not been decided. This was because the Stock Exchange set about building the computer systems:

- before it had reached agreement with the various parties over how the system should operate and what it should do;
- before there had been any attempt to simplify City procedures;
- before the legal and regulatory matters to take account of computerisation had been fixed.

The result was that the software developers were perennially on their knees, awkwardly trying to struggle up the down escalator. And so, once work on the project began in earnest, for every step forward taken by the programmers, the expected completion date for the project seemed to move two steps back. Before long the City was gleefully ridiculing every revised completion date announced by the Stock Exchange.

The obvious maxim here is: **Thou shalt not computerise until the existing paper-based or semi-computerised processes have been simplified, simplified again and further simplified long before computerisation; in any efficiency drive, computerisation is the last thing to do.**

It was almost the same at the Performing Right Society and London Ambulance Service. Vainly, they had hoped that computers would effect reform where humans had failed. In fact the new technology magnified a hundredfold all the pre-existing administrative procedural weaknesses and deficiencies.

If the Exchange had had the benefit of hindsight, it might have realised that the hardest part of computerisation is defining issues that have nothing to do with computerisation – dealing with internal political problems, pulling empires apart, placating sceptics, simplifying paper-based processes and answering what in this case was the toughest question of all: whose jobs would be made redundant by the advent of computerisation?

This needed to be considered in detail before technical challenges were faced.

But the Exchange, like so many other disaster victims, assumed that it could juggle many plates, the regulatory, the procedural and the political, all at the same time as the computerisation.

In Singapore, the opposite was happening. In what became one of the world's most successful major computer projects, the Singaporean authorities built TradeNet to retain the country's pre-eminent trading position, which was being threatened by competition in the Far East, most notably Hong Kong. But nothing was rushed. Nobody went for glory. It was simply a question of the authorities bringing together all those who had a vested interest in improving the country's trading status, and deciding the best way to go about modernisation. So great effort went into simplifying and streamlining documentation and procedures first.

And the design of the computer system was the last thing the Singaporean authorities considered.

Before this stage was reached all those involved in the planning of the project spent some time gaining a full understanding of the existing trading processes and procedures, how they operated on a day-to-day basis and if the administrative rules were followed religiously or circumvented by end-users.

This non-technical task seems to have been as complicated as computerisation yet nobody underestimated the scale of the undertaking. The authorities compiled countless reports from maritime organisations, government agencies, statutory bodies, customs and excise, port officials and the civil aviation executives – all of whom discussed what needed to be done and how they should do it.

These discussion documents dovetailed into a single report, which revealed that different organisations were using a multiplicity of official forms and diverse procedures.

It was decided that computerisation at this stage would not achieve a quality improvement or contain costs. A massive simplification exercise would have to be undertaken first.

And this is exactly what happened. As one of its measures, the TradeNet Steering Committee decided to designate a single form for use in all trade agreements. This would also constitute the basis for a computer specification.

In effect this standardisation and simplification reduced the technical risks, and made computerisation relatively straightforward. The state also arranged a mass education process so everyone knew what was expected of the systems, and of them. Communication between various parties was encouraged, not avoided. There was no need for secrecy, disinformation or cover-ups. Transparency of the decision-making ensured that everyone saw the benefits of participation.

Once computerisation started, changes were kept to a minimum and companies linking into the system were expected to adapt themselves to suit the project. Innovative technology was not introduced into the main project until it had been fully tested in controlled circumstances.

TradeNet went live in January 1989, cost $20 million and met the original timescale – and the objectives were achieved. For example, the turnaround time for processing trade documentation was cut from a maximum of four days to fifteen minutes. End-user companies reported cost savings of 15 to 30 per cent.

But Singapore is an authoritarian country. And in any country where it's a serious offence to cross a road before you're told, people will tend to submit easily to the will of statutory bodies. This gave the country an easier ride across the political and regulatory terrain of computerisation.

The City is not and never has been so tame. Its scepticism of authority has been shaped through the centuries by monumental blunders, such as the South Sea Bubble.

In the City, authority today is represented in part by the Stock Exchange whose approach was the Singaporean plan in reverse.

It began computerising, then formed a scrum of various committees to facilitate communication, and to reach agreement between the amorphous parties involved . . . whereupon simplification became impossible because the evolving technology imposed limitations on what could be simplified.

And, as the computerisation evolved, the design became unimaginably complex as the various vested interests pulled the project in different directions. The Stock Exchange also lacked a coherent public relations approach.

Thousands of registrars, for example, who held share certificates were told what Taurus would do for them: leave them jobless.

So they could hardly be expected to support a project that turned paper share certificates into electronic ones, held on databases, which largely removed the need for a registrar.

And it was all too much in one go. Simplification – if it had happened – would have been a huge task in itself, but well worthwhile. Computerisation of the process by which shares are bought and sold would have been an equally massive undertaking. But a third immense job was also taken on board: that of trying to eliminate share certificates.

This was a similar mistake to the ambulance service's attempt to computerise the key human decision-making jobs at the same time as everything else. It adds immeasurably to the risks, when everything should be done to minimise the risks. (Chapter 19, which is about success stories and includes a Barclays Bank case study, demonstrates the advantages of trying to do as little as possible with as much money as the project leader's ingenuity can muster.)

But apart from introducing innovative, pioneering, technologies there was worse to come. For the Exchange decided to customise an existing package.

As the tailoring work expanded to meet ever-changing legal and end-user requirements, and to surmount technical problems, the main advantages of buying a proven package – simplicity and ease of installation – were lost.

In the end there were small villages of developers building different parts of Taurus, and nobody seemed quite sure where it would all lead.

Clearly, as the project became more complex, it went beyond the ability of anyone to control or understand it.

So when the timetable began to slip, the Exchange's public relations staff invited newspaper and magazine editors to high-level tête-à-têtes designed to make them feel both important and awkward about continuing to criticise the Exchange.

This defensiveness was unnecessary. It was merely a screen to cover the fact that Taurus should never have been allowed to go ahead without more thorough planning and a consensus on the design.

The idea of Taurus was to replace the paper at the heart of share trading, to change the way that most of the stockbrokers, jobbers, merchant banks, even the high-street banks, conducted their business.

The elimination of share certificates was the most radical part of the plan.

For a long time certificates have been shepherded around the City by courier, as shares are bought and sold.

This is time-consuming, costly, unreliable and, in an electronic age, unnecessary. But major 'middlemen' businesses have grown up around the registration of shares and the safe custody of the certificates.

The Taurus project was to cut out the heart of these businesses, turning the share certificates into electronic entities.

The second key aim of Taurus was to reduce the time taken to complete the legal and financial arrangements for the payment of shares that have been traded.

The project was conceived in the late 1970s but work did not begin in earnest until 1987 when a meeting of the world's leading economic nations produced a report which was critical of global securities settlement standards.

Part of the reason for Taurus was to cope with the explosion of computerised share trading after the 1986 'Big Bang' deregulation, which among other things obviated the need for face-to-face meetings between share dealers.

Big Bang also put pressure on those companies that did not have adequate 'back-office' support to keep track of the massive number of transactions, many of them driven by privatisation, which created millions of small investors.

The first plan, dubbed Taurus I, was intended to cover all share dealings, with a single computerised register of shareholdings to be maintained by the Stock Exchange.

But some of the main banks, NatWest, Lloyds and Barclays, who controlled over 80 per cent of the share registration business, did not want to see a centrally based database register. At the time, one senior banking executive remarked of Taurus: 'Turkeys don't vote for Christmas'.

So the most obvious and easiest way to develop Taurus – a centralised database register – was ruled out. The official reason was that no system would be large enough to cope. There were also genuine technical snags to this approach.

A comparison was made with the central database used by the Driver and Vehicle Licensing Agency (formerly the Driver and Vehicle Licensing Centre, or DVLC) in Swansea, which was not performing particularly well at the time.

When the single central database idea fizzled out, the impetus to modernise disappeared.

Then the Bank of England intervened. It set up a committee of the great and good – the Securities Industry Steering Committee on Taurus (or the SISCOT Committee) – which set up a blueprint on how a paperless settlement system would work.

But the City is a dynamic industry. And its shape was changing faster than the SISCOT Committee's plans for the new paperless system.

Yet still the Exchange pushed ahead with the idea that technology could cure all its ills. So three strategic options for computerisation were proposed: T1, T2 and T3. All three were risky, expensive and uncertain, but they were also pioneering and imaginative, and so were considered attractive in their own way.

The safest option was not even seriously considered. The Exchange already had a satisfactory settlement system called Talisman, hardly the most modern of systems, but tried, tested, proven and robust.

More importantly, it was well understood. And there was much computer expertise within the exchange, dozens of specialists having worked on Talisman for years. Many of them felt that Talisman could have been extended to provide a system comparable to Taurus.

But Talisman was rejected out of hand. It was impressively reliable, and much liked, but its biggest shortcoming was that it already existed. Without a shining new technological edifice the Stock Exchange would not be able to convince its critics and the European financial world that it was reforming itself to head off the challenges from European exchanges.

In any case, Talisman was somewhat dated, and developing something new is much more excitingly unpredictable than making better use of what exists.

And so Taurus II, a completely new project, was born.

What the exchange eventually chose was a complex arrangement of fully integrated databases rather than one central system.

Original figures from the SISCOT report put minimum development costs at around £14.5 million with additional capital costs of about £3.5 million.

Software development costs would be recovered over a five-year period on the basis of 20,000 transactions a day through Taurus.

But the figures were not definitive, merely indicative. On the other hand the benefits were widely promulgated. The Exchange announced that Taurus would bring down the cost of dealing in shares, save £54 million a year by cutting thousands of jobs and secure London's future in world markets as a premier financial centre.

But already many of the City institutions who were supposed to benefit from Taurus were soon deriding it. A survey before the project was under way showed that two-thirds of companies believed Taurus would increase their share registration costs.

So the exchange was about to embark on a multi-million-pound project without fully understanding its implications, or without the full support of the prospective end-users.

This defies a basic precept of computerisation: **Thou shalt not impose a new system on end-users without first establishing whether they want it**. Because if they won't enthusiastically back the project from start to finish you'd better abandon it now before you're forced to later.

By now everything was moving gracelessly towards a crisis.

Rather than adapt City procedures to a standard software package, which would have kept the risks to a minimum, or develop a bespoke system that would have been medium-risk, the exchange chose to customise heavily a US package for the UK market.

The selected software was a package from a US company, Vista Concepts, whose products were used widely in the US financial sector. But the choice of a US supplier that had little presence in the UK led to regular exchanges of computer specialists between Vista in New York and the Stock Exchange in London. At one point it seemed that most of the Taurus programmers and analysts were headed either westerly or easterly at 35,000 feet over Nova Scotia.

No sooner was work under way than project deadlines passed with little to show for them; but few people realised there was a problem because sub-sections of the timetable were not openly published.

Meanwhile the most stable element in this revolution of the project was the Stock Exchange's own computer staff. They had been around for many years and had a good grasp of both the technology and City trading systems.

So the next step was to 'dispose' of them. There were no mass redundancies but the exchange set about 'streamlining' and senior figures were encouraged to leave. The casualties included some of the best-known names in the computer industry. The trickle-trickle procession continued for months.

I remember asking the then chief executive of the Stock Exchange, Peter Rawlins, about whether the jobs of remaining IT staff were safe. 'I wouldn't think it's a bad idea for our computer people to keep their eye on the recruitment pages of the computer journals,' he replied.

Before long the exchange was employing large numbers of consultants to replace those who had left. Then came the most controversial step: the remaining IT staff were transferred to the payroll of one of the exchange's main external consultancies, Andersen Consulting, without a competitive open tender.

Andersen, which had been involved in the development of Wessex Regional Health Authority's RISP systems, was given a contract worth about £50 million over five years. It also emerged that Rawlins had some knowledge and trust of Andersen. After all he was a former partner at Andersen, though there is no evidence that this caused a conflict of interests. Indeed, although Andersen ran the exchange's computer systems, it was not involved in the development of Taurus.

The first phase of Taurus, known as INS (Institutional Net Settlement), was designed to enable institutions to settle for all their daily share transactions with one net payment. INS was widely regarded then as a success, but other parts of the project began to fall apart.

For example a security protocol known as Pelican, which would have been a security interface between end-users and Taurus, was dropped. It was replaced by one from IBM, which was commissioned to supply what was called an encryption authentication non-repudiation device. The Stock Exchange did not go out to tender and appointed IBM to write it for personal computers at a price of about £1 million, which ultimately became nearer £6 million.

IBM found it required larger versions of its PS/2 machines than were originally envisaged. Ultimately the protocol was delivered about six months late.

Meanwhile, more compromises were being made to accommodate different interests, which led to exponential system design, and complexity.

As the programmers struggled to cope with the evolving design, the Department of Trade and Industry weighed in with technological, financial and legal constraints to protect investors.

These ministerial firebombs scored direct hits in the trenches of every programming team. What little had already been designed needed redesigning.

And what had started life as a 'distillation of the Central Nominee concept' became a complex integrated hub of networked databases. Soon, the project was riddled with new committees, which lobbied for their conflicting interests.

Rival management consultancies, Andersen Consulting and Coopers and Lybrand, became involved at the Exchange, with

Andersen running the Stock Exchange's day-to-day computer operations and Coopers staff trying to run Taurus.

A timetable produced in October 1991 by the Stock Exchange compartmentalised the Taurus project into a series of 'milestones' grouped by activity. These included the IBM Communications System, Central System Development, RDE Replacement, Market Systems Development, Customer Testing, Taurus Operator, Customer Training, Taurus Rules, Regulatory Arrangements, Dress Rehearsal, Dematerialisation of First Stocks, and Live Running.

These milestones were rarely hit.

The same 'Taurus timetable' document proved prophetic when it went on to warn of a number of 'project risks'.

The document expressed the hope that:
• regulations and rules would not cause major changes to requirements (they did);
• participants would produce good-quality systems and would not encounter too many problems in customer testing (in fact, they failed to produce quality systems, and never reached customer testing);
• there would be no unexpected delays during the final acceptance period (it never reached that stage either);
• IBM would deliver its communications system without further slippage beyond March 1992 and then install it within the 'tight' timescales allowed (the product was delivered late and the timescale slipped);
• the US software house (Vista Concepts) at the centre of the project would deliver a quality product in a timely fashion (the product was late even if, eventually, the quality was up to scratch);
• the outline design would not uncover major and as yet unknown problems (it did);
• there would be no major problems integrating the US and UK software (there were);
• the central software would be tested and prove reliable before being used in customer testing (it did not get to the stage of being fully tested).

The document also expressed concern that there was a risk if the project's acceptance was delayed. It was.

The method of development also became a contentious issue. The Vista global custody system package should have cost only

£1 million, but so much customisation work was needed that the total (unfinished) bill to adapt the package for the London securities market was about £14 million.

And yet the Vista package was chosen before any operating architecture was in place. There was also a considerable learning process before programmers could begin to adapt the Vista package to the UK requirements.

It did not take long before the City's quasi-united front on Taurus began to show cracks, and then fall apart. As early as September 1991, users had a negative view of Taurus, according to a survey by the management consultancy KPMG. It found that some users were unconvinced that Taurus would happen at all, others said it was taking too long, and a third group ruled out any idea that Taurus would eliminate all paperwork.

The survey backed up one of four months earlier, which found that UK companies were unclear about the benefits offered by the system.

Despite the problems, the Taurus project director, John Watson, a genial and experienced professional seconded to the exchange from Coopers and Lybrand, always tried to exude confidence. He was so unruffled by everything around him that he was able to spend a few days on board the *Canberra*, a luxury cruise ship, which was sequestered for the purpose of a city computer conference.

Speaking at one of these conferences – called City IT – Watson declared that the Taurus project was a success and not a fiasco, and that it would save money by replacing an error-prone paper-based system.

But not all computer managers on board shared his confidence. Executives from Guardian Royal Exchange and Swiss Bank said that they could not see any obvious financial return on their internal estimated Taurus costs of between £500,000 and £1 million.

The projected live date of 1991 became 1992 and this became 1993. A survey by the consultancy Touche Ross said that companies had 'little confidence that the Exchange will deliver within the next 12 months' and saw the exchange as the 'main culprit' for any delays.

One registrar told the survey, 'There is an increasing disbelief in the industry that the Stock Exchange can meet any deadlines.' As for the complexity of the project, one custodian remarked that 'the whole project has become a juggernaut with individual organisations unable to influence the timetable, the structure or the tariff.'

Another said he felt sorry for the computer suppliers, 'who have been encouraged by the Stock Exchange to invest on a false prospectus regarding the nature of the system and the timetable'.

Touche Ross commented that there was 'a worrying problem of credibility surrounding the project' because of time slips; and one asset manager observed, 'The goalposts have been moved on several occasions, and now somebody has absconded with them.'

A study on problem IT projects by Imperial College London described Taurus as having an initial design that was defective because there were no clear objectives.

A crisis situation had brought together a 'wide, diverse group of interests', which were unlikely to be conciliatory or looking for the best solution for the City as a whole.

No clear thinking emerged from the committees, which, it is said, failed to understand the scope and complexity of the project. Communication between parties was poor, and there was no control linked to a project-wide process of evaluation. In addition, accountability was often unclear.

One developer of systems for Taurus suggested there were too many 'personal fiefdoms' within the exchange.

At one point the delays had become so worrying that John Watson was forced to put a freeze on all changes because there were so many in the pipeline. Watson did his best but there was little that one man working for an independent computer consultancy could do to prevent a disaster. He could not control the legislation, and there were too many parties pulling in different directions.

The project was finally killed in dramatic fashion by a combination of critical reports and memos from the two competing consultants at the exchange, Andersen and Coopers and Lybrand.

The idea was that when Taurus was developed and running satisfactorily, Andersen would take over its day-to-day operation from Coopers and Lybrand's stewardship.

Ahead of this contract, Andersen was asked by the Exchange's chief operating officer Jane Barker, an associate of Rawlins, to review Taurus operations.

Andersen's report prompted Rawlins to summon one of

Coopers and Lybrand's top information technology consultants, Stuart Senior, to conduct a technical review.

Within a short time, Senior had delivered a report to Rawlins, which suggested that the project would take a further three years to develop, and cost as much again as had already been spent.

Before leaving on a trip to Tokyo, Rawlins left a memo for the exchange chairman Sir Andrew Hugh Smith, setting out Senior's views.

After reading it, Sir Andrew contacted the exchange's board directors to inform them of the full extent of the chaos. They were asked to choose between begging market firms to contribute a further £90 million to continue Taurus – and killing it.

This reminds me of another maxim, one I keep coming back to: **Thou shalt not have any idea how much a new computer project is going to cost until you have planned it meticulously, costed it to the last penny, then multiplied by three**.

The Exchange's board felt it had little choice. The City's goodwill had been exhausted. Taurus was aborted, after which Sir Andrew described the project as building an 'invisible' palace.

'The problem was we built the palace wings first, forgetting to build the central rooms.' He added that the Exchange had been developing and testing parts of the system before the central control structure had been designed.

'To put it mildly, it was imprudent. We had a deeply flawed central system.'

Despite the scale of the Taurus disaster there were few recriminations, but plenty of anger at how the project had been managed. Although there were early threats of litigation, most parties quickly realised that it was pointless. After all, the Exchange consisted only of member firms; and it was the member firms who were worst hit by the Taurus failure. In any case, although millions had been spent to provide system interfaces, there was no contract between the Exchange and City firms.

In total the Exchange is understood to have lost about £75 million, but companies that had been developing systems linking into it are thought to have spent hundreds of millions. Perhaps as much as £400 million was lost.

Taurus failed because, in common with the other disasters recounted earlier, there was:
• too much secrecy;

- no one was in overall charge;
- flawed planning;
- insufficient attention to the business rather than computerisation priorities;
- a high-risk approach to the software;
- an expectation that computers would simplify existing procedures.

It is worth looking at some of these points in a little more detail. With the secrecy went defensive cover-ups of problems as they emerged. This led to project teams not knowing what the others were doing, and institutions having to speculate over the progress or otherwise on the project. It also led to the exchange giving the impression that there were no serious problems when some people knew there were. This destroyed confidence in the exchange's ability to manage the project and alienated the business community.

No one was in overall charge. There was a computerisation project head, yet computerisation was only one part of the reforms, which were largely legal, procedural and political. No single person had overall responsibility.

The Exchange did not provide for regular 'stop-and-go' points at which a decision would be made on whether to carry on or abort the project.

Computerisation was prioritised over business needs. There were so many vested interests keen to ensure that they were not disadvantaged by Taurus, that the common goal for the greater good of the City of London was lost. In the end there were so many compromises that the final system was a shadow of what had been originally envisaged.

The high-risk approach to the software came in tailoring a ready-made package, which is worse than writing bespoke software, which at least can be developed from scratch without limitations. Modifying a package loses all the advantages of off-the-shelf software: that of a proven standardised design.

As for simplifying existing procedures, the simplification should have been started and finished *before* and not *by* computerisation.

The ending of the project was also marked by the departure of one of the Square Mile's more colourful characters: Peter Rawlins, the Stock Exchange's chief executive, a controversial, abrasive figure nicknamed 'Napoleon', who masterminded the project. He left the exchange with a settlement of £174,000 together with his pay and bonus package for the year which was £348,500.

Only the Taurus acronym was a success, if only for the headline-writers: CITY GORED BY TAURUS and BANK TAKES BULL BY THE HORNS were two of the least colourful versions.

Even today the scars remain. One senior executive of a software house that had to make a third of its staff redundant after the débâcle retains a calendar on his desk for March 1993 with the 11th ringed and the reminder: 'Taurus Collapsed'.

The picture portrays a liner sinking in the seas near a desert island with a firm of consultants sailing to the rescue.

The collapse of Taurus bruised London's reputation as one of the world's leading financial centres. Even lesser European exchanges in Frankfurt and Paris have, in the Deutsche Kassenwerein and Relit, the successful paperless trading equivalents of Taurus.

But perhaps the overriding casualty of Taurus was the realisation that the City of London's best financial experts, management consultancies and technical specialists proved unable to bring the system to fruition.

Has the City learned its lesson? Perhaps it has. In 1996, a company set up by the Bank of England, which undertook to build Taurus's replacement, Crest, said that it had delivered the systems on time, to budget and in full working order.

However the Bank of England – and just as importantly the City itself – was determined to get it right. There was an additional incentive for the Bank of England. It wanted to show that it could do what the Stock Exchange could not. That it succeeded, at least initially, is a testimony to its authoritarian project management. Being the Bank of England, an authoritarian approach came naturally. This meant that it had the clout, and the willingness to exercise that clout, to prevent any unnecessary changes to the system. The City had to accept its design, like it or not. This meant that simplicity ruled. The design was frozen at an early stage.

Equally important was the bank's avoidance of a 'Big Bang' implementation. Participation in Crest was voluntary. Dematerialisation – the replacement of share certificates with electronic records – did not happen overnight and, crucially, is not mandatory. It is being introduced gradually. In some ways it is a compromise. Even more importantly, the participants, the end-users in the City, *wanted* Crest to succeed. They had seen the introduction of Taurus as a Stock Exchange project which was designed largely to enhance the reputation of the Stock Exchange. Only when Taurus collapsed did the City realise that it needed Taurus. London, as a financial community, needed Taurus, or rather a replacement of it.

By the time Crest went live, the collective need had smoothed over the conflicts that had torn Taurus asunder. Not that it is an unqualified success. By 1997 Crest was displaying some familiar early warning signs: discontented users, slow transaction times, communications traffic jams and additional costs. Never mind. A Bank of England official was consummately reassuring. He said that Crest was suffering 'teething troubles'.

WHAT THEY SAID ABOUT TAURUS
(before and after the collapse)

'The emphasis in terms of settlement was put on getting in a similar system to the gilts market, that came on stream with Big Bang. The view was that you couldn't liberalise the trading system, which was what Big Bang was doing, and change the whole settlement system at the same time. With the benefit of hindsight, we'd have been better to sort out the settlement system before the trading system. That might have prevented the mess we got into with the bull market of 1986/87.' – *Terry Pearson, Royal Bank of Scotland*

'The Stock Exchange was trying to please everybody i.e. registrars, market makers, brokers, the stock lending community. Every player in the business wanted their particular functionality requirements built in.' – *Pearson*

'When we saw it, we immediately thought, "this is a 0 out of 10, please see the project plan". But we thought we'd live with any changes and give the planners the benefit of the doubt because we honestly thought they would never cancel Taurus. Ultimately, if you put all the delays together, the project would probably have gone live sometime late in 1995.' – *John Wyse, Synergo (a City of London software house)*

'News on the Taurus front has a depressingly familiar theme of further delay and uncertainty. Given the long history of this project, it would probably be unwise to speculate on a likely end date. The delays are clearly disappointing. Given the time, effort and other resources that we have all invested so far, there is a danger that confidence in Taurus is beginning to be undermined.' – *Lloyds Bank Registrars newsletter before the project was aborted*

'By trying to cater for myriads of vested interests, Taurus has become too complex for the first stage. Other countries have avoided such complexities – the full implications were not appropriately understood from the outset.' – *Taurus asset manager*

'Continued delays on timescales are causing potential participants to question the increasing costs of developing Taurus vis a vis the benefits which should be obtained.' – *Institutional Broker*

'The deadlines published have never been believed, causing a feeling that maybe there was more time to prepare than there actually was.' – *Custodian*

'There is a strong sense that inertia has set in across the industry, caused by slippage to delivery dates. Doubts now exist about the viability of the project: indeed the question has been asked "not when but why?"' – *Institutional Broker*

'When it collapsed it was obviously a great disappointment but there was a refreshing feeling that we were not going to look for scapegoats and try to have a witch hunt. The one enduring lesson was: "This is how not to run a project "followed" by "let's see how we get out of this"' – *Pearson*

'The Stock Exchange had no one with the appropriate project management skills for a system of the size of Taurus. There were great hopes of John Watson, the Coopers man brought in to bring the project to fruition. Watson had been the driving force behind the Talisman system developed in the late 70s and he brought in some acolytes who had been with him on that project. John was a very likeable guy, with a large amount of persuasive skills, and he managed to persuade everybody that the project was always on schedule.' – *Pearson*

'The continuing delays are damaging confidence in the system. Taurus is not being taken seriously: there is too much paper and too little useful communication from the Stock Exchange.' – *Retail Broker*

'In terms of overall project management, there was no one on Taurus overseeing and specifying how all individual components would fit together. If you are building a house, if you are putting up your structure, and your panels are coming along later, you hope that the panels and other individual parts will fit. You need someone to ensure that that happens. Taurus never had that.' – *John Wyse, Synergo*

'It was all a miasma. When they got to the published regulations by the Department of Trade and Industry, the Exchange said, "Oh, they won't do that." But they did. How the Exchange got through years of discussions and found that their design did not meet what the DTI was thinking about in terms of legislation, was beyond everybody. There was an arrogance and elitism about the Exchange that smacked of "Of course they'll do what we say."' – *Manager at an unnamed US software company*

'Stalin's maxim, "Trust is good, but control is better", was applicable to many of the problems with Taurus. Maybe there was too much trust that Vista and the contractors at the Exchange were going to deliver the goods, and not enough control of them.' – *John Wyse, Synergo*

'Several of us had serious doubts about it. I became convinced that it was a classical situation of a project doomed, when the project team seemed to bring up diversionary tactics, talking about peripheral issues. There was a tremendous effort to get the listed companies to put the necessary resolutions to their Annual General Meetings to dematerialise their own shares. Now that would obviously come eventually but there was a big effort to get a lot of companies on board ready to do this. It was putting the cart before the horse: a smokescreen to hide the lack of progress on the central core systems.' – *Pearson*

Towards the end of 1990, the Exchange produced a book called *The Taurus Business Requirement,* which, though not a specification, was supposed to offer guidance for firms to interface with Taurus. The problem for would-be users was that there were omissions from it:

'There were "to be advised" sections within it; things that hadn't been thought out, particularly in the area of corporate actions such as take-overs, rights, splits, all instruments that go through the market. I was saying to my team, "Can you start work on this?" And they'd say "No, we have a big chunk missing over here. We can't build this bit without knowing about that bit".' – *Manager at an unnamed US software company*

CHAPTER ELEVEN

The Sixth Deadly Sin: Consultancy (II)

SECOND CASE STUDY

It's incredibly difficult getting computers to do even the simplest things that humans can do. – Bill Gates, founder of Microsoft (television interview with David Frost Sunday 26 November 1995).

The computerisation of Britain's welfare benefits payments was hailed as the biggest computerisation endeavour in Europe; but it will be remembered as the biggest overspend in the UK computer industry's history.

This project also shows how easy it is for lessons of previous mistakes to be forgotten, and that managers responsible for computerisation may deny even to themselves that the problems are serious.

It further highlights the advantages – and cost disadvantages – of hiring armies of consultants to operate and manage a major system implementation.

Many years before the Department of Social Security's 'Operational Strategy' computer project began, the department had tried repeatedly to computerise welfare benefits without success, and mostly without involving end-users because they were seen as too technically naïve to be worth consulting.

These early projects suffered from the same problem that would go on to afflict the Operational Strategy: that of the designers and the promoters having too high an expectation of what computers can achieve.

It was even thought at this time – in the 1970s – that

computers would replace humans. Machines did not go out on strike, never made mistakes and cost nothing in national insurance contributions.

In this context, the public money spent on computers did not seem to matter. It would all be repaid in no time.

So the plans for a Brave New World began with a project to correct human deficiencies by installing computers to tell civil servants when they were miscalculating welfare benefits.

The problem was that whenever the system detected something slightly awry, it spewed out reams of paper asking operators to check what had gone wrong. If nobody addressed the queries within 24 hours, the systems generated an entire batch of new 'error messages' until the users were drowning in paper.

More than two decades later the London Ambulance Service would encounter a similar problem. And it was a similar story at the book distributor Tiptree. Nobody had anticipated the extent to which computers would require precise information on which to act.

Although technology zealots might claim otherwise, humans are still superior to computers in that our eyes and brain can accommodate unexpected situations and make decisions accordingly. With computers, their behaviour must be pre-programmed.* They do not have eyes and even if they did (in the form of electronic sensors) they could disentangle and prioritise only that information they have been programmed to recognise. Any 'data' beyond their understanding will leave them baffled. At Tiptree, for example, the system knew where certain books were kept, what orders existed for those books, how the books should be retrieved from the warehouse shelves and how they should be packed. But tiny human mistakes – which were not predicted by the system designers – threw the system into a spin from which it could not immediately recover (see Chapter 6).

As I have suggested before, tests and pilot trials of computer systems will confirm to you that you have thought of everything. But only when you go live with the new systems in a full working environment will you be humiliated into discovering everything you hadn't thought of.

*Some computer scientists claim that neural networks – networked computers that can 'learn' and improve their responses as a result of experience – are capable of mimicking the lower functions of the human brain. However, neural computing is mainly at the research stage and it will be many years, if not decades, before neural networks can be put to a wider practical use. At this time one cannot see any possibility of their being able to mirror the human brain.

The Department of Social Security was immune to humiliation, however. It had no conscience that could be reproached because no single person was ever in charge. So those early social security welfare systems were scrapped without anyone to take the blame; and the matter was put down to experience. To paraphrase Oscar Wilde, experience is the name we give to our mistakes.

And the Department of Social Security would go on to enjoy a whole series of new experiences.

But first, outside consultants were called in to advise on the way ahead. One of the advisory companies was headed by a member of the then Prime Minister Margaret Thatcher's policy unit at Number 10 Downing Street.

Despite the series of earlier failures, and after much discussion, ministers agreed to let the department have another go at a major computerisation project. It was given the nifty title of the Computerisation and Mechanisation of Local Office Tasks, or Camelot (see Chapter 7). It was a good choice of name because Camelot would never exist except in legend. But it was an expensive phantom of a project. About £6 million was written off but only after all the usual pre-disaster signs:

• the technicians assuring non-technicians that everything was going well when the non-technicians could see that it wasn't;
• when problems emerged they were dismissed as teething troubles;
• a lack of project management skills;
• no individual responsible if the project failed.

Consultants who were brought in to advise on Camelot's failure commented that earlier computerisations had collapsed because of lack of end-user involvement. But Camelot suffered from the other extreme: too much user involvement. End-users made so many requests for changes that the systems tried to please everyone and were soon sunk in a quagmire of complexity (as in the London Stock Exchange Taurus scheme in Chapter 10).

The Camelot project also had failings similar to those at the Performing Right Society in that no hardware was capable of running such unwieldy software efficiently.

By 1981, consultants had recommended that Camelot be scrapped and it was. Some benefit could have been salvaged if ministers had learned that big, ambitious computerisations involving custom-made software and overlong time spans were more likely to fail than succeed.

But, in government, being taught a lesson and learning something from it are worlds apart. So in 1984, two years after Camelot was abandoned, the DSS (then the DHSS, when health was part of its remit) launched yet another welfare project.

This would be much bigger and riskier than anything before. It was called the Operational Strategy, and it promised to deliver the sort of administrative savings and central government reform that had been promised by Thatcher when she came to power.

And it had such high-level patronage that there was never any question of abandonment. It had to work, come what may. So as problems developed on the project, they were blanketed with money.

Outside consultants were employed by the hundred, at a cost of between £300 and £1,000 each a day, many of them on long-term contracts.

This angered civil service computer staff and exacerbated industrial relations problems. As the tension between staff and consultants increased, so more computer consultants were wheeled in, some of them fresh from college, who picked up their skills from the civil servants they would soon displace.

The taxpayer was paying even junior consultants five times the daily rate of the equivalent civil servant.

The main hardware supplier was ICL, which had also installed hardware for the failed Camelot project (though the failure was not ICL's fault). Again, as with Camelot, ICL would receive orders for new mainframe computers without open competition.

Cynics would say that the main purpose of the Operational Strategy was to provide a soapbox for ministers to declare and demonstrate their party's commitment to business efficiency.

Indeed, at every major stage of the project's roll-out, ministers held press conferences to which local and national journalists were invited. Every time, the announcements hailed the project as the largest civil computerisation in Europe.

But the most interesting thing about the announcements was the footnote that accompanied copies of the ministerial speeches.

It was a note to editors about the Operational Strategy – what it was, why it was conceived and what it would achieve. It also mentioned the cost . . . and it was a new figure every time an announcement was made.

At first it was described as a £1.2 billion project. Next it was

£1.6 billion, then £1.8 billion, at which point the press releases and ministerial announcements ceased. The last time I checked, the project was expected to cost £2.6 billion.

A trawl through the public records reveals something else: that when the project was announced to Parliament, the cost was put at £0.7 billion . . . and falling.

This assurance was given at a Parliamentary committee debate on the project long before the system's introduction, when an MP asked the Operational Strategy's then project director whether the cost estimate would rise in real terms.

'No,' the director replied. 'It is unlikely to rise in real terms. The bulk of the costs are in salaries and in fees we pay to consultants. The equipment costs if anything are going to come down.'

What the department didn't tell Parliament was that unexpected changes to the project during its lifetime would inevitably increase the costs substantially.

Yet there's nothing certain in computing except that a major computer project scheduled for implementation over many years will be out of date or in need of major renovation by the time it is due to go live.

Therefore the final cost will always be many times higher than that originally envisaged.

However, even in the context of the increased budget, the government and the department have issued numerous statements about the success of the Operational Strategy, though without breaking down the benefits against the costs.

Although the costs have risen, the department claims that the benefits have risen by the same amount.

In the beginning, when the computerisation was approved by the Treasury, it was on the basis that it would cut 6,000 jobs. By the time the costs had risen to £1.7 billion, the department was claiming that the project would cut 20,000 jobs. When the costs exceeded £2.6 billion nobody was saying how many civil servants' salaries had actually been saved.

A spokeswoman for the department's computer agency, known as ITSA, says that the staff savings from the Operational Strategy 'are a matter for the Benefits Agency'. The Benefits Agency says it is a matter for the Department of Social Security. And the Department of Social Security says it is 'impossible to give any figures on the staff savings'.

All I managed to ascertain was that, between 1991 and 1995, the number of staff in welfare benefit offices, part- and full-time, rose from about 70,000 to 71,000. One national newspaper put the figure at 84,000. The numbers employed in the social services computer division also rose. Far from the operational strategy cutting 20,000 jobs, there seems to have been an increase of staff, though it must also be said that the total number of transactions increased enormously as well.

Suffice to say that the Operational Strategy highlights the fact that computer managers may try to persuade a board to approve technology projects by promising benefits that may in reality be impossible to attain, or too nebulous to verify.

Or the benefits may be so far into the future that whoever has promised them will probably have left by the time anyone notices that the benefits have failed to materialise.

The difficulty for the chief executive is spotting when managers have advocated major computerisation merely because, subconsciously, they want something that takes them out of their humdrum day-to-day existence.

MPs had profound misgivings about the Operational Strategy even before it was launched. They had already examined the failure of Camelot. In 1984, a meeting of the all-party House of Commons Public Accounts Committee commented generally on the dangers of over-optimism about the benefits and timescales of the project.

With presentiment, the committee also 'expressed some unease about the continuing uncertainties in what they considered to be an extremely expensive and uncertain series of related computer developments'.

MPs 'trusted that the Treasury would satisfy themselves that the Department had carried out a thorough and realistic analysis of all the risks involved'.

But no civil servant or minister is compelled to pay attention to a Parliamentary committee. So, five years later, the National Audit Office, which monitors public spending, produced a report that suggested that, despite the earlier warning by MPs, the Treasury had not carried out a thorough and realistic analysis of the risks involved.

The National Audit Office's investigation into the Operational Strategy found:
• serious shortcomings in financial control;

- a failure to monitor the financial viability of the project;
- an inability to establish why costs had risen by 145 per cent,* whether it was mainly because of changes to the project since it was conceived, or because of an underestimation of the costs coupled with an overestimation of the benefits;
- a delay in all major projects between 1984 and 1987.

The auditors also found that benefits had undoubtedly been overstated.

Of course the Operational Strategy was never going to be easy. In 1989 the department paid out over £45 billion a year in benefits people from about 500 welfare offices to more than 24,000,000 people.

Any attempt to computerise a labyrinthine network of establishments was bound to encounter problems and delays; but, knowing that, should the department not have been more open at the outset?

Mandarins and ministers could have decided to computerise incrementally, office by office, learn from the problems, get staff familiar with computers, and decide later whether to go ahead with the entire project. However, as in all the case studies of less successful projects in this book, the possibility of abandonment never seems to have been seriously considered.

Perhaps this is because great reputations are made by great achievements against even greater odds; not by low-profile, small-scale battles in which nobody gets hurt.

So ambitious was the undertaking that most of the welfare computer projects – each of them massively complex and ambitious and requiring bespoke software – were undertaken simultaneously.

The optimism and high expectations of computers can be seen at the time from a speech in 1989 by John Moore, then Secretary of State for Social Security, who declared that a part of the Operational Strategy 'has arrived ahead of schedule, within budget and . . . will prove to be of enormous benefit to claimants, staff and the taxpayer alike . . . staff will be able to call up the information they require at the touch of a button.'

It was not as simple as that. Staff said they coped with the workload only by sidestepping the computers and dealing with claims manually. One MP and member of the Public Accounts

---

* This 145 per cent figure is based on the cost being £1.7 billion. After the National Audit Office report it emerged that the project costs had risen to £2.6 billion.

Committee, Dale Campbell-Savours, reported that the systems had lost money overnight. 'I am told that in one office £25,000 of crisis loan money which was desperately needed by claimants disappeared.'

Internal fault-notification slips recorded 20,935 problems in less than a year. In March 1988, the trade magazine *Computer Weekly* reported that 'social security offices face increasing backlogs because new benefits software runs more slowly than current systems.'

The systems 'take up to four minutes to complete processing which current systems perform in less than 30 seconds.'

Another magazine, *Community Care*, found that the micro-based systems used in every welfare office were 'incapable of generating correct data'.

At the time a government spokeswoman said there had been software problems that the department was trying to rectify. But many managers commented to *Community Care* that they had lost confidence in the systems which were said to be prone to frequent breakdowns and to losing large chunks of monthly budget reports. In some offices, staff were working out budget figures on calculators.

The national press was not enamoured either. The *Independent* reported in 1988 the 'scandal of long waits for benefit claims'.

There were further problems. The department issued £21.3 million, in loans to welfare claimants, that went missing from the system.

The Comptroller and Auditor General Sir John Bourn reported that the unaccounted for £21.3 million 'related to a breakdown in the proper operation of the computer system'.

At one point more than 360 consultants were employed long term on the Operational Strategy. A few of them were staying in the finest hotels on a more or less permanent basis, some of them claiming the sort of expenses that were parodied in Evelyn Waugh's *Scoop*.

Inaccuracies in the department's internal records were so serious that public service auditors repeatedly refused to endorse the books as a full and accurate record of the department's finances.

And since then the computerisation errors in benefits payments have risen, almost without exception, every year.

None of this has ruffled the Department of Social Security,

which never wavered from its assertion that the Operational Strategy was a 'magnificent success'.

The main consultancy on the project even commissioned a book on the Operational Strategy, which described the smooth implementation of the project as an 'astonishing' achievement.

Other observers have been less flattering. A paper on the hazards of major computer projects by Oxford University and Imperial College, London, found in 1994 that the demand to introduce Operational Strategy systems quickly, to support legislative changes to social security, led to smaller projects being cancelled.

But the systems that were dropped were those that would have delivered a better service to claimants. There was also a gap in understanding between the policymakers and the technicians.

On one side of the divide were ministers, who were demanding the systems but were reluctant to equip themselves with an understanding of the technology. On the other side were the technicians and administrators, who appeared unconcerned or were powerless to influence policy decisions.

Several other problems were outlined in the paper. Among them was that many of the in-house specialists who understood the welfare benefits systems were pushed out to the periphery of the project. Meanwhile consultants who had little experience of the department's administration were given the crucial tasks of specifying and designing the systems.

Another was that government-imposed deadlines for projects that were changing shape with each legislative amendment increased the risks of failure. There was end-user antagonism towards computers that could replace their jobs. The project had a 17-year lifespan. In comparison many private-sector computing projects are not given approval unless they provide a return within a maximum of two years.

The authors of the paper concluded: 'Therein we question the extent to which the original objectives of cost savings, system robustness, increased job satisfaction for staff and improved quality of service have been, and can be met.'

Yet, despite all the criticism, the Operational Strategy has been successful to a limited extent. One of its purposes was to deal with claimants as 'whole people'. In other words the systems were designed to give an overview of all the benefits to which an individual was or was not entitled – and not deal with the person on a benefit-by-benefit basis. This, as I write, has not yet happened. In fact each benefit has its own system. And few of the separate systems talk to each other on-line. Another promise was that claimants would be able to walk into any welfare office in the country and have the local staff call up their case history on screen 'at the touch of a button'. This has not happened yet, nor will it in the foreseeable future. Today, however, departmental staff say they could not conceive of going back to manual processes. They enjoy using computers. The system has also undoubtedly cut the processing time of some welfare benefits.

But £2.6 billion is a lot of money to pay for a modicum of end-user satisfaction and questionable benefits for the taxpayer, and yet the money might have been well spent had the department learned from the mistakes of all its computerisation projects, including Camelot, by computerising on a small scale using standardised packages.

Instead it followed up the Operational Strategy by commissioning another major, pioneering, ambitious, custom-built system from suppliers and consultants: the £25 million ASSIST statistical scheme.

That too ended in disaster.

To understand consultants in general is to understand their jargon. I have found that the jargon of many consultants is a sort of verbal abstract expressionism. They will speak authoritatively on matters of which you have no knowledge or understanding, yet will earn your bewildered respect by disguising the poverty of meaning of many of their comments with a sprinkling of what everyone knows to be good common sense. It works as simply as this: about 5 per cent of what they will say makes such utter good sense that the listener assumes the rest of it is equally valid. The reality is that the consultants are paid to *know*; therefore they are more hidebound than anyone else by a need to conceal their ignorance. I have asked some consultants about the case studies in this book, and asked them what went wrong. One or two made some pertinent points, or pointed out things that I had overlooked, but more often than not they did not know and assumed that I *did* know. This would not have mattered but for the fact that they camouflaged their ignorance by seeking to baffle me – and succeeded – by stringing together a concatenation of vague or even meaningless jargon phrases that seemed designed to provoke a change in the subject of conversation. But I am not easily diverted, because I understand so little that I spend my life asking questions that others do not need to ask. Yet after asking many questions of some consultants, I have discovered eventually that they too know as little as I do. Perhaps prospective buyers of consultancy services need to do the same: keep asking questions until you feel you have exhausted, or rather reached the limit of, the consultant's knowledge and understanding on the technological subject at hand. This will manifest itself in a remark such as, 'Er, look, that's not really my area. I'll need to bring in our specialist on that subject.' At that point you can judge whether the consultant is worth the money. In fact the less a consultant professes to understand about an area beyond his or her particular specialism the better. It suggests that that they will give advice only when they know what they are talking about and will not feel compelled to affect expertise in every sphere of the computer industry, a problem that afflicts some of the 'strategic' or 'high-level' consultants-cum-philosophers-cum-visionaries. The thing is, unless you are willing to launch tenaciously and unashamedly into a series of questions to which you already know the answers, you won't discover when consultants are hiding their ignorance.

There's an alternative: question them on the case studies in this book. If they have read them well, they will undoubtedly give you different assessments of the causes of the disasters. You can then make your own judgement of their expertise in the light of your experiences and your own interpretations of the case studies.

CHAPTER TWELVE

The Seventh Deadly Sin: Tailored Software

It's the easiest and the hardest thing in the world buying packaged software: easy because it is off the shelf, tried, tested and probably ready to run; hard because the chances are that it won't do everything you want, but because you have bought a package, there's not much you can do about it.

Therefore sales departments of software development companies have a receptive audience when they claim that it is better for companies to buy their own system, like a tailor-made suit. Worse, there's a trend for salespeople to persuade customers that they should buy a package ('a safe, tried and tested solution for you, sir') and then modify it to meet your needs – the 'best of all possible worlds' solution.

What the sales managers tend not to reveal is the likeness between building your own software and designing a space probe to Pluto.

In each case nobody has done it before, and pioneering excursions have a tendency to end up like Mark Antony's expedition against the Parthians or Scott's advance on the South Pole.

Originally pioneers were foot soldiers who marched in advance of an army, having spades and pickaxes to dig trenches, repair roads, and perform other labours in clearing and preparing the way for the main body.

In the computer industry pioneers are the technology enthusiasts who will obligingly walk into all the ambushes so as to render all the traps harmless to their successors.

That's why *unmodified* packages represent such a good investment. Few of them are infallible but are likely to have fewer serious bugs than any tailored software. Microsoft, with its much-hyped but highly impressive Windows 95 operating system could not be certain it was rid of a plethora of serious bugs when writing the software in its programming 'factories'. Even after extensive internal tests it was still uncertain, so it sold the package to the specialist market and called it a 'beta' test copy, whereupon tens of thousands of end-users put the product on trial, discovered all its shortcomings, and fed the results back to Microsoft.

It was only once all these comments had been translated into corrections, and the corrections thoroughly tested with new beta test copies, that Microsoft launched the product to the world in August 1995.

If it took Microsoft several years and live trials of Windows 95 by tens of thousands of different companies to get it right, is there any hope that software written for a single company, and tested by that one company and its supplier, is likely to be satisfactory first time?

Modifying a package is even riskier than starting with a blank piece of paper because the software, if it has survived the test of time, has probably had its bugs removed through a series of new releases; so once a dealer or software house starts tampering with it, the complications that will ensue cannot be predicted; for **software packages are a friendly moggie when patted gently and a pre-menstrual tigress if manhandled – as the London Stock Exchange, the London Ambulance Service and a countless number of government departments on both sides of the Atlantic have discovered to their cost.**

In fact space rockets such as the shuttle have software programs that are infinitesimal in their size and complexity when compared with a typical commercial word processing package[*].

The reason is that missions into space cost hundreds of millions of dollars, sometimes billions, so it's important to minimise the risks of failure – and all software is a risk. Some programmers say it is almost impossible to write ten lines of code

[*] I was about to include the Ariane space rocket here, but in 1996, it was launched with an unusually complex onboard computer system and crashed. The cause was attributed to software errors in the code which was used to control the rocket's inertial reference system. A back-up also failed. As a result the rocket in effect lost its guidance systems about 30 seconds after take-off. The main computer is said to have interpreted diagnostic information as flight data and, as a result, tried to force the engines into making the craft perform an unaerodynamic manoeuvre. This led to the systems initiating a self-destruct program. The rocket was destroyed along with its $550m payload.

without making some sort of mistake. But there's a difference in economic and human terms between the crash of a word processor and that of a space shuttle.

Yet the caution shown by the US space industry could be usefully copied by the computer industry. It is still too easy for enthusiasts, hardware manufacturers, software houses and consultants to convince prospective customers that building new systems or modifying existing packages represents an acceptably small risk.

The computer industry even managed to persuade the then US president Ronald Reagan of the feasibility of building an impenetrable shield in space against a possible Russian missile attack. The ludicrousness of the Star Wars Strategic Defense Initiative was acknowledged by everyone except President Reagan, and of course the Russians, who did everything in their power to discover the American technological secrets – the real secret being that there wasn't any secret.

So if an American president and the world's second largest country can be taken in by the claims of the technology suppliers, what hope is there for the chief executive of a small or medium-size company?

Naturally the suppliers will not promote their products in terms of their pioneering new features. In fact they will claim that they're using only tried and tested technology, which will be enhanced to meet the customer's needs.

But there's no such thing as a minor change to a software package.

Software is built like a house made of playing cards. Adding or removing one row is likely to destabilise or even bring down the whole structure. It took only the failure of a tiny 'O' ring sealant in the Challenger space shuttle to destroy the mission and the lives of seven astronauts.

Any changes should be made within the confines of the architectural structure of the package. Any features not originally envisaged by the designers should not be added, even if the original designers agree to the changes.

No package is entirely bug-free but it will seem positively bug-*infested* once you start trying to adapt it.

Also, if you adapt a package, you may have to pay extra for the maintenance of a modified package because your version of it will need to be upgraded separately every time there is a general release.

But despite the risks, packages are often avoided for several reasons.

Organisations believe they are unique and it hurts their pride to think that their administrative systems are as common as all the other companies that are buying the same software package. This particularly afflicts public sector organisations who rarely if ever buy packaged software because they simply *know* they are unique.

Software is regarded as infinitely adaptable. That's the whole point of it. So companies cannot conceive of themselves having to change their procedures for the benefit of mere software.

Yet they do not appreciate the vengeful power of software to strike back at those who underestimate its importance to the smooth running of an organisation.

The computer manager knows it will be difficult to convince the end-users or the board of directors of the value of a package if it doesn't do everything that the present systems do. **There's an unfortunate corporate perception that new computers will always do more than old ones. They tend to do less, at least at first, though they will do it on a new hardware platform, or may do a lot of other things besides, so it may be worth sacrificing some of the existing functions.**

Many software suppliers and particularly consultancies exist to build new systems or tailor packages and they have mobilised vast marketing armies to convince prospective customers of the need for their expertise. A mass use of packages by major corporations would do many of the suppliers no good at all.

Customers believe that packages will deprive them of the opportunity to gain a competitive advantage through the imaginative use of technology. This is an illusion. Many companies gain an advantage through *sensible* rather than imaginative use of technology. The competitive edge often comes through the products, services, marketing strategy and quality of people in the companies. The technology only supports this. For example, the imaginative use of technology is often credited in the press as having driven the astonishing success of the First Direct telephone banking service. But the technology is nothing special. What's different about the bank is that there is someone there to answer the telephone, to give you a balance, or tell you your last few transactions, at 3 o'clock in the morning or on

Christmas Day. You can even apply for a loan and get an answer late in the evening. *That* is what's special.

There are exceptions. For example, technology used in some of the dealer companies, say at JP Morgan, does undoubtedly provide a competitive advantage. But the software is developed in-house by programmers who sit alongside dealers and therefore fully understand the business. But JP Morgan, as one of the founding fathers of Wall Street, has decades of experience of computers. Most companies don't.

Undeniably the quest for competitive advantage will continue to drive the software programming industry. And this is often understandable because it is easy, when talking to a supplier's sales staff, to imagine how new systems will transform your business.

In the following case, new technology seemed to offer an obvious competitive advantage. The problem was that the promises of the supplier did not always match the quality of the deliveries.

CASE STUDY

The PRS, Wessex, London Ambulance and Taurus disasters were complete failures – the equivalent of a permanent blackout in a lighting shop. More common are the crashes that debilitate but don't disable.

Less demanding computer users tend not to be greatly harmed by failures because they expect little of their computers and those who have never hoped have never despaired.

But the higher your expectations of the technology, the greater pleasure it will take in consistently letting you down.

A company called Resources International had more than high expectations: it had a vision. It was a pragmatic vision in which Resources saw exactly how the technology could be used for business gain. But the project was held up on the border of theory and practice. 'Held up' is a bit of euphemism. It was mugged.

The project began with the familiar delusion of a paperless, all-computerised office. Resources International is a recruitment company, one of the ten biggest in the computer industry, which finds the right person to fill vacancies in large companies in the UK and overseas. A critical part of its business is having a database of people whose skills can be quickly matched with the jobs on offer.

Achieving this is far from straightforward. Recruiting computer staff is a particularly difficult and hazardous business. Programmers and analysts tend to have access to the most sensitive information in computer systems, which are the heart, soul and mind of large companies.

So most large companies cannot afford the risk of hiring the sort of person who would introduce a homemade virus into the network for fun, or would sabotage the computers if the managing director told him to smarten his dress, or who would tout for bribes to pass secret information to a competitor.

So personnel officers who are recruiting computer specialists need to know more about the lives and backgrounds, skills and suitability of prospective candidates than in some other professions.

To help them find the right people, they hire recruitment agencies – and not any commonplace agency but one that will studiously and imaginatively match the specific job requirements with the potential interviewees on its database.

Doing this exacting job well had given Resources International something of a reputation in the computer industry, attracting clients such as Ford Credit and IBM software houses. But as with all companies with particularly high reputations to sustain, Resources knew it had to struggle harder than mediocre competitors to stay on top.

And in a technological age, the most obvious way to sustain success is to spend a large sum on an innovative, class-beating computer system that nobody else has got, is willing to make the effort to find, or has thought of buying. And that is exactly what Resources did.

The opportunity arose when a long-standing supplier of hardware to the company offered some proprietary software that seemed too good to reject.

But this was a mistake. Even before computerising the company was committing itself to hardware when other systems may have been as good or better. **Customers should always choose the software first and then find the hardware afterwards.** It's so obvious a piece of advice that it will make many of those in the computer industry groan. Yet the choice of hardware so often comes before the software, usually because the main sales thrust is often made by the hardware manufacturer who has already had a relationship with the customer.

In this event the onus is on the customer to dispassionately pick the brains of its main hardware supplier – and ask for a loan machine to try out new software – but use the supplier as only one prospective source. It won't harm your relationship with the supplier to talk to its competitors. In fact your main supplier will fight harder to retain your business.

At that time Resources was spending much of its time on routine administrative tasks, which it felt could be computerised. Particularly laborious was the rekeying of thousands of CVs into its various databases. A new image processing system offered the chance to place CVs onto a scanner which would then automatically convert the text into computer code and lodge it into the database as reliably as if the job were keyed in by hand, but within seconds rather than minutes.

Not only that, but anyone sitting at one of the many terminals would be able to summon from the database, virtually instantly, an actual image and text of a CV on screen, at the touch of a few buttons. This was in addition to the computer identifying from thousands of job-hunters only those few with the required combination of, say, IBM DB2, COBOL, client-server and Sybase skills.

This would be stage one of the company's administrative transformation. Stage two would be a 'centre of resourcing excellence', which would capitalise on the systems investment.

The centre would have a factory environment, the computerised equivalent of a typing pool, where sales staff could have their routine administration taken care of, leaving them free to go out on the road bringing in the business. Among other things, this centre would handle the loading of CVs onto scanners, the searches of the database and discussions with the clients, and would then fix up interviews with candidates or send out suitable CVs.

The highly paid sales staff could then use their time most productively by visiting large companies to discuss their recruitment needs and campaigns for the future.

It seemed such an obviously good idea, like inventing the can-opener, that the company's managing director Warwick Bergin thought that his competitors would surely have thought of it before.

They hadn't – and that was partly why it collapsed. It was

brand-new, untried, untested, unproven – in these respects like the PRS's PROMS system and Wessex's RISP.

Within months, Resources International had moved from its current workhorse of a system, which plodded happily from one place to the next, to a top-price racing stallion with broken legs.

Resources invested £143,000 in hardware and software from its hardware supplier, a small trader.

Bergin had expected that the supplier would provide the systems, but later discovered that they had subcontracted the work to a third party – and then had not managed the subcontractor professionally.

It was only once the old system had been switched off and discarded that the deficiencies of the new came to light:
- it crashed up to ten times a day;
- more than 1,400 hours were wasted trying to get it to work properly;
- it could not handle the number of concurrent users it was designed for;
- the 150-Mbyte back-up tape drive overflowed without warning;
- the system could not search CVs by acronyms – although every other word in the computer industry is an acronym;
- it clocked up 408 faults in 10 months;
- some transactions that were supposed to take a fraction of a second took 15 minutes.

That was the relatively good news; then came the climacteric change of life. Once Bergin had sacked the supplier, taken legal advice on how to recover the £143,000 he had paid for the system and had begun reverting to using a hybrid of the previous system supported by manual methods, the problems multiplied.

His Centre of Resourcing Excellence could not function to anything like its capacity because of systems deficiencies, and so was unable to cope with the high-volume business it was originally set up to process.

Eventually the whole centre had to be disbanded, and the sales staff were held back from selling by handling their own routine administration. Even then the basic, semi-automatic system went down frequently and at times the company found difficulty in identifying and sending out any candidates for interviews.

'If we couldn't extract information on potential candidates from our databases we had very little to submit to a client.

Because the systems were not functioning correctly, the jobs were not being filled as often as they could have been. We were missing out on business we would otherwise have got. The system that was supposed to be giving us a competitive advantage was giving us a competitive disadvantage.'

The fallout from the disaster lasted nearly a year – a year lost in what could otherwise have been a rapid post-recession recovery, said Bergin. But at the time of writing he had retained consultants to help get the limping racehorse back on four feet, and business had picked up dramatically anyway.

He was expecting to increase staff by 50 per cent the following year – and was looking towards buying another complex, ambitious system. Bergin said:

> We have got the present system up to a degree of functionality that no longer gives us any competitive disadvantage but it is not satisfactory and does not give us any advantage. It will not grow with us so we have decided to abandon it and take on one of these new proprietary systems from an American company. Everything that we want can be provided and the performance benchmarks are infinitely better. It is expensive stuff. Over the next two years we will spend possibly another £200,000.
>
> Without question it will give us the edge we originally sought. We will identify people with specific skills instantly. It will cut out paper flow. I will be able to identify you as an individual as being suitable for a job; I will send the text of your CV via the Internet to a given client and/or I can send it directly via a fax without any paperwork. I might be talking to a client in the US on the phone about a particular individual and he'll say: 'Gee, that's very good. I'd like to see that.' In a couple of seconds, while we are still talking, I will be able to send, via the Internet, the text of that individual and so instantly that client will have all the details of the CV and can be looking through it as we talk. That will take no more than 30 seconds to do. Then we can agree that that person should be sent for interview.

Doesn't this sound like another impossible dream? Of course not, said Bergin. 'It will work fine; of that we have no doubt. The two suppliers we are looking to buy from have their products to a high state of development. Their systems have for some period of time supplied the recruitment industry. This story has a happy ending. I don't want people to think, "Oh those poor buggers, they're still saddled with this crock." We've had our crock and now we are coming into a happy ending.'

One moral of the story, he said, is to get a reliable consultant who understands your business.

'We placed too much reliance on the supplier. If you take the analogy of building a house, you don't just have the builder in, you have an architect and surveyor and so forth as well. In this instance it would have served us best to have had independent advice helping us certainly at specification stage. What went wrong was that the supplier had a poor understanding of our business even after they looked at us for some time. They poorly specified the work: the specification documentation and quality were highly substandard. Their choices of hardware and software had some fundamental flaws that were not subsequently rectifiable.'

In this case the suppliers portrayed themselves as experts, but this was not the case. As a result Resources were misled into accepting nascent technology as mature technology. The supplier had intimated that the system was an accepted and acceptable part of its proprietary software product range – and Bergin had believed it.

'The supplier's sales people presented themselves to us,' said Bergin. 'They were already supplying us with hardware. There had been a long relationship with them. In effect they said, "We have just what you need", and put together a proposal, and it seemed fine.

'But we made some fundamental errors. We should have checked out their bona fides better; checked out their track record: we would have found out that they did not have a good track record supplying software. In fact they didn't have any track record.

'Originally we had understood from the supplier that its products were satisfactory and the risks would not be great. However one of the products that this particular supplier produced and said was a marketable item was in fact not marketable and its market position was not what it was intimated to be. It was a catalogue of errors.'

Also, he said, the contract was unsatisfactory.

'We should have had an independent consultant to draft a better list of requirements and functional specifications, and have had better quality control on the suppliers' documentation and understanding of what it is they had to do. We put all our faith in them and they let us down. It was a classic problem and it will never happen again.'

Another mistake, he concedes, is that he bought proprietary packaged software, which was then customised. And, as already mentioned, customised appendages to packages are as useful as dropping a consignment of lead into the basket of a hot-air balloon.

'We will try and avoid customising the new software,' said Bergin, referring to work on the new system. 'We have some specific requirements but we believe that the system already can cater for it. Both of the new systems we are looking at have track records in the States; they are new over here but they have some reasonable pedigree in terms of their initial clients. We have had demonstrations on both of them and they appear to be far, far superior to anything that is locally available.'

Meanwhile a consultant has been hired to try to make the best of the existing badly limping racehorse.

'Some of it now works well enough. We are currently retracing our steps and we will be choosing a replacement soon with new planning and re-implementation during the first half of the year. As far as the existing system is concerned, we will be replacing the whole shooting match; though some of the hardware will be deployed internally – Unisys optical disks, Jukebox, Unix workstations and PCs.'

A pilot will be run on six terminals. If successful it will be extended to about thirty end-users. Bergin said he could not make do with the existing systems because his company is growing too quickly.

Resources International sued its supplier for recovery of the amount spent on the system and the cost to the business of rectifying the problems. A High Court writ seeking £400,000 in damages was issued, which claimed that the system was not of merchantable quality nor fit for its purpose. It was described as poorly designed, unreliable and inaccurate.

'We never did get any compensation from the supplier. They sold themselves out and disintegrated themselves so that they disappeared into the ether from a litigation point of view. There's nothing we can do about it.

'We made some fundamental errors. We should have checked out their financial stability. We just didn't check, and the company wasn't big and strong enough to withstand a knock should they have made a mistake.'

Bergin repeated that there had been a concatenation of mistakes that would never happen again.

'We did see demonstrations of the old system at an early stage but they were appalling. We went ahead with it because of promises of high performance. At that point in time there was nothing else available in terms of CV scanning. The rudiments of it, the principle of it, were good – but as they put the thing together the demonstrations became more and more appalling.'

Bergin believes he has learned the lesson. 'On the new system we have seen the demonstration of the whole thing working. We can actually go to sites and see the whole thing functioning. I am absolutely convinced we won't suffer a disaster again.'

Indeed, nearly two years after this conversation with Bergin I spoke to him again, by which time his company had installed a new system which, he said, had transformed the business – or rather the business had transformed itself to fit the new system. Prior to buying the hardware and software, Bergin had hired a consultant who would understand how the proposed system worked and how Resources would need to adapt its business processes to accommodate the new package.

By the time Bergin signed a contract for the new system, the consultant had become one of the world's foremost experts in the package. Equally important was the fact that the consultant had acquired a knowledge of the business which rivalled that of Bergin himself. This enabled the consultant to document every business and technical process involved in turning on the system in the morning to switching it off at night. It took eighteen months to investigate, identify, assess, train staff and install the system. And to date it is an unequivocal sucess. 'This time we exercised extreme caution, and by changing our business processes we now have much tighter control over them.'

Therefore some of the clearest messages to emerge from this case study are: **don't tailor a package to suit your business, but tailor your business to fit a suitable package. And don't buy the package until you've understood its strengths and limitations as thoroughly as you understand your own business.**

CHAPTER THIRTEEN

The Eighth Deadly Sin: Concealment

I blame Plato for setting a bad example when it comes to openness. In the *Republic* he suggested that censors should ban mothers and nurses from relating tales considered bad or evil. He also campaigned for some unconventional beliefs to be treated as crimes.

Clearly, his liberal ideas had a long-lasting appeal. One of those he influenced, perhaps, was Gaius Caesar. who used to come home from work and get down to his favourite hobby of burning alive those who tried to disseminate bad news. Had the British Prime Minister Margaret Thatcher enjoyed a similar level of authority over her citizens in the 1980s, one wonders whether a pyre might have been built for Peter Wright, a former civil servant who wrote a spicy diary on the day-to-day activities of Britain's secret services.

In corporate life, secrecy is as much a part of history and convention as it is in the government, though there's a difference. Companies tend to be secretive for good commercial reasons. The uniqueness of their products, services and skills is bankable currency to them, and much could be lost if their company secrets became public knowledge.

In government, secrecy is a religion and every civil servant is exhorted to become a fundamentalist. Yet the grounds for secrecy in government are much weaker than those cited by commercial organisations. And it's nothing to do with national security[*].

[*] In the 1990s the Ministry of Defence installed a secure electronic mail system called Chots (Corporate Head Office Technology System) that cost a large sum – £380 million – because it was designed to carry secret messages between defence staffs. But when most of the staff refused to use it because they said it was slow and cumbersome, these

This was revealed in a survey of senior public servants into their attitudes over the public disclosure of a computer and other administrative disasters. They listed their main concern, not as a diminution of service to the public, or an inability to do their job, but that of embarrassment. Perhaps this is because departments want people to believe that they are infallible.

Although there has been no such survey in the private sector, it is not in doubt that in commercial companies there is a tradition of dealing with problems on a departmental level. Any onward transmission of bad news is regarded as an admission of failure, an acknowledgement that middle-line managers have not been able to contain the difficulty.

This is particularly true of the computer department, which, more than any part of the organisation, is perceived as an arcane specialism, and that's the way the computer specialist wants it to remain. For it means that the department is not subject to the same accountability as other parts of the organisation.

At the Performing Right Society those outside the computer department sought, but were unable to obtain, information about progress on the organisation's computer project. At Wessex Regional Health Authority, all the external critics of the massive computer project – including doctors, administrative staff, MPs and journalists – were told not to be so nosy, that everything was fine. Just trust the computer people. At the government's Central Veterinary Laboratory, about £1 million was quietly written off on an overambitious, custom-built software project, but nothing was mentioned in its detailed accounts.

And even as this is written I am being told of new disasters – in two cases involving more than £100 million – which are being concealed from shareholders and the public because of the fear of embarrassment at their disclosure. Ultimately we'll know about them, but only after those involved have left. Meanwhile lack of legally watertight evidence prevents anything being written about them.

Given then that computer sections in government departments and private companies will do all in their power to keep their failures hidden, sometimes even from their boards of directors, it is clear, again, that the onus remains on chief executives to

employees revealed that about 95 per cent of the messages that needed to be sent on the network were unclassified. Had this been realised at the outset of the project, a standard commercial network could have been installed at a fraction of the cost of CHOTS. The other 5 per cent of secret messages could be sent on a smaller purpose-built system.

oversee – personally – large technology projects, if only because they are the ones ultimately responsible for any major failure in their company.

It is the chief executive's job to pry into computer schemes and not to be beaten back by assurances that everything is OK.

The following is one of the more extreme examples of concealment. Interestingly, perhaps, it comes from the US, which in computerisation terms is as inept as the UK but is strangely more open about its cover-ups; they tend eventually to come to public attention. I do not believe that any case similar to the following one would ever be exposed in the UK.

CASE STUDY: It never rains in California

Seven years after the Department of Motor Vehicles embarked on a major computerisation project it had spent nearly $50 million (£31.5 million) – with almost nothing to show for it.

Its one redeeming quality is to show UK disaster victims that they are not alone. US companies also mirror the UK in their unerring faith in consultants, major computer projects and pioneering technologies.

In 1987 the California state department that licences vehicles began a project to redesign its systems and databases. The work was to be undertaken by the Department of Motor Vehicles, which does a similar job to that of the UK's Driver Vehicle Licensing Agency (DVLA), based in Swansea.

In the US, the work of the department was overseen ineffectually by a monitoring body called the Office of Information Technology.

The idea of this department was to keep control over state information technology projects. It didn't – and was later singled out for abolition.

Without adequate monitoring, the Department of Motor Vehicles did what it wanted, which was to build new and pioneering systems – come what may. This fundamentalist approach to computing led to a covering up of cost increases, the overstating of savings, equivocation over technical test results, and even the falsification of records to make an illicit payment to the main supplier, Tandem.

But the nature of the problems might have come to light

earlier if the department had followed a particularly pertinent maxim: **Thou shalt continually seek assurances that a major project is under firm and successful control, and if you believe what you are told without independent verification expect to discover a disaster only when it is self-evident.**

All the department's problems stemmed from one incongruity: it wanted to buy a $3,000 round-the-world air ticket with $100.

Worse, it did not realise it couldn't be done until it had effectively paid 99 per cent of its budget to consultants.

One thing was in the project's favour. It didn't start with a vision. There were perfectly sound reasons for wanting to buy new systems. The department was processing more than a million on-line and batch transactions every day on a variety of large, complex databases, which were supported by thirty-year-old technology. This was intolerable.

Although paper-based processes can have a lifespan of centuries, computer systems are perceived as suffering from dementia after five years. The chips inside the machine can last happily for decades; so can the software. What deteriorates are the skills to maintain software languages that become obsolete.

Suppliers also coerce companies into replacing the old with new, the most persuasive tactic being to charge exorbitantly for supporting ageing operating systems and for hardware spare parts.

So it made sense then for the Department of Motor Vehicles to seek to modernise its systems. Its databases were split into two main functions: driver licence records and details on vehicles; but the two systems were barely compatible, so it was difficult for the department to match personal licence records with those of the vehicles.

This posed a problem when the state tried to pass a law that required the department to refuse to register vehicles whose drivers had been convicted of drink-driving or had refused to pay parking tickets. The department could not match the vehicle registration database with one that held details of driving convictions or parking tickets. So the law was vetoed by the California State Governor because it would have cost too much to link the two databases.

This and other difficulties gave the state an incentive to invest in new technology. The problem was that once the decision had been made to spend vast sums on new systems, the development and managerial teams became obsessed with the project and also acquired a paranoia of failure.

They became computerisation junkies who could not bear the thought of cancellation, and desensitised their minds to the increasing number of problems.

As in nearly every disaster mentioned so far, they became indefatigable in their attempts to scythe a way through the jungle of public relations and technical problems rather than turn back and find the main road.

That the vegetation grew more dense with every step simply strengthened their resolve not to capitulate to common sense.

Originally the department's systems were developed to run on RCA computers but the hardware was later changed in 1981 to Unisys and in 1989 to IBM. In the case of driver licence records, the systems hold more than 30 million entries, and in the case of vehicle registration, 40 million.

Replacing the hardware was fairly straightforward. But in the late 1980s the department decided to change the software, partly because many of the programs were written in a dated language, Assembler, which is no longer in widespread commercial use.

Many of the original programmers had moved on, and it was not easy recruiting people with Assembler skills.

The old age of the systems also made it difficult to extend the software without changes having an unpredictable knock-on effect on other codes in the system.

And there were specific advantages to buying new systems. The technologists would be able to deliver new programs to end-users more quickly using standard software. This would improve the accuracy of records, help collect parking fines and speed up the computer department's responses to irregular information requests. It would also make it easier to modify programs, allow for expansion of the databases and reduce the cost of systems maintenance. The new systems would also meet the political agenda: by addressing the demands of the state legislature.

The new development was expected to cost a mere $29 million, based on a plan to incorporate existing databases into an IBM DB2 relational system, which is used widely around the world – particularly by UK banks such as Barclays and National Westminster.

Had the project managers at least trebled the estimate of $29 million or scaled down the project and bought packaged software, they might have stood a chance of success, for $29 million was far too small a sum for a complex, bespoke system that involved major consultancies and suppliers.

Somewhere along the line, someone seems to have vetoed the IBM DB2 database plan in favour of a shoot-out between IBM and a competitor, Tandem's Nonstop SQL.

To aid a comparison, the department commissioned a simulated database of vehicle registration records. But this was unrepresentative of the actual system because it was too simple.

The simulation contained only 12 to 15 tables of data compared with over 170 used in the actual driver's licence database, so it gave little idea of how the systems would work in a live environment.

The department also scaled down other tests, as if to make the tasks less arduous for either IBM or Tandem. Even at this stage there seems to have been an abject fear that the project might be cancelled, so every effort seems to have been made to complete the tests satisfactorily.

Originally the intention was to carry out 47 operational tests, but there were only 23. The reason given was that there wasn't time to do all the tests; but it is not clear whether the time constraints were imposed artificially because people wanted the project finished, or because there was a genuine need to rush the tests.

No evidence was presented of any genuine need for the rush. The maxim here seems to be: **Thou shalt not set artificially tight deadlines**.

Some tests were deleted because they were considered inapplicable to the products being evaluated. A further ten were deemed to be key tests on which the database would pass or fail.

Of these, six related to system response time, and the other four assessed the system's ability to recover from equipment failures.

Those tests mysteriously dropped included ones that monitored the system's ability to perform certain types of database modifications: update database statistics, upgrade the system's software, recover from an operating system failure, and recover from a data centre power failure.

More ominously, of the tests that were carried out, neither the Tandem Nonstop SQL nor the IBM DB2 passed all of them. Of the ten key tests, Tandem passed nine, and IBM three, and both failed the test designed to show the system's response time while operating in the simulated 'transitional architecture' – a system that would allow the old and new databases to work simultaneously while the new system was gradually phased into operation.

On the basis of this inadequate evaluation Tandem was chosen as hardware and software supplier. So we might add yet another maxim: **Thou shalt not rely on assurances from the supplier that the problems will be sorted out by the time the system is finished**. If the prototype isn't exactly what you want there's no hope for the final system.

Not only did the department guillotine many of the tests, but those it kept were of questionable value. Blatantly, the department set lower performance standards for the new systems than for its existing thirty-year-old ones. In one way this was sensible because it accepted the principle that new systems will do less than the ones they replace.

However this applies only to software features. A company can easily sacrifice, say, a grammar checker in the existing word processor if the new package includes an automatic spelling correction function, but if response times are worse then the new system becomes intolerable.

And the department established a target of 1.5 seconds as the response time per transaction for the new system, even though the current thirty-year-old software already produced response times of between 0.5 and 0.6 of a second, and rarely took more than one second.

Therefore the new system could pass the tests yet lower productivity for both the department's data entry operators and its external end-users.

However, in choosing the relatively slow 1.5 second test criteria, the department was acknowledging that perhaps either the hardware was inadequate or that there was a fundamental problem with the software design and the arrangements for switching off the old and cutting over to the new. These issues clearly needed resolving before further major spending.

Yet, by September 1988, the department formally requested approval from the Office of Information Technology to proceed with the project, saying that it first planned to build a working model.

By December of the same year, only the working model had

been given the go-ahead, and the department was warned not to proceed further with full implementation until the model was demonstrably satisfactory.

But it went ahead with the project anyway, without the sanction of the supervisory Office of Information Technology.

The aim of the model had been to test the software programs, the transitional architecture and a set of new on-line driver's licence transactions; to implement a pilot database; and to confirm cost estimates of subsequent development phases.

The model would also test high-risk features, notably the use of computer-aided software engineering (acronym: Case) tools to rewrite existing programs.

These Case tools were the wonder product of the 1980s. They did not require ordinary mundane programming: the idea was that you told the software what you wanted it to do in simple terms and it would generate the code.

What was not generally fully appreciated was that the code was proprietary. It locked you into the supplier of the Case tool. Any software amendments had to be made with the chosen Case tool. You were a prisoner of the supplier for the life of the software.

Despite this, the department was keen to adopt Case, and commissioned a consultancy, Ernst and Young, to find the right product. A year later Ernst and Young's contract was terminated by mutual agreement after no suitable Case tools were identified.

Unwisely the department did not give up. It tried to continue the idea of moving to Case tools by taking over Ernst and Young's consultant subcontractors.

So by September 1990, the department reported that it had successfully completed the working model, and it was ready to begin full implementation. However the working model had still not successfully achieved its objectives, and the high-risk features had not been adequately tested.

By now, the department had chosen Case tools to rewrite the existing software, but had not successfully determined what the tools were able to do.

A further problem was that the tools worked only with certain versions of the Tandem operating system. So when the department upgraded its Tandem Nonstop SQL operating systems, the new version was incompatible with one of the department's Case tools. Nor could the company that had supplied the tool adapt it to the updated system.

Yet the department was lobbying for the project's continuance by insisting that the new system could save up to $8.9 million a year by the 1998–99 financial year. And it was putting forward those savings on the back of Case tools it was not successfully using.

The savings were not quite plucked out of air – but almost so. They were deduced from a 1981 textbook on software engineering and from a previous pilot study using a different Case tool from the one selected for the project. It took until August 1991 before the department finally admitted that the Case tools selected for the project had failed.

Now facing a project catastrophe because of lack of funds, the department acted decisively: it broke contracting laws to circumvent its budget limits.

It transferred subcontractors working on the project to Tandem; and because it had no money in its existing Tandem budget to pay for the subcontractors, it tried to include their fees under a different budget heading, by amending a maintenance contract between its main data centre and Tandem to include the cost of the subcontractors.

But its parent body, the Department of General Services, disapproved of the idea. It said that it was inappropriate to add consulting services to a maintenance contract.

Still the department did not give up. It sought to conceal the costs of the subcontractors by falsifying records. Later, when Tandem submitted two invoices in September 1992, for $28,000 and $18,000 for the services provided, the department concealed the costs of the subcontractors by showing their fees as a false software purchase order to Tandem for $46,000.

The department also overestimated the potential savings.

It forecast that making the anticipated changes to the driver's licence database would reduce the workload and make thirty existing positions redundant. It also predicted that it could avoid employing a further twenty staff by permitting easier modifications to the driver's licence file.

This saving was not based on benefits demonstrated by the working model, but on a false assumption that these tasks would somehow be made more efficient during the development of the project.

The estimates of the equipment needed were also specious. It predicted that it needed eight Tandem Cyclone machines costing $11.9 million, which were soon delivered.

In reality it needed four times as many Tandem machines, half of which were necessary to meet the department's insistence for continuous availability. So . . . **Thou shalt not buy the hardware until you know exactly what software you intend to use**. When you have chosen the software, test and select the hardware by using loaned equipment from suppliers, at their site or, ideally, yours. And there's no point in blaming the hardware response times if the software is badly designed.

Also, the deception over the tests would have been detected if there had been a regular independent verification or audit, whereby the auditors would report not to the computer department but to the chief executive or equivalent.

In fact there were independent reviews, but they came too late; and even then nobody seems to have taken any notice of their warnings.

Worse still, there is no evidence that the department had allowed for stop-or-go points along the way to provide for early termination of the project.

By October 1991, the project was in such disarray that Tandem offered to validate and where necessary modify the plans for the driver's licence system. The department accepted Tandem's assistance, and the company submitted its report in June 1992, whereupon the department increased the project's estimated costs from $31.4 million to $57.3 million, and extended the estimated completion date by three and a half years, from July 1995 to December 1998.

In April 1993 Tandem, now working jointly with the US computer services company EDS, began cooperating with the department on yet another project plan, which was submitted for approval in November 1993. But by now the costs estimate for finishing the project had soared from the original $29 million to about $185 million . . . more than 90 per cent of it comprising Tandem's and EDS's costs.

Under this new scheme Tandem and EDS would manage the project, and the current systems, and would guarantee that the new development would be completed within a given period.

But the State of California would not sanction spending $185 million when $49.4 million had already been consumed to no useful effect. So the project was cancelled.

The irony of the disaster was that, if the $185 million had been spent, we would probably not be writing now about the failure of the systems. With such a vast budget undoubtedly EDS and Tandem would have delivered satisfactory systems. But would it have been worth it?

When it was discovered that the UK's Department of Employment had spent £48 million on a Field system that was considered unsuitable and was rejected by many end-users, MPs said that public money had been spent on a Rolls-Royce to carry potatoes. If the US system had cost $185 million it might have faced accusations about potatoes and Cadillacs.

After the failure of the Californian project, the State Auditor's autopsy report said that, if the project had been halted after the working-model stage, the total bill would have been 'only' $14.8 million, incorporating $8.3 million to develop the system, and obligations of $6.5 million to buy computers.

Instead, the department laboured to spend another $34.6 million bringing the total amount wasted to $49.4 million, and, crucially, the system failed because of unresolved technical and performance problems already identified during the developmental stages of the project.

Having given assurances to the Office of Information Technology that it would develop a working model of the system, on which future decisions on feasibility could be based, the department had then failed to develop the model; but had pressed on with the project regardless.

It also ignored all the feedback it received on the problems identified from the half-working model; and before long, it was ignoring independent reviews of the project as well.

According to the State Auditor's report, formal quality assurance was non-existent. This would have provided a check on systems development projects 'to ensure an independent and impartial assessment of the project's methods and techniques and of the work products produced'.

This supervision is like the work of building inspectors who keep an independent watch over a construction to ensure it conforms with accepted standards.

Yet at no stage, it later emerged, did the department establish a formal quality-assurance function.

In its semi-contrite response to the State Auditor's report, the department suggested that the project's failure was not in its initiation nor its strategy but in its execution. Specifically, it agreed that the underlying causes of failure were that:

• the 1988–89 operational assessment to prove the applicability of relational technology was flawed;

• a pilot to demonstrate proof of concept was terminated before it was completed;

• three business areas – driver licensing, vehicle licensing and occupational licensing – were wrongly combined into a single architecture, eliminating the need for subsequent feasibility study reports;

• the department believed it could complete the project itself through the use of independent consultants and Case tools.

It also agreed that the project should have been stopped and reassessed in 1990, and that a formal project costs-accounting system should have been used.

It accepted that a fictitious purchase order had been raised, and that contractors had been allowed to begin work before contracts or contract amendments had been finalised.

The California State's Office of Information Technology also responded to the report, admitting its superintendence of the project 'left much to be desired'. It said it had started pursuing new and innovative methods of acquiring information technology that 'reduces financial risks to the State and gives vendors a greater financial stake in a project's success.'

It cited one contract in which the Franchise Tax Board's plan to replace its twenty-year old systems would involve a supplier paying the up-front costs for both hardware and software, and being paid only if the system produces predefined goals for increasing state revenue.

This is one of the best ways to avoid a disaster (although it is not without its risks) whereby you pay nothing until the supplier delivers the promised business benefits.

This is similar to the partnership arrangements suggested in earlier chapters in which the suppliers share in the business profits related to a successful project, or make a loss if the systems fail.

One of the few drawbacks is that many suppliers will refuse to sign such a contract; and if they do the agreement will need to be drafted punctiliously to protect your interests; and these genuine partnership arrangements can cost a premium price because, if the project is successful, you are paying the supplier's costs, its profit margin, plus a share of the return in your investment in the system.

However this is only fair if you are expecting the supplier to take a loss if the project is abandoned.

But the biggest lesson from the department's fiasco was that companies must have ways of ensuring that bad news travels to the top of the pyramid.

And this can happen only if the chief executive takes more than a passing interest in the computer project. Even then the bad news could get hijacked somewhere along the route.

So how does a chief executive know when information is being concealed by line managers? There's a simple test.

The idea comes from a highly secretive and racist political party in the US, which was devoted to stopping immigrants obtaining high office in the nineteenth century.

The party had a coordinated approach to outsiders who asked them about their membership practices and policies.

'I don't know,' the member would always reply. Hence the party became known as the Know-Nothings.

And if, as a chief executive, you question your managers about progress on the latest £10 million project and you find that the computer department is full of know-nothings, perhaps it's time to prepare to panic.

CHAPTER FOURTEEN

The Ninth Deadly Sin: Buck-passing

The subtle avoidance of responsibility when things go wrong is as much a British tradition as greasy fish and chips – and just as healthy.

However there is a marked difference in the attitudes towards accountability in the public and private sectors.

In the private sector there is the natural feeling that, in any disaster, somebody should be willing to take the blame, which is why it is always someone else's fault.

In the public sector whenever something goes wrong, and for some unusual reason it can't be covered up, there will be an inquiry, which will clear *all* individuals of any responsibility.

Indeed, the National Audit Office, which oversees spending on computerisation in government, studiously avoids blaming individuals.

And the organisations it sometimes criticises in its reports always respond by saying they have already addressed the problems identified by the Audit Office. They say this even when the problems recur a few years later and another disaster comes to light that is investigated by the Audit Office. They argue that the disaster was caused by new problems.

Therefore buck-passing has to be accepted because it is part of the British way of life. The standard has been set at the highest level of government and has matured over centuries of practice.

That this is possible is because of the power of the civil service, which has grown through necessity. It can, perhaps, be traced back to Sir Robert Walpole, wrongly regarded as Britain's first prime minister, who worked a clever ruse: he secured a Civil List (pots of money) for the King, ensured that the King retained power over the House of Lords, ensured that the House of Commons retained power over the King, and ensured that he, Walpole, retained power over the House of Commons, which is why he was dubbed prime minister, largely as a slur. As a means of self-preservation and as a check against the autocratic powers of the prime minister and his cabinet, the civil service, over the centuries, has acquired the art of stage-managing the prime minister, as astutely satirised in the British TV series *Yes Minister*. In this, civil servants hold their minister in affected awe, and swell his head with a small number of things they want him to know, so that there is no room for the innumerable things they don't want him to know.

On the 250th anniversary of Walpole's death, the Scott Inquiry (also known as the Arms-to-Iraq inquiry) showed that civil service power has come of age. In this instance, Whitehall was perfectly happy for innocent company directors to go to jail rather than allow them to embarrass officialdom and the government.

And on many occasions, too numerous to mention, officialdom and even ministers have forcefully denied the existence of a grievous mistake in their departments only to find that evidence of that mistake has surfaced publicly, whereupon the minister informs Parliament that he had mistakenly misled the House. Every time the incident is quickly forgotten.

Whether such behaviour is right or wrong is not a matter that should be debated here. Suffice to say that the British system of government and administration is an obstacle to good project management, because the avoidance of accountability is an obstacle to good project management.

It's a not dissimilar story in the US, although the Americans have had less time in history for their administrations to develop a structure that is quite as self-serving as the British executive and legislature. The US system still, in most quarters, enforces accountability, rigorously, to the point where public sector departments become more imaginative and industrious about covering up their mistakes, as at the Department of Motor Vehicles in California (see previous chapter).

In general, however, US disasters tend to be investigated thoroughly and blame apportioned where possible, thus deterring would-be blunderers. After the Pearl Harbor fiasco a congressional committee placed the primary blame on General

Short and Admiral Kimmel, who were declared guilty of errors of judgement. And President Nixon, after a long struggle, was forced out of office for behaviour that might have been regarded in the UK as legitimate political manoeuvring.

That is not to say that nobody is *ever* held to account in Britain. Where there is a public outcry over a monumental blunder then that most vital component of the British system comes into play: the scapegoat.

In biblical history the scapegoat was an unfortunate animal that stood impassively while sinners crowded around it and watched as a priest spiritually transferred their misdeeds onto the goat, whereupon the creature was sent into the wilderness or pushed off a cliff. Thus the failure of the London Ambulance system led to the resignations of the service's chief executive and his deputy but not any of their overseers at the Department of Health and at the House of Commons.

Of course this dearth of regulation, and the haphazard application of convention in matters of establishing responsibility, poses real problems when managing a computer project because it means that when anything goes wrong the fingers of blame will start pointing everywhere and nowhere in particular.

Yet it is vital for someone – a named, clearly identifiable person – to know that their head will roll if things go badly wrong *whoever else is blame*. This gives the named person an incentive to cancel an irretrievable project before too much has been spent on it. But who?

In theory chief executives can appoint someone other than themselves to be the undisputed head of a project; but this rarely works in practice because, if things go wrong, the appointee will blame their lack of authority to make the major organisational decisions that needed to be made, or their inability to extract vital information from uncooperative end-users.

In short – and it has been said before – the buck has to stop with the chief executive.

In acknowledgement of this, some artful chief executives have hired consultancies or other external suppliers to take full responsibility for project management. But this will not tend to work either.

Most likely, a consultancy that is put into an all-powerful position may be unable to resist the temptation to extract for itself a large portion of the project's budget because it has been placed in the position of Chancellor of the Exchequer, the main recipient of the funds and arbiter on how the money should be spent.

So what do chief executives do? Understandably they will want to duck responsibility for computerisation because they have other more pressing duties, such as running the company. *But they adopt this attitude at their peril.*

The following case study is an exquisite example of what happens in a disaster, where the customer blames the supplier and vice versa, and an outsider stands no hope of establishing where the blame really lies. The vague truth, as in all disasters, is that both sides must bear some responsibility for underestimating the risks.

The case also draws attention to one of the most common apparent causes of a disaster: hardware that is too small to deliver decent response times at the terminal.

In fact, as the evidence in this case shows, it is not the choice of hardware that is to blame but an unanticipated change in the demands on the system and a possible underestimation of the predicted workloads.

CASE STUDY

The sunshine state of Florida is one of the richest states in America. And its computer services partner EDS is one of the most profitable computer companies in the world. But it was not a perfect match.

When they joined hands in a contract to manage the computerisation of welfare benefits for the disadvantaged, the two became locked in a vicious court battle that dragged on for years.

The case involved more twists than President Nixon in the final hours of his fiefdom. The $60 million lawsuit also involved the UK's Child Support Agency, whose systems were originally similar to those in Florida. The case also took in a panoply of state courts, which fed a large number of lawyers.

The affair began in May 1989 when the two protagonists signed an agreement for EDS to supply a system, based on IBM 3090 mainframe computers, that would help to support such projects as Aid for Dependent Children, Food Stamps, Medicaid Eligibility, Child Support Enforcement and Refugee and Entrant Assistance.

The plan was to *integrate* six software modules, covering these social and welfare area , but, as explained in earlier chapters, integration is the most dangerous word in the computing lexicon. It's much better to build small self-contained modules that can work independently of each other than be reliant on all the elements working as a homogeneous whole.

In its original specifications Florida said it would prefer a distributed system that would not depend on a single computer processor.

However, when it formally invited suppliers to bid, it gave them the freedom to propose any equipment configuration provided it guaranteed that the system performance could cope with at least a 120 per cent increase in the projected 1993 departmental caseload level of over 2.3 million cases.

It is this forecast that was at the core of the courtroom wrangles.

In documents outlining its complaint against EDS to the Florida courts, the state's Department of Health and Rehabilitative Services (HRS) insisted that, because of the expected growth in social service programmes, the system should have been designed to cope with any future loads without adversely affecting the overall configuration.

The state said that EDS had insisted that its proposed CRIS-E system design offered 'tomorrow's solution today'. The system also promised 'powerful and proven hardware and software components for maximum reliability and performance'.

Also, said Florida, EDS had suggested that, based on the CRIS-E system, an IBM 3090-300E mainframe computer would handle the caseload stipulated in the invitation to tender and still leave 20 per cent of the machine's capacity free. At the same time, it would provide the response times at the terminal that the state wanted.

In addition, the state claimed, EDS suggested that the IBM 3090 series of mainframes would provide more than 100 per cent performance growth over the predicted 1993 volumes.

Florida admitted that it relied on EDS's recommendation that, as the transaction volumes did not flow through the system in an average fashion, the system should be designed to cope with 'peak' volumes, which for modelling purposes, EDS estimated would be 20 per cent above the 'average' volume.

Later in its claim, Florida suggested EDS had underestimated this peak, adding that the supplier should have known that it had got its sums wrong.

It was the state's contention that EDS knew what it was doing because its technical expertise was superior to that of the HRS staff.

But EDS's case against the state was that some caseloads did indeed 'greatly exceed projections' but that it was Florida's fault for drawing up 'erroneous' initial forecasts of cases, which led to an undersizing of the new system.

EDS also claimed in its court statements that 'unfortunately the atmosphere at HRS was not conducive to admitting mistakes'.

In August 1989, three months after signing the contract, EDS wanted to change the agreement, and proposed an amendment that would have changed the system's architecture from a partially distributed one to a centralised one requiring a larger mainframe computer than the IBM 3090-300E originally suggested.

After using an IBM monitoring tool designed to provide a 'snapshot' of the IBM 3090-300E's performance, EDS said the results suggested that a more modern 3090-300J would handle the workload, providing acceptable response times at the terminals of end-users.

Late the following year, according to the state's legal documents, EDS realised it had a problem with the system. The design would not allow it to measure performance in accordance with the response-time categories detailed in the agreement between the two parties. This, according to the state, was one factor in EDS's not being able to predict accurately the loads on the system.

Florida also claimed that, rather than inform HRS that the system design was causing the problem, EDS had claimed that the problem was caused by changes made by HRS to the system. EDS denies this.

By April 1991, when a pilot office system went live, it was discovered that many more transactions than anticipated were going through the system. The state claimed that response times were so poor that EDS's own employees were reported to have complained that they were unable to test the system properly.

The effect on the 3090-300J mainframe was that it reached its maximum capacity at between 1.2 and 1.5 million transactions a day, though the agreed transaction level needed to support

Florida's growing caseload was 3.356 million a day.

Soon the relationship between the two sides deteriorated. Florida said it was unhappy that it was unable to get performance data from EDS on the 3090-300J to see whether the machine was overloaded. EDS found that a 'fear factor' within HRS inhibited decision-making.

To support this claim, EDS quoted from a report by the Florida Governor's Chief Inspector General: 'The corporate culture at HRS seemed to promote and reward those who did not raise problems; and thus the Secretary [head of HRS] was often the last – not the first – to know.'

By the end of September 1991, two out of the eleven HRS districts had begun using the Florida system. The state said that response times were poor, and the other nine districts had not linked into the system.

EDS has always maintained that the problems are not its fault. In a letter to the state's secretary Robert Williams, an EDS vice-president blamed 'the immense increase in caseloads' generated by the state.

A subsequent letter from EDS's President George Newstrom reiterated that the costs would have to be borne by the state.

The partnership continued to break apart, as the two sides tried to find a solution to the capacity problem and Florida's caseload grew inexorably.

Because of the additional cases, HRS's required computer capacity reached over four million transactions a day. Eventually, HRS, EDS, and its subcontractor, IBM, agreed that a bigger machine – a combined IBM 600J/720 system (the 720 was one of IBM's largest commercial mainframe computers appropriate to Florida's needs at the time) – would suffice. HRS would pay 35 per cent of the cost of the computer upgrade.

But the uncertainties remained. Linking the IBM 3090-600J and the 3090-720 mainframes was far from straightforward. The idea was that both machines would be able to handle 4.4–5 million transactions a day.

Florida learned that, to achieve a bridge between the two machines, EDS planned to use an IBM product, IRLM. This would allow both machines to work together as if they were one, and yet still be independent of each other.

There were two drawbacks, according to HRS, which says it discovered that:

- IRLM would not be able to handle the workload demands expected;
- The product would use around 20 per cent of the capacities of the 600J and 720 machines which, in HRS's view, was 'an unacceptable level of overhead'.

What all this was implying was that, as at the Performing Right Society, if the loads on the system are too great, the computer systems can slow almost to a halt.

Early the following year, in March 1992, the two sides clashed again, this time over a benchmark test intended to show that the chosen hardware was up to the job.

HRS alleged that EDS conducted the test on 13 March in secrecy, then transmitted the test results to HRS, saying that the Florida system had passed the test, and demanding payment for the central site computer equipment.

Clearly the relationship had collapsed. As the year wore on, HRS claims the Florida system experienced instability and unreliability problems with frequent crashes.

During these unproductive periods, the state says its system could not be used for any business purpose. Florida also claims it was forced to turn away its customers or claimants who had to stand in long queues for hours to receive benefits. This led to 'innumerable' complaints from both customers and staff, as well as unfavourable publicity over the 'excessive' delays in the issuance of benefits.

By the time the contract was officially terminated on 1 June 1992, HRS was maintaining that EDS had delivered a system based on a configuration that was 'unproven, inflexible and insufficient to meet the capacity requirements, either present or future'.

Two months later, in August, HRS, to try to prevent the system crashes and poor response times, went to IBM for another hardware upgrade which cost over $13 million.

Florida today insists that, because of the problems, some of the older systems have had to remain in use to provide back-up or to supplement existing operations. That, the state says, has led to financial losses because the extra systems should already have been shut down or phased out when districts cut over to Florida.

Three months after the termination of the contract, the two sides resorted to lawyers, beginning a legal battle that lasted more than three years.

In September 1992, EDS sued HRS seeking damages of over $40 million for non-payment of bills relating to development work on the project. HRS immediately counter-sued for $65 million damages, alleging breach of contract and warranty.

Two years into their legal dispute, both sides agreed to 'alternative dispute resolution' (ADR) which avoided a full-blown court case. A 'Special Master' – in this case the former CIA head William Webster – was appointed to adjudicate between them.

His judgement was that the state owed EDS $50 million and, late in December 1995, a circuit judge backed EDS and said the state should be held to Webster's ruling.

The state said it would appeal to the district court and, if necessary, to the state's Supreme Court. It even wanted to prevent EDS doing more business in Florida, and urged other states to take notice.

The view from EDS was that its design was not at fault and that the system problems were caused by the department. The supplier described the state's lawsuit as 'outrageous' and called it a 'smokescreen' to avoid payment. 'This case will cost Florida $13,000 [£8,666] a day in interest until it is settled,' said an EDS spokesman.

Merv Fortney, the president of EDS's state and local government unit, said Florida should pay up and 'stop wasting money on baseless legal manoeuvring'. And EDS's government services spokesman Randy Dove added that the CRIS-E system worked and had been described as functionally rich. He said that the contract had been hindered by changes in the political colour of Florida's administration and by the growing number of cases, some of which had been caused by a number of natural disasters such as Hurricane Andrew.

EDS also attacked the state's 'adversarial atmosphere' and said this helped to destroy the prospect of the two sides 'working together to serve Florida's needs and to gain the fruits of the contract'.

The supplier added: 'The undisputed facts will show that this unworkable atmosphere led EDS to negotiate ... and end its relationship with HRS. Notwithstanding all these problems, the Florida system has been a success for HRS, despite systematic legislative underfunding and despite HRS's difficulties in operating and maintaining the system. Without the Florida system, HRS simply could not have handled the enormous growth in welfare caseloads, at least without an equally large increase in funding and caseworkers.'

There was never any doubt in the minds of senior EDS executives that they would end up as the victor. 'We want to get this case settled, and get our payments from the state,' said Dove. 'Not only have they yet to win a case in court, they have yet to prove they have a case.'

Indeed EDS was awarded much of the money it had sought from the state. Eventually a court ruled that the state of Florida should pay EDS $42.8 million (around £30m) to settle all disputes relating to the system developed and implemented by EDS. This compares with the $55 million originally sought by EDS. The case is now over.

Putting aside the detailed issues in this case, it does not take a Supreme Court judge to see what has apparently gone wrong in this and so many other computerisation failures. There has been an underestimation of the difficulties of computerisation. **Had the state meticulously calculated the cost of the project and then multiplied by three, it would then have been able to afford the necessary upgrades when the forecast workloads increased. Its relationship with EDS might now be unassailable.**

As it was, there appears to have been little room to accommodate large-scale unforeseen changes.

Clearly customers and suppliers should always expect the unexpected and in computerisation projects the unexpected means that there will always be more demands on the hardware than originally anticipated. When this happens, it's usually too late for the customer to expect the supplier to face the consequences.

However, in the Florida case, neither side showed any spark of willingness to quit until it had won a resounding victory. Often this is unwise, because in many disasters the fault does not lie with one party but with both sides underestimating the risks, and with both sides anticipating the benefits too easily and too keenly.

A failure to acknowledge this will lead usually to the buck being passed from supplier to customer or vice versa. But once a legal action has been started it's a runaway train as some of the following case studies show.

CHAPTER FIFTEEN

The Tenth Deadly Sin: Lawyers (I)

During the very early stage of courting, when suppliers are pluming their iridescent feathers to attract customers, much of the chit-chat is studiously not about the terms of the contract.

Neither is it about selling products or services. The early discussions are designed to assure prospective customers of the solidity of the supplier, the quality of support over the lifetime of the product or services, and generally to make would-be buyers feel encased in a womb of professionalism, expertise and caring.

Only once trust has been firmly established are the products and services introduced tentatively into conversations. Later there are the no-commitment demonstrations, presentations to potential end-users, and eventually final negotiations on price.

By the time a provisional deal is agreed, the customer's confidence in the supplier is now as good as it is going to get.

And that is why the terms of the contract are often overlooked: because the customer feels so securely swathed in the supplier's verbal assurances that the contract seems to be a legal interference with the relationship. The mere mention of lawyers is as distasteful as discussing a pre-nuptial financial contract with your would-be spouse.

Once the customer has come so far, and has established a seemingly insoluble partnership, it is impossible to envisage the *possibility* of a breakdown, let alone the consequences of one.

But the supplier has been through it all before, perhaps a hundred or a thousand times, and although the 'standard terms and conditions' seem innocuous enough, they are usually designed to minimise the customer's protection in the event of a disaster.

It may also be worth bearing in mind that when lovers fall out, the animosity is much greater than if the two parties had hardly known each other.

Indeed several of the following cases show that legal actions have more to do with feelings of betrayal, animosity and the desire for revenge than any pragmatic desire for recompense for a lost investment.

In computer cases the law is usually an ass: but the judges are not. Their decisions tend to be surprisingly rational. Judges seem to take the view that those who sue must have a genuine grievance or else they wouldn't go to the trouble of suing (or it could be that judges unconsciously support those who indirectly pay their wages – anyone who issues a writ keeps alive the civil courts system).

It's only a personal view, and I know that some lawyers disagree, but it seems to me that the civil law in the 1990s has shown a marked tendency to sympathise with those who issue the first writ.

This could be why, as soon as a disaster is imminent, the legal initiative is usually seized by the supplier.

The usual sequence of events is this:
• the delivered system does not meet the customer's expectations;
• the customer refuses to pay the bill;
• the supplier sues for non-payment.

This is shrewd because the supplier's writ usually arrives just as the customer is most distracted by the failure of the system and is trying to maintain a façade of commercial respectability to hide an administration in chaos.

The customer has not even thought yet of suing the supplier; but once you have received a writ, you are on the defensive. And there is no hope now of avoiding hours of management time visiting lawyers, answering the supplier's allegations, providing proof of your statements, and counter-suing by drawing up your own list of allegations that look more plausible than those of the supplier. This process can take weeks, months or even a decade, as a later case study shows.

Standard Chartered Bank was one of the companies that, following a project disaster, found itself defending a writ from the supplier.

The bank had hired a major company to supply systems to link its mainframe computers in Hong Kong, New York and London. A £2.8 million project, which had begun in 1987, was abandoned in 1990 because the supplier, according to the bank, failed to supply a system that was operable. But the supplier had taken the initiative by issuing a writ for non-payment of £1.7 million, the cost of the system.

Audaciously, Standard Chartered stole the show by issuing a counter-claim for £9 million and sent a press release to newspapers and business magazines proclaiming that it was suing its supplier.

The bank's announcement declared that its supplier had:
• failed to produce a quality plan until two years into the project;
• failed to manage the project adequately or at all;
• failed to inform the bank that it had assessed the project as high risk;
• completely underestimated the scale of changes that would be needed to an existing system to bring it up to scratch;
• cut corners in unit, system and installation testing of the software.

This was only the beginning. The bank further unnerved the supplier by announcing that the case would be 'one of the largest and most expensive pieces of computer litigation yet seen in the United Kingdom'.

The supplier was thrown back on the defensive, for the bank's resources were greater than its own. And if the bank was willing to sink its money into retribution, there was every reason for the supplier to settle.

Also, Standard Chartered's public declaration ignored the fact that it was counter-suing the supplier. One would easily have thought that it had initiated the action.

If it was another intimidatory move, it worked. The case was settled amicably without Standard Chartered losing any money; though another factor may also have encouraged the supplier to settle.

Standard Chartered suggested that it would award the supplier another valuable contract if a favourable settlement could be reached.

On this occasion the customer proved more wily than the supplier. Usually it is the supplier who knows much more about the law and how to put it to best advantage.

Yet, during the pre-contract negotiations, the supplier may

disingenuously hide the extent of its knowledge and experience, especially when negotiating with a naïve user. It may even feign a mousy timidity.

It may also wax unctuous about the need for a partnership and an in-depth understanding of each other's business. The suggestion is that if the customer's business fails because of computerisation, the supplier will dive into icy waters rather than allow the client to drown.

Not being able to imagine a confrontation with such an honest, sympathetic and reputable company, inexperienced users drop their guard and sign the supplier's contract, which can snuff out an effective comeback over any serious lapse by the supplier.

This credulousness on the part of the customer is more common than might be imagined. At an IBM Computer Users' Association meeting in St Albans in 1994, I was surprised (and so were many members of the audience) at the large number of computer managers who admitted that they had not inserted penalty clauses into their contracts with suppliers.

These are clauses that allow users to seek financial compensation if the supplier breaks any terms or conditions of the contract. The conference delegates said they did not need onerous clauses: they trusted their suppliers.

However, Wessex Regional Health Authority, which had agreed to waive some of its legal protections in return for maintaining the goodwill of suppliers, lost millions of pounds. In one contract it specifically sought the removal of penalty clauses.

But customers often do not realise the extent to which their trusted supplier/partners are acclimatised to confrontation. Some suppliers know that if they issue the writ first, particularly if they suspect they may be in the wrong, the defensive and vulnerable user will be encouraged to settle out of court.

Such an arrangement could be far less damaging to the supplier than if the customer sued first. If that happened the customer would be more than likely to win costs and substantial damages, especially as civil judges are tending to side with the inexperienced user against the worldly-wise supplier.

Not that that makes it any easier for users to sue. It can take years for a case to come to court; and, even if the user wins, the losing party will probably lodge an appeal, which could extend the legal process by a further year or more – by which time the user, if it has not gone out of business, may have lost the stomach for a fight, or simply will not have any more management time to spare on the appeal preparations. Another danger for the customer who wants to sue first is that employing lawyers and 'experts' to substantiate your case could cost a medium-sized business £300,000 – even before the court hearing, which is likely to double this figure. Some experts will tout for business among disaster victims on the promise that they will encourage suppliers to settle quickly. This is highly unlikely. Most major suppliers have greater resources than their customers and are better able to fight a long battle.

In short, justice tends to come down on the party that has the tenacity, money and time to pursue an action. That party might not necessarily be in the right.

In two of the UK's biggest disasters – the Performing Right Society's PROMS project and Wessex Regional Health Authority's RISP scheme – legal proceedings were concluded unsatisfactorily for both sides in each case.

Although Wessex was encouraged by district auditors to seriously consider legal action against suppliers, when it examined the possibility, it found that its contracts favoured the suppliers. In one major deal, Wessex had put forward the contract it had wanted the supplier to sign, whereupon the supplier had amended or deleted virtually every clause it saw as unfavourable and then signed it.

In the end Wessex sued (or, rather, counter-sued) only one supplier – and only after the supplier had issued a writ for non-payment. The case was eventually settled out of court. It is understood that the authority did not even recover all its legal costs.

The Performing Right Society also settled out of court by accepting compensation from one of its suppliers, but again this was less than half of its stated losses from the project's failure.

The court cases detailed in this and the following two chapters show that, although the minutiae of the wording of contractual clauses and their interpretations are argued over during cases, when there is an ambiguity, the judges will usually interpret the wording as rationally as any ordinary person in the street.

Even so, the law remains a lottery to some extent. One of the best descriptions of the processes of the civil courts is given by Jonathan Swift in *Gulliver's Travels*.

He observed that, if your neighbour steals your cow and you go to court to get it back, the arguments will not focus on who owns the cow but whether the 'said cow were red or black, her horns long or short; whether the field I graze her in be round or square, whether she were milked at home or abroad, what diseases she is subject to, and the like; after which they consult precedents, adjourn the case and in ten, twenty, or thirty years come to an issue.'

That was written in 1726 and is as relevant today. The abilities of individual barristers, the strength or otherwise of pedantic legal arguments, contractual ambiguities, the experience or otherwise of the defendants, contention over the weight of certain circumstances and conversations, precedents, the availability or otherwise of witnesses and their credibility in the witness box are more important factors than who owns the cow.

Another factor today is the judge's understanding of computer technology. Some judges are tediously and punctiliously syllogistic in their deductions and seem, like Socrates, to come up with logical answers in the end. Others seem to think that all software should be as robust as Windows 95, which it should be in an ideal world. However few software suppliers have the resources of Microsoft with which to test a new piece of software. Therefore customers must expect most new software products to contain bugs, some serious. The question is: to what degree are the bugs acceptable?

You may say no bugs are acceptable and the law would probably back you up. In 1996 the Appeal Court in London ruled for the first time that packaged software is 'goods' under the Sale of Goods Act. This means it must be as fit for its purpose as a new vacuum cleaner or washing machine. If it is not, you can get your money back – in theory. In practice suppliers can argue that software is not as self-contained as a dishwasher. Software works in conjunction with unpredictable hardware such as power supplies, volatile memory and accident-prone disk drives. So nothing is clear-cut when it comes to the law and software. The law is even murkier when it encounters software that has been modified. The only thing that is certain is that seeking a legal remedy is a hazardous and costly journey.

Also, the law offers little guidance to help customers determine whether they should write their own contracts rather than sign the supplier's standard terms and conditions.

Some cases show that the customer's naïvety went in their favour. If they merely accepted the supplier's standard terms and conditions, and these terms and conditions were deemed to be unreasonable by a judge, the court would probably rule in the customer's favour in any dispute. Conversely, if the user organisation had obtained expert advice in the drafting of the contract, and had renegotiated some of the clauses in the supplier's contract, in law the customer would be left more isolated. It would probably have to suffer the consequences of any legal agreement that was badly drafted or failed to confer adequate protection.

Yet, on balance, it is probably still better for the canniest customers to write their own contract and persuade the supplier to sign it even if the salespeople and their lawyers throw tantrums.

This is because a tightly worded contract that sets out *in detail* each party's responsibilities and the penalty clauses is likely to deter a supplier from taking a case to court in any dispute.

Incidentally the phrase 'penalty clause' is shunned by the legal establishment because of its undoubted clarity. The legal jargon is 'liquidated damages'.

The petroleum conglomerate BP is one of the few companies to draw up its own services contracts for suppliers to sign. For example, it spent six months negotiating a major computer supply contract. On several occasions, during the legal discussions, lawyers acting for the suppliers refused to agree to contractual commitments insisted upon by BP.

When both sides refused to capitulate, the suppliers' lawyers left the room. Once tempers cooled, the suppliers always returned to the table. And BP pushed through its requirements.

At the last minute, shortly before the contract was due to be signed, new lawyers acting for the suppliers intervened and refused to sanction the deal.

Again BP refused to compromise – and its perseverance paid off.

Today, BP has a remarkable contract which, in effect, reduces its payments to the suppliers for computer services if the oil price goes down. That is like having a car that automatically reduces its fuel consumption when the driver is short of money, though it has to be said that BP pays more if the savings from the contract go beyond an agreed sum.

That BP was victorious in its negotiations with suppliers was not merely because of its commercial clout, but because computer companies in the current competitive climate will rarely walk away from potentially good business.

If, even after BP-type bullying, the suppliers still do not sign a reasonable contract drafted by your lawyers, the reason is probably that they do not want to face the consequences of failure. In effect, their rejection of your contract could be an acknowledgement of the likelihood of a disaster.

Some of the biggest user companies have their contracts drafted by lawyers acting on the advice of disaffected former employees of major suppliers. The ex-employees know the tricks of the trade, particularly if they have legal experience.

But even if you have a sound contract and a solid case you may not win a legal hearing. When Resources International sued for £400,000 over the failure of its UNIX-based system, the supplier metamorphosed into untouchable guises. As far as litigation was concerned the supplier became invisible.

Another customer, a furniture retail group called Saxon Hawk, which had 41 stores around the UK in 1992, was luckier. It sued only weeks before the supplier went into liquidation.

Sheffield-based Saxon Hawk, formerly known as Gillow, had a well-drafted contract stipulating that, if the supplier failed to meet any date for delivery of a customised accounting and stock-control system, then the supplier would have to return all the money it had received from Saxon Hawk, without any deductions for costs or expenses.

The contract also set out in detail a timetable and requirements for acceptance tests. Clearly, Saxon Hawk had not signed a standard supplier's contract.

By 1992 the supplier had failed to provide a variety of systems by the required dates. These included:
• a sales-order processing system that showed how well individual salespeople had performed in relation to targets;
• packaged stock-control software to analyse data on prices and stock values branch by branch;
• a sales ledger that included credit notes issued and a refunds analysis;
• a nominal ledger.

Saxon Hawk found that the delivered software contained 'hundreds of bugs'. In one case the system did too much: it posted each and every written line of every order form to the nominal ledger, thereby soaking up processor capacity and unnecessarily using up expensive disk storage space.

Other problems included orders being mistakenly cancelled by the system, trouble with confirming the dispatch of goods, difficulties calculating discounts for early settlement and a nominal ledger imbalance.

The customer gave its supplier a stipulated time to correct the defects, but no remedy materialised. In the end Saxon Hawk terminated the contract and issued a writ claiming back the £88,979 it had already paid as deposit on the £245,000 system, plus two other stage payments – a total of £173,457.

At the time, Richard Adams, Saxon Hawk's group finance director, said, 'It is a disaster in terms of performance. In order to open up new stores we need the new system. We feel quite bitter.' A particular defect he said was that staff were unable to follow through a customer order on the system without encountering an electronic brick wall. The supplier had originally promised that the software would feed back better information about the stock and sales performance in Saxon Hawk's 41 retail stores.

But the failure had left the end-users reverting to their 'old and ponderous' Bull DPS system.

During the court case the supplier fiercely contested the action. But it was an unusually short hearing. The court decided in Saxon Hawk's favour and awarded it £100,000 in compensation.

The supplier paid over the money – and promptly went into liquidation.

After the case John Yates, the solicitor acting for Saxon Hawk said:

The action is typical of the growing number of disputes between suppliers and users. Despite the fact that Saxon Hawk took the precaution of appointing management consultants to help them specify their requirements in writing, they became the victim of the supplier's failure to appreciate the full scale of the development work. To avoid disputes like this suppliers will need to refine their methods for software estimating, project management and quality control.

Yates is right, though perhaps it is also possible to put the problem more bluntly.

Suppliers often sell their software by exploiting the public perception that computerisation is a science rather than what it really is: a skilled, imaginative but sometimes bizarre art form that occasionally impresses and more often doesn't.

However, the courts are growing wise to this. Two cases in particular give a good insight into the attitude of judges in computer litigation.

The cases are also exemplary computer disasters, and so have the following two chapters to themselves.

CHAPTER SIXTEEN

The Tenth Deadly Sin:
Lawyers (II)

Judge John Hicks became an expert on the computer industry during a single trial about an information systems dispute.

In a matter of weeks, by listening carefully to rigorous questioning and surprisingly candid answers, he was able to gain a better insight into the inner workings of the industry than many who have worked in it for years.

The advantage of uncovering the facts of a computer disaster in a courtroom is that people are under oath to tell the truth. This is no guarantee of veracity or even verisimilitude but lawyers can always ask the sorts of question that customers might be too embarrassed to ask their suppliers.

And it is up to judges to decide whether a witness is credible. If they don't think so, they can simply reject the witness's every utterance.

Unlike their counterparts in criminal courts, where they are subservient to juries, judges rule civil courts as effortlessly as Cromwell dominated Parliament.

In this case study, the hearing was initiated by a user company, the marine insurance firm Tindall Riley. It manages a club of ship owners who ensure that, if one ship is lost or badly damaged, the club members chip in to pay the bill.

With its business growing markedly during the 1980s, Tindall Riley decided it needed a new computer system. There was little seriously wrong with the existing Siemens Nixdorf computer, but its bones were beginning to creak, and a new system seemed to offer the possibility of lower running costs, ease of writing new programs and a quicker way to search for and access information on its database of ships.

Not knowing what systems to look for, Tindall Riley hired the consultancy firm PACTEL, which helped to write an invitation to tender.

This was the right thing to do, and indeed, at the time, the buying process appeared to be fairly straightforward – except that Tindall Riley was taking a seemingly attractive shortcut known as Dead Man's Road.

This is where the customer, to achieve a perfect blend between computers and the business, buys software that is built especially for the purpose.

So Tindall Riley was negotiating its way along a lane that, at that time, few other companies had travelled before, which years later would lead to the High Court in London.

What particularly complicated the legal case was the fact that there were effectively two suppliers – the main hardware manufacturer (the US company Unisys) and its local dealer, called DSL.

At first neither Unisys nor DSL was seriously in the running for the contract.

After a competitive tender, a bid from the UK services group Hoskyns had seemed attractive, but pricey. Then Tindall Riley directors heard that they could dramatically cut the price of their bespoke software by using a wonder code-writing tool called Mapper, marketed by Unisys.

There was then a head-to-head comparison between the bids from Unisys and Hoskyns – and Unisys won.

The main pre-contract negotiations between Unisys and Tindall Riley then took place at El Vino's wine bar in London's Fleet Street. And it was about ten years later that some of the same people would meet again virtually opposite El Vino's at the Royal Courts of Justice.

Presiding over the case Judge Hicks was not the sort of judge to allow any intricacies of the evidence or any computer industry jargon to fly over his head.

Describing a software tool as a fourth-generation language was a cue to the judge to seek an analogy in genealogy. He wanted to know in some detail about the ancestors of the fourth generation language, and so gained an extensive understanding of first-, second- and third-generation languages. He would later refer to the languages in terms of children, parents, grandchildren and even great-grandchildren.

In the end the judge would not even take the description of hardware and software for granted.

He went on to hear how Tindall Riley found that the hardware it had purchased was not up to the job of running the newly written software.

But it was not entirely the fault of the hardware. Many problems stemmed from the software – the complexity of its design and the fact that the code was generated by a fourth-generation tool, Mapper.

The judge discovered what many customers learn only after bitter experience: that the latest technology may not be the best technology. Judge Hicks observed that each new generation of software tools adds complexity to the programs; and this in turn requires larger hardware and more storage space. In particular, he said, fourth-generation software tools have 'extensive databases or data dictionaries'.

He added: 'There is a price to be paid in computer slowness, or alternatively in the monetary cost . . .'

Dryly he commented that Mapper had some characteristics of fourth-generation products. He said it was 'very resource-hungry', meaning that it consumed a great deal of computer hardware capacity, and so needed a large expensive machine to run it.

This was a critical point because suppliers can often underestimate the size of hardware needed to run the software efficiently. If they overestimate the hardware requirements, the cost of the system becomes unattractive. If they underestimate, the captive user can always spend more on a bigger machine.

In this case the judge decided that the hardware supplied had been inadequate, though he also concluded that the original design of the software was far from ideal.

Yet the suppliers in Tindall Riley's case put great emphasis on the ease with which code could be written using the Mapper tool. The salesmen also maintained that the Mapper 10 minicomputer, designed for the Mapper software, would be more than fit for the purpose.

It was not Unisys's intention to sell directly to Tindall Riley but to brief one of its franchisees, DSL, to act as the local trader. In this way the dealer would, in effect, become the main supplier and Unisys would be the big-name company in the background providing support.

DSL was a medium-sized software company which at that time, 1984, had been established for six years and employed about 150 people, including freelance and consultant programmers who were self-employed but worked exclusively for DSL.

It specialised in systems for clients in the financial markets, including insurance.

DSL's job was to install Tindall Riley's system, yet it knew little about the Mapper product until it attended a Unisys seminar on fourth-generation languages.

The events bring to mind two of the most common failings of major computer projects:

• The supplier needs to be an expert in the hardware and software businesses and, most important of all, *your* business. If it's not intimately familiar with the hardware and software the chances of success are reduced;

• There needs to be someone working for the customer (ideally the chief executive) who has a good working knowledge of the hardware and software and of course understands thoroughly his or her business. This is the person who should be in charge of computerisation – not someone who works for the supplier.

Even if you know nothing about computers you may know more than the so-called experts. That's because you're sufficiently detached from the technological arguments to see clearly the context of computerisation in the wider context of your business.

DSL's seminar on fourth-generation languages was followed up with Mapper introductory and familiarisation courses at which the DSL people met some senior executives from Unisys.

At the fateful meeting at El Vino's wine bar, all three sides in the triangle – Unisys, DSL and Tindall Riley – discussed the best way to go about replacing Tindall Riley's ageing Siemens Nixdorf system.

The Unisys contingent gave a convincing sales pitch, namely that:

• the Mapper 10 hardware and software had an installed database, with the ability to run do-it-yourself software programs;

• the Mapper database was flexible in use;

• the software substantially reduced the time needed to write programs and hence cut the cost of software development;

• Mapper software made the writing of programs a

straightforward process, which could be carried out by people who had not received special detailed training in the use of Mapper and its techniques.

At the end of the meeting the parties agreed to meet again, negotiations moved towards a contract and soon afterwards a deal was signed between Tindall Riley and DSL.

But, unknown to Tindall Riley or DSL, a Unisys consultant was concerned about the project. As someone who had taken part in the early negotiations on the contract and had some knowledge of the customer's business, and of the hardware and software, his opinion was to be valued.

He felt that, although DSL was a software specialist, it had no practical knowledge of Mapper and would have to rely on the advice of Unisys as to how best to apply the software to Tindall Riley's project.

The same Unisys employee had other concerns about the project, but he did not tell either DSL or Tindall Riley in case it stood in the way of Unisys's sales efforts. His fears were:
• that the design of the database would be critical to the success of the project;
• that it would require skill and expertise possessed only by those who had training and experience in Mapper;
• that the Mapper 10 hardware would be stretched to its capacity and the system would be overloaded;
• that Mapper at that time was unsuitable for major 'turnkey' projects;
• that project success was dependent on the skill and expertise of the programmer;
• that Mapper could not support more than eight to twelve end-users and preferably not more than eight.

Despite all these reservations, the consultant appears to have given Tindall Riley and DSL the impression that Mapper was right for the job. This led the end-users at Tindall Riley to believe that their new bespoke system would be written quickly, easily and to specification.

The Unisys consultant had three important meetings with Tindall Riley. At each of these, he did not tell the whole truth.

At the first meeting he saw his role as giving 'technical weight' to the Unisys sales effort. His felt his job was to give assurances that Mapper was suitable or could replace the Nixdorf system and that the Mapper 10 hardware would also be suitable.

The second meeting was for the consultant to give a demonstration of Mapper to Tindall Riley. The third meeting, to answer a number of Tindall Riley's questions, was attended by the third-party consultancy PACTEL, representing Tindall Riley.

Again the main purpose of the meeting was to assure Tindall Riley about the suitability of Mapper for the conversion of the Nixdorf system.

Exactly what questions Tindall Riley asked at the meeting the consultant could not remember. 'All I can say is that at no point was the answer against Mapper,' said the consultant at the trial.

The local dealer DSL was also reassured by Unisys, and believed that:
- the conversion of the existing Nixdorf system would be no trouble;
- there would be no problem arranging the data on the new system in a similar format to that on the original system;
- the Mapper system was flexible and a forgiving tool.

The inference was that the design could be changed easily at a later date.

The result of all these meetings was that, in effect, Unisys endorsed the new database design as acceptable. In fact the design was less than perfect.

One of the problems would be that the programmers would try to recreate the look and feel of the old system in the new. This was what Tindall Riley wanted, and Unisys had suggested that Mapper was suitable for this.

But this was a particularly risky type of conversion, and internal Unisys documents acknowledged this.

It would have been better to design the database from scratch, allowing the programmers complete freedom to engineer the most efficient format, rather than try to restrict their creativity by trying to superimpose the old design onto the new.

One of the problems with recreating the former way of working is that the old design is known and proven to the end-users, and has been honed over the years. Trying to mirror this effect with a new system will have the same negative impact on people as replacing a much-loved old timber edifice with a modern concrete facility-packed construction.

In short the end-users will resent every change. The new software will be able to do much more in theory but it may also have more screens, more features, more security restrictions, and more complexity, which may usurp the power of the new hardware. All of this will conspire to make the new system seem slower than the old one.

For Tindall Riley, the first problems surfaced not long after the system was commissioned in the mid 1980s. A first attempt at a conversion of data from the Siemens Nixdorf system to Mapper failed.

At around the same time DSL built a prototype that was designed to show how the new software might work in practice.

Usually, a prototype is a cut-down sample of the full software and is constructed quickly and fairly simply to demonstrate some of the programs and features of a final system. A good demonstration of a prototype can give the project team confidence that they are on the right track. It can also give the end-users something to look forward to.

But DSL's attempts at prototyping proved inordinately lengthy, expensive and disappointing.

This was largely because of a poor database design, the ineptitude of some of the programming work, and the excessive demands for alteration by end-users – all the classic prerequisites of a computing disaster.

The failure of the prototyping must have surprised Tindall Riley. One of the reasons it had chosen Mapper was that it had seen the success of the product's prototyping at another insurance company, Aetna Life, one of Unisys's 'showcase' customers.

As part of its sales effort, Unisys had taken Tindall Riley to Aetna Life to see Mapper in use. The show could not have been more impressive. Aetna Life had built a system in six months, using prototyping techniques. This reinforced all the Unisys literature about the ease and speed of programming in Mapper.

But Tindall Riley had no experience of other computing disasters.

If it had, it might have better understood that demonstrations given by other apparently similar user organisations may be useful, but are no indication of whether the systems can be transposed successfully into your business.

Indeed, many demonstrations are exhibitions of computer prowess, which impress sightseers who do not always realise all the problems and how much work has gone into producing what appears to be an effortless and smooth-running system.

It's also worth remembering that producing a demonstration

of complex software on a single PC can be straightforward. But trying to deliver the same system on line to 300 people simultaneously may be rather different. In fact the difference is as great as that between an ant and an army walking on thin ice.

Also, it is a truism that what works for the company down the road probably won't work for you. No two companies are exactly alike, have exactly the same requirements or go about implementing a system in the same way, using staff with similar abilities. Even if all these things match, no two companies are likely to run the same software on the same hardware, with the same operating system, disk subsystems or memory capacity.

Aetna Life was an insurance company, and Tindall Riley was an insurance company, but there the comparison ended. Aetna Life sells life insurance and other policies and financial services.

Tindall Riley operates in a different market altogether, acting as manager for a ship-owning syndicate. Its database requirements were many miles from those of Aetna Life – yet understandably Tindall Riley was strongly influenced by Aetna Life's success with Mapper.

But there was little about the Tindall Riley system which was straightforward.

Particular impediments were the method of 'sequencing' and the database's 'data dictionary', which defined the basic structure of the database in an inappropriate way. An imperative of any computer or paper-based database is that you should be able to access frequently-needed information quickly.

There are two ways to do this: you can browse through the database to find what you want or consult an index. Such an unstructured roam around all the data is time-consuming and makes a heavy demand on the computer's capacity. Therefore, in a paper-based or computer system some kind of index is a good idea.

With an ordinary paper-based dictionary, the sort you buy in the shops, there tends to be only one type of searching method: alphabetical order. A set of book-based encyclopaedias is more advanced, however: it will be laid out in alphabetical order, and will additionally have a separate index. This shows all the references to, say, Indian music, even though Indian music may be mentioned in several different volumes of the encyclopaedia.

A library may go even further with indexing. You may be able to search for books under the subject, the title or the author.

Computer databases are supposed to take indexing several stages further. It is one of their advantages over paper: that they can incorporate a huge number of indices, giving many ways of directing a search and obtaining precise information.

If it works properly an electronic database can, in a scientific library for example, make it quick and easy to obtain a list of all scientists who have ever studied astronomy yet have written papers on a particular medical subject for a particular journal between the years 1910 and 1917, and lived in Scotland.

Some databases are so flexible that their structure is largely irrelevant to the ease and speed with which information can be extracted.

But when programmers constructed the Tindall Riley database they found that Mapper's structure required a hierarchical arrangement rather like that of a filing cabinet. There were 'modes,' 'types' and 'rids' which were described as the cabinets, drawers and files of a manual filing system.

What was not so apparent from the literature on Mapper was that this hierarchical structure dictated the main means of access to the database. So the judge concluded of Mapper that: 'Indexing is possible, but access by that means is less convenient, and the construction and maintenance of indexes requires more forethought, expertise and effort in the development and use of the database than in conventional systems.

'In Tindall Riley's business the most usual starting point for an inquiry was, not surprisingly, a ship's name; but the Nixdorf system was organised by policy year, and within that by area, group, member and ship number. In that system, that structure [of the database] was not apparently a disadvantage, but when carried over to Mapper it was crippling.'

In practice this meant that Tindall Riley staff who had completed their work in a 40-hour week using the Nixdorf system found themselves working nights and weekends with the Mapper replacement – just to get the work done.

Yet, with the old Nixdorf system, there had been no complaints about response times at the terminals, or on the time taken to produce reports.

It was a classic case of a computerisation project that had led to a reduction in productivity.

The development of the new system was supposed to have taken six months but was still incomplete in 1987 – more than two years after Tindall Riley first placed the order for Mapper hardware and software.

Clearly the writing of programs was not always so elementary that it could be carried out by people who had not received special detailed training in the use of Mapper.

In court later, the question of whether Tindall Riley, and the local dealer DSL, had been deceived by Unisys became the main issue.

Giving evidence against Unisys was one of the supplier's former pre-sales consultants. He was asked to give his opinion on the factual accuracy of a Unisys promotional publication, which was supposed to give the 'facts and figures' about the Mapper system and its dedicated hardware, called Mapper 10. The literature had said that, with the new system, managers could:
• decide how to organise and display information specifically related to their needs;
• decide when to update or discard information;
• decide what information and accompanying graphics should be contained in a report.

And they could do it all without the aid of programmers – and without needing 'previous knowledge of computers and programming'.

The pre-sales consultant also told the court that he thought the passage was 'rather ridiculous . . . completely wrong'.

At a separate point in the trial, the man was asked further questions to establish whether the supplier's advice had been misleading or even deceitful.

Q: What were your views as to Mapper's suitability as a vehicle for the conversion of the Nixdorf system?
A: Well, there is no doubt that one could do it. It is just a question of whether it is as easy as you think it is.
Q: Was it?
A: Certainly not.
Q: Why not?
A: Well, conversions tend to – or rather, when people have existing systems, their expectations are much higher of new products. Mapper performed in a limited way in terms of its screen functions and could not, except with great difficulty, supply that same functionality.
Q: Did you say that at that meeting [with Tindall Riley]?
A: No.

Q: Or at any meeting?
A: No.
Q: Why not?
A: I was not asked.
Q: Why not volunteer it?
A: As I said, I did not want to put obstacles in the salesman's way – it was not my job.

One of the most remarkable aspects of the whole trial, according to the judge, was that evidence in support of allegations that Unisys sales staff made misleading or even deceitful claims, came from former employees of Unisys who were, to quote the judge, 'implicated in the conduct complained of'.

In some cases the former employees unwittingly gave false information to Tindall Riley, but in at least one instance they knew the falsity of the claims that were being made.

What was equally striking, the judge said, was that there were no suggestions by any of the lawyers on any side that the former employees had coloured their evidence out of any animus against their former employer.

In the absence of this, the judge said he approached the factual issues on the basis that the witnesses were all endeavouring to assist the court to the best of their ability, subject only to the fallibility of human recollection.

In short the judge declared that some Unisys employees had made claims knowing them to be untrue. These misrepresentations included claims that no new database design was needed and that programs could be written by people who had not had special training.

By the time that Tindall Riley terminated the contract in 1987, the new system had a 'wholly inadequate performance' in that response times for inquiries and reports were 'grossly excessive' and that arrangements for taking back-up or security copies of the data were unsatisfactory.

Tindall Riley had also bought some Unisys hardware, called the Mapper 10, which had sold so poorly and performed so badly that it was phased out soon after it was launched onto the market.

The internal computer department at Tindall Riley had produced a report on the Mapper project's problems. It said that benchmark tests had confirmed that the poor response times of the Mapper system were because of the database design and poor programming, and also because the Mapper 10 hardware 'has not proved to be a reliable machine'.

Even internally within Unisys, the Mapper 10 was considered problematic. One former Unisys City director told Judge Hicks that the Mapper 10 hardware was 'by no means' a successful product.

'It was under-powered. It did not have enough significant disk capacity in a way it could handle it or manage it. The claims for the language which was driving it – if you like, an operating system – exceeded its capability. Effectively, it was under-powered. It was like putting a Mini engine into a Rolls-Royce motor car. In effect that is the best analogy I can think of, in simplistic terms.'

The former director was also asked how soon it was that he came to this conclusion about Mapper 10. Given that the reply was coming from a director of a supplier company the comment was poignant.

'Well, quite obviously, because of the company's circumstances, it did not want to hold its hand up and make a public pronouncement all in one go that the product was inferior and not fit for the purpose it was sold. It sought to change those circumstances by improving the product's performance . . .'

In an even franker admission he went on to state that there were problems with Mapper 10 throughout the country.

'Everybody including the people that were responsible for the sale here was in damage-limitation mode and looking for alternative solutions to the problems.'

Unisys had sold only about a dozen of the Mapper 10 machines in the UK and was phasing it out after only two years in service. Normally a new machine can expect to do four, five, or more years' service.

Faced with all the problems with both hardware and software, Tindall Riley's internal computer department put forward five options for the future:

1. do nothing;
2. rewrite the database and purchase a new machine;
3. upgrade the machine;
4. use a machine belonging to BP for rewriting the database while live operations continued on the Mapper 10;
5. scrap Mapper and start again with another manufacturer.

Tindall Riley decided to rewrite the database from scratch

using BP's machine. It was the right decision. On a recommendation from Unisys, Tindall Riley employed a talented programming expert who redesigned the database and managed to install a high-quality system using improved hardware.

The key to success, it seems, lay in the quality of the database design and the right choice of hardware.

But the eventual success of the project did not stop Tindall Riley taking legal action to recover its losses.

It sued the dealer and won about £550,000 damages and costs for a breach of contract and negligence.

The dealer in turn sued Unisys, claiming a total of £708,592, which included its own costs.

Judge Hicks concluded that Unisys had acted deceitfully, and that it was liable to pay damages for breach of the implied warranty of fitness for purpose in relation to the Mapper 10 hardware.

But the judge also found that DSL was partly to blame for the incompetence of some of its programming work for Tindall Riley.

So he reduced the sum of damages payable by Unisys to DSL to take into account the poor programming work. There was no appeal by Unisys.

So what could Tindall Riley have done to avoid such a disaster?

With hindsight it is easy to see the lesson, namely that there is nothing about computerisation that is easy except, comparatively, taking the decision to spend vast sums on systems that you think will increase your company's productivity.

And any salesperson who says that anything to do with computerisation is easy should be distrusted profoundly.

Tindall Riley will also now know of the risks of tailor-made software. A ready-made package might not have fitted in so well with the business, but perhaps the business could have adapted to a reliable well-established package rather than vice versa.

Also, don't trust the advice of a salesperson merely because it is offered in good faith. Sales staff may have been given false briefings by their superiors.

Sometimes, as in this case, the salesman may say one thing when he knows another to be true. The fact that he works for a major supplier which is one of the most reputable in the world does not guarantee his integrity.

The hardware, too, proved inadequate, as often happens in a

disaster. A rule of thumb might be to buy the hardware only once you know exactly what software is going to run on it. Choosing the hardware in advance of the software is like laying the foundations before you have decided how big the house will be.

Suppliers will often agree to a free loan of their hardware to allow you to test your software, or a cut-down version of the software that you intend to develop. If not, they may agree to you taking your software to their premises.

Even if this proves to be a problem, there are numerous computer bureaux or corporate users who will sell machine time.

A further problem in this case was that the programmers allowed the end-users to make an excessive number of changes to the software. This happens in 99 per cent of failed software projects.

However, the end-users do not know what they want until they see the system gradually forming in front of their eyes. Then their lists of requirements and changes seem to proliferate unceasingly.

And, because project managers tend to know more about the technology than the business, they agree to all the changes, not being able to prioritise suggestions into categories such as 'critical', 'important' and merely 'a nice thing to have'.

In this case programmers admitted that one of the reasons for the overrun of the project was that they acceded too freely to Tindall Riley's requests for additions and variations.

The moral here may be that the project managers need to understand the business much more thoroughly than the technology – ideally both.

In a perfect world, the programmers should spend several months sitting beside end-users to understand their day-to-day work before embarking on code-writing.

Even then, the programs should be delivered in small modules, each one of them self-contained, demonstrably effective and robust, before the company agrees to pay anything.

That avoids the big-bang, all-or-nothing situation whereby the whole system is delivered in one go, and either works or doesn't.

In the end, computer hardware and software should be bought without emotion. **Enthusiasm for any one product is a potentially dangerous thing.** This seems to have been perceived by Judge Hicks, who commented in his judgement on the credibility of one of the expert witnesses for Unisys. The witness had shown such an enthusiasm for Mapper that this had slightly unnerved the judge, who remarked that '… his enthusiasm for Mapper somewhat carried him away, and his opinions on the technical aspects of this case need to be assessed with that in mind.'

The witness had shown his enthusiasm by writing a preliminary report, which began: 'The name Mapper is said to stand for Maintaining, Preparing and Producing Executive Reports. Many users of Mapper prefer the alternative, that it is an acronym for Most Amazing Programming Product Ever Released.'

On this the judge also remarked: 'I must confess that I did not at first sight think that that was intended to be entirely serious, but I now believe that it was.'

So perhaps the most striking lesson of the whole fiasco is provided by this last slightly frivolous but sincere comment by an employee at Unisys. **His comment about Mapper showed how a supplier can become so enveloped in the wonders of a product that it becomes preoccupied with the software's advantages and may not always see its shortcomings.**

A similar lesson has emerged from other failed projects: that computer sales staff are among the most credible people in any industry because their enthusiasm is genuine, derived from seeing at first hand how a well-designed, properly implemented system can transform a business. The trouble is that some salespeople assume that every implementation will be as successful as the last.

In reality computers are like lions. They can purr one minute and kill the next.

The judge's conclusion that Unisys had given deliberately misleading advice about the ease with which Mapper could bring about a new efficient system for Tindall Riley might be a little harsh.

What seems to have happened is that Unisys was simply swept off its feet in a love affair with Mapper. Perhaps its judgement was clouded by its veneration of the product.

I have suggested it in an earlier chapter, but it might be worth repeating: **it is dangerous to trust what computer salespeople tell you merely because they believe it themselves.**

The following is a chronology of the events before and after Tindall Riley's disaster.

1984 – autumn: A marine insurance company, Tindall Riley, decides to replace its ageing Siemens Nixdorf computer system and proceeds to a point where the placing of contracts is imminent. Before the end of the year, a salesman in the City office of the computer manufacturer Unisys hears of the Tindall Riley project. Unisys does not always deal directly with a computer user organisation, and so asks a local Unisys dealer to take part in discussions with Tindall Riley.

1985: Preliminary meeting at El Vino's wine bar in London at which Unisys sales staff seek to persuade Tindall Riley of the virtues of Mapper.

1985 – February 19: A deal is signed between Tindall Riley and the local dealer DSL. The agreement provides for DSL to write a bespoke system to replace Tindall Riley's Siemens Nixdorf system.

1985 – February 26: DSL places an order with Unisys for Mapper 10 and Mapper software, for delivery to Tindall Riley.

1985 – March–May: DSL prepares a functional specification of the new software for Tindall Riley.

1985 – April: DSL's programming team attend a week-long programming course arranged by Unisys to learn about writing code using Unisys's Mapper product.

1985 – June: Programming work on Tindall Riley's new database enquiry system begins in earnest. The project is supposed to take six months. But the first attempt at a conversion of Siemens Nixdorf data to Unisys's Mapper product fails.

1987 – July: Tindall Riley terminates its contract with DSL. Remedial work on the database design begins.

1988 – January: First benchmark tests with new hardware running on a redesigned database.

1988 – April: Second benchmark tests on new hardware followed by a replacement of the Mapper 10.

1988 – July: Tindall Riley sues its supplier DSL and subsequently wins £708,592 in costs and damages. As a result, DSL later sues its supplier Unisys.

1994: A High court judge finds that Unisys acted deceitfully and made misleading sales claims about Mapper's abilities. He decides that Unisys should pay damages to DSL but reduces the sum to take account of DSL's poor programming work for Tindall Riley. It is understood that Unisys did not appeal against the judgement.[*]

* At the time the systems were supplied to Tindall Riley Unisys was called Sperry. Later Sperry would merge with another computer company, Burroughs, and the name became Unisys.

CHAPTER SEVENTEEN

The Tenth Deadly Sin:
Lawyers (III)

After discovering the truth about so many disasters one is entitled to ask: how can so many reputable companies be reduced to idiocy when buying big computer systems?

But imbecility plays no part in it. The most careful and diligent companies, even those who hire independent consultants to help choose the best system, may still find their impeccably planned project disintegrating before their eyes.

One problem is that large organisations are attracted to comparably large organisations. Big user companies tend to trust big suppliers. The customers can let their defences drop when the contract is drawn up, only to find it later turned against them.

This happened when the UK's Inland Revenue signed a £1 billion deal with the American computer giant EDS. The Inland Revenue thought that its thousands of pages of contracts with EDS were watertight until it found that there were areas it had not fully considered and wrote in internal documents that the agreements imposed burdensome duties that the Revenue was finding difficulty adhering to.

It is also worth remembering that the caring, professional salesmen who negotiate the contract are not the same people who deal with any disputes.

In a confrontation the supplier wheels in its heavy-gun lawyers who, on occasions, will punctiliously and unemotionally threaten to enforce the letter of the contract.

This all sounds obvious now but nothing is obvious at the start of a computer project. Areas of potential conflict are overlooked or deliberately ignored because nobody envisages that the project will go so seriously wrong. Nobody can envisage a time when neither the customers nor suppliers will communicate with each other except through lawyers.

Indeed some computer managers have so close a relationship with the main technology suppliers that they fail to acknowledge their supplier's weaknesses. So the chief executive needs to be involved at the beginning, to intervene if the pre-contract negotiations seem too cosy and too easygoing; perhaps even to appoint an independent auditor to oversee the work of the computer department, who will report not to the computer manager but directly to the chief executive.

However, the contract must allow flexibility. A supplier pushed too hard, beyond its capabilities, is bound to fail. Some suppliers believe that they can implement a major project satisfactorily only if they have complete management control. The contract may need to reflect this, but only on the basis that, if the supplier fails to deliver an acceptable system, the supplier gets paid nothing and the customer is entitled to compensation. And what exactly is acceptable will need to be defined with tedious precision early on. Precision is the key word here. For example the use of clear, unequivocal language is particularly important. When a relationship turns sour, arguments will focus not on the logical reasoning behind contractual clauses but the ambiguities in the language used.

In return for agreeing to sign a contract which sets out the customer's reasonable rights incontrovertibly, the supplier may be offered the incentive of receiving a share of the anticipated savings arising from the introduction of the new system – in effect an incentive scheme that allows it to recover its costs, a profit margin and a variable percentage of the savings.

Such a scheme can work only if based on 'open book' accounting whereby the supplier opens up its books to the customer showing its costs and profit margins.

Some major consultancies will agree to deliver a system on time and to a fixed price, and will not expect any payment until the system is demonstrably acceptable. This would be fine if you wanted the supplier to go away and come back with the system in a year's time.

But end-users will want to make changes as and when they see how computerisation can help their work. As the project takes shape, the more changes they will request and the more impossibly complex the project will become; **yet the supplier**

may not warn against more changes because each change not only adds to the cost but provides an excuse to blame the customer when the project is late and over budget.

In any case, it may not be politically acceptable for the supplier to say 'no' to the very end-users who will ultimately determine whether the system is acceptable.

But the problem of poor specifications can be overcome by remembering a couple of the pieces of advice mentioned already:
• do not computerise until the existing paper-based or semi-computerised processes have been simplified, simplified again and further simplified long before computerisation; in any efficiency drive, computerisation is the last thing to do;
• do not assume suppliers or consultants are even close to being called experts until they understand your business as well as you do.

It may even be wise for both supplier and user to agree the scope of the systems and then prohibit any further changes. The trouble here is that end-users do not know enough about what computerisation will achieve until the system is half built – and that is the point at which they will want to make more changes.

If these changes are not made, the end-users will ultimately be disappointed and may even reject the system during the final 'acceptance' phase.

There may be an answer to all this: **do not expect the entire system to be delivered in one go but in small self-contained sections that will work on their own but could perhaps be integrated with each other later**. This *slow*, phased introduction, if well publicised internally, will minimise the expectations of end-users.

I italicised 'slow' because of the dangers of rushing any aspect of the buying and implementation cycle. It sounds an obvious pitfall, yet customers seem regularly to fall into it, as the following case shows.

CASE STUDY

St Albans District Council was always unhappy with the contract it was given to sign by International Computers Ltd (ICL). But it signed the contract anyway.

The council's initial reluctance to sign was because of a clause that limited ICL's liability in any disaster to a maximum payout of £100,000.

The council knew that the potential failure of the system could cost the authority hundreds of thousands of, or even a million, pounds or more.

This was because the system was designed to collect the Community Charge (the controversial Poll Tax) from local residents. Without that money, the council would be deprived of much of its income.

Although St Albans was tempted to query the £100,000 limit on compensation, the authority said that there was a time restriction on the signing of the contract – not a restriction imposed by the council but by ICL.

The supplier, according to the council, had warned that there was a risk that unless the contract was signed by the following Monday the council might lose the hardware that ICL had reserved.

This put the council in a desperate position: it had chosen its supplier after a laborious tendering procedure, and had faith that the supplier could deliver everything promised.

Now it was threatened with the loss of the hardware and a possible delay in the implementation of its system.

Yet it needed the new system in place quickly to collect the Community Charge tax from local residents. So it had two choices:

• it could have rejected ICL as a preferred supplier and considered another company – but this would have delayed the project, led to a re-evaluation of tenders and the adoption of a possible second-best supplier;

• it could have signed the contract under ICL's terms.

As you might expect, ICL made the choice easier. It offered a package: ready-made software, hardware ready to be delivered and a ready-made computer contract.

It was a package similar to that accepted by many users in other organisations. All this seemed to reduce the risks. By way of further encouragement ICL wrote to the council:

'With regard to ICL's contractual terms and conditions . . . our offer is based on these standard terms and conditions, and given the tight time scale, I would advise you to make use of them.

'These standard ICL conditions are accepted by over 25 local authorities, and in no way detract from the business partnerships.'

So St Albans accepted the ICL package, including the standard contract.

But no sooner were the systems delivered, installed and tested than the council's presentiment proved to be well founded.

Something disastrous happened that would cost St Albans far more than the £100,000 ICL was limited to paying the council in compensation.

This was not a tale of a major project failure, but of a small undefined bug in a software program that caused a massive miscalculation of the money the council thought it was owed by local residents.

The bug led to the council overestimating the number of people who should pay its Community Charge. This was particularly serious because St Albans, like other local authorities, had to inform the Secretary of State for the Environment of the number of residents who lived in the district.

This number then determined the amount of government money that the authority received to meet its own financial demands. The figure would also be used to set the authority's Community Charge rate: the tax that it would have to collect to meet its budget.

In addition, the number of people in the council's area would also determine the sum the council would be compelled to pass over to a bigger authority, the Hertfordshire County Council.

But once the population figure had been calculated and notified to the government, there was no way it could be altered even if known to be incorrect.

Like other authorities, St Albans was given a deadline before which it had to tell the government this crucial figure. That date was 8 December 1989.

Dutifully, the council used its new ICL hardware and software (known as COMCIS) to extract the local population figures.

From a trawl of the COMCIS database over the weekend of 2–3 December, the system displayed on a computer screen the figure of 97,384.7. The calculation was not as easy as it seems at first sight. The software had to exclude from its deductions entire categories of people who fell outside the statutory criteria for paying community charge. Only a computer would make 0.7 of a person pay poll tax. But that was not the real problem.

One of the difficulties was that a *hardcopy printout* of the 97,384.7 figure produced a series of zeros.

This suggested to the council's computer department that there was a defect in a part of the COMCIS program. However, it was assumed that the defect did not affect the calculation of the figure. It was simply thought by the council that there was merely a mistake in the part of the program that generated the printout.

Therefore the council was not concerned about the zeros. The figure of 97,384.7 had shown on the transaction processing (TP) screen, and an ICL representative had earlier made it clear to the council that the figures demanded by the government could safely be taken from that screen.

But, unknown to the council, the TP screen figures were anything but reliable.

ICL, it appears, may have been aware of this fault but failed to communicate this to the council.

Dryly, a judge hearing a dispute between the council and ICL would later observe: 'The evidence reveals, in my judgement, some lack of communication on the part of the defendants [ICL].'

Yet to the council, the figure of 97,384.7 looked correct. It compared approximately to an earlier assessment by the council of its population.

So, by the morning of 4 December, the Secretary of State was duly notified of the estimated number of residents living in the catchment area of St Albans District Council.

However, nearly three months later, on 26 February 1990, long after the deadline for altering the figures had passed, the council noticed a printout on its systems that showed a variance with the number of people notified to the government.

Clearly there was a mistake somewhere – but nobody knew where, how, or the extent of it. Could they even be sure a mistake had occurred?

That evening the council's director of finance and information technology told the authority's chief executive that there was a serious problem with the figures. Yet it was now only two days before the council was due to meet to fix the level of local tax.

The chief executive was, to put it mildly, in a fix. At this stage the council suspected that the figures on which it was about to set its level of Community Charge were incorrect. But it was not certain the figures were wrong, and in any case it did not have any definitively accurate figures with which to replace the suspect ones.

At that stage the council was less concerned with what had gone wrong than with discovering exactly how many people lived in its area.

Short of doing a door-to-door census in 24 hours, or analysing tens of thousands of paper forms sent to the council by residents, there was nothing it could do.

To add to the problems, the council was running up against a deadline to produce 97,000 or so bills for the Poll Tax – with the financial year due to end in only four weeks.

In the end the council had little alternative but to accept the original figure as correct. And so the Community Charge was fixed – on the wrong basis.

The software had overestimated the population by 2,966. And, since ghosts tend not pay Community Charge, the council found itself seriously short of money. Apart from the fact that no money would be paid by 2,966 non-existent people, the authority had set the Community Charge tax rate at a lower level than it would have done had it known the true numbers in its area. The receipts proved to be £484,000 less than they ought to have been. This was not the only loss. The 'ghosts' increased the sum the authority had to pay to its higher-tier county council. This was an extra £1.79 million. By the time credits were taken into account the total loss to the authority, with interest, came to £1,314,846.

Worse was to come. The contract with ICL, which the authority said had been signed reluctantly amid considerable time pressure, limited the supplier's liability to only £100,000.

What's more, ICL argued in court that this figure was not strictly speaking correct. The actual limit on liability was only £10,000, a restriction stipulated within ICL's 'Application Product Development Service Agreement', which was inserted into the body of the main contract.

The addition of this appended agreement puzzled the judge, who remarked: 'Precisely how the Application Product Service Agreement lies within the main COMCIS agreement is not entirely easy to see.'

The judge decided that the £10,000 figure was not an appropriate sum in the circumstances. Neither was he inclined to sympathise with the £100,000 limit. He expressed his views in fairly colourful language.

'The defendants [ICL] were one of a limited number of companies who could meet the plaintiffs' [the council's] requirements, all of whom dealt on similar standard conditions. The defendants were therefore in a very strong bargaining position. The plaintiffs were over a barrel because of the tight timescale.'

Citing various legal precedents the judge decided that ICL's £100,000 liability limit was not reasonable in the circumstances and in effect declared it null and void because:

• St Albans and ICL were of unequal bargaining power;
• the limit was too small in relation to the potential risk and the actual loss;
• ICL had insurance cover against product liability (to an aggregate of £50 million, though this sum had to cover all of ICL's contracts with all of its customers).

Then the judge made a pronouncement that will strike fear into the hearts of all computer suppliers, namely that the party that stands to make the profit – ICL in this case – should carry the risk. This is what he said:

> On whom is it better that a loss of this size should fall, a local authority or an international computer company? The latter is well able to insure – and in this case was insured – and pass on the premium to the customers. If the loss is to fall the other way, it will ultimately be borne by the local population either by increased taxation or reduced services. I do not think it unreasonable that he who stands to make the profit should carry the risk.

All the above factors outweighed, in the mind of the judge, counter-arguments put forward by ICL. These included the fact that the authority went into the contract with its eyes open, that liability limits are commonplace in the industry and that the COMCIS software was an area of developing technology, which was subject to the vagaries of evolving legislation and extremely tight interim deadlines imposed by government departments at short notice.

At the end of the day, said the judge, the onus was on ICL to establish that the exclusion clause, which limited to £100,000 ICL's liability to pay compensation, was 'a fair and reasonable one'. In his judgement ICL had 'not discharged that burden'.

In conclusion the judge observed that the COMCIS software contained an error; that ICL was in breach of contract in that the software did not correspond to the description in the tender documents; nor was it of merchantable quality or fit for the purpose for which it was required.

He also decided that a comment to St Albans by an ICL representative, who had indicated that the council could safely take the population figures from the TP screen, was an unwitting misrepresentation which was tantamount to negligence. This put ICL in breach of its conditions of service.

The judge further decided that the council was not at fault either for failing to discover the error earlier or for failing to take different steps once it was apparent that there was a problem. He decided that there would be a judgement in favour of the council of £1,314,846.

ICL's pain did not stop there. It was also required to pay the council's costs.

Virtually as soon as the judgement was declared, ICL announced its intention to appeal. The result was that the Appeal Court in 1996 upheld the original judgement but ruled that the council had over-stated its losses and reduced the damages payable by ICL to the authority by about £600,000.

So what are the lessons?

Two key points were made by St Albans at the end of the appeal: the council stressed the importance of keeping clear and detailed written records of all communications and conversations with suppliers, and the dates of them; and the need to include in a contract all relevant supplementary material such as the invitation to tender. One of reasons for St Albans's success had been the clarity and simplicity with which it had stated its requirements in the invitation to tender. This made absolutely clear, for example, the need for the chosen supplier to deliver systems that would have to meet legislation that had not been finalised. The tender stated that suppliers would be expected to 'give a firm commitment' to supplying a system to meet a 'large number of statutory instruments/regulations that still have to be laid before Parliament'. This was quite a challenge, but ICL agreed to it.

Other main issues in the hearing had included the speed with which the contract had to be signed. As we've already seen, many computer suppliers impose a deadline, sometimes legitimate sometimes artificial, to induce users to commit themselves to a contract, sometimes before they are ready to do so.

On occasions, false deadlines imposed by suppliers can be

Crash

exploited by the customer's computer department to persuade the chief executive to agree to funding a major purchase without proper consideration of whether the purchase is strictly necessary. It is not unknown for the computer manager to collude with the supplier to deceive the chief executive.

This happened in an organisation whose computer manager was later sacked. It happened in another organisation whose computer manager and supplier put a perfectly rational case to the chief executive for a new £1.5 million mainframe to run alongside the existing machine. It was only when the chief executive ordered an independent assessment of the computer manager's business case for requiring a new machine, that auditors discovered that the existing mainframe was only 10 per cent used. The other 90 per cent of its time was either idle or used by programmers to resolve software problems that had not been correctly analysed and investigated.

The other side of the coin is that it takes a bold chief executive to question both the computer manager *and* the word of a multinational computer supplier that is presumed to have grown big by always doing the right thing by its customers.

There was no evidence of any deception or foul play at St Albans but the judge was concerned about the way in which the council suddenly found that it had to sign ICL's standard contract quickly or lose its reservation on some vital hardware. In short, said the judge, the council had 'no realistic option other than to accept' ICL's terms.

Indeed the council said that it was not told until 19 October that the hardware could not be reserved beyond 24 October. This put it under additional pressure.

One of the ironies of the case was that ICL had originally won the contract, seeing off its main competitor IBM, partly because of the attractiveness of its terms and conditions. ICL's terms and conditions had scored 18 out of 20 in an independent evaluation of bids, compared with a score of only 12 out of 20 for IBM. The judge commented that there was no evidence that Coopers and Lybrand, which had helped to evaluate the bids on behalf of the council, had given 'any serious consideration to the terms limiting the defendants' liability.'

Yet, in the end, the judge found in favour of the council partly because he considered the contract unreasonable: and here there is a strong similarity with the Tindall Riley case in the last chapter. **In both court hearings, the inexperience of the user company counted in its favour against the supposed wisdom of the computer supplier.**

Perhaps the moral of this case, then, is that users who can prove their inexperience and can pitch this against the supplier's wisdom would be in a good position to sue if everything goes wrong – if the disaster has left them with a spare £500,000 or more for expert reports and a High Court hearing.

CHAPTER EIGHTEEN

The Tenth Deadly Sin:
Lawyers (IV)

There was nothing unique about the scene outside the High Court. It was one that had been witnessed many times before, and is seen regularly on television or in the newspapers.

The winning side, with its coterie of lawyers, spill out of the High Court onto the streets of London, all smiling broadly: the losing team follows shortly afterwards, shunning publicity.

But the two sides that emerged into the late October London sunshine from the Official Referees Court in 1992 – it has to be said into rather less than a tumultuous throng of well-wishers and media scrum – knew that the judgement was one that could prove to be a landmark in the short history of the UK computer industry.

It was one of the first times that a computer user had taken its IT supplier to the High Court over the large-scale failure of a system and won. This was not a protracted row followed by an out-of-court settlement that keeps publicity to a minimum. This was a trial that was watched keenly by the business press, so there was little that was gentlemanly about the accusations and counter-accusations.

At the end of a year-long case, in which the legal costs had been more than £1 million, the Salvage Association, an organisation better known for its marine insurance and surveying business, had proved to the High Court's satisfaction that its computerisation project had been a failure.

In return for its effort and courage in persisting all the way to court, the Salvage Association was awarded damages of £662,926 against the French-owned computer services company CAP Financial Services. In his judgement, Judge Thayne Forbes said the association was 'fully justified' in terminating its contract with the supplier.

CAP appealed against the judgement but lost this also.

So just how did a reputable supplier of computer services, with a reputation for successful project management, end up losing an acrimonious court case, the result of which left suppliers anxiously poring over their contracts?

The customer said that it ordered custom-made software and received a wreckage of a system. The supplier retorted that the end-users had made so many changes that they had committed professional suicide.

Although many of the claims and counterclaims are not unlike those in other chapters, they are worth recording to show that, although many projects seem unique at the outset, by the time they have ended up as a disaster, they all sound remarkably similar.

In its statement of claim against CAP, the association demanded the return of £291,388 paid under two contracts, as well as £432,004 for alleged wasted expense, and £139,674 worth of management time allegedly thrown away.

After completing foundation and definition work costing over £30,000, the association commissioned CAP to design, develop and install the system by July 1988 at a cost of £291,654 plus VAT.

But the association said the work had been carried out without reasonable care and skill and by incompetent personnel. The project was claimed to be the first that CAP had undertaken using software from the US-based Oracle company.

It was also said that staff who carried out systems test preparation had no experience other than that acquired on a one-week course on the software. The system was allegedly incapable of producing audit reports, balancing nominal ledgers, taking on initial data, or matching the debtor's ledger system.

At the time, the choice of Oracle was a bold one, for it was a new technology. Like Mapper (in the Tindall Riley case in Chapter 16), Oracle was a fourth-generation product, but one with a short track record at the time, and therefore there was little historical information about the success or otherwise of implementations at other sites.

Appropriately, innovative systems are often called 'bleeding-edge' technology because blood is on the floor before experience on how to use the product is obtained.

An older, third-generation language would have been more reliable, but the association was reluctant to use one because it felt that such languages were 'outdated', according to the court evidence of the CAP project manager, Graham Dickens.

Nevertheless, the association was warned that such a 'naked Oracle system' with no part of it written in third-generation languages would 'freeze to death'.

CAP admitted that the Oracle software was a 'relatively new system' and that few large projects had been completed with it. It also agreed that the company had comparatively little experience of using Oracle, but rejected the claim this was one of the prime reasons that the system was eventually implemented with 629 analysis and programming errors, which gave it a response time of minutes rather than seconds.

When the system was guillotined in July 1989, the errors had been cut to 78, but that was still too many.

While accepting that there were problems with the system, CAP blamed the end-users. They had inflicted problems on themselves by wanting to make too many changes that were not part of the original specification, said CAP, which also insisted that the Salvage Association had had a 'change of heart' over its original specifications, but had failed to make clear the functions it wanted.

In addition, CAP maintained that it had pointed out that the Oracle technology was largely unproven, even 'riddled with bugs', but still the association chose it in preference to third-generation technology.

Oracle too became embroiled in the case. It claimed in an audit for the association that CAP's original design was poor. In response, CAP's project manager said that, for all the software's trumpeted user-friendliness, 'Oracle were reluctant to admit that there were significant developmental problems with the package'.

But the association exonerated Oracle. Its project manager, Peter French, claimed in court that the Oracle software was not at fault. It was the way that CAP programs used the software that caused all the problems, he added. In a list of complaints over the system, he alleged that:
• user manuals were 'totally inaccurate', requiring operators to have a 'very detailed knowledge' of the database structure and Oracle software;
• the huge volume of manuals were 'generic and general' and

the keystroke-by-keystroke instructions were not specific to the system;

• eight users dealing with invoice production experienced maximum response times of 350 seconds – 'clearly far beyond the response times normally expected of interactive on-line systems';

• CAP staff were incapable of performing 'full multi-user tests' because they had only nine visual display units (VDUs) at their offices, compared with the association's 23.

When the problems with the response times emerged, the association was assured that remedial work would be completed by 1 January 1989 yet, by that date, the supplier had failed to correct errors or improve performance 'by a noticeable degree'.

Eventually, after a series of tense meetings between the two parties, the contract was terminated by the association a year after the implementation date, in July 1989. Legal proceedings began nine months later.

In his reserved judgement, Judge Thayne Forbes said:

> 'In my opinion, it is difficult to exaggerate the seriousness of the situation that faced the Salvage Association in July 1989 when it terminated the second contract.
>
> 'After two and a half years and payment of a total of £298,388, not to speak of the cost to the Salvage Association of the considerable time and efforts of its own staff, the system which had been delivered by CAP was still unusable. And, to the extent that the performance of the system could be tested, it had been shown to be very unsatisfactory.'

The judge added that he was 'not only satisfied that the association was entitled to terminate the contract and dismiss CAP, but that the decision . . . made perfectly good business sense.'

The case then hinged on the judge's interpretation of limited-liability clauses in the association's two contracts with CAP. The clauses restricted the total liability to £50,000, despite the fact that the system cost six times as much – about £300,000.

But the judge ruled that the limited-liability clauses came into effect only on the acceptance of the system; and the association had never accepted the system because it did not work.

After the case, the French-owned services company Sema, which had acquired CAP, questioned the judge's interpretation of the contract terms. It said that Sema was struggling to defend the conduct of a contract signed over four years earlier, under a different name, with a different management team, and different staff.

There was even another change of managing director before the current incumbent, Harry Fryar, took over.

'I have never previously had to go to court to sort out a problem with a customer,' said Fryar, who added that changes in Sema's personnel since the signature and subsequent cancellation of the Salvage Association contract had made Sema's case more difficult to justify.

'People who did the work in 1987 and 1988 are no longer with us. We had to try and persuade them to come to court and talk about their work with a previous employer. And all that is costing the time and money of their current employer.'

The outcome of the case has worried suppliers who are disputing poorly designed and developed systems with their customers.

Shortly before Christmas 1994, a medium-sized building and development company, Robert Hitchins, based at Cheltenham, issued a writ against ICL seeking nearly £2 million in damages, which the supplier said it would defend vigorously. The case was later settled out of court, after Hitchins decided to accept a lump-sum payment, from ICL.

This and the hearings detailed in earlier chapters suggest that it is worthwhile suing suppliers. But none of the victories were won without considerable pain.

The Salvage Association, for example, was hampered by the death of its chief accountant midway through the case, while Sema lost a legal adviser who went off to have a baby, and a solicitor from its legal firm, Herbert Smith, returned to Australia.

But High Court writs are not the only way to seek redress after a failure. Growing in popularity are 'alternative dispute resolution' methods. These include arbitration whereby the supplier and user agree to abide by the decision of an independent arbiter. Most major suppliers have a provision in their contract which allows for arbitration, one attraction being the fact that the press is not allowed to attend.

Although it is quasi-legal, the costs of such arbitration are lower because there is no need to hire barristers and QCs; and the legal processes are less involved. The Centre for Dispute Resolution, which strongly advocates arbitration rather than High Court action, says: 'We've been trying to improve awareness of the tremendous costs involved in litigation. There is the cost in management time, secretarial time, and research that's sucked in, as well the effect of publicity on the company's reputation. The legal costs are the tip of the iceberg.'

In one dispute, a chief executive found that 40 per cent of his time in a single year had been devoted to a case. It is conceivable, therefore, that in chasing a loss of £50,000 a medium-sized company could damage itself out of all proportion with the original loss.

And justice can take a long in coming. In the case of the Salvage Association the time between commissioning the system and receiving compensation was about ten years.

CHAPTER NINETEEN

Success at Last

THE WISDOM OF SIMPLICITY

If it is easy to see in retrospect why projects go wrong, it is just as easy to see why they sometimes go well.

The new customer system for Barclays Bank was big but simple.

Even the project name was simple – Customer System. Compare this with project names that were affectedly stately such as the Department of Health and Social Security's 'Computerisation and Mechanisation of Local Office Tasks' (which failed).

Barclays succeeded by doing everything against all the best-known marketing precepts. Normally companies sell their new project internally as the system to beat all others. This is accompanied by some nebulous internal marketing abstraction along the lines of: 'We have always delivered a superb computer service but this new system will provide an even better service and a new focus to our business.'

Barclays did the opposite: it denigrated the existing systems and lowered user expectations of the new ones. The reason was simple. The lower the user expectations of the software, the less they would be disappointed by it.

A clearly written information leaflet to all staff about the Customer System said, 'Current systems and practices hamper our ability to serve the customer in the way we would like to. It is difficult to concentrate on providing a high quality service when we have many complex procedures and little by the way of systems support to help us.'

And while most companies seek to pay as little as possible for as big a system as possible, Barclays paid a vast price for seemingly little.

Everything possible was done to reduce risks. It invested up to £110 million to build from scratch a new single IBM DB2 database which would bring together scattered information about customers and their accounts.

Prior to the project going live, the bank had two main systems, one based centrally and the other distributed in 2,000 or so branches.

The first system held details of customer balances and transactions. This produced bank statements but did not show a full account history, or provide a picture of the customer's business with the bank, which could include a variety of different accounts as well as pensions policies, life insurance, a Barclayloan personal loan, a Barclaycard credit card account, or other products or services offered by the bank.

These customer details were held locally, branch by branch. In effect the customer became the property of the local branch managers, who owned all the information about those clients who banked with them.

One of the main purposes of Customer System was to bring together all the locally held information about customers onto a single, central DB2 database.

This would mean that the local branch managers no longer 'owned' all the information on a particular customer's business. And that information would be brought back to the centre onto a master database. So the local branch customers would become the central bank's clients.

And all branches with access to the new master database could then view a customer's profile and records in other branches.

Where the account was held would become immaterial.

Customers could make amendments to their accounts from any branch. The new system would also produce a range of standard letters, using optional phrases, that could be dispatched centrally, bearing a facsimile signature, or produced locally if required.

None of this was anything particularly special. Newer banks, such as First Direct (part of Midland Bank), were already offering a fully computerised telephone-based banking service whereby bills could be paid, balances given, the last few transactions read out, or a loan decision made on the spot simply by making a call to one telephone number at local call rates wherever you are in the country – 24 hours a day, every day, throughout the year. And statements could be sent out weekly rather than monthly and be printed by cash-dispenser-type machines.

This may sound like an advertisement for telephone banking services, and I don't mind if it does. First Direct and Trustee Savings Bank are particularly good examples of computers being used for the direct benefit of customers. Their rapid success has encouraged bigger and more traditional banks such as Barclays to orientate their services towards the customer, while reducing operating costs.

To its credit, Barclays has not moved particularly swiftly. Caution has been its watchword.

The Customer System was left mainly in the hands of Andersen Consulting on the simple basis that if its consultants failed to deliver they would not be paid and would never work for the bank again.

Unsurprisingly then, the scope of the systems was extremely limited, particularly phase one.

In other companies the temptation might have been to try to leapfrog technologically all the competitors and introduce something innovative and grandiose that would swell the egos of the most senior project managers. That was never on the cards at Barclays, however, partly because bank employees tend to earn Brownie points for displays of circumspection, not entrepreneurialism.

Yet, although phase one would in fact deliver less than the existing computerised services offered by smaller banks such as First Direct, it would give Barclays a lead over some of the other major high street banks. And it was a big step for Barclays.

The objective was to introduce new systems into 1,000 branches in October 1994, each branch running a new IBM RS/6000 server linked to the master database.

Ideally the bank would have liked to run the old and new systems in parallel until everything was working satisfactorily. But the machine capacity required to run two massive sets of systems in tandem made the idea of parallel running impractical and uneconomic, especially as every amendment to existing information would have needed to be entered onto both systems simultaneously, and the two sets of databases reconciled.

It would have been a nightmare to administer. So a Big Bang

approach – switching off the branch systems and moving over rapidly to the new master database linked to 1,000 locally based servers – was considered to be the only feasible option.

The weekend chosen was 8–9 October 1994. All the old branch systems were brought down on the Thursday before. After that, staff were unable to gain access to them until the new systems came on stream four days later: Monday the 10th.

No sooner was the countdown under way than a disk head crash at the bank's Gloucester datacentre threw the timetables into a spin.

'Our systems prove reliable at least 364 days a year – and the one day we have a head crash is during the countdown to live day,' said one senior Barclays executive at the company's computer headquarters at Radbroke Hall in Cheshire.

The date for live day, 10 October, had been set eighteen months earlier, although the preparations began in earnest on the Wednesday, 5 October, when software systems started automatically merging 25 million customer records held on separate databases onto the single master database.

By mid-morning on Monday the 10th, it was hoped that nearly 1,000 branches would go live with the new system.

Up to 100 Barclays computer staff and 50 people from Andersen Consulting had been working on the project since 1992.

But the head crash, combined with a software bug, put the schedule back by two hours. To recover the lost time, Barclays prevented more than 10,000 branches logging into the branch systems for two hours on the Thursday morning before 'live' Monday. This allowed centrally-based staff to commandeer the central mainframes and to continue funnelling customer records onto the new database.

By the end of Thursday the project was back on time.

Everyone was casually dressed and calm for the crucial night shift that would check the integrity of the data going into the new database. One quality-checker, Nicola Edney, looked at her own account details and found errors – but only because of minor mistakes in the original data.

More impressively, she found that the new system had cleaned up and eliminated from her records details of defunct accounts.

By 4 a.m. staff were an hour away from making a decision on whether to abort or continue with the project. There had been some earlier problems with configuring the RS/6000s in local branches. Some of the branch staff had incorrectly configured the systems, with the result that they could not communicate with the master database. But the problems were small and isolated.

So a decision was taken to go ahead.

The bank had provided for stop-or-go points along the way, which allowed for the early termination of the project.

'Things are not perfect,' said Nicola Edney, 'but we have met the criteria.' Remarkably, the decision on whether to stop or continue the project was left to the shop-floor staff. In fact the go-live day had been planned on the assumption that it would fail. Staff had only to run down a checklist to see if the project should be postponed or not.

Yet by noon on Monday, 800 of the planned 1,000 branches had gone live. The remainder had local problems configuring their systems, but these were resolved, and by February 1995 nearly 1,800 branches were linked to the master database.

With the new systems running, branch staff found that little had changed and they might have wondered what the fuss was all about.

But phase one was 80 per cent technical change and 20 per cent business benefit. The second phase, by the end of 1995, delivered the remaining 80 per cent business benefit.

Its features touched on the trickier management issues such as automated credit scoring in local branches, which reduced the need for highly experienced bank managers, because the computers, and not people, took over decisions on loans and overdrafts.

Even phase two did not quite bring Barclays up to the technological level of First Direct, but it gave it a secure base on which to build new and innovative systems. It also greatly reduced the bank's administrative costs and the risks of holding inaccurate data.

For example, under the old systems a change of customer address needed to be entered and re-entered for every account in the customer's name – on loans, credit card accounts, statements, pension, life insurance and other records. With 25 million accounts, making amendments to them was time-consuming and costly. Under the new system, the modification was made only once.

The run-up to the Big Bang at Barclays may sound too good to be true, but there was never any panic, not even signs of duress, partly because the bank *had not set artificially tight deadlines*.

I was in the control room at the bank's Radbroke Hall datacentre headquarters all night during the all-important switch from old to new systems. Staff were allowed to talk openly about the problems, and how they were being solved. They felt part of the decision-making process.

Barclays had not imposed a new system on end-users without first establishing whether they wanted it, and also whether they would enthusiastically back the project from start to finish. In addition, it kept the end-users fully informed about all the problems all the time. It didn't allow them to make changes unless they were deemed vital, but let them feel part of the decision-making process.

If everything had gone badly, the changeover to new systems would have been postponed for another weekend until all the problems had been resolved. If major deficiencies had persisted, Andersen would not have been paid.

As it was, the testing and experimental runs had been exhaustive.

All the processes to be computerised were documented, kept simple and were fully understood. But the *pièce de résistance* was the internal marketing documentation, which was more impressive than any of the technical aspects of the project.

There were presentation packs, videos and single-sheet leaflets written in clear, jargon-free English, none of it doctrinaire, which explained exactly what Customer System would offer, when each phase was expected to go live, and what was expected of individuals in the branches.

Every imaginable question was posed and answered. There was even a 'what if' section, which set out the contingency plans if, for example, the main software tapes did not arrive in the branches for loading onto the RS/6000 servers.

Most importantly, staff were not assured that everything would have to be perfect first time. One of the questions asked in the internal literature says: What happens if Live Day goes wrong?

'Extensive testing has already taken place,' is the reply. 'Some of your colleagues may have been involved in this. Everything possible has been done to avoid problems but should something major occur we will revert to existing systems.'

But the big bonus points go to Barclays for the dogged refusal of managers to countenance changes requested by end-users unless the modifications were deemed absolutely vital.

'This made us quite unpopular with the end-users,' said a senior bank executive, 'but it helped to keep the final design close to the original one.'

The bank ensured it was not computerising a moving target.

Equally important to success was the post-mortem exercise, which was carried out in 1995 after phase one had been completed. This examined every managerial and technical aspect of the project, looking at what had gone wrong, why and how it could be avoided in future. And this was on a successful project.

The post-mortem was so crucial because it was a beacon to staff, warning that their every action and decision during the introduction of a major project would be scrutinised at a later date.

This introduced accountability without oppression, and is preferable to the attitude in many parts of the public sector where, if something goes wrong, all effort is directed at suppressing news of it.

In short the Barclays Customer System was a success because the bank had anticipated failure. Every contingency was in place, every possibility considered, particularly the human and business consequences of major change.

And at no time did suppliers try to market their system as a spaceship to the distant planets. Barclays would have known better, having spent thousands of millions of pounds on information technology in the last twenty years. And, being an experienced user of consultancies, it understood the need to manage them.

In many respects Barclays management was as competent as Andersen's senior consultants, which raises the question: why employ dozens of consultants? They were brought in to supplement the in-house skills. Barclays did not want to hire extra people only to make them redundant when the project was completed.

There was no possibility of serious problems being suppressed because everyone was encouraged to talk about difficulties as they arose.

In addition, senior business (*not* computer) managers ran the project, so they were healthily sceptical of the technology.

Also, there was no expectation that the new systems would lead to massive job cuts, only to an improvement in the speed and flexibility of services to the customers, as well as reducing the costs of the bank's computer operations.

There again, success did not come cheap; and the systems have their limitations. Few companies implementing computer projects will be wildly excited about the idea of spending tens of millions of pounds on scaling a technological molehill. But if you measure success in terms of pragmatism and not in glory, who needs to scale an Everest?

CHAPTER TWENTY

Another Rare Success

An unusual computer project this: the company commissioning the system gained more than the company supplying it.

The end-user company was the Abbey National building society and bank. A fixed-price project was completed to budget and on time in February 1994 from an original business proposal in 1991; and the project's success virtually guaranteed future business for the suppliers.

The scheme did not follow the Barclays Bank model set out in the previous chapter. Barclays paid a large sum for relatively little; in effect it paid a premium to lower the risks of failure.

Abbey National paid the minimum. However, for a major project, it could not have been simpler.

Most important of all, it started with a clean sheet of paper.

There was no long-established 'corpocracy' to burden the project with an inveterate business or technological culture. This left Abbey free to plan the procedures, discuss the staffing and training, and decide what exactly the business needed to gain from the new systems without internal political strife, or having the choice of new products restricted by the need to marry them with extant hardware and software.

In short, it was a 'green field' development. Yet, despite the simplicity of the approach, it was not without appreciable difficulties, although these were all overcome.

The Abbey National, until 1989, was the UK's second largest building society with 5.5 million shareholders who were also account holders.

It went public that year by floating on the Stock Market, and became the country's fifth largest bank. After the usual wave of small-shareholder selling, the number of investors finally settled at a steady 2.7 million, each of whom receives a dividend twice a year.

All public companies need by law to keep track of everyone who owns shares. This is not a simple job because shareholdings can change virtually on a daily basis; and every change is weighed down by a plethora of legal and regulatory requirements.

Sometimes companies do the job of share registration in-house, often run by the computer department, but, for the flotation and soon afterwards, Abbey decided to employ Lloyds Bank to keep the register, though the arrangement was far from ideal.

'They offered us a very competitive price,' said Phil Hallatt, Abbey National's director of shareholder service, who was responsible for managing the logistics of flotation and setting up the register. 'And we went there because they were the market leader and, because of the risk and the timescale, we couldn't do it ourselves. But we found that they didn't handle the register very well, and it was also extremely expensive.'

With one of the largest shareholder bases in the UK, and possibly the world, and seeing the possibility of gaining a competitive advantage, the Abbey commissioned a strategic analysis of what it ought to do.

What emerged were seven good reasons for keeping the register in-house:
1. to improve customer service;
2. to have better control of the database;
3. to capture and use management information;
4. to create more operational flexibility;
5. to cut costs;
6. to remove reliance on Lloyds;
7. to develop a profitable share registration system.

How should it be done? It could either use a package-based system or seek a bespoke solution but was not sure which.

Hallatt's group was given the go-ahead to produce a business plan to investigate the marketplace for a mainframe-based registration system.

The original intention was to make use of the City's plans for the Taurus paperless share settlement system, but Abbey dropped the idea when Taurus was cancelled (Chapter 10).

The new system would manage the business of keeping a

shares register. This would entail handling changes of names and addresses, keeping details of investments held and all financial reporting. It would also be used for preparing an annual return and dealing with enquiries and correspondence.

From day one, the system would have to handle:
- 16,000 mandate forms
- 6,000 items of legal correspondence
- 5,000 changes of address
- 2,150 items of general correspondence
- 1,350 dividends stops
- 2,000 non-market transfers and
- 4,000 phone calls a week.

'Our analysis of what the various packages provided showed that the top-scoring package offered us a maximum of 60 per cent of what we were looking for,' said Hallatt. 'We would therefore have had to develop the package considerably and that would have affected the finances. It was better to build it ourselves.'

A package would have represented the lowest risk, an adaptation of a package the highest risk. A bespoke development without the encumbrance of 'legacy' systems is medium-risk.

Hallatt considered that the packages on the market were fine for companies with a relatively low number of shareholders, but not for Abbey National's 5.5 million customers.

One of its requirements was to computerise the three-stage process by which its clients are sent a form, are asked to return it with details of their banks, and then share dividends are paid directly into their accounts.

Putting some of the details of the customer's investment on the bank mandate forms before sending them out is part of the service – but it would be too laborious a process by hand.

However Abbey could not find a ready-made software package that handled 100,000 bank mandates for dividend payments.

Also, it wanted document imaging systems. These would allow the bank to scan the paper share certificates and automatically transfer the information on the certificates into a database, so saving the manual keying in of a huge amount of data.

'We wanted something to help us with the front end of the business, such as dealing with large volumes of shareholders. We wanted to provide a level of service that we didn't believe you could get anywhere else,' said Hallatt.

Having decided to consider a bespoke development, the bank sent out a request for information from potential suppliers. It chose deliberately to conceal the exact nature of the system's purpose, relying on the responses to demonstrate suppliers' capabilities.

One of the would-be suppliers was the Italian company Olivetti. Its marketing manager, Yvette Randriamalaza, said, 'We didn't even know it was a share registration application. The invitation to tender was a very high-level thing; it did not talk about the business, it just talked about the image-processing requirement, and Abbey's projection of the numbers of documents. We put in a response in which we tried to imagine what they were trying to do.'

Eventually, the Abbey National told Olivetti's account manager that it was a system for share registration, and asked him and the other shortlisted supplier, NCR, to be more imaginative in their proposals.

But by this stage Abbey had a good idea of what it wanted. It was a formidable force, pushing the suppliers into delivering what Abbey wanted, not the other way around.

Already Abbey had visited US sites such as that of the retailer J.C. Penney and had seen how other share registration systems worked. These US sites bore little resemblance to Abbey's type of business but that did not matter. Abbey used the visit as a fact-finding mission, to see what was technologically possible and to get a feel for how other companies ran share registration schemes.

'It was the business processes that we saw that triggered our imagination,' said Hallatt. 'We were the driving force with the ideas as to how this technology could be used to our own benefit. We used Olivetti as the contractors and in the end they came round to our way of thinking.'

Randriamalaza's role was to take a business requirement and interpret it into a technical solution, and then use the computer programmers to produce the system.

'We knew we needed to do things like optical mark recognition because Abbey National had a lot of forms they wanted to process, and the key for them was that they wanted to use technology to provide productivity savings,' she said.

Olivetti then spoke to companies that could provide technologies such as bar-code recognition and low-speed image-processing. It then set out to negotiate a deal with Abbey.

'We had a team of developers working on the project, and we were coming up to a big exhibition at the time, and we decided we would build a prototype of what they wanted at the exhibition,' said Randriamalaza. 'Our team was so highly motivated that one of them who had had an accident and had his neck in a brace still came to the show and did the demonstration. That seemed to clinch the contract for us.'

At first Olivetti was selected only as preferred supplier. Final acceptance of its bid would come only after it provided a projected cost of the systems. This put Olivetti in a difficult position.

Normally it would go through a detailed analysis, including a cost-benefit analysis to calculate the figures, but Abbey wanted a cost projection quickly. Any delay might have held up approval of the project by the Abbey National Board.

'It is only at that point when you define the functionality that you are in a position to do an estimate of how much the project is going to cost. In this case, we were being asked to produce a figure way before that,' said Randriamalaza.

This was a potentially dangerous flaw in the process. The supplier was being rushed into producing a cost estimate. And the setting of an artificially tight deadline is a common denominator in many wrecked projects. Indeed the rushed pricing requirements did prove to be a problem – but for the supplier, not Abbey.

Urgent discussions took place between Abbey's project manager and Olivetti's account manager based on the demonstration models that Olivetti had built of the project in the pre-sale period.

And an estimate was given on which a fixed-price contract was awarded. In the end the project cost 25 per cent more than the fixed-price figure – a shortfall that Olivetti decided it would have to bear.

'A lot of people said it was wrong to do that estimate, and that we shot ourselves in the foot, but in the end we were able to come out of it not too badly off. We underestimated, because at that time, Abbey said they had their business procedures defined, which they did not really have, and so we had an extra phase.[*] It would have been a different financial story had it not been a fixed-price contract. But we have a very close strategic

[*] This was to define the requirements more clearly.

relationship with the Abbey National, and things came out probably in their favour.'

In this case, possibly because of its commercial muscle, the deal worked out well for Abbey National. It was able to wash its hands of the responsibility for the underestimation of costs. A smaller user company with little corporate clout might not have been able to negotiate a similar risk-sharing arrangement with its supplier. And, even if it did have such a fixed price contract, the supplier might still have tried to pass the extra costs back to the customer on the grounds that the original requirements had changed.

But Olivetti wanted Abbey's custom badly. So Olivetti's project and account managers found themselves working hard to justify the company's continued involvement in the Abbey project to Olivetti's management.

They won their endorsement by emphasising the importance of the strategic relationship with Abbey, and the potential business that this could generate.

Once the project was underway, Hallatt's prime task as project sponsor was to manage the scheme's passage through his organisation, ensuring that staff were aware of what was happening, what the problems were, and how they were being solved.

His team went through the laborious but vital process of ensuring that his executive committee were aware of what the plans were, and agreeing the budget. To keep open good lines of communications, there were regular progress and steering group meetings, some of which were attended by all the senior people in Abbey's business groups. So everyone was aware, at a policy and strategic level, of the major issues and how the project was progressing.

One of the chief causes of the failure of projects such as the London Ambulance Service's was the lack of any consultation with those who would use the system. Abbey bent over backwards to court the end-users, asking for their comments and securing their commitment, so that when the system went live, they would have an emotional equity in its success.

'We are not professional registrars but because of the problems we had with our previous registrar, we were thrown into contact with that area of work far more than probably any other company secretariat. What we did was bring on board people with the right "can-do" attitude who had strong ideas about customer service.'

Hallatt brought in staff with good project management skills from a London-based consultancy, CMG, which has specialised in running share registration systems.

CMG helped to handle the central mainframe-related aspects of the project while Olivetti worked on the document image-processing front-end system.

'At all stages, the users had an influential role and were moving things in the direction that they wanted. We had progress reviews, and the team reviewed every piece of work very thoroughly. This ensured we all understood the work so far and believed we were getting everything we asked for.'

It could all have been a disaster, however. There were two main suppliers, Olivetti and CMG each of which required managing to avoid conflicts and misunderstandings which could have jeopardised the project.

However, Abbey was prepared – and experienced – in managing suppliers. It also had a clear idea of what the business was trying to achieve, of the technology available, and what it wanted the suppliers to do.

Moreover, it understood what the suppliers were capable of delivering.

What should also be remembered, however, was that Abbey had little to lose. If the project had failed, it would simply have carried on using the Lloyds registration system. And it would not have paid Olivetti any money under the contract.

The project was also made immeasurably simpler by the absence of any need for a Big Bang or cut-over decision.

'If the operation was already up and running, then there would have been far more work required in terms of redesigning the forms and the documentation. They would probably have vast amounts already in stock, and there would be existing processes in place which would need to be reviewed. When we started they had no processes in place,' said Randriamalaza.

As it moved towards the final stages of the project, Abbey went through extensive user-acceptance testing. Then the bank said in effect to Olivetti: 'We've tested the functionality and it meets what you said you were going to deliver. Now let's see if it works for the sort of volumes we want to put through the system.'

Although it was up to Olivetti to prove that the system could deliver the claimed performance, equally there was an onus on the bank to provide the correct information on which to base the volume tests.

It is worth remembering here that many projects flounder because users fail to show sufficient commitment to them and fail to provide enough information for the supplier to build a system.

Abbey's responsibility to Olivetti was to give figures on exactly what volumes the system would have to cope with, at normal and peak times, and allowing for growth.

The Abbey team therefore had to approach Lloyds, the registrar it was abandoning, to get information on the volumes of work. This was not easy: and neither was the volume testing.

'We found that the level of Filenet software we were using was causing us problems with performance. So we spoke to Filenet about it, and they told us that there was a new release coming out which we were able to use to improve response times,' said Randriamalaza.

With the volume tests completed, Abbey then set up an area to run as a real production office – a model office. So it was able to test how the business procedures ran in a real office environment.

In the end the new system proved to be the most tested in use at Abbey National: it is also the one with the fewest operational problems.

The bank had proceeded with a punctilious caution, which may seem to cost more and take longer than doing it all in one go, but the cost and time disadvantages are more than offset by the reduction in the risk of failure.

The bank also found that 25 to 30 fewer people were needed to maintain the new systems than it first envisaged. This brought follow-on savings in terms of space, furniture, equipment and support costs. The total savings on the budgeted costs were £2.5 million.

However, Abbey and Olivetti suffered 'people' problems that could have held up the project. Hallatt's difficulty was that, with the project nearing completion, staff had to be moved from a project into a management role where they would use different skills.

'You have to ensure that people are free from the project to start training and start managing their own areas and be ready for the launch. That was a complicated issue, and some people were released into their management role later than we would have liked. We had to be aware of who was going to do what and provide them with the maximum opportunity to be released from the project.'

Olivetti's staff problems were equally tiresome. Some key staff were promoted or left the company. Also, when Randriamalaza finished her business analyst role to become involved in product development, her former job was filled by a replacement member of staff – who soon had to leave the project because of pregnancy.

'Someone took over my role and did a good job and it was key for her to stay on. Then she became pregnant, so they videoed her training sessions because they did not know if she would be around later. There were an awful lot of long hours being worked by people who Abbey thought were key to the project.'

Hallatt believes the project has been one of the bank's most successful information technology projects. 'We launched the in-house register on 28 February 1994, and one of our objectives was ultimately to offer this service to other companies,' he said.

'But we couldn't do that until we had proved to both ourselves and other companies that we could manage our business. We now have a record low level of complaints, and we have customer satisfaction levels which exceed anything I have ever seen.'

So why did this project succeed? The following helped:
• a realisation from the outset that there would be problems and mistakes, and that there should be processes to ensure that everyone knew about them;
• recruitment of people with the right attitude and skills, matched with recruitment of contractors with whom the users could work closely;
• strong management of suppliers;
• tight planning and regular reviews to identify easily any variances and issues that may lead to delays further along the line;
• clear project management structure, featuring close monitoring of change, progress and testing;
• good communications – minutes were kept of all meetings so that actions were not made on the basis of word of mouth;
• cohesive team structure – Audit, IT and Human Resources departments were all involved in the project, so everyone was motivated by a common purpose;

- clear buy-in to the project by business end-users and top-level board sponsorship based on precise benefits to the business offered by the system;
- comprehensive risk and cost/benefits analyses, which led to a mandate from senior executives for the project to go ahead.

However, the project made a successful sea crossing because the sun was shining, there were no waves, the crew was motivated and the distance was so short that the captain could see the other side before setting sail. And if it had all gone badly wrong, there was even an on-board helicopter – the existing Lloyds Bank service.

Despite all these advantages, the crossing was far from straightforward – which says a great deal about most projects in this book, which set sail in hurricane-force winds, in complete darkness, the navigator disorientated, and the captain and crew torn asunder by internal power struggles.

The following chapter describes just such a journey – in fact a series of them.

CHAPTER TWENTY-ONE

The US Experience

Welcome again to the wonderful world of US government computing where $25 billion (£16 billion) a year is spent on computer systems, many of which are often incompatible, obsolete and inappropriate for their users' needs.

In the last ten years, it is estimated that a total of more than $200 billion (£129 billion) has been spent on systems that have left the US government administratively and financially worse off than prior to computerisation.

At least before computers the US government was able to access most of the information in its files. Today much of the data it needs is unavailable, incomplete or unusable.

It is remarkable how the US and UK governments have unconsciously mirrored and regularly repeated each other's flaws.

Each project disaster comes as a surprise, a minor setback which can be forgotten by launching a fresh project which re-motivates staff and managers.

US illustrations of failures tend to be more graphic because of the openness of the administration. And everything is on a much grander scale.

Nobody talks of losses in millions, or even *tens* of millions. To be worthy of special attention in an official report you must have lost billions, preferably a few hundred of them.

For example, the Department of Defense accounting systems are less than accurate. At one point $41 billion of payments made by the department could not be matched with invoices from suppliers. The department rained down money on suppliers; some of the suppliers didn't know what to do with it and some sent the money back. In a six-month period in 1993 suppliers, entirely of their own volition, sent back $751 million because they said the department had overpaid them.

The Federal Aviation Administration – the US equivalent of the Civil Aviation Authority – saw costs on one part of its air traffic control system rise from $2.5 billion to $7 billion. Now the whole scheme, begun in 1981, is likely to cost over $30 billion.

The Department of Veterans' Affairs, which processes welfare claims from US military veterans, has spent ten years trying to modernise its systems. At one point it spent $206 million to reduce the processing time of compensation claims from veterans from 180 to 106 days. But two years into the programme, the processing of claims went up to 225 days – almost eight months.

One cause of the problems is the US government's belief in its uniqueness. It shuns the simple in favour of the esoteric, hoping that computers will slip into the clothes worn by the manually based processes.

And it failed to fully appreciate that moving from the decades-old way of working to the computer age was no less of a challenge than General Hannibal's trek across the Pyrenees – and just as successful ultimately: Hannibal committed suicide rather than be handed over to the Romans.

The problem for governments and technology is that computers work so much more quickly than people and do not bend so much as a millimetre to accommodate human caprice, error, changes and all the procedural idiosyncrasies that comprise the soul of public-service administration.

Problems that used to be simple to circumvent when procedures were manual prove time-consuming, expensive and complicated to work around once computers are installed.

Yet the US and UK government departments continue to think that computers can and should achieve anything that humans require of them. For example, in the Gulf War, the US military authorities provided TV film showing how computerised missiles could find their targets so precisely that they could follow streets, climb buildings and zip down chimneys. What they were less willing to discuss were the number of times these ultra-intelligent missiles mistook friendly forces for the enemy.

But self-deception is an intellectual lacuna in the field of vision of any project manager.

It may also help to explain why departments operate in isolation: they all think so highly of their own administrative processes that they usually do not want to know how others work.

So, despite the good intentions of the individuals who work in government, the institutions themselves are too big, too self-satisfied, often too self-admiring and usually too reactionary to be capable of reform.

And to outsiders, departments will continue to appear as if they regarded profligacy as a virtue, indeed as the best way to retain existing empires and build new ones. Frugality is a torment to be suffered only in the private sector. In government, if a system is not platinum-plated it is not worth buying.

In this respect, and others, the UK and US governments are alike.

A series of US reports shows that projects are characterised by the inordinate length of time between conception and delivery, and the extraordinary effort used to develop programs that avoid any commercially available products.

The reports also show how it usually took longer to acquire the systems than was spent developing the technology used in them.

And by the time the systems came into service, if ever, the technology had long been superseded.

Yet the US government knows that its laborious bidding competitions will yield prehistoric systems.

So now it habitually signs contracts, then ditches the original proposals and orders the latest technology.

The result is that the winning bidder then becomes a monopoly supplier of a system that has not been the subject of open competitive tendering.

This enables the supplier to charge the government virtually what it likes for all changes to the contract – which are numerous.

To win these 'monopoly' contracts losing bidders are prepared to spend millions of dollars appealing against the contract decisions. This holds up the buying process even more, thus ensuring that by the time the appeal is heard, the original contract specifications will have fossilised.

The costs of these appeals are significant. They involve court proceedings, delays to the project, the need to deal with an incumbent contractor, and the tying up of a department's procurement personnel, who need to prepare a legal argument in defence of their decision to award a contract to a particular supplier.

For example, the Department of Commerce spent around $1 million defending its decision to award a contract worth $12.3 million. And the Department of Labour believes it lost over $300,000 in productivity gains due to project delays caused by four legal cases over disputed contract awards.

Merely protesting against a decision can be lucrative for a supplier. Government departments and agencies faced with potential cancellation or delays to their projects have been known to pay 'Fedmail' (sweeteners) to firms that drop their protests against the award of a contract.

It has even been suggested that 'winning' firms have paid off 'losing' contractors to prevent them protesting against the contract.

The reward to the taxpayer for all this effort is that many of the systems installed at government departments do not talk to each other; and there are no government-wide standards that mandate communications between departments.

For example, the Department of Veterans' Affairs has 150 different computer systems; the Department of Housing and Urban Development has about 75; and the Agency for International Development maintains 45 different systems around the world to track its property, but most cannot share data with each other.

The worst offender is the Department of Defense. It operates over 160 different 'major' accounting systems and hundreds of 'minor' systems on old mainframes.

A report on the 'chaotic' state of US computing by a US senator, William Cohen, described public-sector systems as antiquated, expensive to operate and incompatible, contributing to 'vast inefficiencies in government management.'

The Department of Defense's systems contain programs that are thirty years old; the Internal Revenue Service (the tax-collecting US equivalent of the Inland Revenue) spends nearly $1 billion a year operating its existing systems; and the Federal Aviation Authority's air traffic control systems have scarcely been updated since the mid sixties.

Some air traffic control technology is so dated it relies on vacuum tubes from Poland. In comparison, the UK's Civil Aviation Authority has sprinted from the Jurassic to the more modern Cretaceous period by replacing its IBM 9020D air traffic control system at West Drayton near Heathrow Airport with two newer, but scarcely leading edge, IBM 4381 machines. This is sensible because the 4381s are proven and reliable.

In the US, as in the UK, poor project management, together with unrealistic expectations, are identified as the main causes of failure.

But the US differs from the UK in that it has a strong and influential supervisory agency, the General Accounting Office, which not only peers into the hole once a project team has plunged into it, but tries to find all the holes in advance of a project's approval.

But the GAO's philanthropy rarely seems to make any difference, because it cannot be everywhere simultaneously.

Within the last four years, the GAO has reported on 74 computer systems developments, and complained mostly about vague requirements analyses, the poor quality of general management, and the lack of benefits.

None of this is new: the GAO's equivalent surveys in the mid-60s commented on similar managerial problems and led to Congress demanding centralised systems purchasing.

The most common problem, according to the GAO, is inadequately defined requirements: in other words departments do not know exactly what they want, or cannot put it on paper.

Perhaps they have something to learn from Abbey National (see Chapter 20), which knew far more about the business and technology requirements than its suppliers.

But in the US, agencies have been trying to update their systems in advance of rethinking and reforming their business practices.

Far from simplifying and simplifying again, departments have been tinkering with the edges of the existing procedures to try to adopt a more creative approach to setting out systems specifications. This has made things worse.

The requirements have become so ludicrously detailed that unless they could fill the space of a public library they were not considered fit for issue.

This esotericism rules out the purchase of commercial off-the-shelf packages, which are cheaper than tailored programs, and take less long to develop.

In contrast the private sector in the US is much more likely to use off-the-shelf packages. It also benefits by having an average purchasing cycle of around thirteen months, against four years in the public sector.

A computer industry maxim is that processor technology doubles in power every eighteen months, so a four-year public procurement is likely to span two leaps in technology.

One department with particularly deep-rooted problems is the Federal Aviation Administration. Its role includes making air travel safer, ensuring a competitive airline industry, and undoubtedly the most difficult task: modernising air traffic control systems.

The sums involved are almost too high to comprehend. By the year 2000, the Federal Aviation Administration is expected to have spent $32 billion modernising US air traffic control systems.

Of the 200 projects included in the Administration's modernisation programme, only 3 per cent have so far been completed. Even in 1992, a GAO report was bemoaning the fact that 'twelve major projects, accounting for a third of the cost of modernisation, have an average schedule delay of 5 years'.

One of the Administration's biggest computer-related projects saw its budget rise from $2.5 billion to $7 billion. Its scope was then curtailed. An independent evaluation of the programme found that:
• the Administration did not have the necessary management and engineering expertise to undertake such a large programme;
• the management process lacked authority and discipline;
• responsibility was not clearly assigned;
• accountability was absent.

The report went on to say that the Administration's leadership did not enforce milestones, assess performance, or fix individual responsibility. And, as at the London Ambulance Service, there was a failure to fix all the problems that had been identified early in the project.

A Congress view of the Advanced Automation System which was supposed to replace air traffic controllers' workstations and PCs suggested that the implementation was hindered by:
• an over-ambitious development and implementation plan put forward by the Administration and IBM;
• inadequate oversight by the Administration of IBM's performance – eventually another US contractor, Loral, bought out IBM's Federal Systems Division and took over the project;
• the Administration changed requirements and failed to resolve issues as basic as the format of electronic flight data strips to be

used by controllers.

Aviation officials were also criticised for awarding a contract that, according to the GAO, should not have been awarded. The background to the deal shows graphically how easily the rationale for buying new systems can be manipulated by the managers, who are anxious to win approval for a project.

The project was called Corn (Computer Resources Nucleus) which, it was hoped would meet the FAA's general-purpose information technology needs for ten years and help to run other parts of the Department of Transportation.

The estimated cost of Corn was put at around $1.5 billion.

If all went well, it would replace an existing network called the Common System, which comprised an IBM 3084 mainframe and 22 Data General MV/15000 minicomputers distributed around twelve sites – headquarters, nine regional offices and two data centres.

But the new scheme would not comprise replacement hardware and software.

The FAA argued that it was not feasible to upgrade existing systems because they were a 'hodgepodge of widely varying equipment that were inefficient and wasteful of critical staff and funding resources'.

Instead the FAA decided, controversially, to 'free itself from the administrative and technical burdens involved in acquiring, managing, and operating its own general purpose facilities'.

What this meant was contracting out everything to a supplier, who would provide, operate and maintain a new system to be defined by the contractor on the basis of a ten-year Federal Aviation Administration plan. The existing Common System would be closed down.

The chosen contractor would then convert the existing programs and data to the new system on a fixed-price basis. It would also prepare documentation, provide technical staffing, support and training to agency end users, select and manage subcontractors and implement system upgrades.

In the meantime, the authority's remaining information systems staff would transfer from managing an in-house system to helping business end-users meet their information needs.

The FAA was in for a surprise. The GAO, unlike its equivalent in the UK – the National Audit Office – has the power to stop contracts before they are awarded.

In this case, the Federal Aviation Administration's plan to contract out all its computer operations was ridiculed by the GAO, which was asked to investigate by a senior Congressional committee.

It emerged that the FAA had exaggerated the problems of the old system to justify the new.

For example, aviation functionaries had claimed that the Common System users were getting inadequate response times because the computers had reached their capacity; but this claim was not supported by any evidence.

Indeed, the FAA had 'virtually no data' to prove that there were unacceptable response times to end-users, or that there was a lack of processor capacity.

Even the assertions that Corn was necessary because the agency's information technology needs would increase faster than its ability to upgrade were rejected.

The GAO told the FAA that the data and methodology used to make its growth projections were 'inadequate', raising further doubts about the necessity for the Corn approach.

In a 32-page report, the GAO told the FAA that it had not justified the need for Corn, and accused the agency of:
- gathering insufficient data on current system performance
- failing to provide enough data on response times
- using ten-year projections based on sparse, inadequate data
- making unsupported assumptions of level of service needs
- adopting a validation strategy that would not adequately test Corn systems
- providing unreliable assessments of conversion costs and the level of staff support required for this.

Specifically, the GAO discovered that the FAA lacked a 'central capacity and performance management program for the Common System, even though this was important to ensure maximum use of existing resources and to provide adequate capacity for growth'. In plain English this meant the authority did not know how much hardware it was using, and how much it needed in the future – so how could it know it wasn't enough?

There is a federal government regulation that requires agencies to work out their hardware needs. It is called officially 'performing capacity management activities in planning, acquiring and using computer resources'.

But the GAO found that the FAA had not done its capacity

planning homework. It therefore condemned the FAA's claim that poor response times were caused by insufficient hardware capacity.

In fact an analysis by the GAO of response times showed that the interactive, time-sharing options subsystem was giving more than adequate response times of less than a second.

The GAO went on to suggest that the FAA's slow response time could have been caused by reasons unconnected with the processor capacity, namely:

- inefficiencies in the design of software programs;
- contention for peripheral devices such as disk and tape drives;
- problems in the Administrative Data Transmission Network communications system linking users and the Common System;
- inefficient management of current system resources.

The GAO found that the mainframe system contained an operating system module that was designed to optimise the trade-off between throughput and response time. The module was like a set of transaction traffic lights. It gave control over which batch jobs were allowed into the computer's memory and at what point they were allowed in. This improved the efficiency of the system. However, the authority in effect turned off the traffic lights. It denied control to the module by not allowing batch jobs to be initiated during primetime hours. Therefore, the GAO suggested, there were instances of computing tasks using only hundredths of a second of processor time, yet waiting hours before they were initiated because the traffic lights to the processor were set at 'red'. In one case, a job waited eighty hours at the traffic lights but, once it was allowed to go, the task used only 0.06 of a second of processor time.

The GAO also found that the FAA was unprepared for converting its existing code to the new system. Another US government supervisory agency, the Federal Software Management Support Center, had warned that software conversion is 'labour intensive, management intensive, machine resource intensive, and deadline intensive. In short it has all the wrong attributes for a successful enterprise, and many problems will arise.'

It was considered that the Federal Aviation Authority's Corn project would involve the conversion of nearly 290 software programs, comprising 15 million lines of code. At best it was likely to be costly, disruptive and time-consuming. At worst it would be a disaster.

The GAO suggested that the conversion would probably cost 'substantially more' than the planned $74.5 million estimate which was based on an unreliable inventory of programs and excluded the cost of fixing major documentation deficiencies.

Between 1987 and 1989 differing estimates put the number of software programs that needed to be converted at between 200 and 500. Similarly, estimates of the number of lines of code ranged from 10 million to 18 million.

Even project officials admitted that, in a briefing document on Corn, conversion would not be easy because 'the FAA's knowledge of what currently exists to be converted is far from perfect'.

By February 1989, the uncertainty over the inventory of software programs was such that the FAA received complaints from would-be suppliers who claimed that the Corn specifications were 'incomplete, confusing, and did not provide an adequate basis for making a fixed-price offer.'

Two months later, the Administration conceded that its documentation was neither adequate nor accurate. Its own analysts reported that the documentation contained obsolete versions of applications, and applications that were no longer in use.

As if to exacerbate the confusion, between February and August 1989, the projected number of programs to be converted oscillated between 247 and 279, and the number of code lines rose from 12.8 million to 14.8 million.

By the following February, the estimate had risen even further to 289 applications. The conversion cost estimates also omitted the cost of enhancing, updating or rewriting the out-of-date documentation.

Originally, the FAA's officials maintained that the additional costs of correcting the documentation could be offset by a decrease in the number of lines to be converted following a review of the program inventory.

Eventually, though, they conceded that the additional documentation would add close to 10 per cent to the original $74.5 million cost estimate.

The catalogue of errors eventually gave the GAO little option but to recommend that the Corn contracts should not be awarded.

In theory the GAO had prevented a disaster.

Its reasons for stopping the project were damning. It accused the FAA of several things.

• It had done a poor job in tracking Common System utilisation, monitoring the systems performance, optimising the use of its current resources, and identifying the causes of perceived response time and performance problems.

• It could not make a reasonable projection of its anticipated growth in general-purpose data processing over ten years. The figures it had produced – a projected growth rate of 30 per cent per year compounded for ten years – were based on inadequate data and oversimplified analysis of the agency's workload. The estimated Corn contract value had then been increased by about 40 per cent to accommodate the 30 per cent annual growth rate.

• It had not provided would-be suppliers with important information on the performance of the current system to enable them to develop a coherent proposal to meet the FAA's needs. Suppliers were being asked to work blindfold with their hands tied behind their backs. Without the correct information, suppliers would have had to make assumptions about crucial characteristics of the current systems in order to model their solutions to the agency's needs.

• It had not provided agency management and Congress with reliable information on the funding, staff resources and time frames of the conversion. The cost estimate of $74.5 million was unreliable and incomplete, and the conversion timetable originally specified a quick eighteen-month effort. This was then extended to three years after the project was approved, with the costs likely to run as high as $105 million.

• It had overstated the likely improvements to software programs. Problems currently found in databases were likely to be transferred to the new system at considerable cost.

The initial project was a chimera which was itching to inflict damage but which had been killed off because the GAO had adhered to the unwritten rule that chief executives or their auditors should continually seek assurances that a major project is under firm and successful control and not believe the assurances they are given without an early independent audit. Worryingly, the business case, naïve and inadequate as it was, would probably have been approved in the UK because there is no body such as the GAO which goes

around destroying inchoate project disasters.

The Federal Aviation Administration provides a particularly good case study of a computer department that wants to launch a new project without a good case for doing so. But this was a disaster averted. The same cannot be said for the following.

The Federal Deposit Insurance Corporation abandoned development of a workable system to track asset values and calculate interest payments, despite having liquidated hundreds of banks with computer systems that performed these functions. The organisation was unable to collect loans, and failed to maximise revenue for the government in liquidating bank assets.

The Resolution Trust Corporation designed its computer systems without consulting its users, leading to millions of dollars in wasted investments and lost opportunities to track and dispose of more than $100 billion in assets.

The Department of Defense's failure to modernise its systems is said to have had a serious effect on military readiness and the department's ability to buy major weapons systems. Its Corporate Information Management programme is one of the largest technology initiatives ever undertaken and is designed to streamline systems and avoid duplication. The DoD had claimed that up to $36 billion could be saved from efficiencies generated by the technology programme by 1997, if the three services – Army, Navy and RAF – could agree how to work more efficiently. So far, inter-service rivalry, together with inadequate planning and ineffective management and incompatible systems, has afflicted its progress. The DoD has more than 1,700 computer centres where there are literally thousands of incompatible information systems. It is little wonder the DoD relies on its suppliers to tell the department when they have been overpaid. The problems have become so acute that the DoD has even bought $30 billion of spare parts it did not need because of problems with inventory systems.

The Federal Crop Insurance Corporation began working on a new computer acquisition before adequately determining its needs. So far it has spent $62 million, money that will be wasted if, as expected, a proposed reorganisation within the Agriculture Department changes the way the program works.

The Internal Revenue Service has been developing incompatible systems without first considering how the hardware it is buying will fit into an overall system. Inadequate planning and strategic changes of direction characterise some of its massively expensive projects. Between 1993 and 1997, the Revenue Service planned to spend $7 billion on computerisation; and a further $16 billion before 2003. Its Tax Systems Modernization Plan was criticised by a government agency for using old cost estimates, and for its overly optimistic technological assumptions. To make the point, Congress carved $340 million from the $989 million that President Clinton had wanted for the project. Further, battles over funding of the systems are certain.

The US National Weather Service relies on old systems to help protect lives and property. According to an internal report, improved systems could have given earlier notice of the floods of 1993, reducing human suffering and saving millions of dollars in damage to property. A programme is in place to replace the systems, but costs have risen from $1.4 billion to $4.6 billion, and the project may be halted because the GAO considers the modernisation is inadequately planned. The Meteorological Office in Britain has also spent heavily on new supercomputers to improve its performance, largely on the back of its failure to predict the hurricane-force storms of 1987.

Jack Brock of the GAO says much of the problem with US government computing stems from the management of information technology within individual agencies.

He believes none of the agencies within the US government can consistently say it has implemented projects effectively.

Brock spent a five-year stint at GAO looking widely at the problems of US systems implementation, before moving on to look more closely at the DoD, the State Department and NASA.

He feels that departments must better understand that information is a resource that has to be managed. He admits he has 'not seen giant strides in the management of information, but I did see some recognition of it'.

The GAO has made it clear to departments that information does not manage itself, nor can it be left only in the hands of technical staff.

The biggest difficulty, according to the GAO is the 'separation' between the top management of an agency and its computer operations.

This is also a common problem in the commercial world.

Directors give approval for a project, and direct its strategic direction, but the computer managers are not empowered to cancel it, or even to question its future.

Theirs is not to reason why but to try to get on with the development as well as they can. Also, there is no link between information-technology spending and what it is supposed to achieve.

The GAO said it recognises that there are lessons that can be learned from the private sector, notably that information technology is an investment that needs to be controlled like any other corporate investment. In other words there must be a rate of return.

Some documentary guidance on achieving best practice has now been issued by the GAO which is littered with executive-speak, but it's pretty worthy stuff. It lists at least nine things that companies should do.

1. Make line managers accountable for the impact of IT, and get them involved in information management decisions.

2. Pick internal project champions to shepherd day-to-day improvement actions, and establish incentives tied to successful resolution of performance problems identified by top management.

3. Anchor strategic planning to customer needs and mission goals. This demands the ability to match the needs of external and internal customer groups with specific products and services, because without a customer focus any organisation risks ignoring what matters to key stakeholders.

4. Measure the performance of key delivery processes. Such a measure means gauging the service provided to key customers and embedding performance measures in management processes such as planning, budgeting, investment selection and even the appraisal of individual staff. This will influence decision-making and support continuous improvement.

5. Focus on process improvement in the context of an architecture, bearing in mind that IT projects that do not take account of business processes are doomed to fail. Process improvements using IT pursued in an uncoordinated fashion can result in chaos and incompatibility. Therefore senior management needs to lead a high-level analysis of the organisation, and to appoint a business and information architect to facilitate the

design and maintenance of an organisation architecture that takes into account work processes, information flow and technology.

6. Manage IT projects as investments. This requires linking IT decisions closely to programme budget decisions, and establishing a high-level investment review board to help make key decisions throughout a project's life cycle. It also involves making projects as narrow in scope and short in duration as possible to minimise risk and increase success probability.

7. Integrate the planning, budgeting and evaluation processes. Managers should put all five elements of the strategic planning cycle in place: long-term strategic and information planning; systems life cycle and project level planning; budget review; performance assessment; and architecture management. This means that sight of critical projects is never lost and is treated consistently, despite disparate management processes. This helps link IT efforts to the organisation's mission, provides tight controls during implementation, and allows regular assessment to ensure benefits accrue from the investment.

8. Establish customer/supplier relationships between line managers and IT professionals. To achieve this means making line managers responsible for identifying critical information and performance needs, work requirements and the economic benefits of mission improvement projects. Then IT professionals need to be made responsible for the support of line managers, acting as suppliers of support efforts to meet a management objective, make a critical decision, or solve a business problem. Increasingly, as well as providing systems, this can involve supplying advisory services. This is all designed to achieve specific missions, goals and objectives, rather than satisfying sometimes unrelated user requirements.

9. Appoint a Chief Information Officer as a senior management partner. This will bridge any gaps between top management, line management and IT staff and can design and facilitate the implementation of new organisation capabilities by articulating the role of information systems in mission improvement. The role demands a combination of leadership ability, technical skills, business process understanding and communication skills.

But, though advice like this is commendable, it has been circulating for more than a decade with no influence on the failure rate of computer projects in the UK or US.

In Britain, Whitehall's computer agency, the CCTA has in the past churned out books of similarly solid advice to little practical effect. Perhaps the problem is that there is too much generalised guidance and not enough specific help.

The above fine words are more abstract, more conceptual and more difficult to remember when you are trying to implement your own computer project and run a business at the same time.

Also, they are not sufficiently proscriptive and so allow too much margin for interpretation and therefore error. They need to state unambiguously what does and does not work.

But without being too negative, it is hard to imagine that the sort of advice given in this book will make the slightest difference in government, where faces change, accountability is a mission statement only, and collective responsibility is the whitening liquid that comes out of the stationery cupboard whenever disaster strikes, to protect the names of the project's 'visionaries'.

In Britain there is a leaflet which is given to new employees of Her Majesty's Treasury in London's Whitehall. It applies equally to the US Treasury when it states: 'Mistakes never happen but there are readjustments, corrected forecasts, re-projected estimates and unavoidable cost increases'. The leaflet goes on, 'A layman would say that Treasury estimates are always wrong. This shows no understanding of the way public money works. So how does public money work? By adding noughts. Noughts should be added to the end of any estimate to bring it into line with reality.'

That there are success stories in government computing is not in question. Nobody is claiming that departments always get it wrong, only that they tend not to learn from past mistakes.

As the Treasury leaflet states: 'There's always enough money to pay for things. If you run out of noughts apply for some more. And remember that the bigger the sum is, the less criticism it will arouse.'

The leaflet is clearly a spoof − except that I don't know a single person in the US or UK Treasuries who regard it as such.

CHAPTER TWENTY-TWO

The Experts

This one is short but irresistible. It is the US antithesis of the earlier success story at Abbey National.

The reason Abbey National's project was a success was that it knew exactly what it wanted, what technology was on offer, and what its chosen supplier could deliver. This is unusual. Many user organisations know what they want and assume that any competent supplier can deliver it. Naïvely, they throw up their hands in ignorance and tell the chosen supplier: 'It's over to you . . .'

This doesn't work. There's usually an insurmountable gap between what the customer thinks the systems will do, and what the supplier thinks the customer has asked for.

The more abdication of responsibility by the user, the less successful the project. This is because the supplier knows its own skills and software inside out, but has little idea of how these will fit the customer's business. The customer knows the business inside out but has little idea how the supplier's skills and software will fit.

Reconciling these differences is the key to a successful implementation.

And the way to do it is for the customer to take the time to learn about the supplier's level of skill and its software; and for the supplier to take the time to learn about the customer's business.

The following short tale shows the dangers of leaving everything to the supplier, in this case a consultancy.

In 1995 an eighty-year-old engineering company, UOP, issued a $100 million fraud lawsuit against a multinational computer consultancy, Andersen Consulting, which we first met in relation to the Wessex fiasco in Chapter 4.

Based in the USA, UOP is an $800 million engineering company that develops technology used in oil refineries. It hired Andersen to streamline its engineering specification and cost estimating processes, and also to develop a series of client/server software programs.

Three years later, UOP's president and chief executive officer, Michael Winfield, claimed that 'the difference between what Andersen promised us at the outset and what it actually delivered was staggering.'

Eugene Schmelzer, director of support systems centres at UOP said, 'From the beginning, we were not included in the actual development process. Andersen kept us at arm's length and insisted on using their own staff for coding and software work. They also kept re-estimating the number of man-hours it would take to complete the project.'

According to the lawsuit, Andersen deployed inexperienced staff who delivered incomplete and largely unusable systems.

'Many of the things they gave us were software modules that were incomplete and we couldn't even run tests on them. The way it was coded made it impossible to maintain the software over the long run.'

Meanwhile Andersen's periodic progress reports to UOP indicated all was going well, according to UOP officials.

Andersen has refused to comment on the specific allegations but in a statement issued after the suit was filed on 21 March 1995 it dismissed UOP's accusations as 'completely without merit'.

The US magazine *Computerworld*, which reported the case in detail, said the project was not unusual. Nor were the problems exclusive to Andersen. It quoted an unnamed competitor of Andersen's. 'Consulting and services is 100 per cent people based. You could have great success in New York and an absolute disaster in Los Angeles, and it is the same firm.'

Computerworld also quoted another disaster project at First Union Corp., a bank based in Charlotte, North Carolina, with $77 billion in assets, which ended its $6 million contract with the consultancy after the first phase was finished because 'work had become a struggle to complete'.

Although the bank said Andersen's work was not always

adequate, First Union also accepted some of the blame. Judge Fowler, senior vice-president and director of systems development at First Union, said:

'We've learned that projects don't do well when you expect someone else to manage them.'

CHAPTER TWENTY-THREE

Putting Theory into Practice: A Five-step Guide

All the earlier chapters look at the lessons from past failures and successes. How do you now apply these lessons in practice?

There is no off-the-rack method for implementing a successful computer project, only general rules on what you should do and particularly what you should not do.

Specific advice is often in short supply because every computer system, every project, every business is different and every chief executive's expectations of technology are different. However the following gives some step by step suggestions:

SUGGESTION ONE:

Your predicament: you have a computer system running largely standard software, but the equipment is approaching the end of its useful life.

You know this because the maintenance engineers are making ominous noises about spare-parts availability, and there is little potential to expand the system at a reasonable cost, or there are a growing number of transactions that the computer cannot cope with. For example, you need a new system to handle a new business that was acquired recently, yet you are not enthusiastic about changing the computer.

Ideally you would like to run your existing software on a new piece of equipment, extended to cope with additional transactions, but otherwise have the reports and screen formats look the same. But the company that sold the original systems has gone bust and nobody else wants to touch your software. They want to sell you something new.

At first you resist but eventually you like the idea of buying new. The latest technology seems to offer everything you have ever needed and wanted. So you set about acquiring a new system.

STEP ONE

Ask yourself: do you really need a new system yet? You should look for ways to avoid it because, once you are committed, the project will absorb far more management time, and give you more ulcer-inducing problems than any recalcitrant staff.

There may be ways to avoid it. Erasing or archiving all the files you don't need can save acres of disk space. Upgrading your existing hardware by buying a larger second-hand machine may be much cheaper than upgrading through your existing supplier. The computer industry is full of reputable, long-established brokers – but watch out for rental and leasing deals that seem cheap in the short term but lock you into a contract that proves expensive in the long term.

You may not need to upgrade at all. Perhaps you can run the new transactions on the existing system by ceasing to do so much system management work on the processor. You may find, if you have an independent audit, that your mainframe, minicomputer or whatever, is spending 50 per cent of its time looking after itself (i.e. running its own system management and utility programs) rather than running your business.

When you have cut down on this, and *simplified existing procedures* to ease the processor workload, or diagnosed bottlenecks in the input/output, and rewritten or replaced loosely written programs, you may find that you have the equivalent spare capacity of a new machine.

So you won't need to consider a new system for the time being.

If, however, your computer department is ultra-efficient and the system is running as leanly as possible by spending 80 per cent of its time devoted directly to servicing end-users, and you have simplified procedures so much that you could describe how your business functions, from top to bottom, on two sides of a sheet of A4, and you still want a new system, move to step two.

STEP TWO

The first thing to realise is that buying a replacement system is great fun for everyone but the chief executive. The computer manager and staff will be motivated anew. So don't expect them to do much else while they have an official remit to go out shopping for computers.

They should avoid any hardware or software that is highly proprietary – in other words, it locks you into a specialised hardware or software architecture. Many earlier computer problems turned into disasters because the user organisation had written software using a highly specialised tool that generated its own code, effectively locking the customer long-term into the product.

When things went wrong, the users wanted to sack their suppliers but found themselves unable to continue the work in-house because they did not have the skills to use such specialist products. Nor could they afford to go to the market to buy in the expertise because skills in the product were rare and universally expensive.

Also, proprietary hardware and software looks cheap to start with but when suppliers have a large captive market, with big investments in the systems, they tend to raise prices arbitrarily. In 1995, for example, there was a rebellion by IBM AS/400 customers in the UK over upgrade charges: some users refused to pay and others, such as National Car Parks, decided to develop new systems using alternative hardware and software.

But how can you avoid proprietary systems? You can't. Virtually every product on the market is proprietary despite what suppliers tell you about their products meeting 'open' OSF, AP11, BS9000 and all the other international standards.

Manufacturers have a habit of tweaking components, protocols and codes so that their product offers a unique selling point but also turns a standard product into a non-standard one. The director of 'open systems' at a major multinational computer supplier said with a canny smile: 'There's no such thing as open systems. Every product is a different brand of barbed wire.'

However, because of widespread and growing use, certain proprietary hardware and software is more acceptable than others.

Five years ago, for example, the IBM AS400 was all the rage in minicomputers. Then it was the IBM RS6000 workstation running the AIX operating system. This was followed by uncertainty in the user community about the future of AIX, and much discontent about the cost of AS400 software.

Today, the technology focuses on 'client server' systems. In essence these are usually medium or large computers (the servers) which run software that controls and feeds a network of work stations or PCs (the clients).

Client server systems are often based on the Unix operating system which was universally popular a few years ago, but although it is being used to impressive effect by some businesses (Churchill Insurance for example) many end-users want to reduce dependence on Unix and run Microsoft's Windows systems, which have become desktop standard.

Although Unix and Windows can sit together, they don't feel comfortable with each other's company.

But Windows-based systems are far from perfect. I have known them crash with stress-inducing regularity, but so much Windows software is available, much of which is generally well-written and superbly flexible, that it is a good bet for the time being; but there are other choices.

The important thing is, if possible, not to consider transferring your existing systems to your new chosen technology. This is the highest risk strategy. Instead, keep your existing system running and buy new hardware and software to handle the extra transactions or new applications.

Once you have looked at a few systems it is obvious that they all have their own strengths and weaknesses which makes it hard to decide what to buy. After seeing demonstrations from various suppliers, you end up with three or four who seem to have reasonably suitable products and sales representatives you feel comfortable with; so you form a small committee, perhaps you, the finance director and computer manager, to try to choose between the shortlist of systems.

Everyone seems to be offering a standard package, and promising that they have a vast number of established users for their products, and that there is no pioneering work involved, but they suggest that, to meet your needs exactly, some small modifications will be needed.

DANGER! DANGER! DANGER!

There's no such thing as a small modification. Software is like a house built with a pack of playing cards. Modify the position of one card, and it may have a profound effect on the whole structure.

In contrast a good software package has had all the bugs removed through other peoples trials and errors. It is now as robust as it'll ever be. Do you really want to modify it? It would be much safer to buy the package that most closely fits your needs and tone down your expectations of what the systems will do or adapt your business to suit its software's limitations. Go and see similar systems elsewhere – but remember these are only a very rough guide.

It's much better to realise that, no matter what the supplier and computer supplier say about the number of successful users a product has, assume that your installation will be different.

Therefore caution will be your watchword. And remember that consulting and services are 100 per cent people-based. Your prospective supplier could have had great success in New York and an absolute disaster in Los Angeles. But you'll probably never find out about the Los Angeles system.

STEP THREE

If you find it all too complicated, and you know someone who plays golf with the partner of a management consultancy who apparently knows everything there is to know about computers, you might want to arrange a meeting.

Johnson Highphee, a senior partner, mentions not a word of jargon, hardly even uses the word computer. It all sounds so simple: just a question of a couple of consultants having a look around and recommending the best system for the job.

They say they don't have any ties with hardware or software companies and so must be staunchly independent. What's more Johnson Highphee has seen it all before. His customer list features most of the companies in Fortune 500. Yours is a small company in comparison with most of his multinational clients.

But you'll be charged next to nothing, just the cost of one or two consultants coming round to check things out.

On Monday morning one consultant arrives and is conscientiously unobtrusive. By Thursday, there are two consultants and the following week nobody notices when the two are aided by two or three of their colleagues.

Two months later Johnson Highphee meets you and explains in detail why you have a big problem that's easily solved. The trouble is that your computer manager is living in the past, the systems are obsolescent, are not giving you a competitive edge or even value for money, and he strongly recommends 'business re-engineering'.

This means that your business needs to be rebuilt from the foundations upwards. It sounds expensive but the partner persuades you it'll save twice what it costs – guaranteed.

You don't even need to go out to competitive tender, because that would mean imparting all your company's secrets to a whole new set of consultants who may be talking to your competitors.

Much better to limit the knowledge of your company's problems to Johnson Highphee. What's more, he'll write off all the costs of the consultancy so far – tens of thousands of pounds. All you need to do is agree to pay Johnson Highphee on an hourly basis and he'll see to everything.

He sounds honest, well-meaning, knowledgeable, and seems to understand your business. Who better to have the contract?

Without your knowledge, Johnson Highphee gradually takes over the running of the computer department. Nobody dares question him. After all, he has the ear of the chief executive. In no time, complex purchasing deals are arranged which, without your realising, lock you into proprietary software. Johnson Highphee was right in saying that his consultancy receives no commission from the sale of the software or the hardware – but he knows that this particular software product is a technological straitjacket – an impressive product that can be installed satisfactorily only by the most knowledgeable (and expensive) consultants. It's an area of expertise in which Johnson Highphee has particular skills.

At first the product is used in a small way and is demonstrated. It looks tremendous. It can transform your business. Johnson Highphee says he'll draw up some specifications and, once they're completed, you can have a fixed-price on initial release of software implementation contract.

Sounds fantastic. The bills have been reasonable so far.

So you trust the consultants. Instinct tells you that Johnson Highphee will get it right. In any case he cannot afford to go wrong, not if his company wants to keep its reputation. It doesn't occur to you that if things do go badly wrong, you'll have as much a vested interest in keeping it as quiet as Johnson Highphee. Do you want shareholders to know you've botched a multi-million-pound project?

Highphee tells you he's bought a tried-and-trusted package that will form the nucleus of the new systems. *Danger*! Any phrase along the lines of 'the package will form the nucleus of' probably means that the package is going to be modified. This is a high-risk approach. Yet Highphee convinces you that the 'package' is very powerful and the consultancy is pretty experienced in installing it. Nothing ever goes wrong, you are told. Three months later the project seems to be going well, but there's no date yet for when the fixed-price element will start.

By this time end-users have heard about the new system and have started recommended changes. Johnson Highphee tells you he's restricting some of the changes, but a few are pretty important.

DANGER! DANGER! DANGER!

The design of the software should be frozen before any development work begins in earnest. The aircraft manufacturer Boeing freezes the designs of its passenger jets three years before rolling them out. Of course computer software has a much shorter payback period than aircraft and so development times should be much shorter, but the principle of not allowing late changes holds good. Apart from destroying the integrity of the original design, late changes will give the consultants or supplier an excuse, if the project subsequently fails, to blame you or your end-users for all the late changes that, it will be claimed, destroyed the integrity of the original design.

Shortly before you're expecting the initial phase of software to be delivered, Highphee tells you he's found some problems with your systems that weren't apparent earlier. It has put the schedule back a bit. One or two aspects of your business have changed as well. These will need to be incorporated into modifications of the software, but everything is firmly under control. Oh, by the way. The finance director saw a demo and thought it was great, but he's only now thought about linking invoicing to stock control. I don't think it's strictly necessary, says Highphee, but the finance director is adamant that better integration of the two systems will deliver a major business benefit. It's difficult to argue with that, says Highphee, who adds that 'we'll be able to move to fixed price shortly, I expect.'

Two or three years later the system is nearly finished. You've been told it will be nearly finished every week for the past year.

Some of the extras requested by the end-users and finance

director haven't worked. Highphee's organisation says it cannot be blamed for delay. End-users say they've hardly made any changes. It transpires that a countless number of changes have been made informally and nobody can remember who instigated them.

Your company solicitor tells you that if you sack Highphee you'll have a legal dispute on your hands that could go public.

In any case you've spent two and half years on the project and you're committed to a single brand of highly specialised software that only Johnson Highphee or Johnson Highphee lookalikes will understand. You can't give up now . . . or can you? You are advised that the best option now is to contract out the whole computer department and use this as an excuse to review the IT strategy and start again.

To avoid this or similar, you might consider that some of the most successful consultants include one-man bands and small companies operating in niche markets who give you a list of *all* their present and past customers and can corroborate their promise that they always deliver on time and to budget.

One small and highly successful consultancy pays its staff double their salary rather than delay delivery on a contract. This leads to its consultants working sometimes all night.

Another way to avoid trouble is to pay the consultancy nothing until it delivers not only a satisfactory product but the promised benefits from the new system. An arrangement similar to this was signed at Barclays Bank.

STEP FOUR

If you cannot find a good consultant you trust, and you have chosen a supplier you feel comfortable with, remember that you are increasing the chances of failure if you abdicate responsibility to the supplier or to the computer department. You need to know what the new systems are supposed to do and how they are supposed to do it.

What you expect from the systems is not what the supplier expects. No supplier knows exactly what you want, however much you tell it.

If you think the supplier is going to understand your business as part of its pre-contract sales effort, think again. Few companies can afford to give away that much effort for free in these straitened times, when the profits have been squeezed out of hardware and it is hard to make software profits compensate.

All the supplier will do is estimate the fit of its software to your requirements. If you attempt to tie it to a fixed price before a detailed investigation of your requirements has been completed, it will probably give you a fixed price for the changes it can foresee and leave itself scope to charge extra for what is not yet obvious. And yet when you come to make the changes – as inevitably you will – you may have to pay large extra costs.

Also, do not get a partial fixed price and fool yourself into thinking you have cost control. This will not be achieved until the scope of the system has been fully defined.

The best way to control cost is to divide the development into two projects. In the first, you ask the supplier to work with you to decide what is going to be in a system that will satisfy your requirements. Make sure that that information is written down; you want a specification that eventually you will pay to own.

You may also want to have an agreement that does not commit you to a second contract, for the purchase of software and hardware, until the specification document is written to your satisfaction.

Alternatively you may agree to a second contract provided that the supplier does not increase the cost estimates more than a given percentage following finalisation of the specifications.

If there is a significant rise in prices, you can go back to the market with your requirements specified in writing.

Once the specification is written to your satisfaction, the main thinking is done. You have the benefits stipulated in writing so you can negotiate from strength.

By then you are the customer everybody wants to deal with, the rarity who knows what they want. However it is also your job to choose the hardware. Don't leave it to the supplier. It should be your responsibility if things go wrong. You can try out the software on a loan machine or at the supplier's premises.

Some suppliers, to militate against any possibility of disaster, will even supply software on a three-month licence so that you can try it out. The licence may cost £15,000 or more merely for a trial but it could save a fortune.

If your new system is business-critical, you should go live in small stages, always having a back-up system running in case of failure.

Each software module should work impressively on its own,

independent of other parts of the project.

STEP FIVE

Once the new system is installed and functioning don't expect miracles. At first it will be worse than you expected. You'll suddenly notice that it does not do some fundamental things you had stipulated. Never mind. The software has dozens of bugs. Never mind. It is slower than you had imagined. Never mind. As long as it is not a *complete* disaster, and produces *some* benefits, the problems can probably be ironed out over time with fine tuning.

Above all *keep it simple*. Don't expect the software to transform or completely run your business. You may find it is better to computerise only the parts that will most benefit from automation.

If you computerise everything you must realise that the rigidity of system design means that you may be unable to do as much as you were able to do previously. It is also worth bearing in mind that sometimes a disaster is a disaster only because the user expectations are too high. No major system has ever come close to being perfect. The realisation of this could make the difference between accepting and rejecting your new system.

CHAPTER TWENTY-FOUR

Perfection?

This is one of the most successful projects I have encountered, but it won't appeal to every chief executive, particularly as it circumvented the computer department almost completely.

Due to the sensitivity of the project, the manager would talk to me only on an anonymous basis, which is ironic, as I have named names in all the disaster projects and, now that I come to the quintessential success, I can only refer to the parties pseudonymously.

Even so, I think this one is too important to overlook.

Wiry Canadian Lien Carter is not everyone's idea of the perfect project manager. He is what some people might regard as vulgarly self-assertive: rough, harsh, excessively active, dryly witty, intolerant of anyone who does not bend their will to his, penetrating of intellect and perception and unimpeded by even a smidgen of self-doubt, which makes him daring beyond the aspirations of the most dynamic business executive. More importantly he is a business manager who, to use an oxymoron with plenty of truth in it, is a cynical enthusiast when it comes to technology.

Having long realised that one of the reasons that his company had become a multi-million-pound success was the quality and range of the intelligence information it had gathered on competitors, he wanted to build a computer system that would gather together all the information held on various paper files in various filing cabinets, and in a variety of stand-alone computer systems.

What's more, the information would need to be accessible by a number of senior executives and directors in a variety of the company's offices around Canada and the UK; and the information had to be capable of being updated across the network in real time (that is within a split second), accurately and securely.

More than anything the response times at the terminals had to be quick. The executives of this company would not use the system unless the response times at the terminals were razor sharp.

Carter trusted nobody but himself, and particularly not consultants or the computer department; but protocol demanded that he ask either consultants or the computer manager to commission the new 'intelligence' system.

This was not a problem, only an irritation; so as an initial step he invited a major consultancy to meet the board.

When the day arrived, Carter met the consultancy's managing partner and his second in command from the lift on the 24th floor of the company's executive suite of offices.

Oleaginously, he ushered them to the leather Chesterfield and buttoned armchair in the waiting room while he went into the lobby and knocked on the boardroom door.

Inside was an exaggeratedly long, oak boardroom table, which did not allow communication from one end to the other without amplification. He went to the far end, where seven directors were seated, with unmarked paper pads and pens in front of them, and, almost in a whisper said, 'They're waiting outside. I'm sure they won't suggest anything too elaborate, but just in case they do, I think you should be aware that big computer schemes have a high death rate. I've read chapter and verse on some horrendous computer disasters in the trade press but so long as we keep it small and simple I don't think we can go wrong.'

Then he departed and returned moments later with the consultants, who, when pleasantries were dispensed with, soberly explained to the board that they might want to seriously consider the benefits of the extensive management information that would be available from the integration of their subsidiaries worldwide as part of a homogeneous networking project, which would break even in a year and would yield a return of several millions of pounds within four years.

'You should have seen the look on the board's faces,' observed Carter.

The consultancy dismissed, Carter arranged a meeting with the computer manager, told him what system was needed, and watched the manager's face crease with anxiety.

No, the manager was not optimistic of the early implementation of such a complex project. It would require detailed planning and discussion to ensure compatibility with the existing infrastructure and IT strategy.

Carter remembers little about the rest of the conversation, only that 'none of it made any sense'.

Carter added: 'Everything sounded so complicated, perplexing and involved; and every time I asked a question there was this sharp intake of breath.'

As the computer manager expanded on the apparently abstruse technical difficulties Carter, far from showing his irritation, maintained one hand on his elbow, the other supporting his chin, and listened seemingly intently.

'Leave it with me,' said Carter when the manager's earnest whine droned to an end. 'I've got a few ideas of my own. I'll let you know when it's all finished.'

Now free of any further obstruction Carter began to plan the project, but not entirely on his own. First he visited a colleague in another department who, like himself, was a senior business manager.

They formed a partnership of opposites: Carter, the excitable, petulant, daring and resourceful entrepreneur and his stolidly calm colleague, an Ivy League graduate, who would not buy a can of beans in a supermarket unless he had read a quality-assurance report on it.

The two worked perfectly together: Carter made all the decisions, verbally pummelling his partner into reluctant acquiescence while reassuring himself that every decision had been reached democratically.

Neither Carter nor his partner was a computer scientist, but both used PCs and were familiar with popular software packages such as Access, Excel, Word 6, Lotus Notes and Lotus 1,2,3.

After talking to several suppliers, Carter confirmed what he had already suspected from the start: that the new intelligence system should be based on Lotus Notes.

But Lotus declined to have anything to do with the project, though it suggested the names of third-party consultancies.

Before making any commitment, Carter visited major Lotus Notes sites, some of which were using the product on a global basis. He even went to see a competitor's implementation of Notes, using as an excuse the fact that he was considering acquiring the company.

Impressive though these demonstrations were, the biggest Notes sites had large investments in hardware, way beyond Carter's budget. He resolved then to calculate what hardware would be needed for a given number of users.

Normally calculating the hardware needed to run software that has not been completed is a black art, if carried out without experience or knowledge. Lacking both experience and technical knowledge, Carter decided to acquire it quickly.

Borrowing hardware, he set up a small-scale implementation of the system he wanted. Although resolving minor technical issues was more time-consuming and irritating than he had envisaged, the experiment gave Carter the knowledge and experience he needed to embark on the project in earnest.

In particular he soon found, by simple mathematical extrapolations, that a forty-user system could be run economically.

'Any number over that, and you were talking about big-money hardware.'

Restricting the users to forty was the hardest part of the project management. Carter found that as soon as he demonstrated his system to the board they suddenly saw all sorts of uses for it, and asked to be included on the network. Carter said no.

Other business managers soon heard of the new intelligence system and also asked to participate. Again, Carter had the authority and self-confidence to say no.

It was his determination to restrict the scope of the project and to 'manage down' end-user expectations, which made the difference between success and failure.

So who would do all the work? All the disparate information on competitors needed to be entered into the system; data from financial information sources had to be fed automatically into Notes, which would also need to identify information on a competitor and append it to an existing file.

And a design for the format of the Notes records had to be considered at length and turned into a workable system.

After seeking Lotus's advice, Carter hired a small consultancy and signed a fixed-price contract, but only after specifying exactly what he wanted.

Most importantly Carter resolved not to make any changes, knowing that this would invalidate the fixed-price contract.

In fact he realised halfway through the project that more data feeds had to be added, so an enhancement was paid for separately, the details set out in contractual form, and a written undertaking given by the supplier that the modification would not impair its ability to deliver the contract on time and to budget.

Not everything went smoothly. 'We'd planned to have all the paper-based stuff converted automatically in a Notes format. It wouldn't work. All the file sizes were different, as was everything else. So we got some companies to quote for physically re-keying all the information in our files into Notes. We found a bureau that probably exploits Indian immigrants, which did the whole conversion for less than if we'd bought a licence on the automatic code converting tool.'

As the estimated completion date neared, the consultancy asked for more money because work had been more complicated than anticipated. Carter said no.

Live day was not a ceremonious occasion. The project was too small for that. Only twenty users went live because Carter was determined that the other twenty would not be added until all bugs and any other issues were solved.

At this stage, if the worse had come to the worst, the project could have been cancelled without large losses, only a loss of pride.

In fact it was several months before the whole forty-user system went live – an unequivocal success.

It would be easy to write off this case study as too small and too simple to liken to major computerisation projects; but that is the very reason that it is exemplary. It could easily have been like so many disasters in this book –

IF the original consultants had been allowed to build their global, business re-engineering, pioneering project;

IF Carter had not had the authority to say 'no' to requests for a bigger system to cope with more users;

IF more users had greatly increased the hardware requirements, perhaps uneconomically so;

IF Carter had insisted on trying to convert automatically the existing files into the Lotus format (he realised that what seemed at first to be the hardest way was in fact the easiest – hiring a bureau to re-key all the information manually onto the new system);

IF Carter had not known exactly what he wanted (he had seen for himself what technology was available, not merely by visiting one site but several);

IF Carter had tried to modify the existing code (all the programming work was achieved within the confines of the existing package);

IF Carter, as project leader, had not been a business manager first and a technologist third – and in between mediated between the business and technology requirements (had he delegated, a subordinate wouldn't have had the authority to say no; neither would he have had an overview of the business).

What all this suggests is that there is nobody better to oversee a computer project than the chief executive or at the very least someone whose position in the organisation is *dominus factotum* – one who controls everything.

CHAPTER TWENTY-FIVE

And Finally ...

Disaster avoidance is not a science. It is the elimination of error through trial – in which case we owe thanks to all the victims in earlier chapters for their trials and errors.

One lesson is obvious. Computerisation is still an art form that is best practised by those who have learned from their own painful mistakes. By this definition, this book contains many expert disaster-avoidance practitioners who can be legitimately described as experts.

The value of being once bitten, twice technophobic is underlined by the fact that, with the exception of some public bodies, most of the computerisation casualties in earlier chapters have gone on to build exemplary systems next time round.

This suggests that companies which are planning a major computerisation should expect to develop the same system twice. And if budgets will allow, this is among the most useful lessons that can be learned from this book. A word of caution, however: the second system may be successful by overcoming the weaknesses in the first project, but it doesn't follow that the third scheme will also be successful. Some organisations which have grown complacent as a result of a succession of successes have been known to be floored by one catastrophic failure.

So if one lesson could be said to be glaringly self-evident it is this: there is no sure-fire way to avoid a disaster.

What you *can* say is that ignoring the obvious increases the chances of failure. In other words it's easier to say what *not* to do: I can advise would-be Rodins not to shape their Gates of Hell using an electric drill, and I can suggest that budding Michelangelos should demonstrate their skills in neoclassicism using something other than a paint roller.

And what doesn't work in computer projects is, by now, obvious, I hope. By the same token I hope it is clear why the Barclays, Abbey National, Singaporean TradeNet and Lotus intelligence projects are outstanding successes.

For example, all the successes were simple projects that were clearly understood by all those involved, the reverse of all the failures that fell into the following three categories:
• the project continued interminably, with no hope of satisfactory completion;
• the software needed rewriting from scratch;
• no matter what remedial steps were taken, the response times at the terminal were appalling.

If any of your projects meet the above criteria you are facing a disaster – but all is not lost. As a doctor might say, serious problems need not always be ruinous if addressed early enough; although so often the signs of impending crises are not recognised and are not brought to the attention of the chief executive until it is too late.

Every disastrous project in this book was presaged by clear early-warning signs: for example, senior managers being told by the project managers that everything is going swimmingly. No computerisation goes swimmingly. Other key warning signs include:
• the computer department resisting your idea of an independent audit of the project;
• problems that *you* think are potentially serious are always dismissed as teething;
• Whenever you ask questions a seven-year-old would ask, such as 'Will it ever work?', you get the distinct impression you're being treated like a seven-year-old.

So, if facing a disaster, what do you do?

Sometimes the best treatment for a bad head wound is decapitation. It's a harsh step, admittedly, but a certain cure for headaches. In the United States, the General Accounting Office is actively looking to put moribund computer projects out of their misery.

Identifying and exterminating no-hope projects in the early stages will end more serious pain and suffering for taxpayers or shareholders later on. If the lessons are learned, money spent on the aborted project will not have been wasted.

After the Tiptree disaster an executive connected with the company said, 'Edison's first lightbulb was pretty much a disaster but the second one was a success.'

If death is too severe a remedy, you can probably turn a disaster into a success by spending twice or three times what you have already paid for the system so far.

The Department of Social Security's ASSIST project, the Californian driving licence system, Wessex Regional Health Authority's RISP and the City of London's Taurus scheme might all have been successes if their original budgets had been multiplied by three; although if they had spent more money on a project that had locked them irrevocably into highly proprietary hardware and software they would have compounded the folly.

At the Department of the Environment (Northern Ireland), for example, euthanasia was the only solution because, when problems arose, managers discovered that all the software had been written using a highly specialised coding tool. Writing more software using the same tool might have ironed out some of the immediate problems; but it would have left the department even more beholden to the proprietary tools supplier. This was not a good idea given that skills in the use of the software tool were rare.

It was better for the department to abandon the whole project and start again by breaking the requirement into small manageable parts and computerising each of them using low-risk package systems – which is exactly what the department has now done.

Other companies can recover from the brink of disaster by a psychological trick. Instead of encouraging end-users to idolise computers, they should be reconciled to the inadequacy of technology, and particularly to schemes that integrate systems. The company can then go on to build small, networked systems that meet immediate business needs.

Embark on a major computerisation only if you have so comprehensive an overview of the business and technology that you know the strengths and weaknesses of each – in other words, you understand what made Lien Carter. (See Chapter 24 – 'Perfection?') such a successful project manager.

It is also a truism that one should understand other people's mistakes so as not to repeat them, and that is one of the main reasons for writing this book.

But, while learning from past mistakes – and the mistakes of past generations – sounds easy, humankind rarely does it. And, indeed, if we applied *all* such lessons, life would be unendurably dull, for there's little to separate Utopia and melancholy.

However, it's not perfection you're striving for, not even a semblance of it, but the avoidance of a catastrophe.

Yet the achievement of this will require the striving for perfection, and this is rarely appreciated.

So many project managers, it seems, underestimate the risks of failure. This might explain why organisations, particularly in the public sector, seem to skip unconscionably from disaster to disaster.

The London Ambulance Service went straight from one large aborted project to another. So did the Department of Social Security. Staff change, the flaws of others are scoffed at, and you assume that you will not make the same mistakes.

There are some honourable exceptions in the public sector. The Central Veterinary Laboratory, for example, which lost £1 million on an overly ambitious computer project, then decided to buy smaller systems on a piecemeal basis, at a lower cost and much reduced risk.

That projects are rarely a success first time around owes much to the resistance of the technicians to any notion that they might fail. They are the professionals, the ones who understand computers. If *they* don't know what they're talking about, who does?

One programmer who has experienced failure said, 'Once work gets started, everyone at the sharp end can see things going wrong but you dare not say anything. You assume those upstairs know what's going wrong but they don't; so the programmers just end up digging the company deeper into a hole.'

This can be avoided by identifying and discussing *all* the risks before the project is under way, and then encouraging criticism so that when a risk turns into a reality, everyone is telling each other the truth, and an unemotional consensus view can be formed on the way forward.

Often the board is as much to blame as the computer or project manager. **Directors suspect that their grand computer edifice is being constructed on marshmallow pillars but do not say anything for fear of showing their ignorance.**

Yet the most ignorant questions are always the best

questions to ask. Earlier chapters show the fallacy of believing that because millions of pounds has been committed to a computerisation the people running it must know what they are doing.

Sooner or later somebody in seniority has to face up to the fact that it may all be going irreconcilably wrong. Then the temptation will be to pour money into the project in the hope that shareholders will not ask too many questions while there is the verisimilitude of a successful project.

The continuance of an irredeemable but limping system may be politically more expedient than killing it off, and will seem to serve the short-term interests of the project leader, staff and perhaps the board, but only at the expense of the long-term interests of the organisation.

It is one of the toughest decisions any project or computer manager and chief executive will ever face – when to stop and when to go on.

The dilemma will be aggravated by the forces which are vigorously opposed to abandonment – most often the project managers. They will be motivated by all the wrong but understandable reasons:

• They have spent two years on the project and cancelling it will make them realise that they could have spent the past two years more productively on a beach in Bali.

• They know the project has stalled, but think it is only because of the teething troubles that everyone has with a new system. Everything will work itself out; the suppliers are absolutely confident of that; all they need is a little extra time and a small increase in the budget, say 50 per cent, and it'll be all right on the night. And by the way, all the extra costs will inevitably be recovered by the anticipated benefits of the system.

• They need more time to mass-circulate their CVs before the dirt hits the fan.

Yet giving up computerisation and using ledgers and quill pens is better than funnelling more millions into the drain of a hopeless computer project.

The London Ambulance Service, for example, improved its service as soon as it abandoned full-scale computerisation, so much so that many patients found themselves being taken to hospital in time for treatment.

All this sounds rather negative and one could ask why this

book doesn't pay more attention to organisations that have benefited from the use of computers.

However, although success stories can teach us a thing or two, humankind seems to learn more from its errors. The plane that kills everyone on board teaches us more than the one that lands safely. And the safest planes today are the ones that have crashed most often.

For example the DC-10 passenger jet had a tendency at one stage to dispose of its doors and the passengers at around 30,000 feet; but the aircraft has fallen out of the sky so many times that it has been honed to near-perfection and is now among the most dependable aircraft in commercial service.

In contrast, some of the latest fully computerised aircraft do not have enviable records in terms of fatalities per air mile.

In general, however, computer crashes do not always kill people, so the lessons are not disseminated. A major public incident such as a plane or train crash, in which many people die, often leads to a public inquiry, which seeks to find out exactly what happened, who was to blame, and how a similar accident can be prevented in future.

WHY DISASTERS ARE HUSHED UP

When a major computer project fails, the first priority is to suffocate news of it.

This is made simple by the ease with which directors can hide write-offs in the annual accounts.

In fact this book is notable if only for the number of cases which have not been mentioned because the companies have managed to cover up the details by denying categorically that they have suffered any problems.

Understandable though this reaction to my enquiries was, the reluctance of large corporations to discuss their project problems, even within the computer industry, gives people the impression that computerisation is easier than it is, which suits suppliers.

A computer manager told a meeting of the IBM Computer Users' Association in 1994 that he regarded himself as successful in his job if he managed to keep his name out of the press. But this secrecy, and the selective use of reference sites, fools many a client into trusting their supplier. Even the 'satisfied' reference account customers can be suspect: many canny suppliers retain the goodwill of a number of key reference sites by channelling extra resources into keeping them not merely satisfied so as not to repine, but making them feel self-consciously special, even if this means in some cases making little or no profit on the account or even losing money.

These customers, who may have received subsidised or free systems and services – and may have been promised more – are of course more inclined to give a good reference than an entirely candid answer when asked awkward questions such as 'Has your system cost much more and done much less than you thought at the start?'

Yet, despite all the suppression of bad news, in researching this book David and I have been dazed by the choice of case studies, even disregarding those companies that do not own up to a major mishap.

Many of the failures have been so momentous that they cannot be hidden; for example, the loss of £75–400 million in the City of London on the imaginatively titled Transfer and Automated Registration of Uncertified Stock – or Taurus – project (see Chapter 10).

Nobody was sued after the collapse of Taurus, despite the hundreds of millions of pounds lost. The reason no action could be taken is that, as in so many projects, blame is directed and deflected all over the place, like a laser beam in a hall of mirrors.

As with air safety, which improves year on year, largely as a result of the excellent procedures for the reporting and dissemination of all known information relating to accidents, computer project management can be improved by studying the common factors in disasters which are easy to see when many projects are viewed together. That is one reason for this book.

WHEN THE BUCK STOPS NOWHERE

Of course David and I are not qualified to pontificate on what makes a computer project successful. We are mere observers of computer projects.

But we have been motivated to chronicle them, and to ransack the truth, because every time we thought that the industry would learn from its mistakes it produced bigger ones.

The most momentous faux pas used to cost tens of thousands of pounds. Now they waste millions, tens of millions and sometimes hundreds of millions.

Meanwhile the British government spends more than £2

billion a year on computers and staff and one report said that it obtains value for money on one pound in every hundred. This much?

But the business world can be much richer for a disaster. When schemes are successful, directors learn little or nothing; the computer department simply takes the credit for doing its job properly.

But, if the computer industry is to gain more from its failures than its successes, then it must proudly admit its project disasters and declare loudly that it has learnt from them. Yet when a multi-million-pound project crashes, it is always amusing to count the number of people who knew nothing.

Ignorance pervades every nook of the organisation. The chief executive sets the example. They insist that they were always kept in the dark and then look to their directors for an explanation.

The directors postulate irritably that they were misled by being given only good news by senior managers. The information systems executives also shake their heads. They maintain that all their questions about the project's progress were deflected by line managers.

The line managers say the same thing about their staff. And the staff are contractors who have already left. So the buck stops nowhere; but if someone has to be made a scapegoat it is usually the head of information technology, who, when cornered, argues justifiably but in vain that an implementation failed because the hierarchy had never shown sufficient – or sometimes *any* – commitment to the project.

But it is clear from some earlier case studies that the lack of board interest in a project can deprive those below of the ability to make important decisions and can lay the ground for the creation of a middle-ranking group of emasculated, secretive managers who are more likely to be fighting power battles and admonishing each other than considering the welfare of the organisations that employ them.

In some companies, managers will tend to keep alive incurable projects artificially for political expediency. A shrewd chief executive can spot this tendency by asking the computer manager how a project is going and ask for a list of the *original* (not the updated) project costings and development timetable and find out whether the technical milestones have all been reached on time.

If you ask clear questions and the reply is swathed in technobabble, you know the project is done for.

HAS THE CIVIL SERVICE MISLAID £5 BILLION?

Public-sector computing aberrations are different. Nobody has a need to plead ignorance, accept blame or point the finger at culprits because it is only public money; and who genuinely cares about public money except those who provide it, or receive it?

The taxpayers ought to be more concerned, but they are kept in uneasy ignorance by Britain's closed system of government. Over the past 250 years, the civil and public service has gained a reputation for efficiency by masking its inefficiencies. When something goes awry, a form of collective irresponsibility prevails, and the hundreds of cogs that make up the mechanics of government suddenly slide beautifully into gear to ensure that nobody outside finds out.

The Scott Report, published in 1996, showed how the government machine was prepared to let innocent men go to jail for the sake of political and administrative expediency.

Only rarely will someone blow the whistle. When that happens the administration turns into John Bunyan's dreaded Giant Despair, seeking out anyone who conspires against it. In one instance – not a case study in this book – an organisation was driven so frantic, not by its computer problems but the media attention given them, that it hired private detectives in an attempt to identify the person who was giving information to a journalist.

Rarely is there is any incentive to put the problem right – only a determination to plug any leak of information about it.

As a citadel against the scrutiny of outsiders, London's Whitehall works as effectively as the Kremlin during the height of the Cold War – except that Russia is now part of the 'free' world with its KGB files open to public view, so the UK's continued introspection and defensiveness ensure that our administration stands out as a model of intolerance.

This bodes ill for the future of computerisation because a mistake-prone civil service, as in a mistake-prone business, can command the sort of loyalty that keeps order on a pirate ship.

Even when information is leaked that seems to be incontrovertible proof of a disaster, press officers will be assigned to do their duty: say nothing or lie.

Well not lie exactly, but subvert the truth. The policy is to convert the simple into the unintelligible, because convolution is the best cure against public understanding.

The following conversation with a government press officer shows how defensive an organisation can be when confronted with the possibility of publicity over a computer catastrophe.

It happened when I was leaked information about the demise of a £25 million project in a major UK government department. At first the department upset a long government tradition and told me the truth.

'Yes it is true,' said a junior press officer. 'We've stopped paying the supplier and we won't resume payments until the system is delivered satisfactorily.'

The following day the same department regretted its openness. I was telephoned by the young press officer's senior manager.

'I'm sorry' he said. 'You were given the wrong information yesterday.'

'So your press officer was lying to me?'

'She was not a press officer. She was a secretary.'

'But she said she was a press officer. And she works in the press office.'

'Sometimes she takes press calls. But she's a secretary. She shouldn't have spoken to you.'

'But she's given press statements before – many times. She's well known as your press officer.'

'Well you were not given reliable information.'

'So she was lying to me?'

'No,' said the manager. 'She wasn't lying – but she gave you the wrong information.'

'So you haven't cancelled the project?'

'I didn't say that.'

'What are you saying?'

'You were given the wrong information.'

'What was wrong with what she told me?'

'Everything.'

'So you're continuing to pay the supplier?'

'I didn't say that.'

'Well you're either paying the supplier or you're not.'

'Computer contracts are never black and white.'

'But I was told that you weren't paying the supplier and payments would not resume until a satisfactory system is delivered. Is that true or not?'

'It's difficult to say. Things are never simple given the complexity of our computer contracts. There are many facets which we could not possibly go into.'

'So what we've been told is untrue?'

'I didn't say that.'

'I'm happy with what the press officer told me, unless you can tell me what is specifically wrong with what she said.'

The manager sighed audibly. 'We have hundreds of contracts with dozens of different suppliers and all the matters are highly complex and all of a sensitive and confidential nature. We do not discuss these with people like yourselves.'

'So what we were told was right but she shouldn't have told us.'

'That's one way of putting it.'

'What you're saying is that your press officer made a mistake in telling us the truth.'

'Yes.'

He was not even sheepish about the final admission.

In the end, it was possible to confirm what had really happened only because a public-spirited member of staff supplied a memorandum of a series of managerial meetings at which the problems of computerisation were discussed.

I have added up the sums involved in this and other public-sector projects in the UK that have floundered or been abandoned and it totals about £5 billion.

But, rather than try to reduce the sums lost, government departments have been allowed to spend seemingly unrestricted amounts of money on private-sector consultants; so failures are now more costly than before.

The Department of Social Security's Operational Strategy, the largest computer project in Europe, exceeded its cost expectations by nearly £2 billion. It employed hundreds of consultants – and it is now the major consultancy firms that tend to run rather than merely assist in the biggest projects.

In the public sector, consultants can serve a particularly useful purpose. Rarely is a department asked to explain how its consultancy fees have been spent, because it is assumed that the money will have been well spent.

Yet the Department of Employment's Field system employed 200 consultants from a variety of companies, but MPs were unable to discover what they had been employed to do. Parliament determined that the project wasted up to £48 million.

WHEN IT'S BETTER NOT TO KNOW

None of this should be cause of concern for most sensible taxpayers. They can avoid needless angst by not thinking about how their money is spent because, whatever complexion of government they vote into power, there seems little hope of the bottomless pit of waste suddenly gaining a bottom.

The problem is that nobody is in overall control of computer projects. Decisions are taken on high by those who don't understand the intricacies, perplexities and contrivances of a day in the life of the computer industry; so the consequences of high-level decisions feed down to diligent and competent computer managers who then struggle conscientiously to try to adhere to the unrealistic deadlines and strategies imposed by uninitiated officials several civil service layers above them.

The computer managers do not have the authority to control the project, change direction or cancel it, only to implement it. This communications gap can be filled to some extent if systems are not imposed on end-users – instead, they are made a party to the decision-making – and there are regular stop-or-go points along the way that allow for the early termination of the project.

It is particularly important that the regular stop-or-go decision is taken both at the highest and lowest levels in the organisation, by the chief executive and the ordinary business end-users, who will often see fundamental flaws more readily than middle management.

ACCOUNTABILITY

The regular review of a project's future or otherwise introduces a level of accountability that has shown to be lacking in most disasters, particularly those in the public sector.

In many government departments there are generally only two people in each department who can be held accountable for a major faux pas: the minister and the permanent secretary, but they are rarely in office long enough to account for their decisions or non-decisions.

In any case, even if they remain in office for a long time, which is extremely rare, their careers are unlikely to face even a minor scratch.

When a department has lost millions, and public auditors get to hear, the House of Commons Public Accounts Committee may hold an inquiry. If this happens, the permanent secretary, supported by an army of civil servants, will then face questions from MPs who have only a vague idea of what has gone wrong.

Anyone who attended these hearings regularly will know that they are a one-sided, serio-comic affair. The civil servants are extremely well briefed and sit at the end of a horseshoe-shaped table answering questions from MPs who have been told only what civil servants want them to know.

That is a little unfair. The MPs are briefed by civil service auditors who have tried to get to the truth, but the auditors are sometimes given only limited information by other public servants. One leaked report written on Department of Transport headed notepaper in 1996 was marked 'Not to be seen by the National Audit Office'. It revealed information about problems with rail privatisation.

Even if auditors have had access to all the papers, their report goes through several drafts of sanitisation (the so-called correction process) before MPs are allowed to see it.

But once the final report is published, MPs have little or no time to read it in full. They already have a host of other reports and cannot fully assimilate all of them. Their job is like that of a London building insurance claims assessor during the Blitz. Where do they start?

Mostly the MPs study reports on non-computer-related ineptitude, but they are increasingly looking at computer disasters.

They find that every time a permanent secretary or equivalent appears before the committee, he laments the problems of the past and praises his department for resolving them, and assures MPs that new procedures are already in place to prevent a recurrence.

Every government computing disaster that has come to the attention of MPs has led to a permanent secretary or equivalent giving assurances that all the problems are in the past and have been rectified.

The reality is that departments such as the Department of Health and the Department of Social Security have had so many techno-crises, and are now so adept at handling issues of accountability that arise from them, that they seem to have developed a genetic immunity to fear of failure.

Inevitably, after each disaster, some MPs forget all the reams of advice and warnings they have previously given to departments and issue the same advice again. This is compounded by the regular changes of membership of the relevant committees. New MPs learn afresh about the problems of computerisation and often have to accept at face value the assurances of senior civil servants that everything is all right now.

As every minister and permanent secretary knows, the trick of holding office and retaining respectability is to hold your predecessor responsible for any failures; so ministers and mandarins tend to move around departments like rugby players avoiding a tackle.

No sooner have they taken office and collected their peerages or knighthoods than they have retired or perhaps have joined a private company that had been a supplier to the department.

This revolving door is in perpetual motion. As I write this, the current Tory government has embarked on a series of new, amorphous, pioneering computerisations.

Yet, if any of the projects fail, we cannot find out until all those involved have long departed because ministers cannot admit of any fundamental failing in the system without undermining the government's credibility – a credibility founded on the premiss that it is always right.

Nobody can question this premiss because secrecy is a way of life.

This leaves top civil servants safe to make whatever decisions they can persuade ministers to accept, knowing that they can rarely be held to account if those decisions are wrong.

Even when, on rare occasions, information leaks out about a financial disaster it is an ephemeral matter. Public concern lasts no longer than the few seconds it takes to read the story in a newspaper. Few, if any, civil servants have ever been sacked for incompetence, and while ministers resign occasionally over irrelevancies in their private lives they never lose their jobs over something important like the loss of a few tens of millions of pounds within their departments.

Even ministerial lying to Parliament is of little consequence. The minister apologises and carries on as before. And, when the civil servants see how MPs give false information to questions in Parliament (one minister, William Waldegrave, admitted that 'in exceptional circumstances it is necessary to say something that is untrue to the House of Commons), the civil servants feel not only that it is right for them to hide the truth, but that it is their duty. They are only servants who follow the example set by their ministers.

All this power without accountability gives ministers and top civil servants a genuine belief in their own invincibility. They can laugh at criticism by promoting those who are criticised by MPs. Sir Robin Buchanan, whose decisions were criticised by MPs in connection with the failed regional information system plan at Wessex Regional Health Authority, was able to command political support at the highest level, and he left the health authority with honour, dignity, a knighthood and promotion.

Against this background, House of Commons committees can only tinker with the edges of the system. They can recommend a tightening up of procedures but they cannot enforce it.

Committees have no executive power, leaving me to suspect that nothing effective can be done to prevent further computing catastrophes without an opening up of the whole system of government.

Only then would ministers and civil servants be deterred from blundering because those blunders would become public knowledge. But genuine US-style open government would require so radical a reform of the British system that it would be tantamount to a constitutional revolution.

At present UK taxpayers cannot even find out all of the computer contracts that are awarded with their money, let alone assess from the price whether they represent value for money. Were open government a reality, ministers should publish all the contracts that it awards, the prices of those contracts, who was awarded them, on what basis, what are the promised services or products, when and how they are supposed to be delivered, and what the penalties are for non-compliance with the contract. At present it publishes only the minimal information it is obliged to publish by the European Parliament. Even then it has been circumventing the disclosure rules by using exemption clauses and umbrella or 'framework' contracts.

Full disclosure is mandatory in the USA, but I cannot see it happening in the UK. Therefore another Wessex is only a matter of time.

THE US EXPERIENCE OF DISASTERS:
THE BIGGER THE BETTER

All this suggests that learning the lessons from public-sector disasters is as easy as swimming in treacle.

But in the US, the administration is becoming incomparably more open. And it is beginning to make a difference. Firm action is being taken on a government-wide basis to kill off troublesome projects. This comes only after a seemingly endless series of reports on computer disasters.

Officials there have little interest in writing a disaster report unless it is more macabre than the last, so each successive blunder is dissected more gruesomely, more enthusiastically. This makes sense, because no American wants to be lumbered with an ordinary failure. Think big.

One investigative US report by Senator William Cohen found that the defence budget had been cut on the basis of phantom savings of $36 billion from a new corporate information management computer program.

Despite the Defense Department's trillion-dollar investments in information technology, it could not reconcile $41 billion in payments with any invoices. In fact, more than thirty US government reports identified projects wherein agencies had no idea what new computer systems would eventually cost or what they would do.

More remarkably, US government officers did not know when they had overpaid suppliers. They had to rely on being notified of overpayments by clerks working for suppliers who could not reconcile the government's cheques with invoices.

In a six-month period in 1993, computer suppliers voluntarily returned $751 million in overpayments. How much *wasn't* returned?

A typical US computer project was one at the Department of Veterans' Affairs, which pays welfare to Vietnam and other war veterans (see Chapter 21).

It spent ten years trying to modernise its systems to cut the time taken to process compensation claims from six to three and a half months only to find that the delay was extended to nearly eight months.

But the US is coming to terms with its failures. Its openness means that it is no longer too embarrassed to admit its mistakes; and so will not perpetuate a moribund project, no matter how much has been spent so far.

Indeed auditors are actively looking for problem projects; they will even investigate the business case for major computerisations *before* the project is given approval, and will have no compunction in saying no if they believe that the need for new technology has been based on mendaciously optimistic premisses.

SUBLIMINAL MESSAGES

In the end, it is not the hardware and software that tend to be at the centre of a disaster: it is the managers. And the London Ambulance Service provides one of the best examples of how not to manage the implementation of a computer system (see Chapter 9). It did not buy a package: it sought to pioneer, but set a budget of less than a quarter of what was required; it saw end-users as the enemy, so hardly talked to them; it did not test the new software adequately; it threw away the old before the new was running satisfactorily.

The one thing it did right was to try to improve its organisation before the introduction of the new system; but its plans were so radical that the staff opposed the changes; in any case they weren't properly consulted or briefed on them.

Managers had relied on computerisation to reform the organisation, which is like investing in a new wardrobe of smaller-sized clothes in the expectation you will lose weight.

One wonders how this and so many other failures were allowed to happen; why so many major corporations sequaciously followed each other off the cliff. The reason seems to be that people believe that computers and efficiency are analogous.

No self-respecting business feels that it can survive, or at least retain its commercial machismo, without the latest technology. The First World is technology crazed. Computers control everything from aircraft to toasters, but the technological revolution has happened too fast for cynicism to set in.

We have so much faith in computers that we entrust our lives to them in aircraft, trains and now even rollercoaster rides. Some passenger jet manufacturers have convinced us that computers are safer than humans: so some pilots in certain circumstances can no longer directly control their aircraft.

But unlike, say, the financial services sector, the computer industry is largely unregulated; so it is up to suppliers and users to set their own standards, which is acceptable if manufacturers do not cut corners and always put quality before cost. But isn't this allowing too much to chance?

What if we replaced criminal and civil law with a voluntary code of conduct?

Yet widely differing interpretations of the law, the off-chance that news of a disaster will leak out, self-regulated ethics and conscience, are among the few checks on the behaviour of the computer suppliers.

Public and corporate scepticism of computerisation would be a more effective control. But we are told that computers don't make mistakes. When money disappears from a bank account and a cash-card customer complains of computer error, known as a phantom withdrawal, the bank is incredulous and insists that its equipment is infallible, as if the software were written by programmers cloned without the human disposition to err. Is it any wonder that a technology sceptic today is made to feel as socially acceptable as a sandal-wearing, dog-biting misanthrope?

Technology services suppliers could not have more effectively impregnated the mind of Mr Everyman if they had been given a public service broadcasting licence to transmit indefinitely the subliminal message that 'a good diet, exercise, and faith in computers contribute significantly to a long life'.

No such subterfuge is necessary of course. The shelves of newsagents' shops are full of computer magazines that propound the wonders of technology. Few computer suppliers *need* to show the advantages of computers over the previous half-automated or manual processes: it is taken for granted. So suppliers need show only that their product is better than that of their competitors.

This strengthening of the credibility of the computer supply industry could explain why technology suppliers can afford to be among the biggest spenders on TV and poster advertising – although at least perhaps the advertising is becoming more pragmatic.

In the early 1980s IBM cleverly bastardised an aphorism of the French philosopher Descartes – 'I think therefore I am' – and turned it into 'I think, therefore IBM'. Now advertising is more attuned to the everyday needs of computer departments: it deals with the problems created by technology.

A more recent full-page advertisement in *Computer Weekly* read: ICL TEAMSERVERS KEEP YOUR NETWORK FROM CRASHING.

THE LURE OF CONSULTANCIES

There is no going back to the pre-computer era, however – not that anyone would want to. Used sensibly, which means without blind fanaticism, computers can make life simpler, but only if one understands their disadvantages.

New systems feed the need for more systems; and businesses are now so scared about falling technologically behind their competitors that they buy expensive advice on what to do next.

So lucrative is computer consultancy that the firms that used to audit company accounts exclusively now have computer advisory subsidiaries, which in some cases make more money than the original auditing business.

For example, Andersen Consulting, which grew out of the US auditing company Arthur Andersen, is now one of the largest management consultancies in the world. It earns between 50 and 70 per cent of its turnover from management consultancy.

Its success, and that of its competitors including Price Waterhouse, KPMG Peat Marwick, Ernst and Young amongst others, are proof of the evangelical zeal with which companies are trying to use technology to leapfrog rivals.

And this is exactly what the suppliers want, because, as soon as one company has installed major new systems and is confident it has the edge over competitors, another company, which has lagged technologically behind for years, becomes conscious of its apparent inferiority and invests in all the latest of everything.

With so many companies now running breathlessly on a treadmill, one has to ask whether more is being spent on computers than can be justified by the benefits.

Technology has become an end in itself, rather than a tool that is much like a sophisticated calculator. And with so much uncertainty around, it is easy for hardware, software, service and consultancy companies to prey on the fears of chief executives.

In the 1980s, computer suppliers sided with the information technology department in persuading chief executives to invest millions, and in some cases tens of millions, on upgrading old systems that would soon become unmaintainable.

In the early 1990s, the recession led to chief executives questioning why they were spending so much on computers, and for what benefit.

Artfully, the suppliers have now retorted that the information technology departments are not putting computers to good use, and that the entire department, including staff, should be put into the safe hands of a technology services specialist – often themselves.

So companies are now spending millions on contracting out their entire computer departments (including staff) to outside suppliers. It is called facilities management or outsourcing, and is a perfect arrangement for suppliers: they have even more control over their customer's computer operations than ever.

Wessex Regional Health Authority contracted out its computer operations to a private supplier to save money but ended up paying more than before; and one of the authority's computer managers, Robin Little, worked for the public service and for its main supplier at the same time.

In ten years, in another swing of the pendulum, chief executives may wonder why contracting out costs so much in relation to the service given.

At this point suppliers may argue that companies should not have contracted out, that they should have invested in a new in-house computer operation which offered more flexibility and control.

End-user companies will then consider contracting in their computer services, and hiring staff again. This will then bring a fresh wave of investment in hardware, software, services and consultancy – for change is the reason that the computer supply industry is now one of the world's fastest-growing professions.

It is an industry that sustains itself by promoting the notion that commercial survival means change.

CHANGE FOR CHANGE'S SAKE?

In my home, my PC was upgraded to the latest, fastest and most expensive domestic hardware. My word processor ran so fast I could barely see the actions initiated by my keystrokes.

Then the hard disk, of such ample capacity that I felt it had to be put to good use, was loaded with such an array of new Windows-based software packages, offering multifarious new and exciting facilities, that I became entranced with the appendages and almost gave up doing any useful work on the machine.

I can imagine how many of these new features, if you thought about it long enough, could be applied effectively. But that's like buying a set of magnificent iron front gates in the hope that one day you'll purchase a house to match them.

That is not to decry the quality of the new software. It was all clever stuff – ingenious in fact – but for me largely useless.

The packages consumed memory and processor capacity so rapaciously that my word processor began to run in slow motion.

Of course the word processor was still impressive. I can change the look of the type from calligraphic to italics, from the illegibly small to filling an entire page with one letter. I can insert ready-made diagrams and graphs effortlessly, while splitting the screen into eight and moving between word processing, electronic mail, spreadsheets, the Internet and databases; but all this functionality, as it is called, makes me less productive.

The computer takes longer to power up and crashes often, and the software does not allow me to do some things as quickly and easily as my prehistoric word processor, WordStar.

Yet my ossifying DOS-based WordStar program uses about 0.4 of a Mbyte of disk space, and the latest Word 97 program requires nearly 50 Mbytes – about 100 times as much disk space.

What I gained in software functions I lost in speed, simplicity and productivity. Yet Word 97 is so impressive and flexible that I would not want to go back to WordStar.

In any case, Windows-based programs today are virtually indispensable. Speed and invulnerability to crashes are not their strengths, but Windows programs can run small to large businesses because of the quantity – and it has to be said the quality – of software packages and programming tools.

Customers include many of the world's biggest businesses, among them American Airlines and BP. National Westminster Bank has the best of both worlds: it runs tried and tested IBM mainframes for its main databases but its future development is based heavily on the Windows NT operating system.

But it has to be accepted that in five years we will probably be told that we should not have Windows-based programs in the twenty-first century because they have been superseded.

For the time being, however, it is *the* technology.

But Windows-based products will improve business efficiency only in the rare event that the programming is carried out by those who really understand the work of the end-user. However, programmers cannot expect to acquire a profound knowledge of the work of those who are going to use the system from a piece of paper that sets out the written specification.

There is only one way to ensure that programmers know how

the business works and therefore what the programs need to do: **they should become the business end-users for a week, a month or a year if necessary**.

They need to sit down at the desks of the end-user and do their work with them. Only then will they see what the business end-user really needs. They will also see how the business works on a day-to-day basis – for example, how the end-users steer around blocks in the administrative system.

If this does not happen, programmers could base their software design on old administrative processes that people no longer use, with the result that the new system will slightly improve a company's textbook way of working – but not the *actual* way, leaving end-users to complain vociferously that the old way worked best.

But once you have accepted the need to invest in the latest systems, you will also have to accept that you are not buying hammers and chisels that can be replaced almost anywhere at any time.

New systems are highly specialised and incorporate proprietary items of equipment that will deliver you helplessly into the hands of the computer supply market.

Such is the nature of the symbiotic relationship between hardware and software suppliers that hardware manufacturers will improve the power of desktop computers so that software suppliers can write ever more complex programs which require ever larger hardware to run them. And, despite such misleading jargon terms such as 'plug and play', each new stage of the technological process makes the systems harder for ordinary people to understand.

So if you can resist the entreaties of salespeople to upgrade, the status quo may not only save money, it may give you a more dependable, faster and useful system than your competitor, who may be investing millions of pounds in a complex, new and pioneering system.

It is ironic that you can now obtain a competitive edge by standing still technologically and watching the opposition flounder as it pioneers the use of software that will have most of its bugs removed only by years of trial and error.

It is also a heresy for me to criticise computers for their lack of flexibility, for they are often sold primarily on the promise of their ability to facilitate change. The reality is that larger systems can – usually but not always – hinder reform.

Before computers, when there was a new business requirement, you could change office procedures in a few minutes; but, once globally installed computers are running that activity, the principal procedures can be changed almost as easily as moving a skyscraper.

Local authorities in the UK spent £300 million on computer systems in the late 1980s to cope with what was then a new tax called the Community Charge, or Poll Tax. When there were persistent public protests, and Community Charge was replaced with the Council Tax, councils were persuaded by suppliers that their £300 million systems could not be adapted to cope.

So councils spent a further £200 million on council tax systems, and because residents still owed money from the old tax, authorities had to pay service suppliers maintenance and support fees to keep both systems running. In fact, because of business rates, some councils found themselves supporting three separate tax computer systems.

But these changes are small in comparison with those that will be needed to cope with the year 2000. Almost every major company in the world is having to buy new systems or modify sometimes thousands of lines in hundreds of different computer programs to allow them to recognise the change of date from the year 1999 to the year 2000.

This change exercise alone is expected to cost billions of dollars worldwide.

In addition, every legislative change has an impact on publicly owned computer systems. The computer supply industry in the UK is extremely grateful to the present British government for the 2,000 legal amendments it issues annually.

The strange thing is that when a project goes horrendously over budget, as in the Department of Social Security's £2.6 billion Operational Strategy, the suppliers and the end-users fall in behind the same explanation: that unforeseen changes were to blame, as if nobody was expecting the requirements to change.

So the unforeseen must be foreseen – not literally, of course, but it should be realised that the technology and the requirements will inevitably have moved on between specifying the system and completing its full implementation.

This suggests that there should be a minimal period between specification and delivery of the system – but if it is a large development this places an unacceptably tight restraint on the supplier or the in-house IT department, a situation that could precipitate a disaster. **The answer then is to keep the project to a maximum of a year – ideally six months – by** *keeping it simple.*

It is worth remembering that the software in the NASA Space Shuttle is simpler to understand than the software in a typical bank cash-dispenser network. The reason is that NASA cannot afford to allow its onboard systems to crash.

Likewise, the company that allows a supplier to build in complexity may have to forfeit the luxury of 100 per cent availability of the system. And it might be a lot less than that. At times the systems used by the UK's Child Support Agency reached only 70 per cent availability during the week. That means, in theory, that sometimes the systems were down for nearly one hour in every three.

Of course computers will help to take the drudgery out of stock control, compiling trial balances and an ageing history of company debtors. They will identify business problems as they occur, for example accounts over a credit limit, and provide management information at little extra cost once a system is set up, or allow share deals to be matched and paid for quickly, enable passengers to check the availability of aircraft seats from any telephone in the world, and facilitate the flow of news and information around the world. These are long-established and proven systems – *the sort that many businesses are persuaded by suppliers to avoid.*

OFF-THE-SHELF VERSUS TAILOR-MADE

In any case, user organisations do not always *want* to learn from other people's mistakes. They believe sincerely that they are unique. They often cannot conceive of any other organisation that would be foolish enough to have such an idiosyncratic way of doing things.

This conviction of individuality is enthusiastically endorsed by private-sector consultants, because uniqueness requires unique computer software that has to be tailored to the organisation's idiosyncrasies – and custom-made software is expensive, risky and requires the specialist skills of consultants.

Another benefit for consultants of tailor-made software, or a package that is customised, is that projects can continue interminably because nobody knows how much they should cost or how long they should take to develop.

But from the computer department's point of view, the greatest appeal of tailored software is that it reduces the chief executive to a baffled, helpless and pliable victim of incomprehensible systems. He will then be grateful that he can be delivered safely into the hands of a knowledgeable computer manager and supplier.

Yet one can also sympathise with the predicament of the computer manager who wants to avoid a tediously effective, seamless implementation of technology that will go unnoticed by the board.

In comparison, a complex, long-term, custom-built system which can be completed only with technological ingenuity and upwardly mobile budgets and timescales is bound to keep technology high on the agenda at board meetings.

The alternative is to be a forgotten computer department that is contracted out or is axed during the next round of rationalisation.

However, even the major suppliers are themselves beginning to turn to packages, at least for internal consumption. A leaked report outlining proposals for a new information systems strategy at the consultancy Coopers and Lybrand says that in future off-the-shelf packages will be recommended, and that the customisation of packages will be avoided.

The disadvantage with off-the-shelf software is that the organisation loses the chance to reform itself. The jargon-obsessed computer industry calls it business process re-engineering, which simply means changing the way things are done.

But reform can take place, and indeed should take place, without considering the need for computerisation.

The disadvantage here is that not rushing ahead with computerisation will leave a company feeling it is being left behind – but should it care? A field is not idle when it is fallow.

Barclays Bank for example is far from obsessed with state-of the-art technology, yet its systems run productively.

This is because the bank manages its suppliers. Much more commonly, suppliers and the computer department manage the chief executive and the board. And one of the preferred means is through the use, or rather misuse of the language.

HOMOGENEOUS COMPUTER-INDUSTRY-
-SPECIFIC TERMS (JARGON)

Perhaps the most far-seeing writer this century, Bernard Shaw, suggested that all jargon is a conspiracy of the professions against the laity; but there is no simple antidote.

The greatest tragedy of jargon is that, like illness, it delivers you into the hands of a profession you so mistrust. The less you understand what salespeople and technical support managers are saying, the greater your dependence on what is opaque and possibly meretricious advice.

I receive telephone calls almost monthly from consultants and computer managers who ask for an explanation of the industry's latest jargon words for contracting out: externalisation, outsourcing, facilities management, cosourcing and smartsourcing.

They ask me for a detailed definition of each word and are surprised when I say that they all mean the same thing – they are speciously profound jargon words for making something simple sound like the novel answer to an obscure set of insoluble problems.

Yet the widespread use of jargon – the lexicon of which grows weekly – is perfectly understandable. No supplier can be seen to offer the same service as a competitor, so, as they all offer a similar service, each calls its brand of product by a different name, like the manufacturers of washing powders.

Suppliers will disagree violently with me, and will offer punctilious explanations for the distinctions between their jargon words, but often their arguments can ultimately be reduced to marketing, pedantry and grandiloquence.

All this is symptomatic of a computer industry that has an aversion to things being told the way they are.

The following is a selection of phrases that can ensnare and intimidate chief executives – phrases that sound important and give their speakers an air of authority but mean little in theory and even less in practice. All are taken from the latest brochures or papers of major suppliers:

- 'our system offers incomparable price-performance'
- 'it is a seminal enabling technology'
- 'we'll help you develop a strategic framework'

- 'you need to manage change in a narrowly focused way which achieves your objectives and mission goals'
- 'we can leverage your budget'
- 'our product is truly open'
- 'proprietary architectures in open systems are indispensable to competitive success'
- 'manufacturing skills may well be essential for success in architectural contests'
- 'achieving world-class performance involves moving an organisation's processes, people and technology forward in an integrated way'
- 'change is always an opportunity'
- 'we have developed tried and tested techniques which have achieved flexibility and sustainable business advantage'
- 'there is a need to exploit new technologies to deliver real business benefits'
- 'using the levers of change'
- 'our management practice draws upon an unmatched breadth of expertise. It blends the management skills and methods from process re-engineering to making outsourcing work in any organisation with intimate functional and industry-specific experience'
- 'Simply stated, competitive success flows to the company that manages to establish proprietary architectural control over a broad, fast-moving, competitive space.'

This last one takes the biscuit – and its clever use of the words 'simply stated' ensures that anyone who *doesn't* understand what it is saying feels inadequate.

The above are among the least technical examples of affected language that I could find. The technical examples are even more pitiable. The following is a real example, from a consultant who is saying in a hundred words what could be said in six, namely: the system doesn't work at present.

From the results of the first benchmark and the failure to improve the resource usage of the 4GL/RDBMS in the second benchmark there was little point in re-running the 4GL applications in the original configuration. Extrapolating the results of the second benchmark using the MIPS ratio from the first benchmark, indicated that the hardware would need some 50 MIPS to run the RDBMS

with the applications written in C. Even allowing for
extrapolation uncertainty, it was obvious that the RDBMS
would have to run across several 14-MIP CPUs in order to
cope. Fortunately the RDBMS supplier had an unreleased
symmetric multi-processing version of its product under
test . .

Jargon is not the only enemy. The computer industry is
bedevilled by 'execu-speak' – an indirect euphemistic language
which sounds credible and uplifting but actually says nothing. I
quote the following further example of vagueness, taken,
ironically, from an official booklet on avoiding computer
disasters.

Particularly appropriate for your needs, in the light of
the rapid pace of innovation in information technology, is
the procurement of a broad-based agreement on better
management models that could help you build the
information technology base you need to dramatically
improve your operations and more effectively serve your
end-users population.

So now you know how to avoid a computer disaster. These are
ideal phrases to kill off general understanding and thus confer
gravitas on the speaker. So beware those who commit verbicide
(murder of the language). The culprits tend to be those who least
understand what they are trying to say, and most hope that you
will not ask for an explanation. Those who know their subject
clearly will try with painstaking effort to explain what they mean
using the simplest most direct language.

In short, those who have an impressive grasp of technology
are more likely to explain it in plain English, because it is what
they are saying that's important, not the way they are saying it.

Not all suppliers try to confuse. Some believe genuinely that
they offer a better service than their rivals, but they fall in with
the general practice of girding their self-belief in what Jonathan
Swift called the corruption of 'enthusiastick jargon'.

Computer managers may find themselves doing the same
thing with their chief executives. It's a form of elitism and job
protection.

There is, however, an infallible way for the chief executive

to expose the technobabblist. Simply saying: 'I'm sorry, I don't understand' repeatedly will infuriate the impostor. The last thing they want is for you to get the right end of the stick.

At the other end of the scale, David and I may be accused justifiably of oversimplification by suggesting that adherence to a few epigrams can prevent a disaster.

Of course there is no talismanic solution; but the Ten Deadly Sins cover the main shortcomings which recur in most of the failures researched for this book. There are secondary points to watch for, and they are just as obvious.

What I am particularly anxious to avoid, however, is painting a picture of a computer industry that is crawling with inept or embittered, Faustian suppliers who will sell their integrity to Mephistophelean computer managers for an easy buck.

There are some computer managers who would all but sacrifice their jobs for the benefit of their organisations, just as there are suppliers who would lose money to deliver a system that protects the reputation of their customers.

But there are also some managers who would do anything to retain their power base, and some suppliers who regard ethics as something to be taken out of the inside of their jacket pocket when someone asks to see their credentials.

The problem is distinguishing the good from the bad. It is a pity that the most unprincipled suppliers go undetected because their directors are shrewd enough to front the organisation with some of the most honest, credible, charming and sincere but undistinguished sales and marketing managers in the computer industry.

The user organisation negotiates only with the delightfully sensitive account managers, but rarely sees the hands controlling them.

That said, the integrity of most suppliers is beyond doubt – even though they may sometimes mistakenly employ charlatans as senior executives.

One can forgive a supplier for making mistakes – and usually those mistakes are made through nothing more sinister than defective judgement – but now and again, when mistakes put money into the bank of the supplier, and those mistakes are repeated, one wonders whether what is sometimes passed off as genuine blundering is really an excuse for profiteering.

However, neither computer managers nor suppliers can be

blamed for protecting their livelihoods, though the unwary chief executive should be aware of all the slightly submerged factors that may openly or insidiously influence major investment decisions.

That is one of the main purposes of this book: to prevent failures that could have been avoided had the facts of similar disaster been widely known. There's no need to be shy of change – indeed no company will survive without change – but you cannot be too cautious when planning changes that involve major computer projects. In this respect let other companies be reservoirs of daring, waiting to be drained by technological experiments.

Ignorance may be bliss – as all the lobotomised will testify – but knowledge is cheaper in the long run.

APPENDICES

Appendix One

SECTION ONE: 165 years of disaster

Some of the biggest calamities we know about, and a summary of the background events, are listed below, as a chronological compendium of human and technical failed endeavour.

1830–1980

1830: Charles Babbage invented the first computer called the Difference Engine. The project went over budget and ended up being abandoned, which set the style for computerisation in the latter half of the twentieth century. It would have been a success had Babbage adhered to the maxim of meticulously calculating the cost of a project, then multiplying it by three.

1969: The UK civil service began experimenting with the idea of using computers to run entire departments. The results are keenly awaited.

1970: The politically influential computer manufacturer ICL urged the UK government to spend more on computers. It warned ministers that 'this country is falling behind in the use of computers and this trend must be halted'. Dutifully, the government decided to put public money where ICL's mouth was, and today the UK government spends £2 billion annually on computers and employs 20,000 information technology staff. ICL is the government's major hardware supplier.

1979: The government's computer advisory body, the CCTA remarked that delays and aborted projects had characterised attempts by the Inland Revenue to computerise its assessment and collection of taxes. The problems were attributed to lack of overall project management in the early 1970s. An official report said that systems had to be completely redesigned and software rewritten after the Revenue decided to buy ICL 2900 mainframes instead of earlier 1900 systems. The problem was that generations of technology had come and gone while the Revenue was developing its software.

There is no easy answer to this one except to covet simplicity. The following is a basic guide to what's simple.

Level one computing

This is the epitome of simplicity – and the lowest-risk form of computerisation. The processes to be computerised are simple, well refined and intimately understood by the system designers. The software can run on networked PCs and PC-servers, using the all-purpose Windows 95 or Windows NT operating systems, or IBM's OS2 equivalent, though none of these are a substitute for good project management. The software in effect locks you into the supplier of the operating system software, who will regularly upgrade the code so that you will be encouraged to keep building new programs to take advantage of technological improvements. And every new program will soak up more memory – and will be more processor-hungry, so the hardware will need to be regularly updated.

For example the Windows operating system changed fundamentally in 1995, which accelerated the ageing process for much of the software written under the previous version of Windows (3.11). The new Windows software (Windows 95) requires at least twice as much memory (at least 8 Mbytes of RAM) and much faster processors (i.e. a Pentium chip or a 486 running at 100 MHz) to exploit fully the new operating system's features. It also uses large quantities of disk space. But the advantage of PC-based systems is that, for example, Windows-related skills are in abundance, the costs can be fairly well contained, or at least predicted, and the power of servers means that PCs can now run medium-sized businesses, provided that the software has been designed economically – in other words, is not wasteful with hardware resources.

Although there is a large central management overhead in running PC-based networks, particularly through help-desk queries, a big attraction of smaller systems is that large numbers of users can be catered for by 'distributing' the software to servers linked to groups of users. Most important of all, if the worse comes to the worst, PC-based software can be thrown away without large losses.

Level two computing

This is a more specialised form of computing for medium and larger businesses, and allows for more intensive input/output transactions. It includes larger PCs or workstations, and perhaps minicomputers. The most common operating system in this bracket is Unix, or IBM's equivalent, AIX, and there are adaptations of Unix for hardware such as IBM's AS400, RS6000 and similar systems. These tend to be medium- to high-risk systems. The Performing Right Society lost up to £16 million on a failed Unix implementation. And Britain's Ministry of Defence spent £380 million on highly specialised Unix systems that were regarded as old-fashioned by the end-users, even before the whole system went live. What seems to be clear from many of the case studies in this book is that these medium-sized systems can work superbly (Churchill Insurance in the UK has one of the most efficient systems in business today based on Unix), but they are not always suitable for loosely designed or highly complex software, which may need larger, much more powerful hardware, such as a mainframe.

Implementations at level two are medium- to high-risk because Unix, AS400, RS6000 systems may seem at the start to be big enough for the job – but if they prove later to be too small, the write-off costs may be enormous. It is best to try an *actual* version of your intended software (*not a modified version*) on a large Unix, AS400- or RS6000-based system and extrapolate the performance under a heavy load by simulation. Most hardware suppliers will let you try out your software on a loan machine if it increases their chances of winning an order. Also, some software suppliers are beginning to offer products on a three-month licence so you can see if it really works as well as they say. This may cost £15,000 or more for the licence but it could save a much larger sum in the longer term.

Level three computing

This is for larger businesses that require mainframes. Companies in this category will already be using mainframes, and may have done so for years. Mainframe computers can handle highly complex, intensive transactions – and even smooth over ineptly written software that's been patched up for years. There is a trend towards disposing of the mainframe for smaller 'cheaper' equipment. However some major companies have found that, although the maintenance cost of mainframes is high, they are a low-risk way of running complex software across a large number of end-user sites. Therefore, companies seeking to keep their computerisation risks to a minimum are investing heavily in additional mainframes, particularly second-hand equipment.

Some even believe that smaller footprint mainframes are, to some degree, making a comeback. In fact buying mainframe-based software may be lower-risk than a Unix, RS6000 or AS400 system because mainframes allow a considerable margin for error in judging hardware capacity. And today, second-hand mainframes can be bought for little more than the cost of a few high-end PCs. However the operating systems software for mainframes can cost more than the machine and, despite what the salespeople will tell you, locks you into the supplier. At computing levels one and two, you may need consultants to advise you. With level three computing you will definitely need them unless you have dependable in-house advisers.

So the most attractive of the three levels of computing is number one.

PC-based networks can serve many major businesses – but it is not always in the interests of the computer department, large suppliers and consultancies to recommend PCs because they are cheap, widely available, do not usually require a high degree of specialist knowledge, and there is much packaged software on the market. However, PCs can require a great deal of central management to prevent the proliferation of large quantities of incompatible versions of different software, and also to ensure the security and integrity of the systems (keeping them free of viruses and so forth). But the ideal solution is not necessarily level one, two or three. These levels describe only the technology. The key to project success lies not in the choice of technology but in the approach to its implementation. Provided that most of the lessons from the earlier case studies are acknowledged, any one or a mixture of the levels should help ensure that a project is successful. Above all, don't consider the technology first and the business afterwards. For example, a business that gives its staff the latest computerised diary, spreadsheet, contacts database and word processing software will, in return for a large capital investment, find that the newly empowered employees will spend much of their time:

- trying to access everyone else's computerised diary;
- learning how to keep their temper when the system keeps crashing due to disk-space overloading;
- plunging into manuals to discover how they can better link their database to the spreadsheet;
- trying to figure out why the printer works only when someone else is using it.

In short, computerisation could lower productivity. **Yet, because of the natural inclination to consider technology first and the business afterwards, companies may have overlooked better ways to achieve a competitive advantage.** A daily newspaper, for example, may spend millions on new systems for writers and achieve little business benefit compared with negotiating with its printers to cope better with late-breaking stories so that front-page deadlines could be extended by an hour.

If, however, you have done everything possible to simplify and improve business processes, and you understand fully the limitations of new computer systems, now is the time to computerise if you are still confident that the benefits are quantifiable and that you have considered the implications of the project going wrong.

At this point your plans will be confounded by the pre-existing systems. This may be a mistake. It is difficult to design the perfect house if you have to adapt an existing one. Much better to start with an undeveloped piece of land and a drawing board. New and spectacularly successful companies such as First Direct, Churchill Insurance and Direct Line have built new systems from the foundations upwards – systems that are startlingly simple in their operation, maintenance and software, yet are highly efficient. One reason for their success was that they were not encumbered with ageing 'legacy' systems.

Another approach is to buy hardware on a services contract. Under this scheme you own the hardware but the supplier takes the risk of the technology becoming obsolete. In effect you pay for computing power in the same way as you buy electricity – according to the amount of processing capacity you need. This avoids having to invest in machines that may quickly prove too small. Not all suppliers will readily agree to these services contracts – but they can be persuaded. Royal Insurance and National Westminster Bank are among the sites that have negotiated such deals.

SECTION TWO: 165 years of disaster (continued)

1980–1990

1982: A 'massive' project called Camelot to computerise welfare benefits was scrapped with losses to the taxpayer of £6 million. The main lesson was that big projects are more likely to fail than succeed. Henceforth, the government set about designing bigger welfare systems.

1983: The biggest computer disaster of them all. A project to equip RAF Nimrod aircraft with computerised air-defence early-warning systems was abandoned when it was found that the computers were too heavy for the purpose-made bulbous nose section of the aircraft. About £800 million of taxpayers' money was wasted. The alternative to developing Nimrod was too ghastly to contemplate. The British would have had to buy the American equivalent of Nimrod, the AWACS aircraft (which it eventually bought anyway).

1984: The UK government aborted the Camelot welfare benefits system (see 1982) and replaced it with the Operational Strategy, which was later described by a Secretary of State for Social Security as 'the biggest and most complex computerisation programme in Europe'. Never has there been a more shameless condemnation of a project before it has begun. In 1984 the Operational Strategy project director told Parliament that the project would cost £713 million. MPs were sceptical and asked the director whether this figure would rise in real terms. 'No,' he replied. 'It is unlikely to rise in real terms. The bulk of the costs are in salaries and in fees we pay to consultants. The equipment costs if anything are doing to come down.' By 1988, the project cost £1.2 billion. A year later the costs had risen to £1.7 billion. The latest estimate was £2.6 billion. But, as the costs rose, so did the putative benefits. The department says that the strategy has saved more than £3 billion, but has not provided any evidence as to how.

1984: The UK Ministry of Defence embarked on a £250 million project to computerise all its main offices, including the main building near Downing Street in London. The idea was to replace pre-war typewriters and a hotchpotch of old and new machines with a common, highly secure network of systems. The Corporate Head Office Technology Systems project (CHOTS), to supply departmental Unix systems and 10,000 terminals, was born. It took seven years to determine the specification and how the project should progress, whereupon the contract was awarded, on a single-tender basis to the UK company ICL. At about the same time Parliament was informed that the whole project would be completed by April 1995. By then, however, the cost had risen to £380 million, and the project was nowhere near completion. This was not the main problem, which was that many officers were refusing to use CHOTS. They viewed the system with repugnance, and argued that each terminal cost £38,000 compared with £800 for a high-street equivalent that was much more advanced and could run all the latest packaged software such as Windows for Workgroups.

However the MoD countered that the CHOTS network was highly secure and could be used to send secret messages. But MoD officials argued that, for most of the time, they did not need to send secret messages. The debate within the MoD over whether Chots is a success or a £380m disaster continues.

1986: The Central Electricity Generating Board spent centrally £100 million on computers without deciding exactly what they should do. End-users complained that their locally bought systems did more and cost less than the new centrally imposed computers, which were usurping cupboard space, clogging up hallways and spilling over the edges of desks. One station manager at Oldbury power station wrote to the corporate headquarters in December 1986 warning that he may have to acquire more office space merely to accommodate all the extra terminals. 'Your proposal,' he wrote to the board's headquarters, 'will result in yet more different terminals in offices which already have a number of terminals for other purposes. In one of the offices there is now no space available for additional terminals and an extension to the office would be necessary.' He added, 'There are now three different terminals required to obtain access to the various regional and corporate systems. This is a clear departure from the 'one per desk' policy.' Faced with such harsh criticism the board reacted swiftly. It launched a molehunt to find the source who had been leaking information to a journalist; then it gave approval for a string of further computer projects costing tens of millions of pounds, only to kill them off when the CEGB was split up and privatised.

1987: The shipping insurance specialist Tindall Riley & Co wanted to develop a bespoke system, and did everything according to the textbook: open competitive tendering, supervised by an independent, reputable consultancy. But the company's system, which was to have been completed within six months, took more than two years, and was still incomplete when Tindall Riley terminated the contract. It successfully sued its local dealer – and the dealer later succeeded in an action against the manufacturer Unisys.

1987: The Inland Revenue assured Parliament that an eleven-year-old project to computerise tax collection was under firm and successful control. Soon afterwards the project was abandoned.

1989: St Albans Council proudly used its new Community Charge system to work out how many residents were living in its ancient city. But a bug in the software led to the council's losing nearly £1 million. It sued the system supplier and its main arguments were upheld by the Appeal Court, although the amount of damages was reduced.

1989: The Home Office conceded that a £10 million switch from manual to computer systems at the Passport Office 'has not gone as smoothly and as easily as we had hoped.' A Permanent Under-secretary told MPs, 'We underestimated the difficulty of the transition . . . there have been technical problems over the capacity of the system and staff have taken longer to attune themselves to it.' MPs criticised the Home Office for needing to bring in consultants to make up for bad planning, and that 'computerisation is not yet yielding the expected benefits.' During the summer of 1989, delays in issuing passports were worse at computerised offices than at non-computerised ones. By 1994, even if applicants went directly to the main passport-issuing office near the Home Office in London, the wait for a new passport could be eight hours or more. Counter staff openly inveighed against the systems, saying that processing took longer than under the old manual regime. However, this was not a fault of the supplier, but perhaps of an unrealistic expectation that major benefits always flow from big computerisation projects. Years later the supplier would argue that the Passport Office was able to cope with the increase in transactions only as a result of the new systems.

1989: A £3 million Foreign Office London Integrated Office System project, designed to link British embassies and consulates worldwide, was scrapped. And two years later the department's accounts could not be reconciled because of a series of further computer-related disasters. The Foreign Office's most senior civil servant admitted to MPs that his staff had been 'cavalier' in ignoring advice from the government's computer advisory agency the CCTA to install adequate back-up systems. The Foreign Office also conceded that it over-relied on the professional expertise of Price Waterhouse, one of its main consultancies and suppliers. After the succession of failures at the Foreign Office, the House of Commons Public Accounts Committee chairman Robert Sheldon issued a warning to all government departments about the 'dangers of computerisation.'

SECTION THREE: 165 years of disaster (continued)

1990–1995

1990: MPs were told that only seven of the 26 computer systems at the Intervention Board for Agricultural Produce had gone live after eight years' work on them. There were no plans to take legal action against the suppliers. Guy Stapleton, chief executive of the department, told MPs that the department 'would have had a stronger claim in any actions against suppliers if the department had had tighter contracts'.

1991: An entirely serious announcement by the government's computer advisory agency the CCTA declared that the public sector led the private sector in the quality of strategic planning of information technology.

1991: A government department, Her Majesty's Stationery Office, sued the computer supplier ACT Logsys after it supplied a £198,000 system for the House of Lords that allegedly cost more than £1 million on top of the expected price. The supplier had been hired to computerise editing and publication of the Hansard reports of debates in the House of Lords. The department thought it was a textbook procurement: it even hired independent consultants from the CCTA to help order the equipment and software. However the systems as delivered were said to have had slow response times and to have needed more powerful hardware than originally envisaged. The software was ten months late and also, according to the writ, was unfit for the purpose, having failed an acceptance test. The government sought to reclaim from ACT Logsys the cost of hiring another contractor to edit and produce the Hansard reports. This cost an extra £7,000 a day between May 1989 and March 1990, a total of £1.4 million. The case was settled out of court in May 1993.

1991: A major supplier, GEC-Marconi, sued one of its biggest customers over the non-payment of bills for a major command and control system. The writ was issued against the London Fire and Civil Defence Authority. According to GEC-Marconi, numerous changes to the specification contributed to delays of more than four years and led to the original price of about £3.2 million rising to £8.09 million, with the result that the authority refused to pay £4.6 million of the bill. Changes to the system were alleged to have led to the lines of code increasing from 80,209 to 156,167. This was said to have created the need for more powerful hardware than that envisaged originally. Eventually the case was settled out of court but neither side is willing to discuss the outcome.

1992: A top-secret defence project, codenamed DOJAC, went over budget having been awarded on a fixed-price basis. As commonly happens in major projects, the end-users and the supplier, in this case ICL, could not easily agree over whether the delivered system was acceptable or not. The MoD refused to meet the final instalment on the cost of the system. The dispute was settled when the ministry agreed to pay ICL the remaining 20 per cent plus a further sum to compensate ICL for an eighteen-month delay and the extra work involved in bringing the system up to a standard accepted by defence end-users. Incidentally, I spent weeks trying to find out the meaning of the DOJAC acronym, only to discover that it signified nothing. It seems the project was classified as top secret only for the same reason that most defence computer projects are top secret – so that nobody outside need find out if they go wrong. The moral here is not to assume that there's safety in a fixed-price contract. Ideally award your chosen supplier two contracts – the first on an hourly or daily rate to determine the exact specifications, and the second, to develop the specified system, on a fixed-price basis.

The first contract will allow the supplier to devote time to understanding your business as thoroughly as you know it yourself. Once the supplier has imbibed all the knowledge it needs to deliver a satisfactory system, it should sign an undertaking that it understands all the requirements and will be wholly responsible for delivering a system that meets those requirements.

At this point the fixed-price contract for delivery of the system can be signed with confidence. You must then leave the supplier to deliver the system and not make any changes to the specification. Do not pay for anything until the delivered system passes an acceptance test, the criteria for which have been defined fastidiously during pre-contract negotiations.

If the delivered system is not up to scratch the supplier cannot blame you for changes, and neither can it argue that it has not understood your business. It will be under a legal obligation to make improvements at its own cost. If, after all this, everything still goes horribly wrong, you have spent only the cost of the first contract – and in return have received a detailed written specification which can then be taken to another supplier.

The second attempt is likely to be more successful because you will have understood the lessons from the first failure. The danger with fixed-price contracts is that you cannot make a material change without in effect nullifying the fixed-price contract, unless you have the full agreement of the supplier. Even then, you may be charged a premium rate for changes – and the more demanding you are, the more you are likely to jeopardise the supplier's ability to deliver a satisfactory system. It will then be the supplier's responsibility to make sure that the finished product serves 1,000 end-users as well as the prototype served just one user – you.

Alternatively, enter into a Japanese-style partnership deal with the supplier – but beware suppliers touting partnerships. Partnerships can be the most reliable and lowest-risk way to implement a major project (though not the cheapest) – but many so-called partnerships are nothing other than a pretence by suppliers to have the customer's interests in mind when it is overcharging them.

The only genuine partnership is one in which the suppliers and customers share the risks of implementation or providing a service. At its simplest, the customer hands over responsibility for computer development and operations to a supplier or consortium of suppliers. That supplier then has responsibility for delivering the computer service, along with the promised business benefits and cost savings. If it achieves the level of savings and service promised, the supplier recovers its costs plus an agreed profit margin. If it delivers more than the promised savings and/or a better service than originally agreed, it receives a share of the savings, plus its costs and profit margin. If the service and/or savings are lower than planned or non-existent, the supplier receives no profit and may even make a loss on the contract. This is a genuine partnership in which the supplier has a vested interest in the customer's welfare.

There are dangers in these arrangements. Japanese partnerships are bonded almost spiritually – personal and corporate honour prevents either party damaging the other. One or two sheets of A4 paper are sufficient to tie a Japanese customer to the supplier. Western partnerships, on the other hand, may need a 500-page contract to protect both parties' interests.

In short, the user organisation needs highly experienced computer-industry lawyers. The partnership will also require 'open book' accounting – whereby the supplier and customer show each other their accounts – so each side knows how much the other is making on the deal. Only then can the profits or losses from the system be verified and distributed between the supplier and customer.

BP Exploration has exactly the type of partnership arrangement explained above – and is more than satisfied with it. What must be remembered, however, is that partnerships are never particularly cheap – because even if they are successful the supplier is going to share some of the savings that ideally you would like to keep for your own company. However, this may be a small sacrifice to make to ensure the success of a new project.

May 1992: A Channel 4 *Dispatches* programme produced evidence that between £200 million and £400 million which had been spent on computers in the health service had been wasted. Paula Proctor, a former nurse who chaired a committee to select nursing systems, said, 'I have found that there are many people who will buy because the salesmen are good.' At a health computing exhibition she watched as doctors, midwives and nurses walked into the hall as if it were an Aladdin's Cave and stared wide-eyed at the rows of shiny machines and free gifts. 'As a nurse I felt sorry, because I felt there were a lot who would not be asking the right questions. They were like lambs to the slaughter.' Within the health service 'computers were springing up left, right and centre but few people knew what to do with them.'

1992: A £20 million criminal information system for the Metropolitan Police went four years behind schedule, was not compatible with systems being developed by other police forces, and led to a dispute between the police and the supplier, the US services group EDS, which had acquired the system's original supplier. Legal action was threatened against EDS, which issued a counter-claim, arguing that the Metropolitan Police had changed the specification outside the contract. Delays to the project – called Cris – led to criminal intelligence officers spending 40 per cent of their time keying data into alternative systems. However, the differences between supplier and customer were eventually resolved and the Cris system went live successfully in 1996.

1992: The Salvage Association, a marine surveying group, took its former computer supplier, CAP Financial Services Ltd, to court over a failed £291,000 computer project. CAP was allowed two years by the user to rescue the project, but eventually the Salvage Association lost patience and terminated the contract. It issued a writ claiming a breach of contract, damages and interest. As in the St Albans council case, the supplier had sought in the contract to limit its legal liability to the amount of damages it would pay in any disaster. But a judge ruled in the Salvage Association's favour and it was awarded substantial damages and costs. Sema, CAP's owner, appealed against the decision but settled the case before the appeal was heard.

1992: The furniture retail chain Saxon Hawk, formerly known as Gillow, won a High Court action against its software supplier and was awarded £100,000 compensation – which the supplier paid before promptly going bust.

1992: The Department of Employment's computer system

accidentally duplicated a £3 million payment to the National Association for the Care and Resettlement of Offenders (NACRO). By the time the error was discovered, NACRO was in no position to pay back the money in one go. As with all major government computer projects, the problems were said to have been rectified by the time they came to the attention of MPs; but two years later, in 1994, the same department wasted up to £48 million on new systems for Training and Enterprise Councils.

1993: A £90 million book distribution company, Tiptree, installed a £1.5 million warehousing system to speed up the supply of books to booksellers and also to cope with an anticipated increase in demand. It adopted a 'Big Bang' approach, and did not have an adequate back-up system to cope with a failure, the result of which was that Tiptree, having been voted the British Book Awards' Distributor of the Year, became so unpopular with some of its customers that a few sought large sums in compensation for what they claimed was poor post-computerisation service. The problems were resolved completely, but only some months later. The claims for compensation were settled privately.

1993: The wisdom of Confucius's remark that people divine the future from studying the past was demonstrated as a spectacular fallacy by the London Ambulance Service, which, having already experienced a computer disaster a few years before, embarked on a new disaster, which repeated some of the earlier mistakes. The bug-ridden system was scrapped after squabbling between various suppliers and distrust between senior administrators and staff, and claims that the deadlines were unrealistically tight, the budget too small, and the software too complex.

1993: The London Stock Exchange's Taurus system, designed to replace paper share certificates with an electronic trading and settlement system, was abandoned at a cost to the exchange and its customers of between £75 million and £450 million. It was too big, too ambitious and too pioneering. It modified an existing package – the highest of high-risk strategies – and failed to secure the support of end-users.

1993: The government-owned Student Loans Company decides to scrap a £12 million mainframe computer system that inaequately specified by the company. The supplier had won the contract in 1989 with a price believed to be 40 per cent lower than the nearest bid.

1993: Meanwhile in the USA, the Department of Veterans' Affairs had spent ten years trying to modernise its systems. It had spent $206 million (about £135 million) trying to reduce the processing time of compensation claims from six months to two months, with the result that processing times increased to eight months.

1993: Also in the USA, the California Department of Motor Vehicles abandoned a system that had cost taxpayers tens of millions of dollars. The hardware was inadequate to cope with the complex software and response times at the terminals were ten times slower than when the old system was in use. The project was scrapped when it emerged that the problems could be rectified only if the original budget was trebled.

1994: The £500 million spent on computers in the National Health Service to reduce administration and staff costs over a ten-year period coincided with a 40 per cent increase in the number of health service administrators.

1994: *The Times* reported that government departments had spent more than £4 billion on new computers during the past five years without achieving any significant reduction in civil service numbers. Armed with such alarming figures the government decided to set aside a further £6 billion for computerisation over the next six years.

1994: The Department of Social Security, which had repeatedly declined to admit publicly that there were any major problems on a £25 million statistical system known as ASSIST, suddenly abandoned the project and sued the suppliers. The case continues.

1994: Customs and Excise postponed twice the date of its plans to go live with an £80 million system linking Customs officers to 600 air freight companies around the UK. Customs and Excise said that the systems were performing magnificently and that any problems were teething. But end-users in freight companies refused to link into the systems, claiming they were bug-ridden. This prompted Customs and Excise to threaten to charge the end-users large sums for the additional costs of running the old systems.

A letter to Customs and Excise from the British International

Freight Association, which represented more than 1,000 end-user freight companies, said, 'It is generally accepted that the December and January trials designed to prove the systems were ready, were a disaster.' But Customs organised briefings for television and other journalists to explain, with the aid of flip charts, how the planning and execution of CHIEF came close to perfection: that it was a model computer project.

The exact truth never emerged, though the systems' problems were eventually ironed out.

1994: The Performing Right Society (PRS) sent a letter to one of its main suppliers requesting a cheque for £16 million to cover the costs and consequences of the society's computer failure. The project had been big, ambitious and pioneering. In an out-of-court settlement, the main consultancy agreed to pay the PRS about £2.3 million.

1994: North Thames Regional Health Authority issued a writ reclaiming £1.4 million in fees paid to the consultancy firm Ernst and Young over the failure of a 'basic' payroll system. The writ also claimed £9 million in damages and interest. The authority complained about the consultancy's management of the project, alleged unjustified fees, excessive development costs and the cost of buying alternative systems. But the case was not due to be heard in the High Court until nine months after the authority was due to be abolished by government decree.

Instead of choosing off-the-shelf software, the authority agreed to the customisation of a package. A pilot project was due to finish in October 1989, but by September 1991 Ernst and Young was said to have managed to get only an incomplete version of the software running in two of the authority's thirteen districts. One individual connected with the scheme said: 'We kept being told that the project was only a week late for years.' Eventually the authority ran a simplified version of the system, ten months after the contract with Ernst and Young was terminated. Ernst and Young denies the allegations.

1994: A success story. A £55 million Eagle Star computerisation project went over budget by only between £5 million and £8 million, which was described by the consultancy, Andersen Consulting, as a 'tremendous achievement' given the complexity and scale of the project and the changes it effected within the user company. A partner at Andersen said that the cost containment was 'nothing short of a miracle', that the estimates were 'broadly' the same as in 1989.

1994: The Central Veterinary Laboratory, part of the Ministry of Agriculture, Fisheries and Food, did not mention in its accounts that it had lost up to £1 million on a system designed to integrate the results of tests on animal blood and organs. Part of the computer project's purpose was to improve the laboratory's efficiency at monitoring the spread of diseases including bovine spongiform encephalopathy (BSE, or so-called mad-cow disease) and salmonella. But it was abandoned as too complex and unworkable.

'We were dealing in a completely new area,' said an executive at the laboratory. 'The suppliers, ourselves and the CCTA (the government computer advisory agency) have made mistakes.' But this was a government department with a difference. Not only did it admit making mistakes (after leaks to the press) but showed that it had learned from them. After the first system's failure, the laboratory went on to commission smaller, PC-based systems modelled on unmodified packaged software, which reduced the costs and the risks of failure.

1994: The recruitment agency Resources International sued its computer supplier because a system that was bought to provide a competitive edge put it at a competitive disadvantage. 'It has been quite an appalling exercise,' said Resources' managing director, Warwick Bergin. Among the problems was the poor response times at the terminal, due to the uncontrolled growth of the database, which failed to archive old data. Even the prototype had never been impressive, although the supplier had assured Bergin that everything would be fine on the night. Resources sued the supplier but did not win any compensation. The supplier disappeared. Resources has since successfully installed new systems.

1995: The Canadian Transport Minister, Doug Young, described the country's $834 million air traffic control computerisation project as a mess and threatened to cancel it. Taking accountability to an exemplary extreme, Young asked the Auditor General Denis Desautels to investigate his own Transport Department. To help rescue the project, the Canadian federal government set aside an extra $100 million from a contingency fund. The project was already two years late and over budget. An audit in 1992 had blamed the problems on the department's senior bureaucrats, who had buried the supplier, Hughes, in an avalanche of changes to the original contract specifications.

1995: The UK government planned more big, ambitious, pioneering computer projects founded on bespoke software, built to unreasonably tight deadlines, and with the target moving, as if it resolved to repeat all the most spectacular faux pas from previous disasters. The Inland Revenue, for example, was instructed by the Chancellor to introduce a £200 million tax self-assessment project by an artificially tight deadline of 1997. Wisely the Revenue refused to disclose the final costs of the project.

1996: The National Audit Office revealed that the National Health Service had spent £106 million over several years on hospital information support systems that had yielded only £3.3 million of benefits. The savings were less than the central NHS administration costs of running the scheme.

1996: Various parts of British Gas suffered from a series of computer disasters as it sought to go live with systems which had been developed to an artificially tight deadline. Hundreds of clerical staff were drafted in to cope with complaints from customers.

APPENDIX TWO

Here we publish replies by Lord Jenkin of Roding and Andersen Consulting to allegations in a District Audit Service Report, published by the House of Commons, over Wessex Regional Health Authority's Regional Information Systems Plan. A response by Sir Robin Buchanan, former Chairman of the Wessex Regional Health Authority, is also published.

Lord Jenkin of Roding submitted a note to the Committee of Public Accounts on 28 May 1993, which read:

On February 11, 1993, *Computer Weekly* and the *Independent* carried articles apparently based on leaked copies of two confidential reports by the District Audit Service for the Wessex Regional Health Authority. In these articles, my name figures prominently and it was implied that acting as a business adviser to the consultants, Arthur Andersen & Co., I had improperly put 'intense pressure on the Authority to accept the bid made by Andersen in partnership with IBM.' The papers quoted an extract from one of the District Auditor's reports to the effect that a note of the conversation I had with the then Chairman of the Regional Health Authority (RHA) Sir Bryan Thwaites, 'suggests that Arthur Andersen would appear to have had knowledge of rival bids which should not have been available to them.'

On the same day, a Member of Parliament, at Prime Minister's Question Time, ended a supplementary question by referring to 'corrupt computer deals involving former Cabinet Ministers.' In an adjournment debate on 15th March 1993, another Member said that I 'clearly had unusual knowledge of rival bids which the District Auditor implies were wrongly obtained through other Andersen consultancies with Wessex.' At the time, of course, I had not seen copies of either of the two confidential reports; I had been given no opportunity by the District Auditor or the Regional Health Authority to comment on the passage or passages where my name is mentioned ...

Although the events referred to took place almost seven years ago I can state categorically that the role I played in this affair was extremely small and entirely proper; and that, to the best of my knowledge and belief, I and Andersen Consulting acted perfectly properly throughout.

I resigned from the Government on 2nd September 1985. In October of that year I received an approach from Arthur Andersen & Co. through one of their Partners, Richard Simmons, who had been known to me for a number of years. He suggested that I should meet his Senior Partner, Mr Don Hanson, to explore the possibility whether, in return for a modest retainer, I might be available to advise the firm from time to time. After discussing the matter with Mr Hanson I felt it right in the light of the legal proceedings by the Northern Ireland Office against Arthur Andersen & Co arising from their audit of the De Lorean company, to consult the Cabinet Secretary, then Sir Robert Armstrong, as to the propriety of my entering into such an arrangement ... Sir Robert Armstrong agreed that this was a perfectly acceptable arrangement. In November an exchange of letters took place between Mr Hanson and myself and I was quickly involved in advising them on a number of matters including the Data Protection Act, the Financial Services Bill and the privatisation of Unipart etc etc.

Towards the end of April 1986 I was contacted by Mr Jim Sweeney, an American partner seconded to the UK, with a deep knowledge of the use of computers in healthcare. Mr Sweeney led the Andersen team on the Wessex computer project. He explained to me that Andersen and IBM, in response to a tender document put out by the RHA, had submitted a joint bid which they were confident would fulfil the Region's requirements. I was given to understand that Andersen's American branches had a wide experience of health service computerisation and had been involved in a number of successful computer projects in the States. Mr Sweeney went on to say that, while the appraisal process was not complete, they had been notified that Digital Equipment Company (DEC) were currently regarded as the preferred supplier and that the AA/IBM bid seemed unlikely to be accepted. It was Mr Sweeney's professional view that the Region was thereby heading for trouble, both because of the manner in which the tender, and the subsequent appraisal, had been conducted and because of the Region's ignorance of the American scene. During the appraisal, for instance, it had become apparent to Andersens that there was no nurse on the Region's appraisal team, something which Andersens would have regarded as essential for a computer system in which nurses would have a major role to play. Mr Sweeney also told me that no member of the Regional team had been to see any of the Andersen systems operating in America; and based on his wide understanding of the industry, he strongly suspected that none of the possible software suppliers who might be associated with the DEC bid actually had a successful system up and running. In short it was Mr Sweeney's professional view that the Region was heading for a thoroughly bad decision, mainly because the team in charge was not competent to reach the right decision.

I was therefore asked whether in my view there would be any purpose in seeking to draw this impending bad decision to the attention of someone higher up in the Region, and I was asked if I knew anyone there. Now, it so happened that, in 1981, towards the end of my period as Secretary of State at the Department of Health and Social Security, I had had to select someone to be Chairman of the Region from 1st April 1982, and from the names submitted to me, I had selected Bryan Thwaites (now Sir Bryan) who had been known to me for a number of years both in his capacity as Principal of Westfield College, London University (where I had been on the Council) and as a competent Area Health Authority Chairman in Brent, London. I had a high opinion of Mr Thwaites, and I recommended his name. I left the DHSS in September 1981 and my successor, Norman Fowler, duly made the appointment.

I therefore indicated to Mr Sweeney that I would be willing to contact Mr Thwaites, and on the basis of the information he had given me, there would seem to be every reason to do so. The tendering procedure was not yet complete – it had only been indicated so far that DEC were the preferred supplier – and given a steer from the top, it was possible that wiser counsels might yet prevail. Accordingly, on 30th April 1986 I found an opportunity to catch Mr Thwaites at home and spoke to him along the lines of the briefing I had had from Mr Sweeney. Mr Thwaites made a record of this telephone call, and on 10th March 1993, in response to a request from myself, a copy of this note was supplied to me by Mr Jarrold (of Wessex Regional Health Authority); I attach it as an Annex to this Note, and it speaks for itself. Though the call took place nearly seven years ago, I believe that the note is an accurate account of my conversation with Mr Thwaites, who gave the impression of being grateful for being alerted to what was happening; as the note records, he also indicated that there would be no possible objection to Arthur Andersen contacting the 'JP' referred to in the note. I also took this as his reaction that there was nothing remotely improper in my having alerted him as to what was going on.

I duly reported back to Mr Sweeney the fact that I had had this conversation, and so far as I was concerned, that was the end of the matter. Until the press reports appeared on 11 February 1993 I never gave the matter another thought.

Nevertheless when stories based on the leaked reports appeared in the press, I was immediately concerned to satisfy myself that Andersens had in fact conducted themselves properly throughout. From the intensive enquiries I have made, I am indeed satisfied. Andersens can explain better than I the precise sequence of events but they have satisfied me that at no point did they make improper use of unauthorised information, or that they had secured information about rival bids which should not have been available to them. I have had considerable dealings over the years with many Partners in AA and I would regard it as inconceivable that they would risk their reputation as leading accountants and consultants by engaging in questionable professional activity ...

I remain firmly of the opinion that in responding to Andersen Consulting's request to put their concerns before the Regional Chairman, I did nothing that could be open to the charge of improper conduct which has been levelled at me in the press and Parliament.

The following is a note by Sir Bryan Thwaites of a telephone conversation between him and Jenkin.

Patrick Jenkin, the last Secretary of State DHSS, rang me this morning in his role as one-day-per-month consultant to Arthur Andersen.

He had been briefed in detail and it was one of the trickier conversations since he was, of course, plugging the value-for-taxpayers-money line. Also that where Wessex leads, others will follow.

Here is a brief summary of his main points:

that no nurse/s had been involved in the assessment (that is, of the Hospital Patients Project which of course was the central subject of his conversation).

that no-one had been out to the USA to see for themselves the AA/IBM/etc package working.

that the DEC package is not working anywhere and so is not available for hands-on trial;

that the DEC package fails to do certain things – in particular electronic communication of certain clinical order/reports – that the AA/IBM/etc does; and that this is a most serious point against DEC.

that we are now in a flat spin because DEC is not coming up with the enhancements that we were requiring of them.

He asked whether Arthur Andersen could contact JP and I said that anyone could write to anyone as far I am concerned. How much notice will be taken is another matter. But his list of points was so detailed (and these will be repeated in the letter that you – JP – will no doubt receive in the next few days) that I myself shall be grateful for a report on them.

End of report on what was a long early-morning conversation.

And the following is the response of Andersen Consulting to the events at Wessex Regional Health Authority between 1983 and 1988:

> In 1983, Andersen Consulting (AC) which at the time was known as Arthur Andersen Management Consultants (AAMC), part of Arthur Andersen (AA), was asked by the Department of Health to do work on the National Health Service Corporate Data Model. As a result of this work, we were introduced to the Wessex Regional Health Authority (WRHA) and asked to help WRHA with data analysis and support of its Regional Information Systems Plan (RISP).

Role as Advisor 1983–1984.

> We served as advisor to WRHA on the RISP programme between late 1983 and late 1984. During that period a number of pieces of work were separately entered into; we commented on the information requirements and the information plan that the Regional Health Authority had prepared, assisted in the development of an implementation plan and advised on risk control mechanisms, organisational steering arrangements and the scope of each of the projects needed to achieve these goals.

> It is worth noting that the District Auditor commented favourably on this initial work to manage the development of RISP, calling it 'clear cut and comprehensive.' The Regional Health Authority, however, did not follow much of the advice offered.

Role as Tenderer/Preferred Vendor for Feasibility Studies: late 1984–1987

> We last worked in an advisory capacity in late April 1984 and received but turned down a request by WRHA for us to become the project management consultants.

> Subsequently we bid for five feasibility studies. We did not gain the work on the Hospital, Manpower or Financial feasibility studies. We were, however, appointed to work on the Community Care and

Estate Planning feasibility studies. The work on the Estate Planning study began in February 1985 and ended with the submission of a final report in October 1985. The Community Care feasibility study was concerned with the use of information systems in community services. Work began in November 1984 and the feasibility study was provided in July 1985. In October of that year we began a feasibility project to develop and design from the users' viewpoint a community information system. This work was completed with the submission of the design report in March 1986.

Role in First Tender for Three Core Systems: November 1985–April 1986

In November 1985 AC was shortlisted to tender for implementation of the Hospital, Manpower and Financial Systems. Each of the detailed proposals for the three systems was submitted separately. The Manpower and Finance proposals were submitted in December 1985; and the Hospital System proposal was submitted in January 1986.

The District Auditor's report of July 1992 says the decision to appoint Digital Equipment Company took place in February 1986. We were told about DEC becoming the preferred supplier in late March or early April 1986.

WRHA took considerable care to ensure we were not provided with any information which was not generally available to any party during the tendering process for the implementation of the three core systems (Hospital, Manpower, Financial). We understood the RISP tendering process required fairness. We respected it completely. We are not aware of ever having any sensitive information.

Role of Lord Jenkin: April 1986

In late 1986, we asked Patrick Jenkin (now Lord Jenkin of Roding), in his capacity as business advisor to AAMC, for counsel on how best to move forward given the circumstances.

The circumstances were: we had been told DEC was the vendor of choice and WRHA was in the process of protracted contract negotiations; we had a great deal of experience in health service computerisation through our American Practice and the insights of the Partner responsible for our bid, an American seconded to the UK, who had in-depth knowledge of Hospital Systems; there was genuine concern in this Partner's view that the Regional Health Authority officials whom the team had contacted were making an error of judgement because of their limited knowledge in this area and particularly because of their exclusion of end-users in the evaluation process. This had been evident in our February 1986 meeting when we met the selection panel for the Hospital System.

In his report, the District Auditor was surprised at the level of knowledge we had of the hospital system software to operate on DEC equipment. We did not find it at all surprising since we had conducted extensive research here and in the United States on available packages and we had extensive practical experience from our world-wide health care practice.

We therefore knew the DEC product in detail. We deduced DEC would be unable to meet the Invitation to Tender specifications because the software suppliers which we thought might be associated with the DEC tender did not have a system which could demonstrably meet the Invitation to Tender specifications. IBM was the leader in health care related systems at this time and the market leading software was all designed to run on IBM. This is why we had decided to bid jointly with IBM.

Lord Jenkin felt comfortable calling Bryan Thwaites (now Sir Bryan) in his capacity as Chairman of WRHA, to tell him of our genuine concerns, so that Sir Bryan could satisfy himself with the decision being reached by WRHA.

We were comfortable having Lord Jenkin call Sir Bryan on our behalf as Sir Bryan was the most senior decision-maker for WRHA and the core team who had prepared the bid did not otherwise have contact with him. With Sir Bryan's agreement we did write directly to our WRHA contact the very next day, to provide similar comments.

Comments have been made that this was improper. In our view we were bringing legitimate concerns to the most senior member of the Regional Health Authority so that he would be aware of those concerns and could satisfy himself of the correctness of the course of action on which the Authority was embarked. We do not believe that this was improper. Nor do we believe that Lord Jenkin would allow himself to be party to improper action.

We did not see any competitive proposals. We were not privy to any inside information. We have not operated in any unethical or illegal fashion.

Role in Visits to DEC Software Suppliers in US: June 1986–September 1986

In June 1986 AC received a call from Howard Natrass, the Winchester District General Manager responsible for the Hospital System. We were told WRHA was having difficulty in locating software for use with DEC hardware, even with the help of another major consultancy.

According to Mr Natrass he did not believe they had the in-depth knowledge we had of the US market conditions. Given our experience in health service computerisation, Mr Natrass thought we could help WRHA identify more than the four options provided by the other consultancy. Mr Natrass sought to retain AC on a fee paying basis. The proposal was submitted. It made clear that we understood that our bid had not been accepted and our role was to provide information on DEC-based solutions. The proposal was submitted on 1 July.

We provided a long list of software vendors, on sites in the United States, as potential suppliers of hospital information systems on DEC equipment. The Region decided to visit the most promising sites.

The trip was conducted in mid-July. AC personnel in the US were available at the visited sites to help with technical questions. They did not introduce our proposal solution nor did they take the WRHA to any sites that had any components of what we had offered. No one from the UK practice was in attendance.

Our limited role in this exercise ended with a letter written on 3 September to Mr Natrass in which we identified two alternatives, based on the visit, to make the DEC solution work. These were: use of third party hardware facilities which would allow the McDonnell-Douglas HOMER system to operate on DEC equipment; and the selection of British Medical Data Systems (BMDS) software on the basis of the backup and future development plans of the parent SMS Corporation. We identified strengths and weaknesses of the alternative approaches.

Role in Second Tender for the Three Core Systems: September–November 1986

In early September 1986, we were asked if we would revalidate our original bid and confirm that it remained open. We did this and subsequently demonstrated the proposed Hospital System to an evaluation group. We were then asked to enter contract negotiations which extended over most of October 1986. On 11 November 1986, the contract was signed between Wessex and AC.

Our bid was not altered in any respect related to our recommended solution. There were cost increases which had occurred in the year since we had submitted the original bid. We did make Wessex aware of the new information, specifically that due to a contract won by Technicon from the US government, they were upgrading the functionality of their software for Defence hospitals in the US and Europe and these improvements would also be available to Wessex. AC was contracted as prime contractor with responsibility for all aspects of the work including hardware and software. IBM entered into a separate and parallel contract for the provision of the hardware needed. We subcontracted Technicon Data Systems and McCormack and Dodge for initial work. Later they negotiated their own contracts with WRHA.

Role in Implementation of Three Core Systems November 1986–May 1988

Highlights of the work undertaken by AC within the fixed price contract include the following:

Hospital (patient) Management System in Winchester, including design and installation of a Basic Patient Register which was seen through to completion. It was the first successful implementation of a full hospital system anywhere in the UK. It was later installed in one further hospital.

Financial Management System in Basingstoke including design and installation. It was then rolled out across the region.

Manpower System in Salisbury including design through to testing and acceptance of the agreed system. As a result of the functional requests from WRHA and the District Health Authority, the system ended up being more complex than initially appreciated by any party. Consequently, AC incurred substantially more costs than originally planned to complete the system. We absorbed these costs. The WRHA eventually chose not to use the system in live operation.

Other Considerations

From the start of our work with Wessex in 1984, and throughout the implementation work for the three core systems, we advised WRHA of the importance of project management and the need for communications between the Region and its Districts.

Whenever we did raise project management issues, we were consistently told this was a matter for WRHA and to limit our thinking to technical areas in our role to deliver software.

We agreed to build the systems because we believed and still believe the vision of RISP is viable. The implementation efforts have proven the technical feasibility of the Manpower, Accounting and Hospital Systems.

We are disheartened about issues which overshadowed very good and worthwhile work. We were not responsible for the broader issues, nor can we take responsibility for them.

We can take responsibility for the work undertaken by us which was successfully completed, approved by WRHA, and paid for on the basis of a fixed-price contract.

The following is a response by Sir Robin Buchanan to the House of Commons Public Accounts Committee:

In view of articles published recently by *Computer Weekly* and the *Independent* concerning the evidence I gave to the Committee at its hearing of 5th May, I felt that I should write to clarify a number of matters raised by these articles.

There have been assertions made in these articles about two particular issues examined by the hearing; whether or not I conducted contract negotiations with the computer services firm, CSL; and whether or not I had detailed knowledge of Wessex Regional Health Authority's original contract with Wessex Integrated Systems Ltd to provide computer facilities management to the authority.

It has been suggested that I misled the Committee and that my answers to questions on these issues were ambiguous and incomplete. That was not the case and I would be extremely concerned if members had interpreted my remarks in such a way.

With regard to the first Wessex Integrated Systems agreement, you asked whether I had been aware of the circumstances surrounding a number of issues being examined at the hearing. I indicated to you that I had been fully aware of the circumstances surrounding the renegotiated second agreement with Wessex Integrated Systems and wished that I had known more of the other issues when I became Chairman in 1988. This theme was also picked up by Mr Couchman [an MP on the Public Accounts Committee] later in the hearing when he asserted that I had not been fully briefed on the first Wessex Integrated Systems agreement and I agreed with him.

As both the *Independent* and *Computer Weekly* have pointed out I was, indeed, aware of some information about the first Wessex Integrated Systems contract and had been at a meeting when it was being discussed. However, as I have consistently stated, I was not involved at the beginning of the negotiations – they started prior to my appointment – and I was never in a position to be fully aware of all the issues raised by the contract.

As far as CSL is concerned, I was asked by Mr Denzil Davies [MP] if I had negotiated with this company to which I replied that I had not. That reply was entirely accurate. Although I negotiated with Mr Philip Sellars [Chairman of CSL and Wessex Integrated Systems] in matters concerning the second Wessex Integrated Systems Ltd contract, I was addressing him in his capacity as

Chairman of Wessex Integrated Systems, not as Chairman of CSL. It is true that he was Chairman of both companies, but the distinction between his role was perfectly clear to me.

May I assure you that I have been dismayed to read assertions that I have been anything other than completely frank and honest with the Committee. Such assertions have no substance.

BIBLIOGRAPHY:

Banking Technology magazine, 'Taurus – an uncertain future', November 1991

Becker, Saul, 'Monitoring the Social Fund', *Community Care* magazine, July 1988

BuyIT Guidelines – a set of guidelines written for chief executive officers and their management teams – Department of Trade and Industry in association with the Information Society Initiative, London

Committee of Public Accounts, Eighth Report, 'The Proper Conduct of Public Business', HMSO, Dd5062021 1/94 C8 3398A 4235 273982

Committee of Public Accounts, Wessex Regional Health Authority: Management of the Regional Information Systems Plan; minutes of evidence, 5/5/93, HMSO

Ennals, Richard, *Executive Guide to preventing IT Disasters*, Pub. Springer Verlag

General Accounting Office/RCED-94-167FS Air Traffic Control: Status of FAA's Modernisation Program

General Accounting Office/T-AIMD/GGD-94-104 Tax Systems Modernisation: Status of Planning and Technical Foundation

General Accounting Office/T-RCED-94-188 Advanced Automation System: Implications of problems and recent changes

General Accounting Office/T-RCED-95-193 Perspectives on the Federal Aviation Administration's Efforts to Develop New Technology

General Accounting Office Study, 'Denver International Airport – Baggage Handling, Contracting and other issues', August 1995

Griffiths, Catherine of IC-Parc, Imperial College, London and Wilcocks, Leslie, of Templeton College, Oxford, 'Are Major IT projects worth the risk?'

Hilton, Christopher, 'Crises . . .? What Crises?', Focus magazine, November 1996

KPMG Management Consulting Summary Report, 'Who's Afraid of Taurus', August 1991

KPMG Management Consulting: 'Runaway Projects – causes and effects', January 1995

London Ambulance Service, Appendices to the Report by the Review Team, January 1995, South Thames Regional Health Authority

London Ambulance Service, Report of the Inquiry, February 1993, HMNT [MC] LlnC, London

Monopolies and Mergers Commission: 'Performing Rights', HMSO, Dd5065804 2/96 C15 Ord. 343664

National Computing Centre, 'User Protection in System Procurement', (Legal Group Conference), September 1994, Manchester

Northern Ireland Audit Office: 'The management of Information Technology in Government Departments in Northern Ireland', HMS0, Dd.750903.C8.2/92, 14567, Gp. 118

Performance Software – The guide to the world's greatest software mistakes and how to avoid them, Devon House, Slough

Senator William Cohen Investigative Report: 'Computer Chaos: Billions Wasted Buying Federal Computer Systems'

Standish Group Chaos Study into Project Development Disasters, January 1995

Vevers, Maureen (principal consultant with KPMG), 'How to have a computer disaster without really trying'

Warner Group Management Consultants, 'State of California Department of Motor Vehicles – Business Applications and Information Technology', Independent Study (Final Report), May 1995

Commonly used initials/acronyms are placed first, followed by full name in brackets, except for government departments, which are given in full as Department of . . . . . **Bold** numbers indicate Case Studies or main references.

Crash

First Direct banking service 210–11, 290–91, 293, 377
First Union Corporation 324–5
Fletcher, Ewen 48–51
Florida State **236–42**
Forbes, Judge Thayne 283–4, 286–7
Foreign Office 381
Fortney, Merv 241
Foster, Jim 72, 74
Fourth Estate 105
Fowler, Judge 325
Fowler, Norman 393
Frankfurt Stock Exchange 189
Freegard, Michael 48, 51
French, Peter 285–6
Fryar, Harry 287

GAO (General Accounting Office, US)
    see under audits/auditors
Gates, Bill 32, 195
GEC-Marconi 382
General Motors 115
Gillow *see* Saxon Hawk
government *see* United Kingdom government;
    United States of America
Guardian Royal Exchange 185
guided missiles 308

Hallat, Phil 298–305 *passim*
Hanson, Don 392
hardware *see* computers
Havant 61
Herbert Smith (solicitors) 287
Hewlett-Packard 44–6
Hicks, Judge John 253–69 *passim*
Hiscocks (insurers) 58
HMSO (Her Majesty's Stationery Office) 381–2
Hoare, John 86, 91–2
Home Office 380–81
HOMER system 400
Hoskyns group **127–42**, 254
hospital information support systems 96
House of Commons/Lords *see under* United
    Kingdom government
HRS (Health and Rehabilitation Services, Florida)
    237–42
Hughes company 390

IBM (International Business Machines)
    air traffic control system 311
    communications system 184
    and Dept of the Environment 117
    and DSS ASSIST project 127–8
    and Federal Aviation Administration 313
    and Florida HRS **236–40**
    minicomputers 329–30, 375, 376
    and National Westminster Bank 363
    security protocol 183
    slogans 17, 360
    and Wessex Regional Health Administration 61,
        64, **70–81**, 85, **391–400**
    also mentioned 212, 223, 280, 290
IBM Computer Users' Association 246, 348–9

ICL (International Computers Ltd) 71, **127–42**,
    198, **273–81**, 373, 374, 379, 382
Imperial College, London 186, 203
Independent 202, 391, 401, 402
indexes 260–61
Inland Revenue 271, 373–4, 380, 390
INS (Institutional Net Settlement) 183
Internet 21, 216
Intervention Board for Agricultural Produce 381
Intuit company 66
IPS personnel system 88
IRLM bridging system 239–40
IRS (Internal Revenue Service, US) 310, 319
Isle of Wight 87–8
ITSA (Information Technology Services Agency,
    DSS) **125–42**, 199

Japan 120, 383–4
jargon *see* language/jargon
Jarrold, Ken 88, 89, 90, 91 *bis*, 394
JC Penney company 300
Jenkin, Patrick (Lord Jenkin of Roding) 72, 73–4,
    81, **391–403**
Johnson, Marilyn 109
JP Morgan 211
Jukebox company 218

killing a project 344–5
Kimmel, Admiral 234–5
KPMG consultancy 185, 361

language/jargon 90–91, 111, 204–5, 272, 294,
    368–71
    computer languages *see* own heading
Last, Chris 102
law, computer 18, 248
lawyers *see* litigation
LBMS (Leamonth Burchett Management Systems)
    42, 52–3
Leaning Tower of Pisa 38
litigation 119–19, 218, **243–52**, **271–3**
    Florida vs EDS **236–42**
    Salvage Association vs CAP **283–8**
    Tindall Riley vs Unisys/DSL **253–69**
    UOP engineering vs Andersen **323–5**
Little, Robin 88, 362
Llewellyn, Kelvin 105
Lloyds Bank 180, 191, 298, 303, 306
London Ambulance Service 26, **143–67** 235, 302,
    346, 347–8, 359, 386
London Fire and Civil Defence Authority 382
London Stock Exchange 27, **174–93**, 349, 386–7
Loral company 313
Lotus **339–42**, 344

McConnell, Anthony 107
McDonnell Douglas 71, 77, 400
McGuinness, Paul 33
MAFF (Ministry of Agriculture, Fisheries and
    Food) 122, 389
Major, John 92
mainframe computers *see under* computers
management 295–6, **320–22**, 359

410